BAKEMONOGATARI

OH!GREAT
ORIGINAL STORY:
NISIOISIN

ORIGINAL CHARACTER
DESIGN: VOFAN

10

MAIN CHARACTERS

Koyomi Araragi

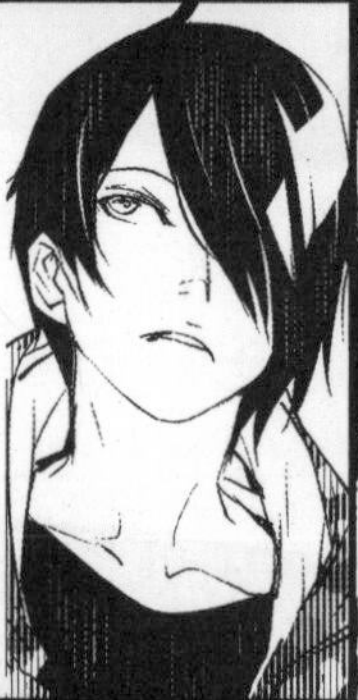

A boy who became Kiss-Shot's thrall after saving her. To regain his humanity, he must now fight three vampire hunters.

Tsubasa Hanekawa

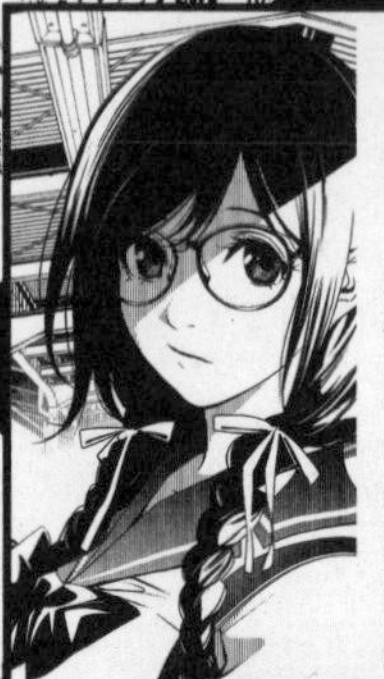

Koyomi's friend who goes to the same school as him. Though an honor student that no honor could sufficiently describe, she goes out of her way to get involved with Koyomi for some reason.

Kiss-Shot Acerola-Orion Heart-Under-Blade

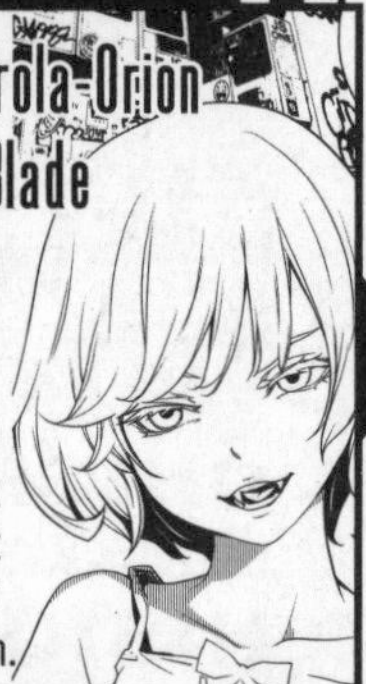

A vampire powerful enough to be called the "king of aberrations" who Koyomi saved from the brink of death. Having lost her powers, she now takes a childish form.

Mèmè Oshino

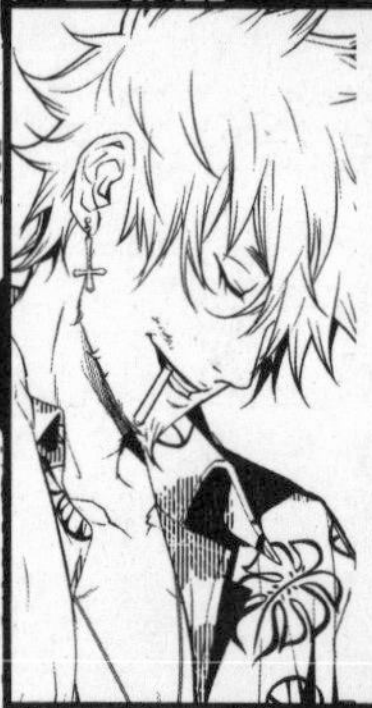

A self-described expert on aberrations who suddenly appeared before Koyomi one day. He offers to act as a go-between for Koyomi and the hunters.

Dramaturgy

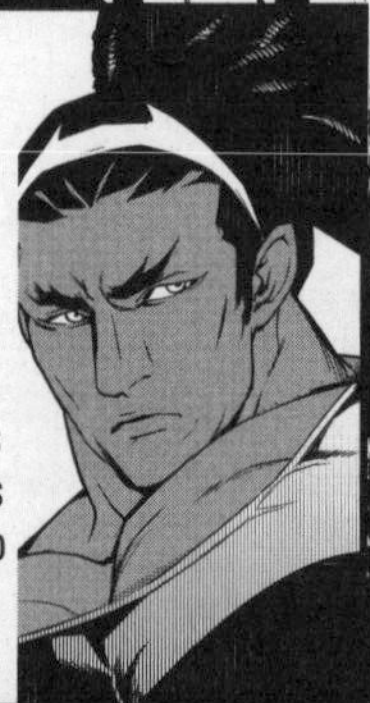

A vampire who hunts his own kind. A mass of manly muscle who carries an equally massive sword.

THE STORY SO FAR

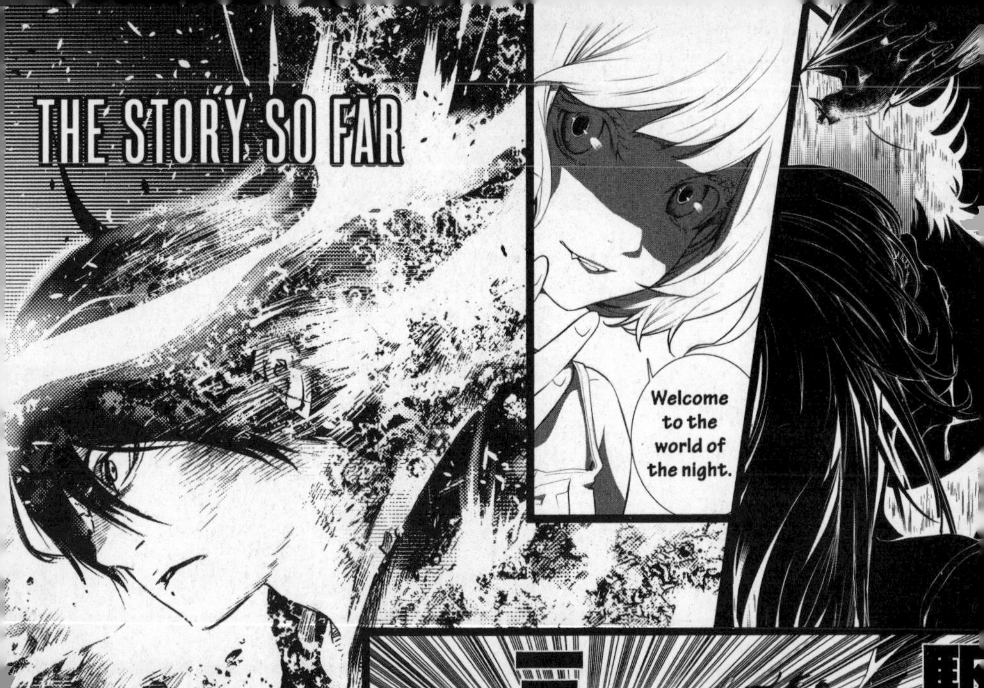
Welcome to the world of the night.
駆除
EXTERMINATIO
三陣
TRI-FORMATION

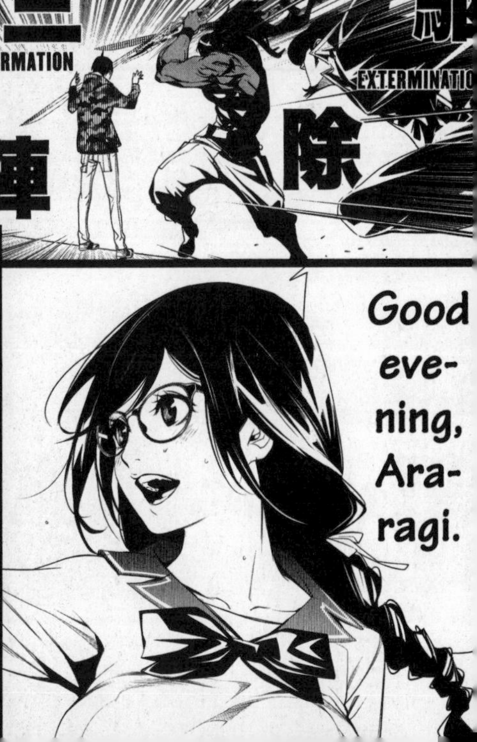
Good eve-ning, Ara-ragi.

During spring break, Koyomi Araragi saved the vampire Kiss-Shot Acerola-Orion Heart-Under-Blade. He was fully prepared to die for her, but instead finds that he has become her vampiric thrall. To become human again, he must now fight three hunters who are after Kiss-Shot. Koyomi curses his fate as he heads to battle, but just before he reaches the site of his first duel, his new friend, Tsubasa Hanekawa, appears before him for some unknown reason...

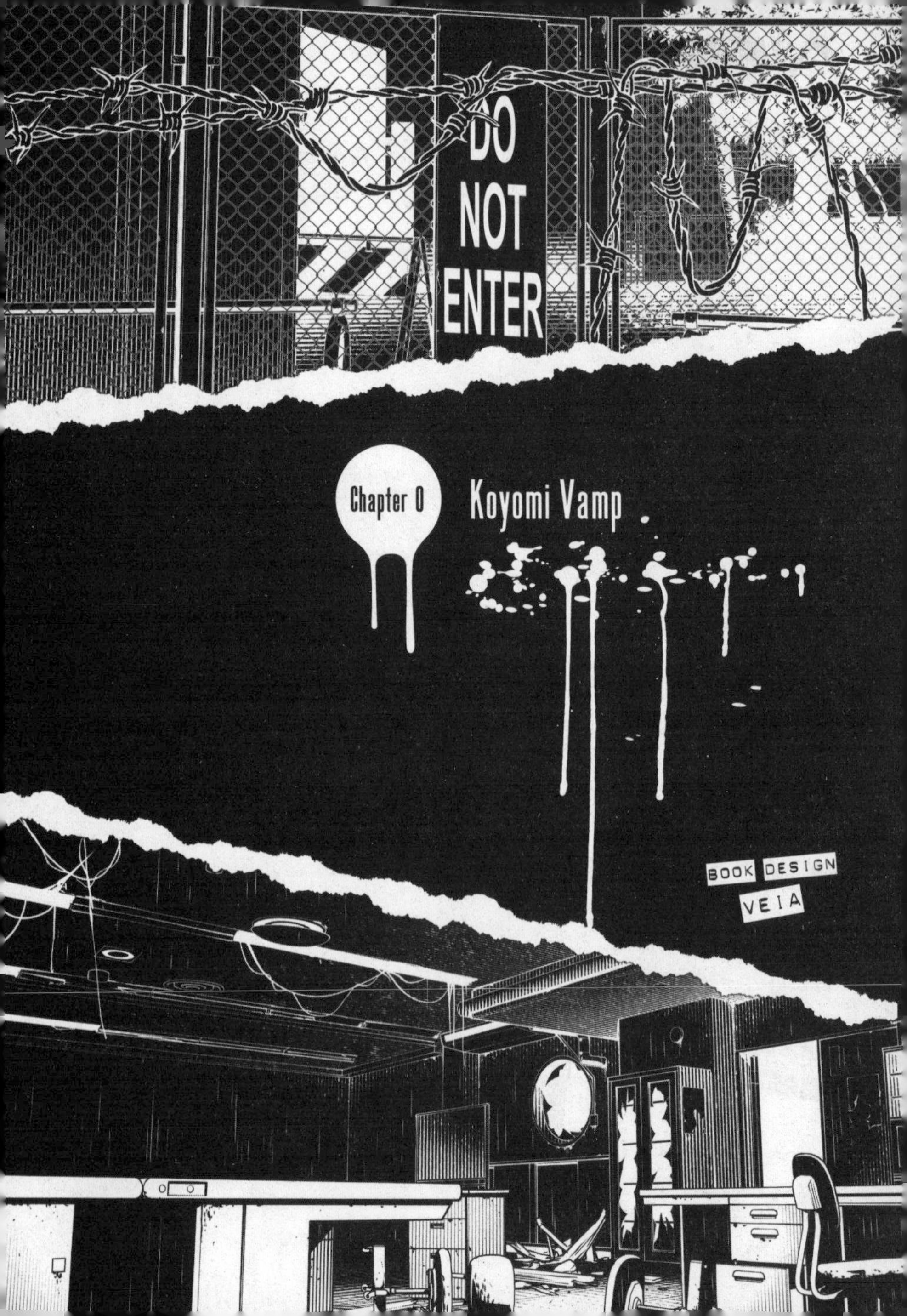
DO NOT ENTER
Chapter 0
Koyomi Vamp
BOOK DESIGN
VEIA

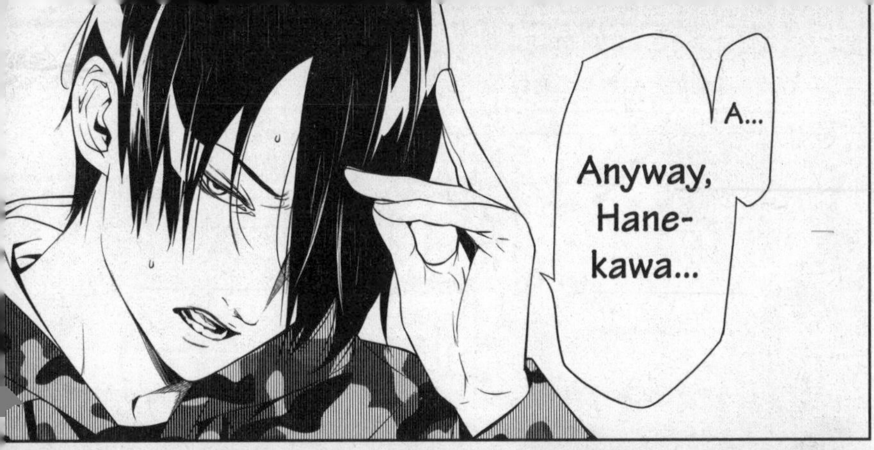
A...
Anyway, Hanekawa...

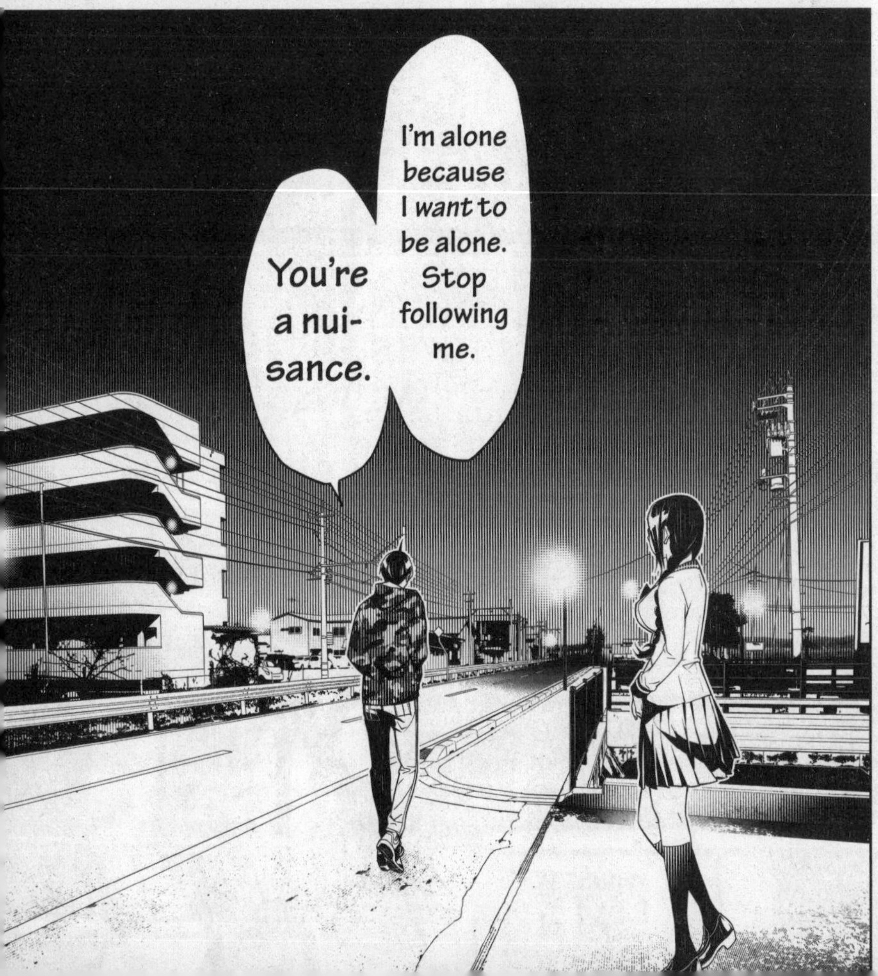
I'm alone because I *want* to be alone. Stop following me.
You're a nuisance.

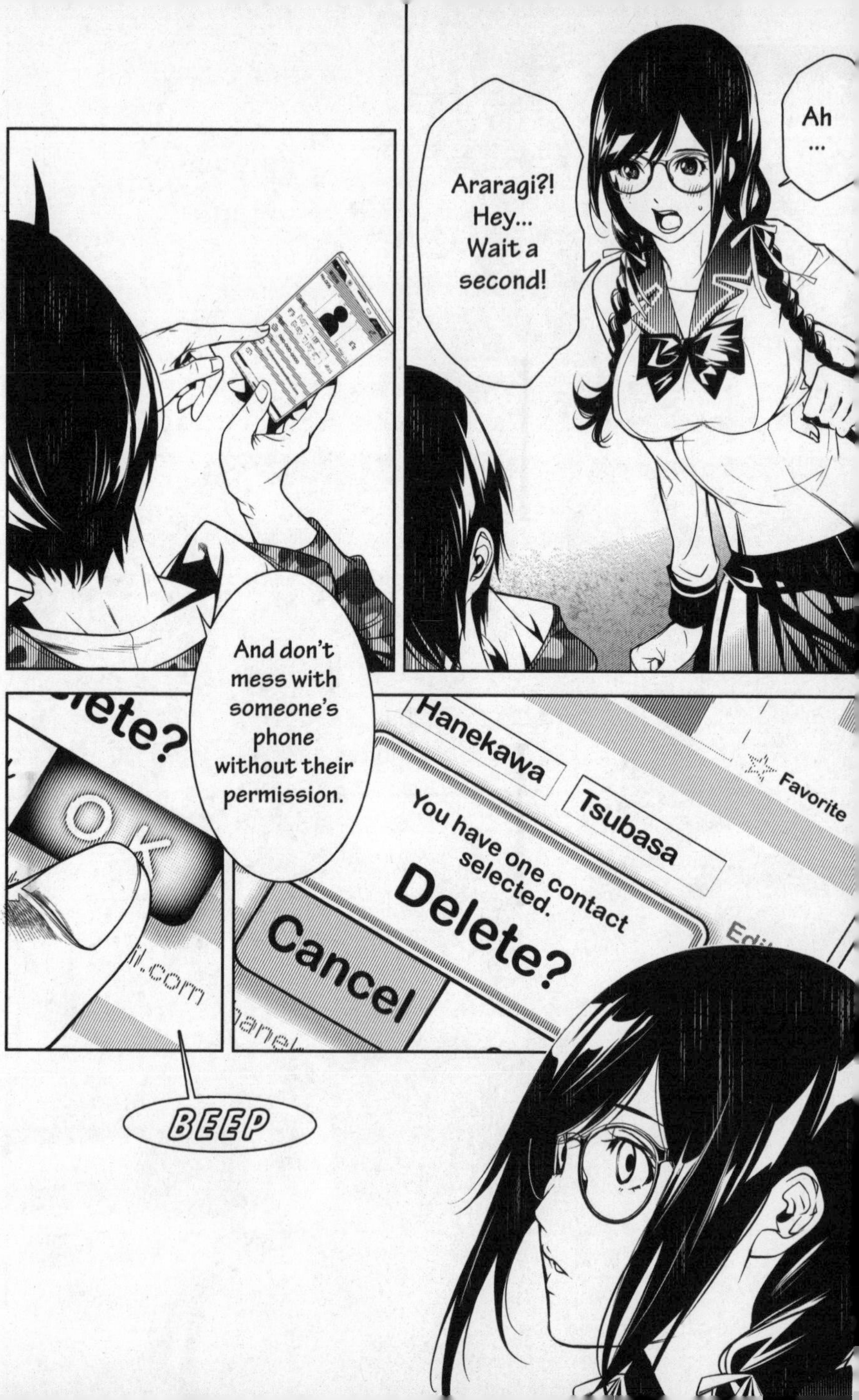
Ah ...
Araragi?! Hey... Wait a second!
And don't mess with someone's phone without their permission.
Hanekawa
Tsubasa
Favorite
You have one contact selected.
Delete?
Cancel
OK
BEEP

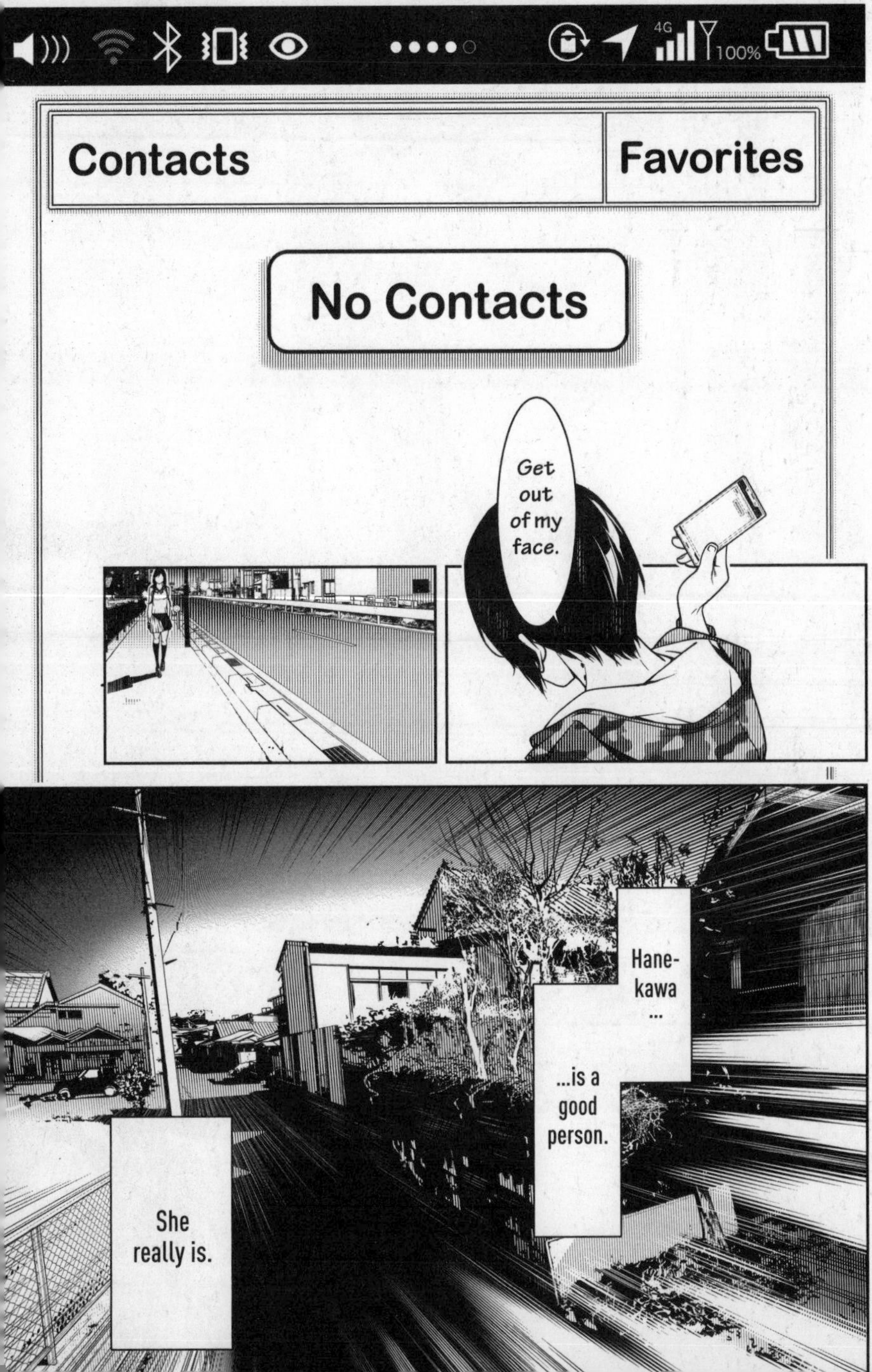
Contacts
Favorites
No Contacts
Get out of my face.
Hane-kawa...
...is a good person.
She really is.

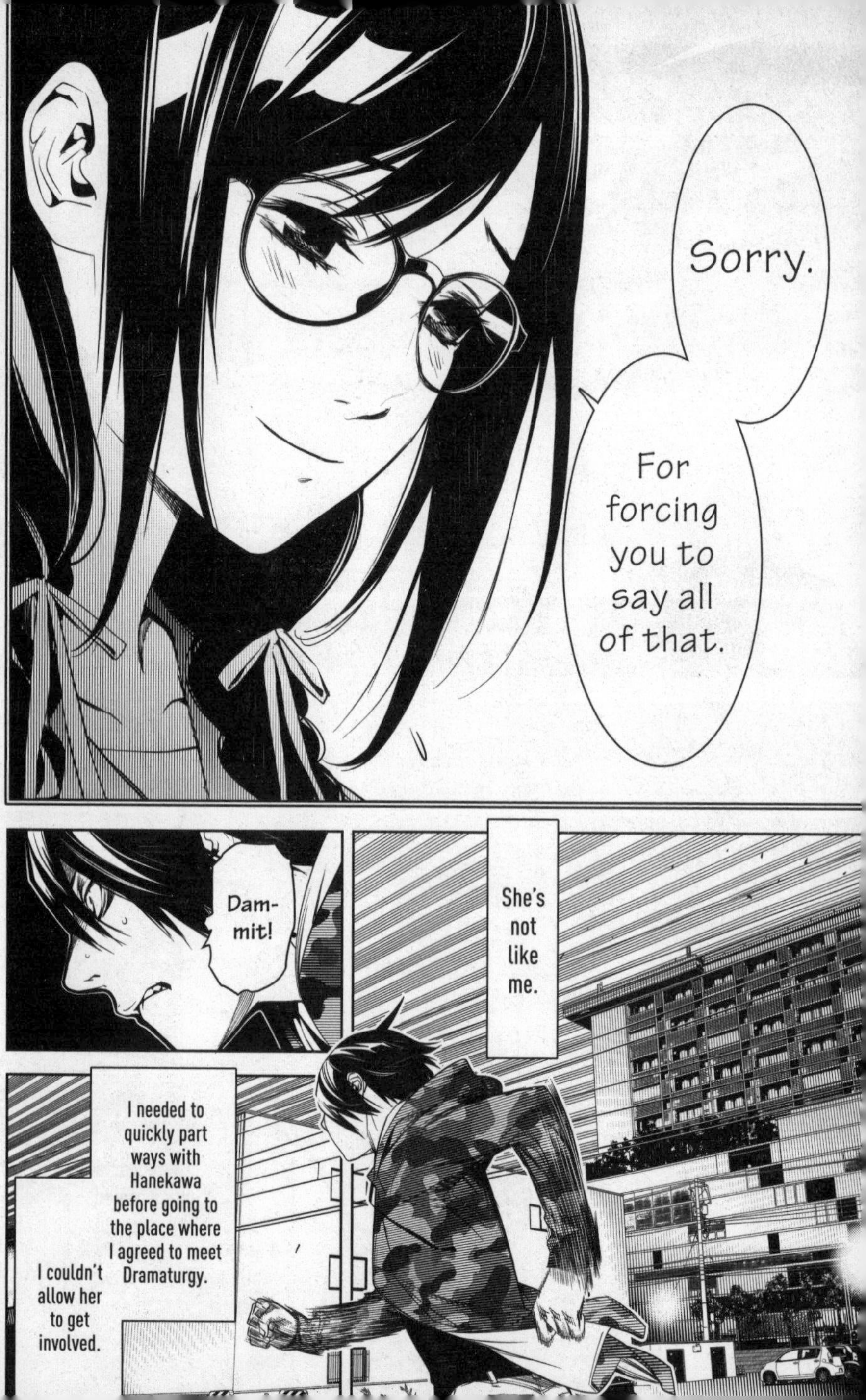
Sorry.
For forcing you to say all of that.
She's not like me.
Dam-mit!
I needed to quickly part ways with Hanekawa before going to the place where I agreed to meet Dramaturgy.
I couldn't allow her to get involved.

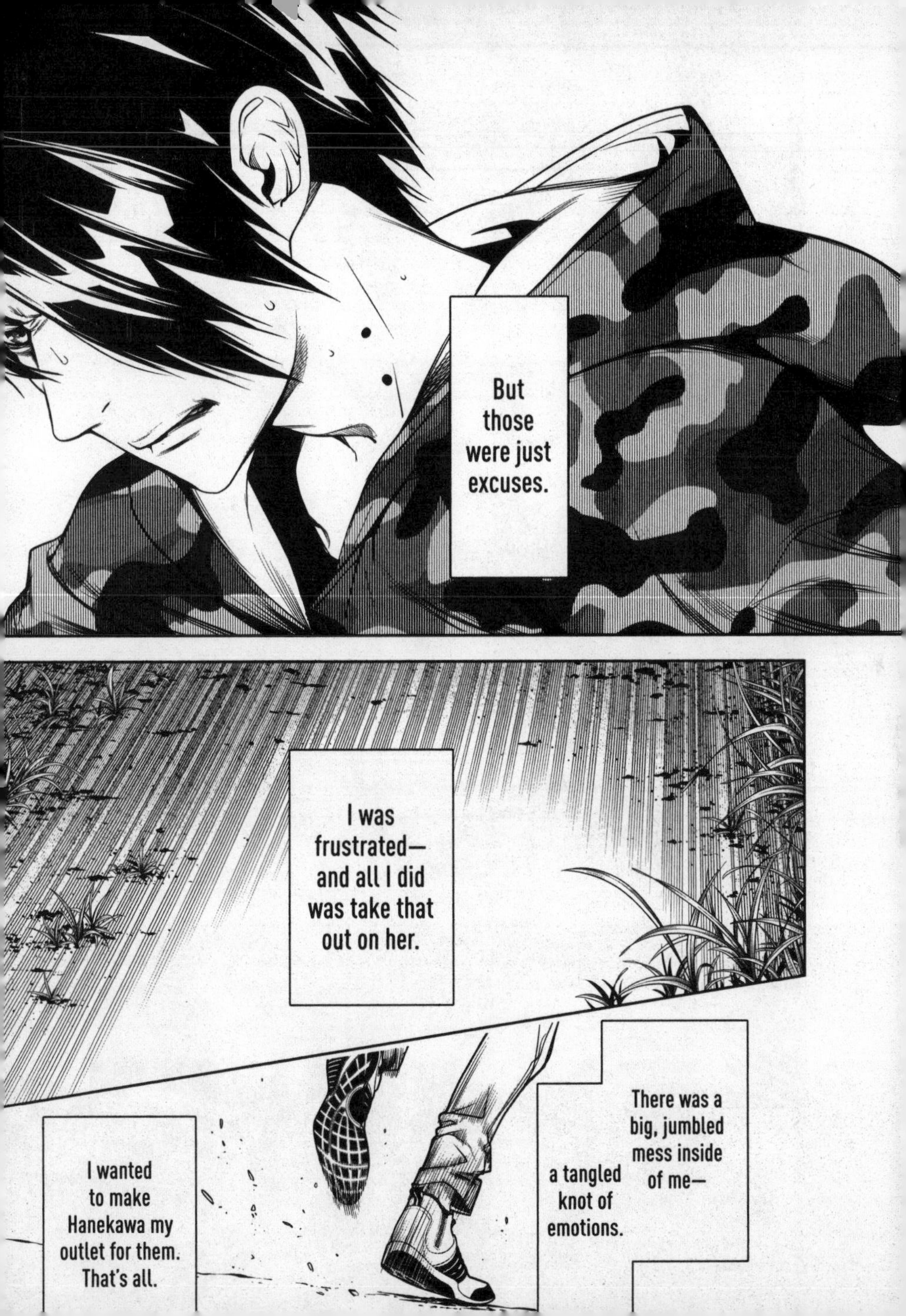
But those were just excuses.
I was frustrated—and all I did was take that out on her.
There was a big, jumbled mess inside of me—
a tangled knot of emotions.
I wanted to make Hanekawa my outlet for them. That's all.

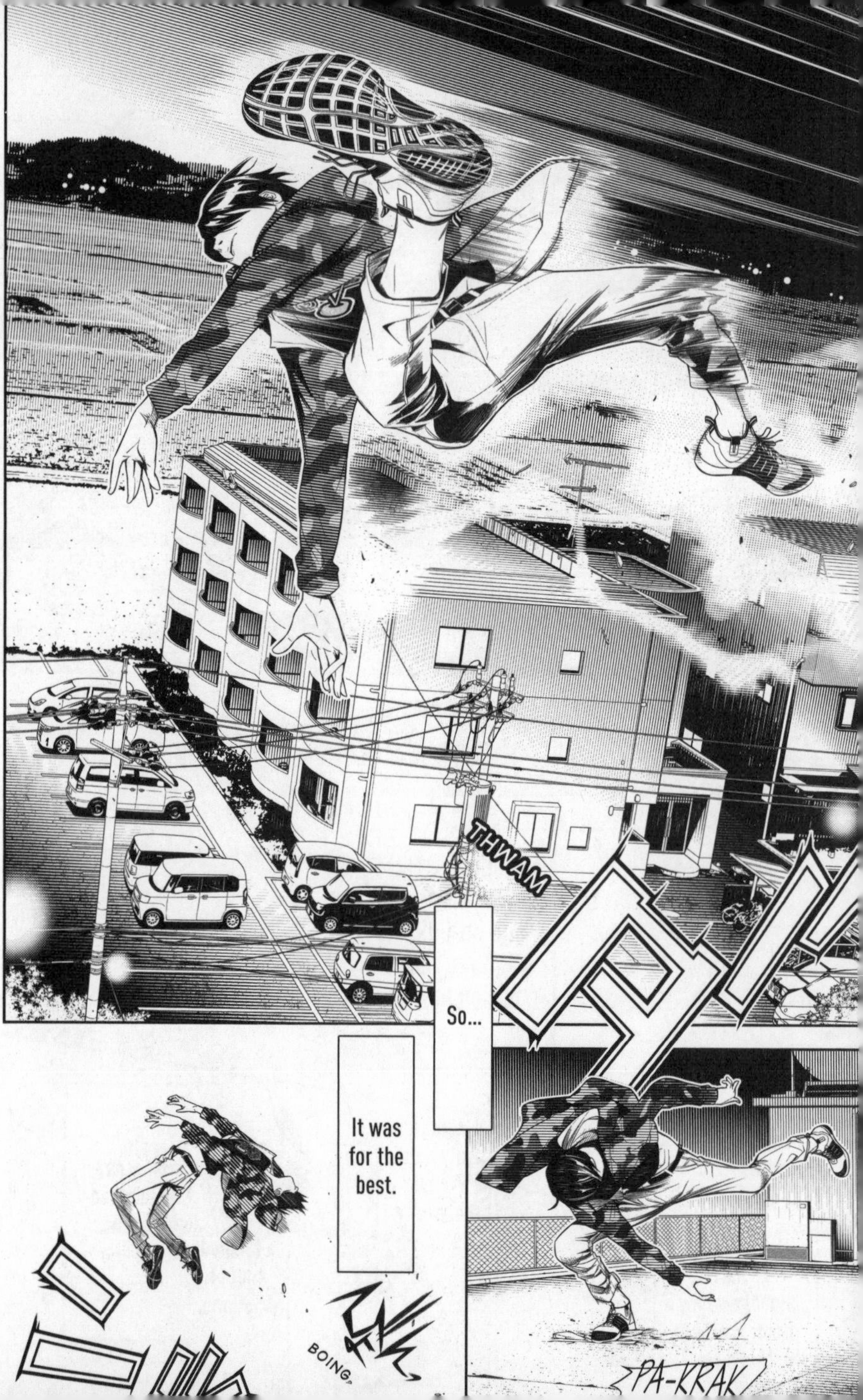
THWAM
So...
PA-KRAK
It was for the best.
BOING

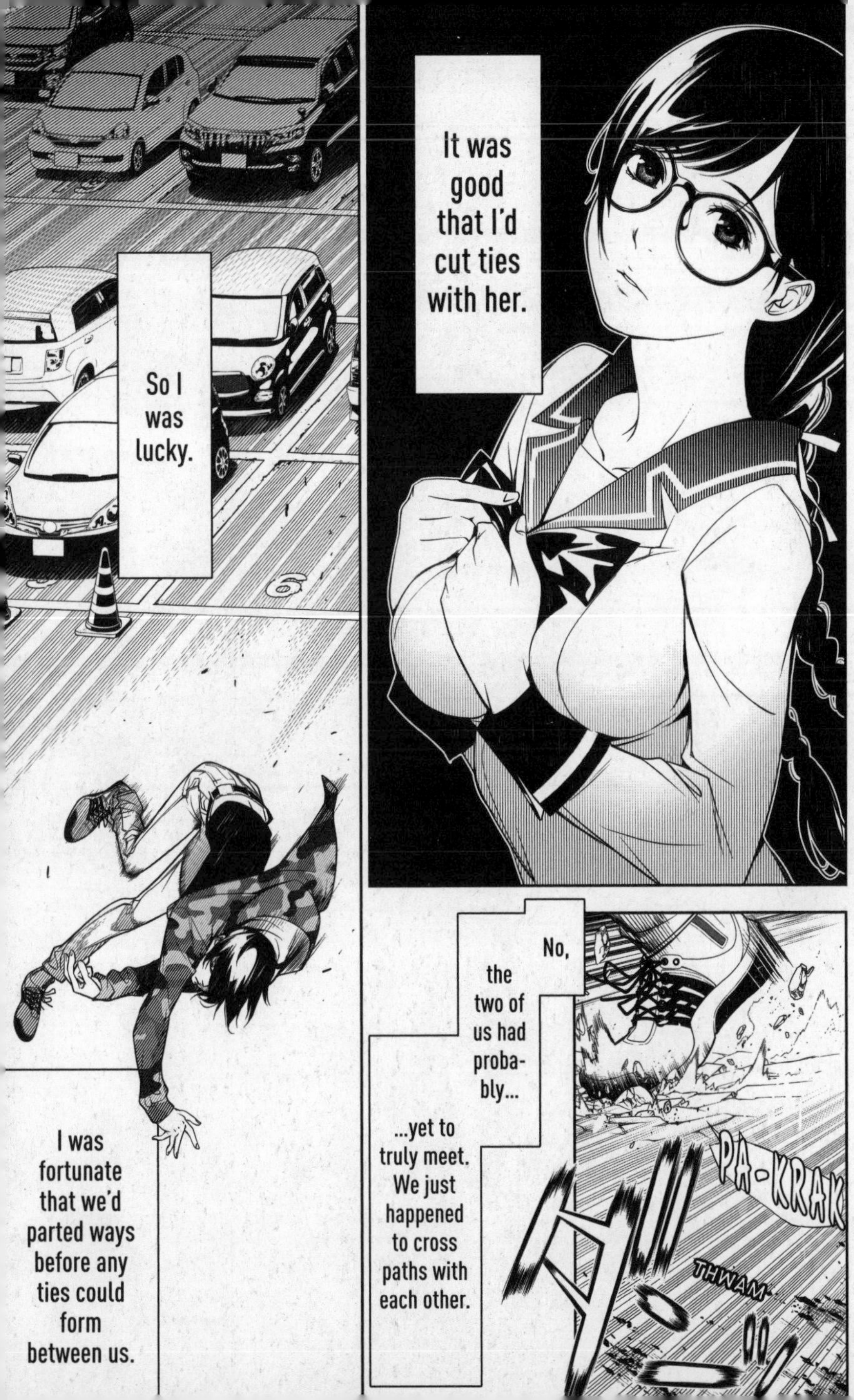
It was good that I'd cut ties with her.
No,
the two of us had probably...
...yet to truly meet. We just happened to cross paths with each other.
PA-KRAK
THWAM
So I was lucky.
I was fortunate that we'd parted ways before any ties could form between us.

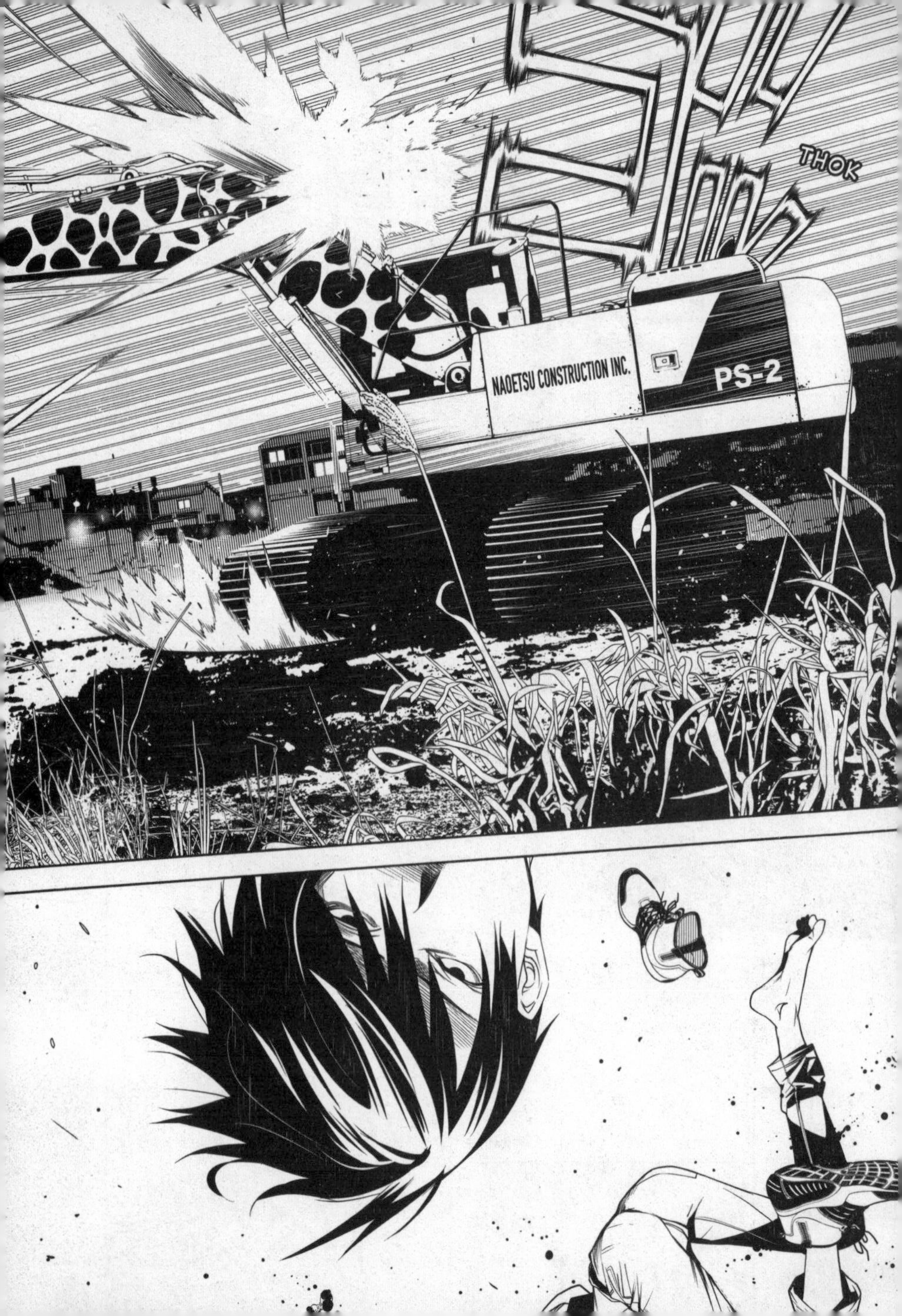
THOK
NAOETSU CONSTRUCTION INC.
PS-2

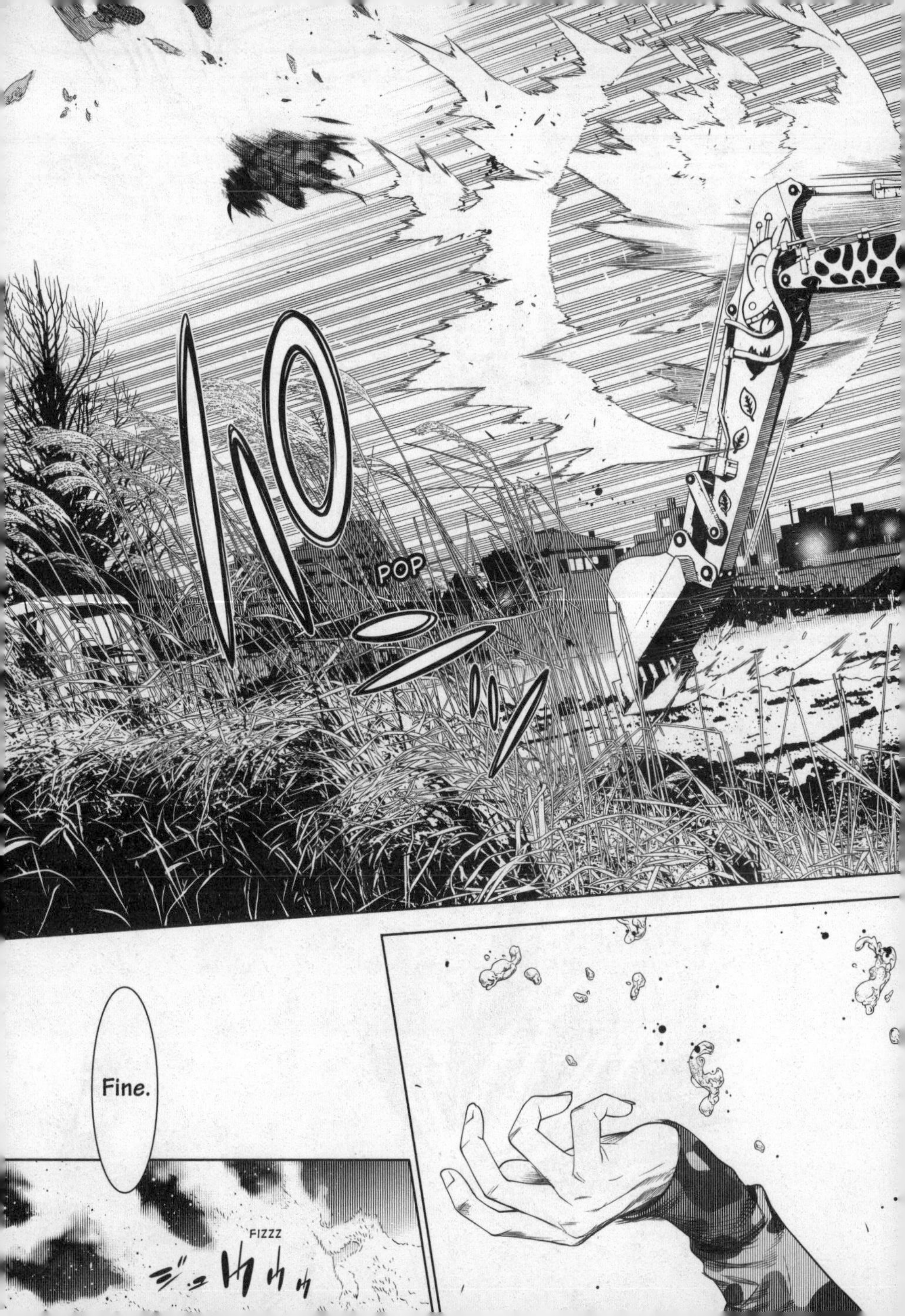
POP
Fine.
FIZZZ

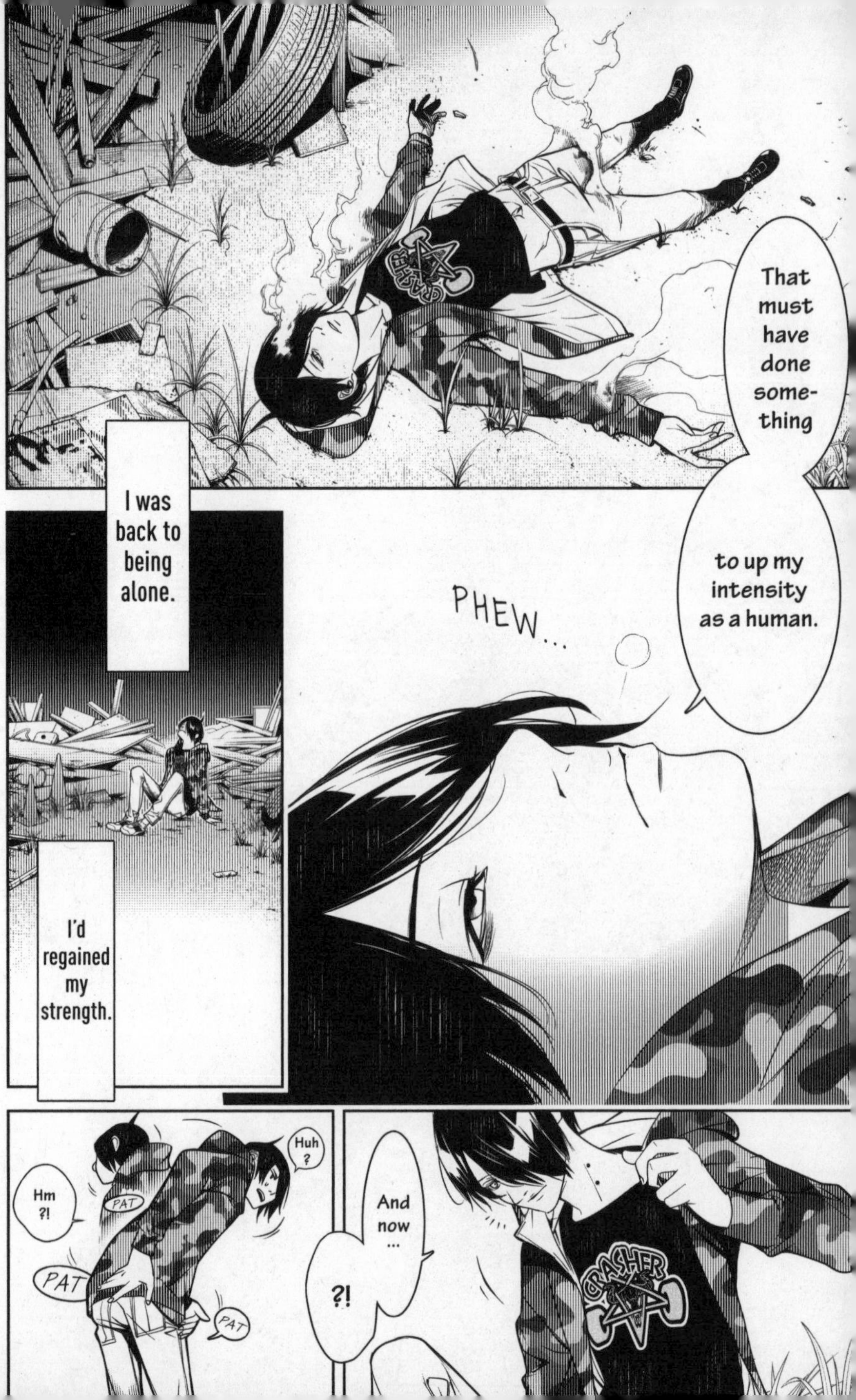
That must have done something
to up my intensity as a human.
PHEW...
I was back to being alone.
I'd regained my strength.
And now...
?!
Huh?
Hm?!
PAT
PAT
PAT

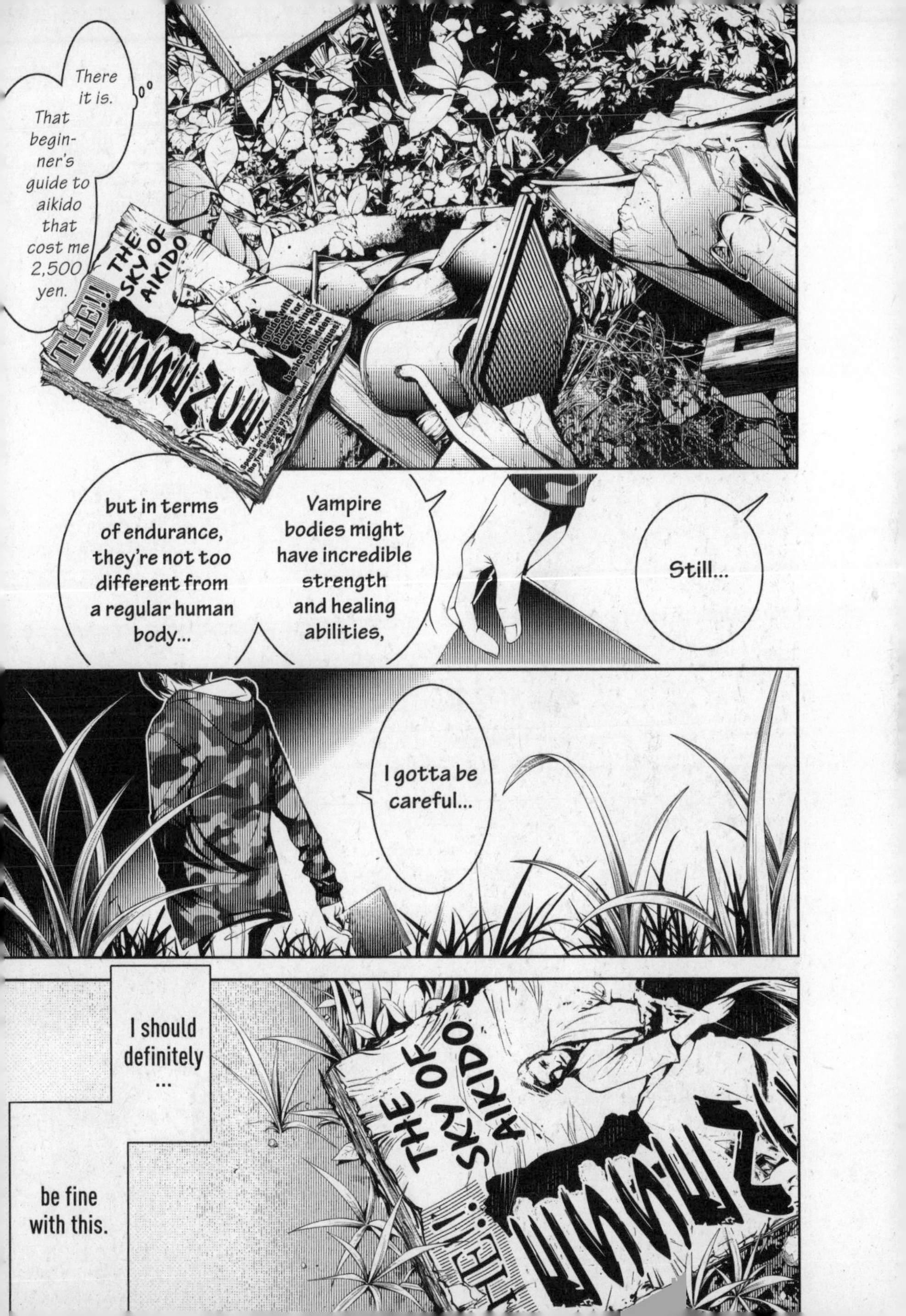
There it is. That beginner's guide to aikido that cost me 2,500 yen.
THE! SKY OF AIKIDO
A guide with photos for everything from the basics to hidden techniques!
Still...
Vampire bodies might have incredible strength and healing abilities,
but in terms of endurance, they're not too different from a regular human body...
I gotta be careful...
THE SKY OF AIKIDO
I should definitely ...
be fine with this.

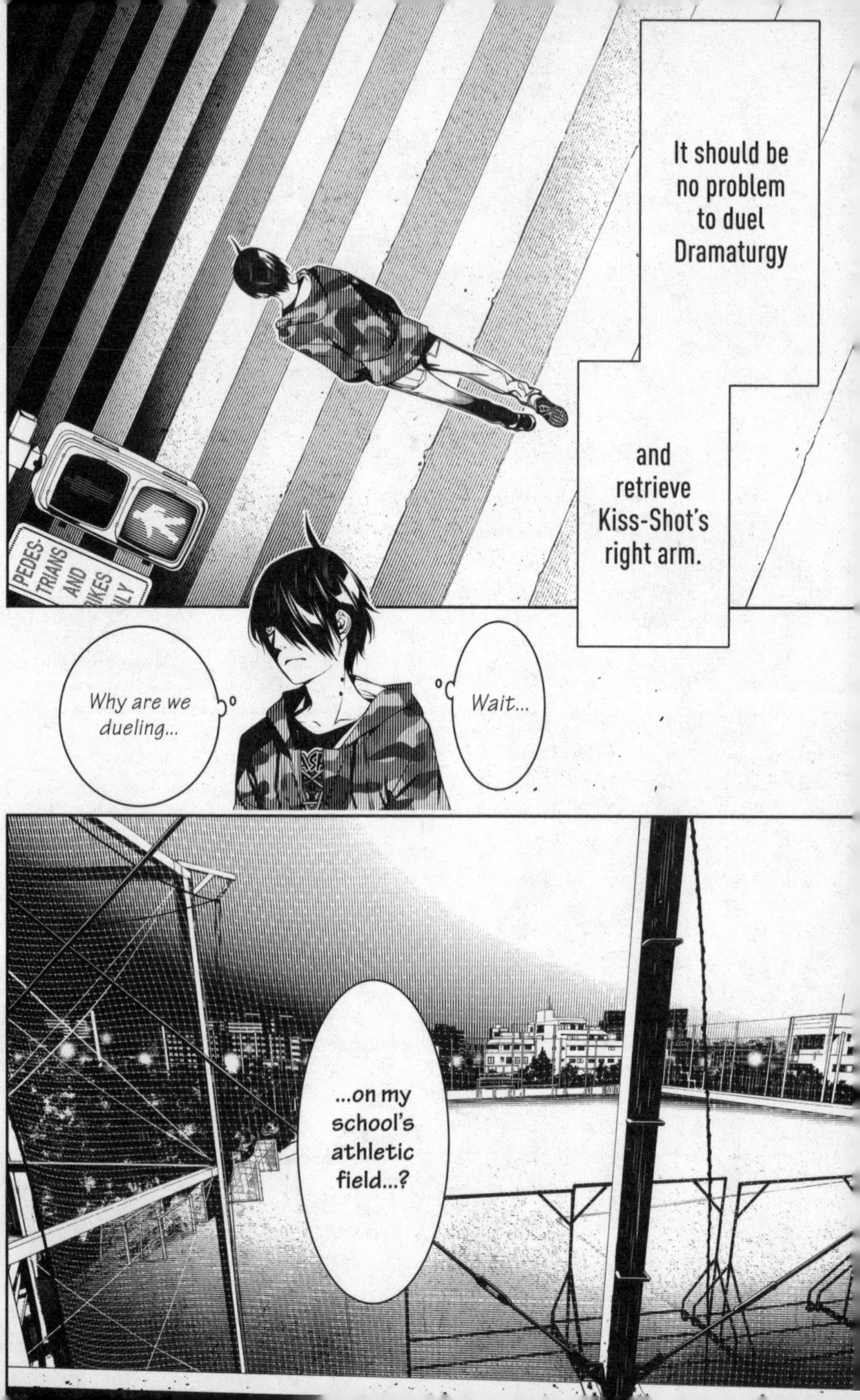
It should be no problem to duel Dramaturgy
and retrieve Kiss-Shot's right arm.
PEDES-TRIANS AND BIKES
Wait...
Why are we dueling...
...on my school's athletic field...?

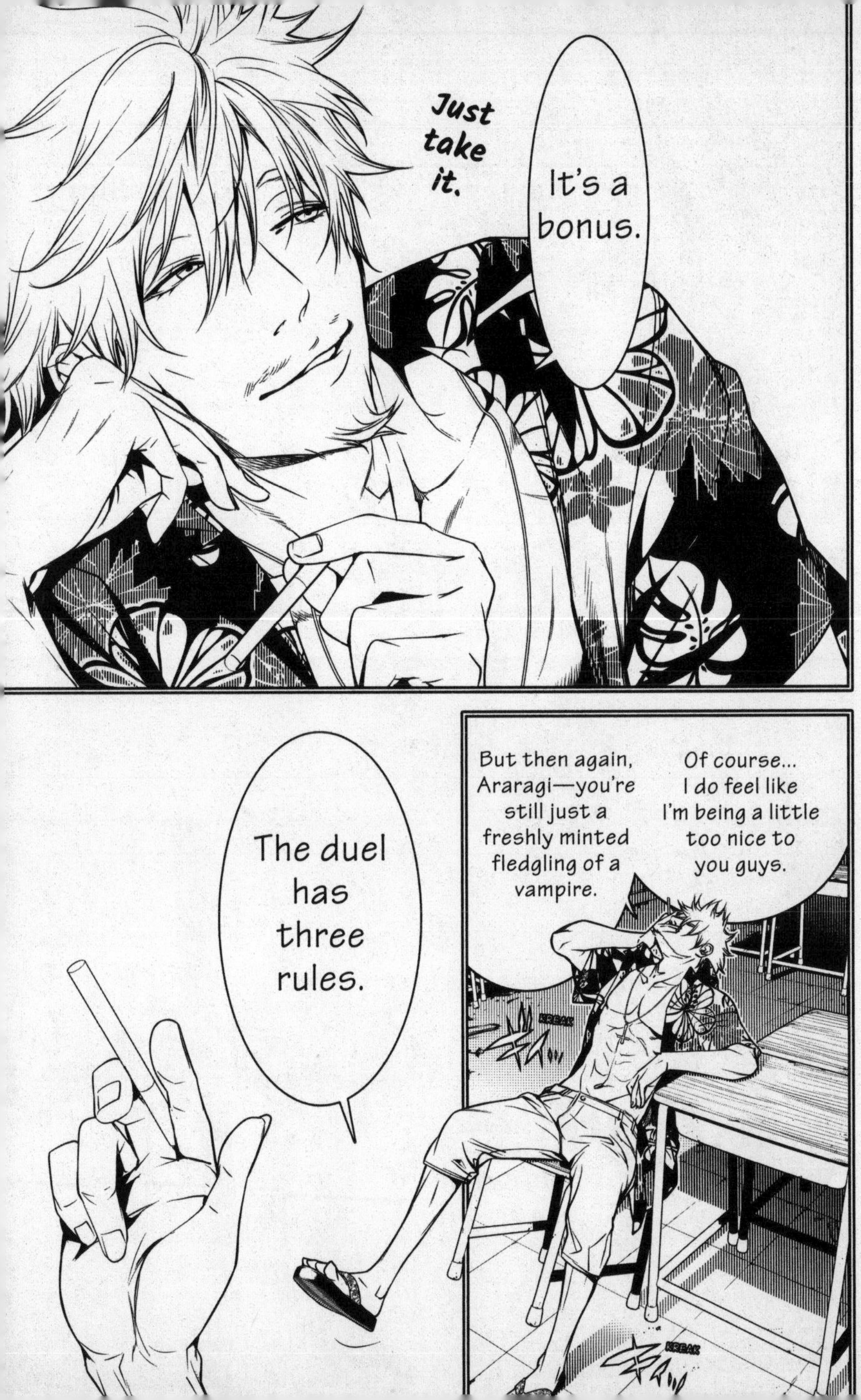
It's a bonus.
Just take it.
Of course... I do feel like I'm being a little too nice to you guys.
But then again, Araragi—you're still just a freshly minted fledgling of a vampire.
KREAK
KREAK
The duel has three rules.

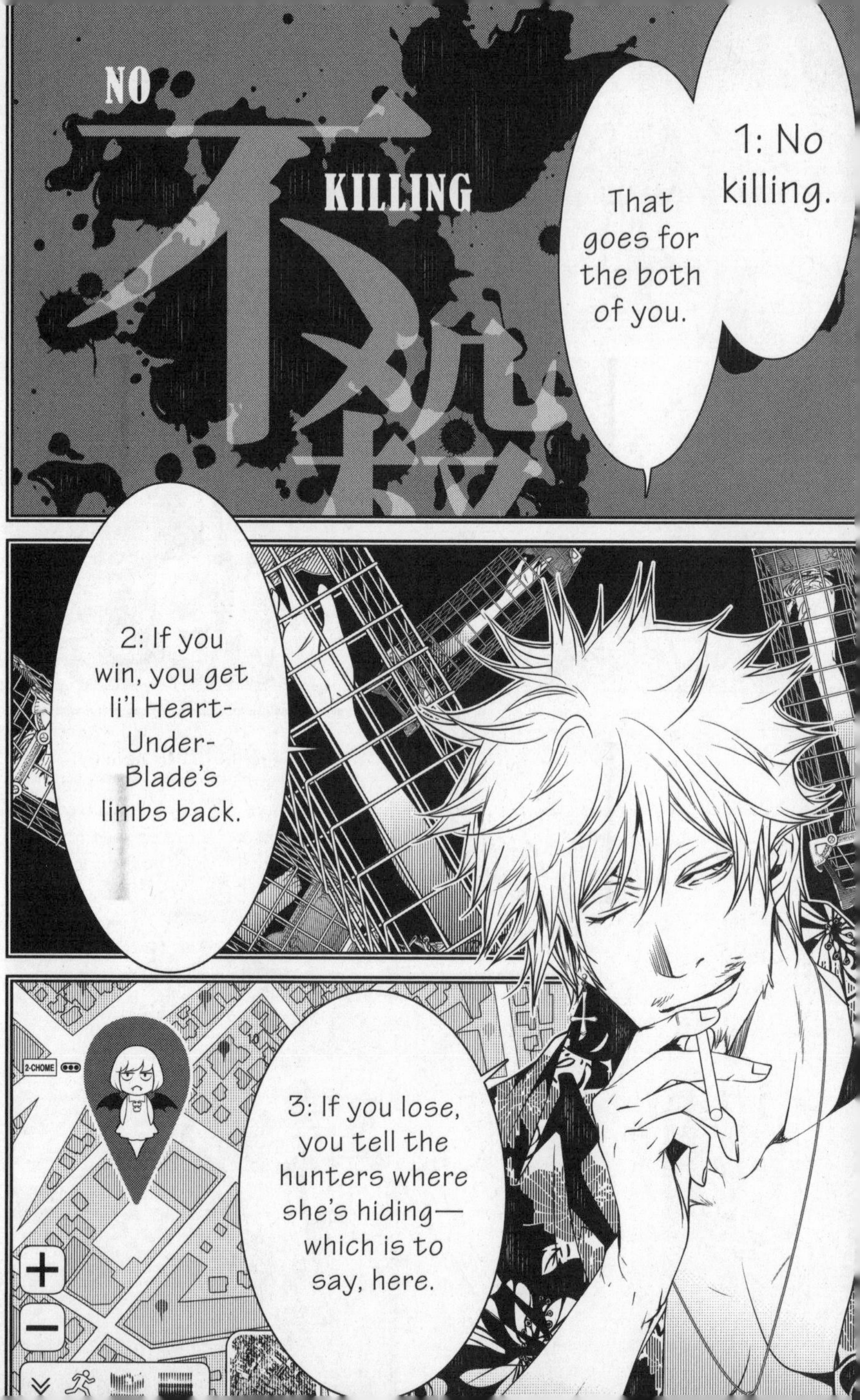
1: No killing.
That goes for the both of you.
NO KILLING
2: If you win, you get li'l Heart-Under-Blade's limbs back.
3: If you lose, you tell the hunters where she's hiding—which is to say, here.
2-CHOME

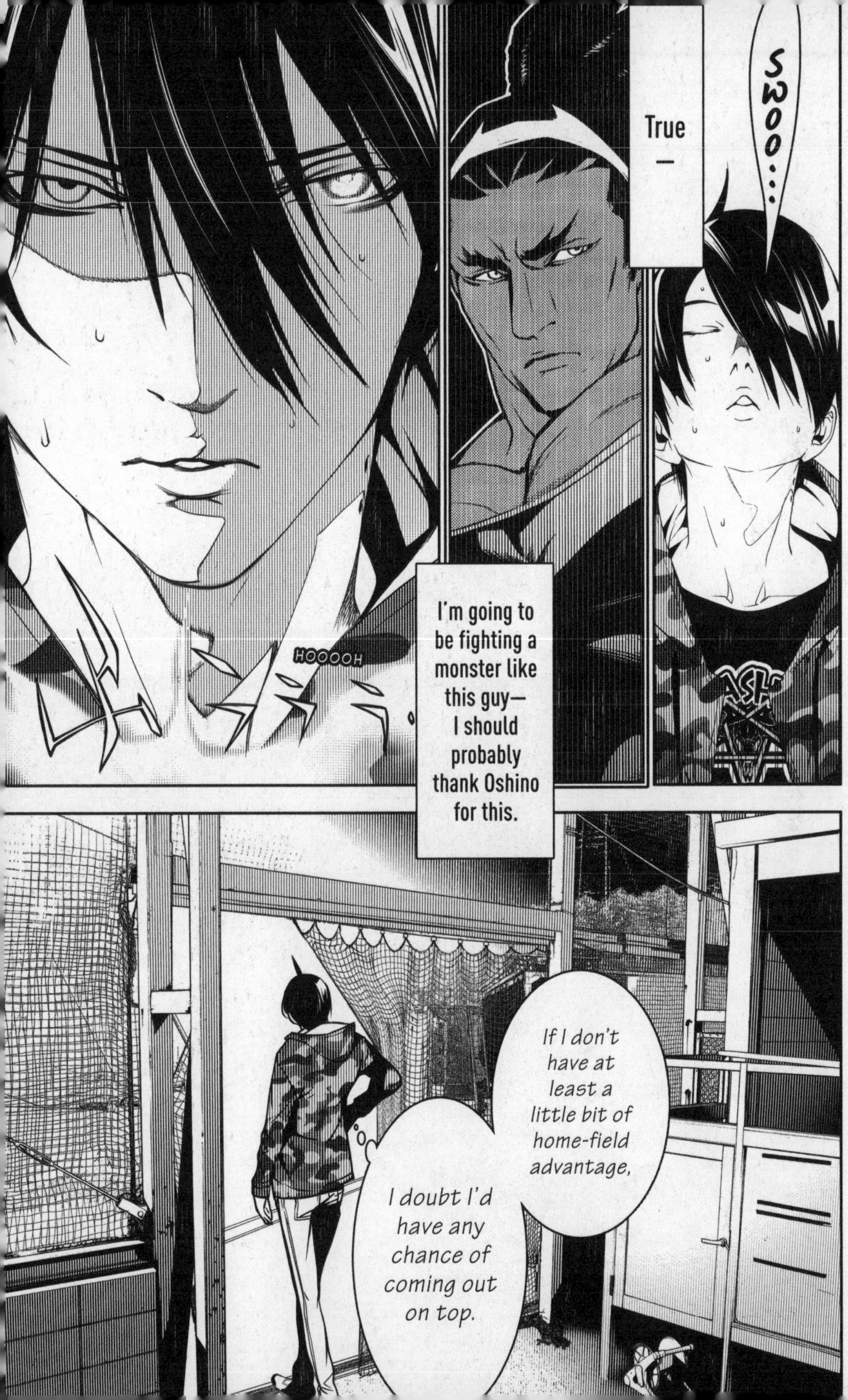
SWOO...
True —
I'm going to be fighting a monster like this guy— I should probably thank Oshino for this.
HOOOOH
If I don't have at least a little bit of home-field advantage,
I doubt I'd have any chance of coming out on top.

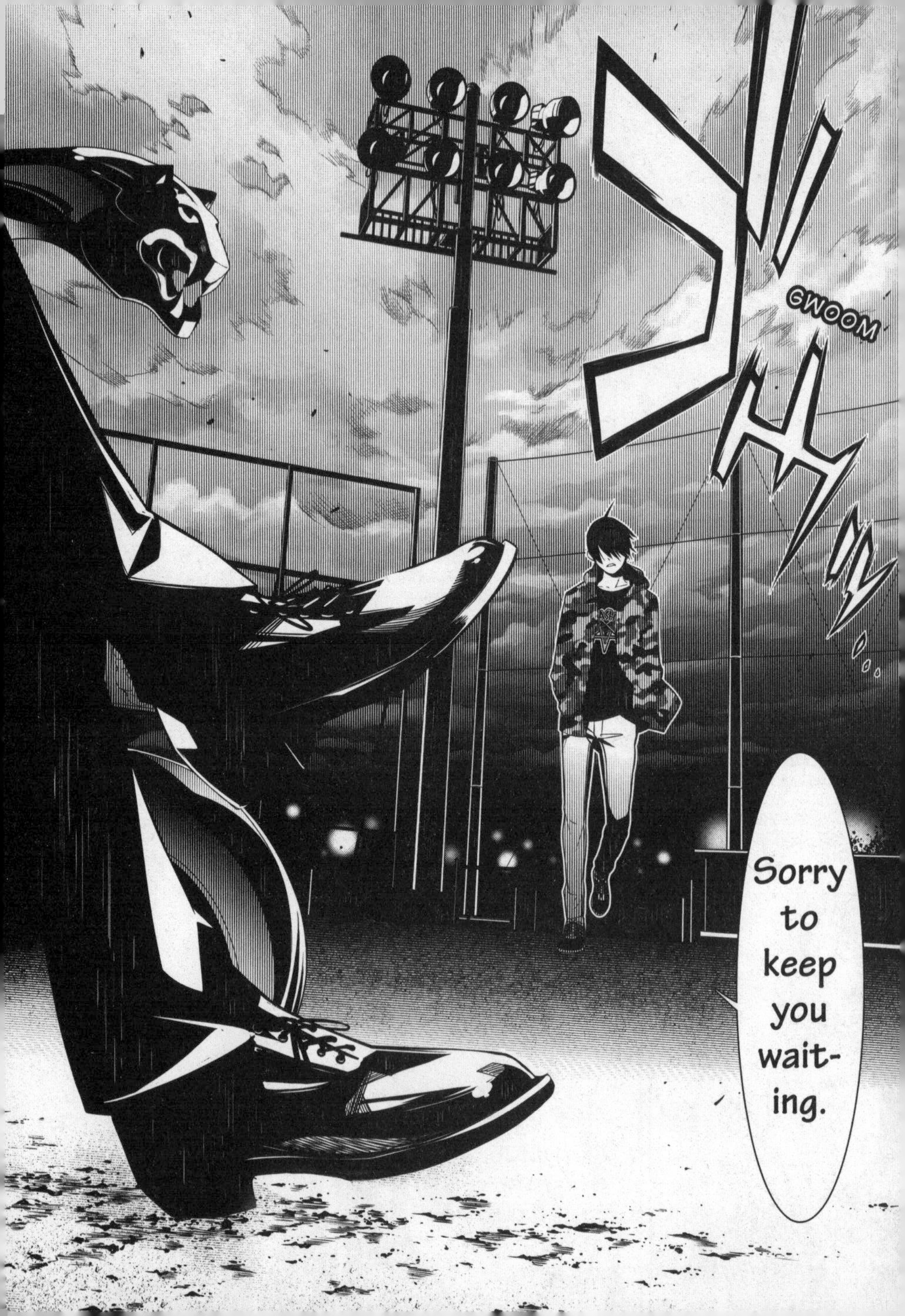
GWOOM
Sorry to keep you wait-ing.

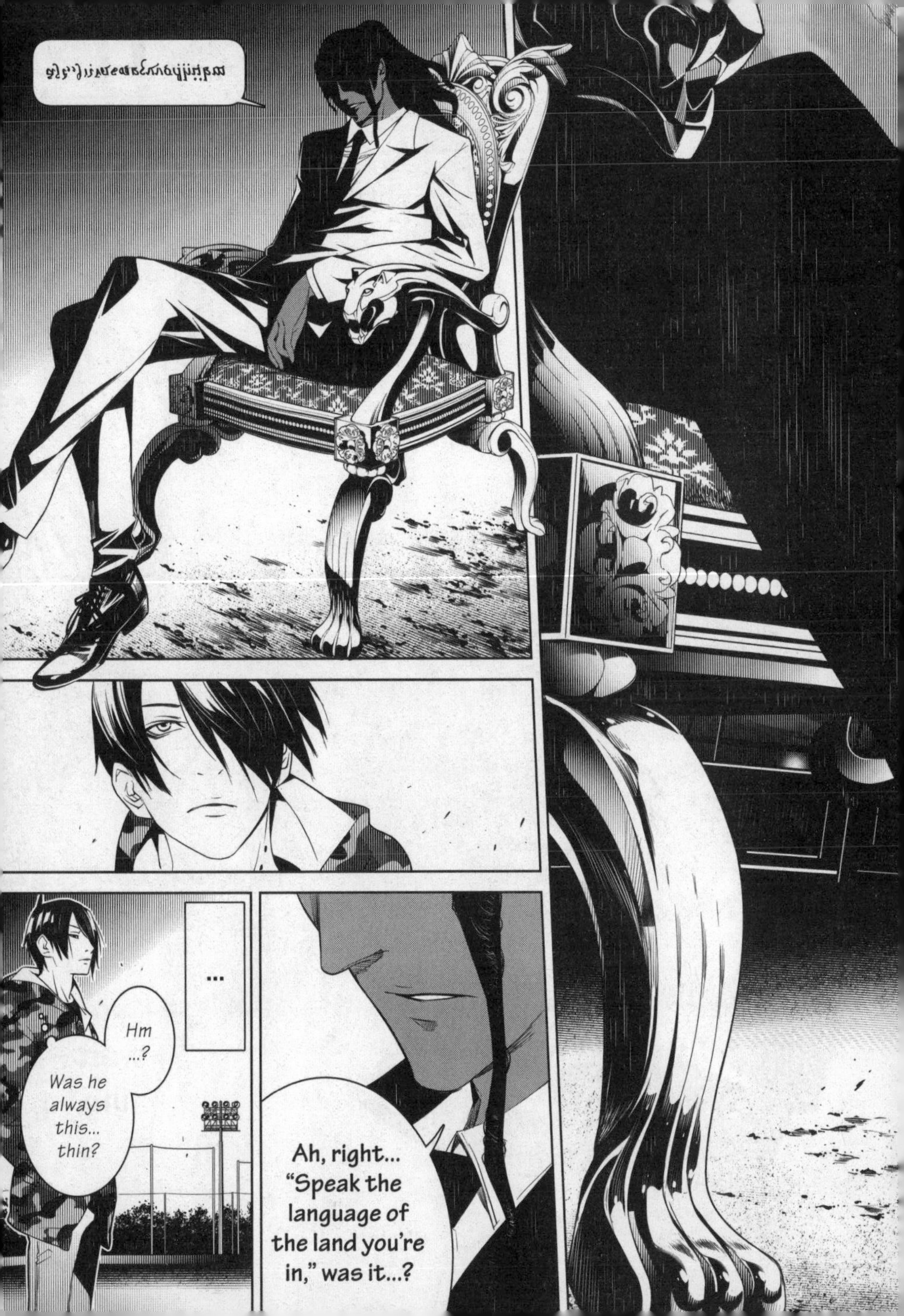
Ah, right... "Speak the language of the land you're in," was it...?
...
Hm ...?
Was he always this... thin?

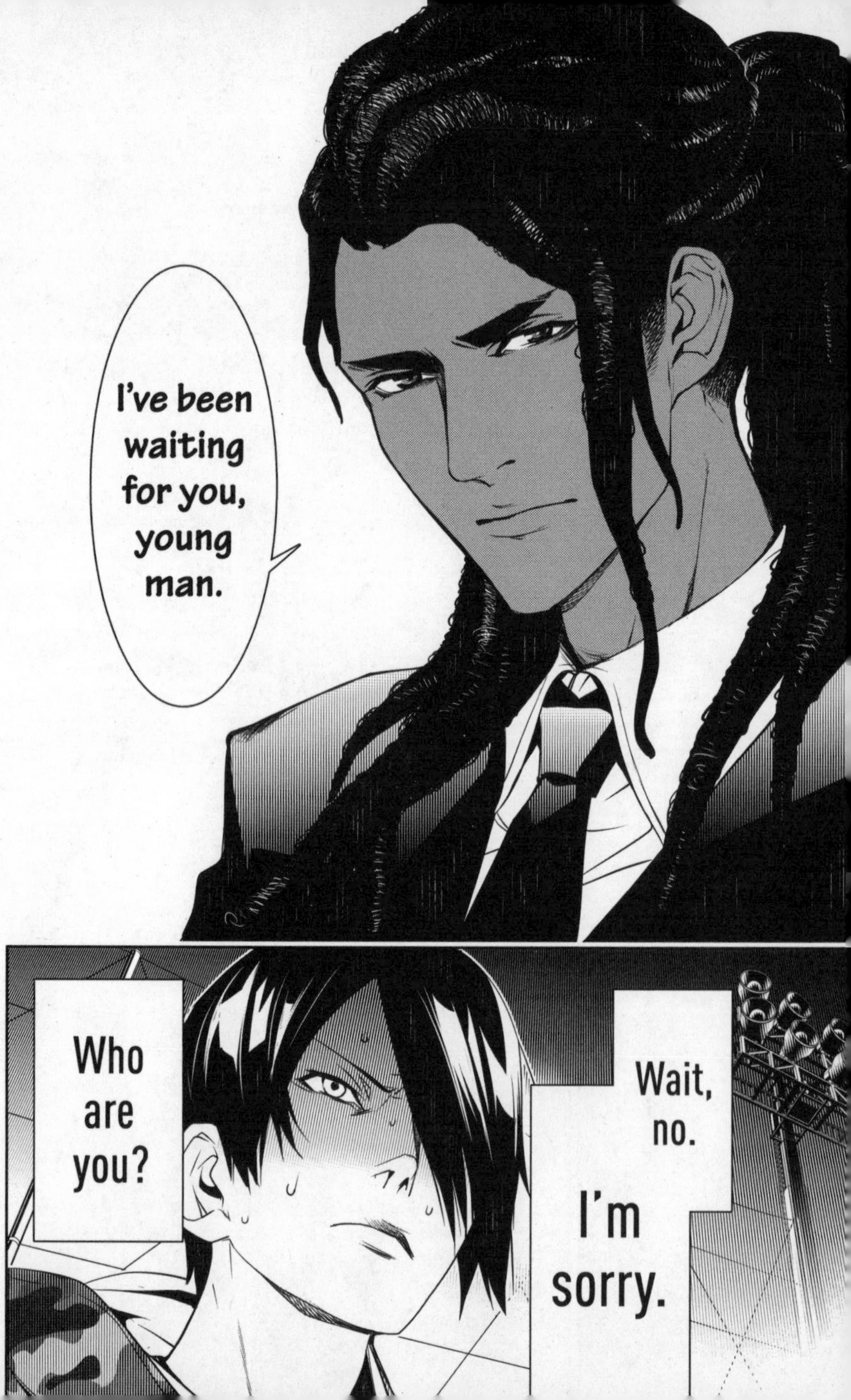
I've been waiting for you, young man.
Wait, no.
I'm sorry.
Who are you?

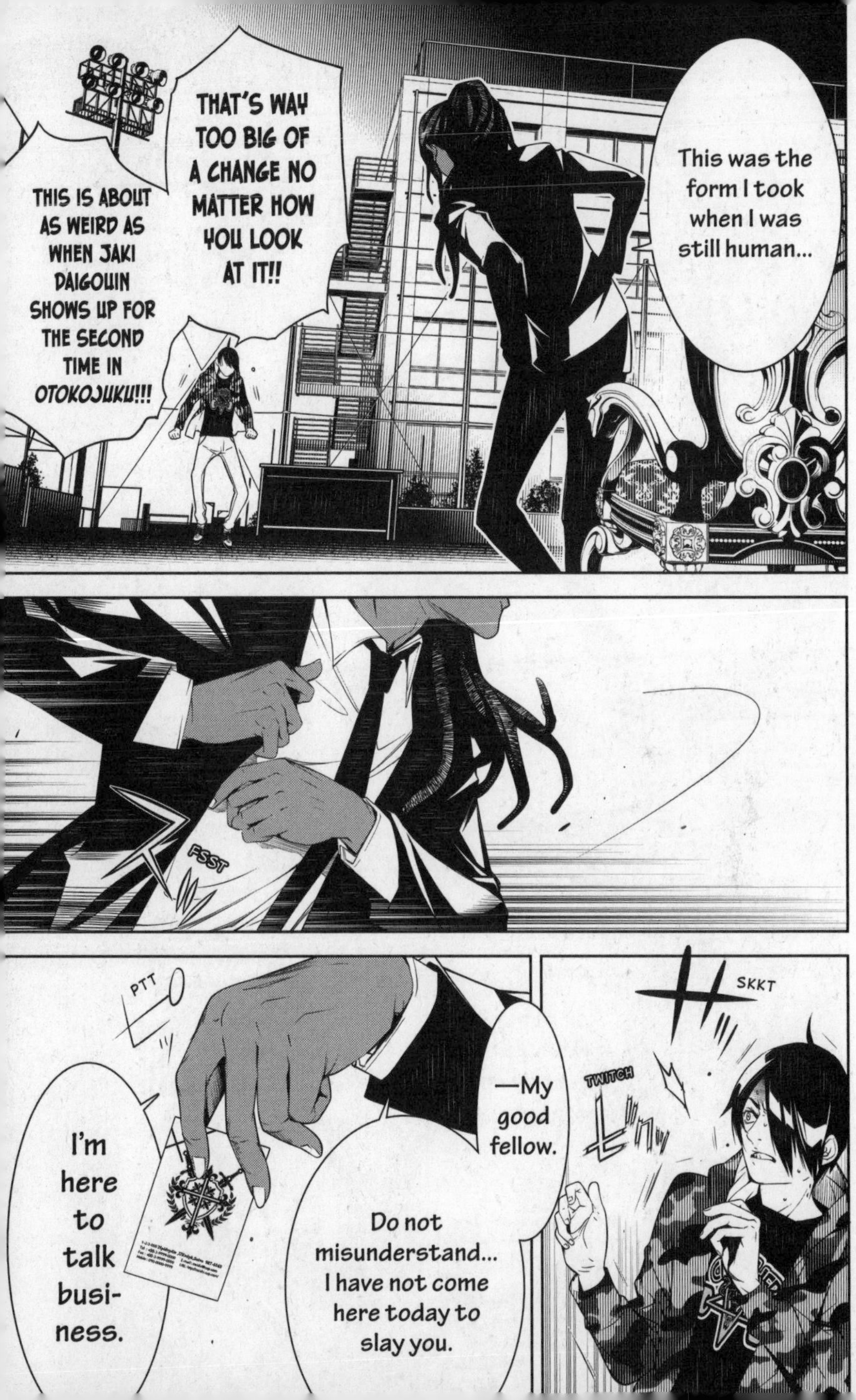

This was the form I took when I was still human...
THAT'S WAY TOO BIG OF A CHANGE NO MATTER HOW YOU LOOK AT IT!!
THIS IS ABOUT AS WEIRD AS WHEN JAKI DAIGOUIN SHOWS UP FOR THE SECOND TIME IN OTOKOJUKU!!!
FSST
SKKT
TWITCH
—My good fellow.
Do not misunderstand... I have not come here today to slay you.
I'm here to talk business.
PTT

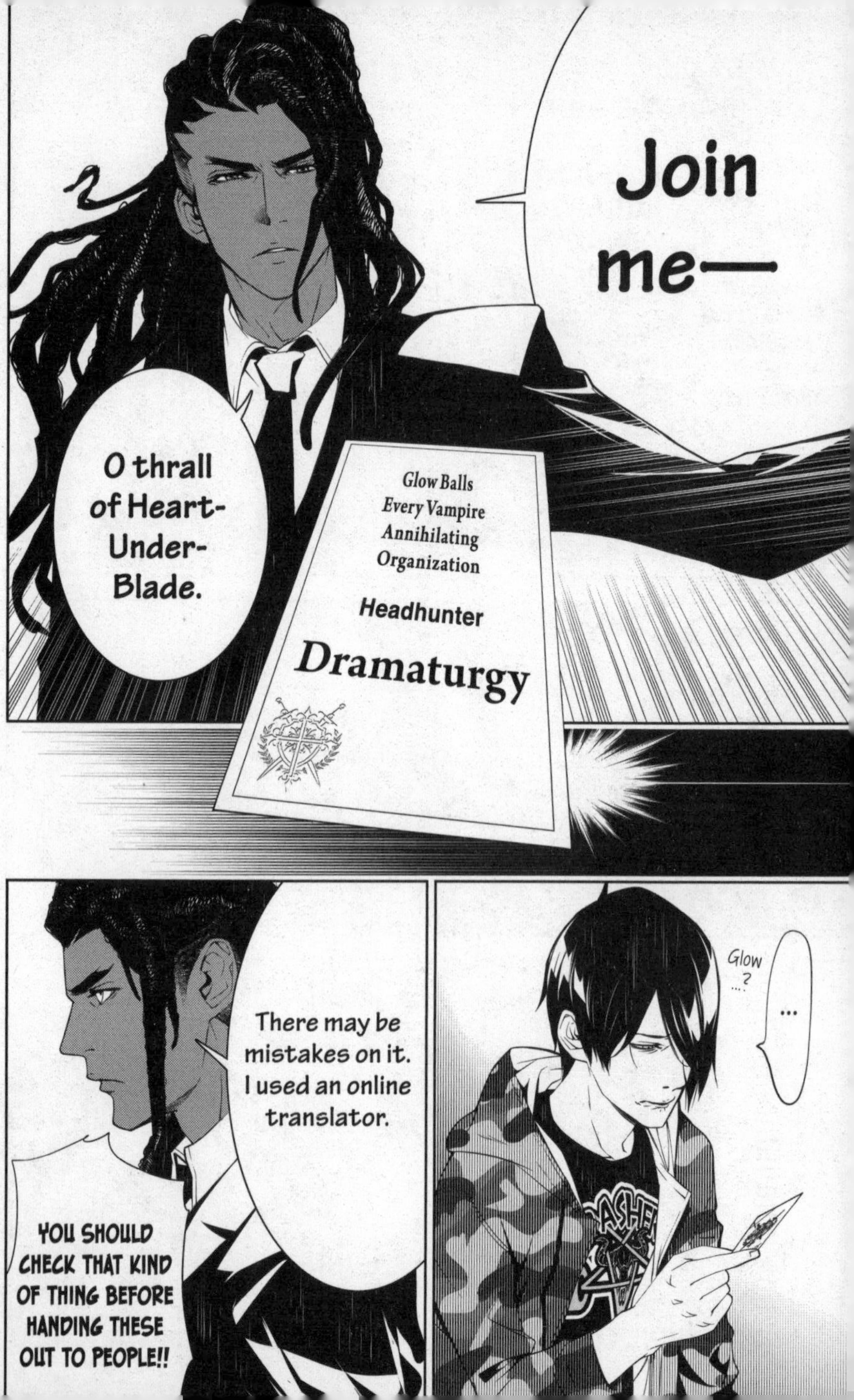
Join me—
O thrall of Heart-Under-Blade.
Glow Balls Every Vampire Annihilating Organization
Headhunter
Dramaturgy
Glow ...?
...
There may be mistakes on it. I used an online translator.
YOU SHOULD CHECK THAT KIND OF THING BEFORE HANDING THESE OUT TO PEOPLE!!

化 *bake*

物 *mono*

<u>*KOYOMIvamp*</u>
10

語 *gatari*

語 *gatari*

物 *mono*

$$\frac{10}{KOYOMI vamp}$$

化 *bake*

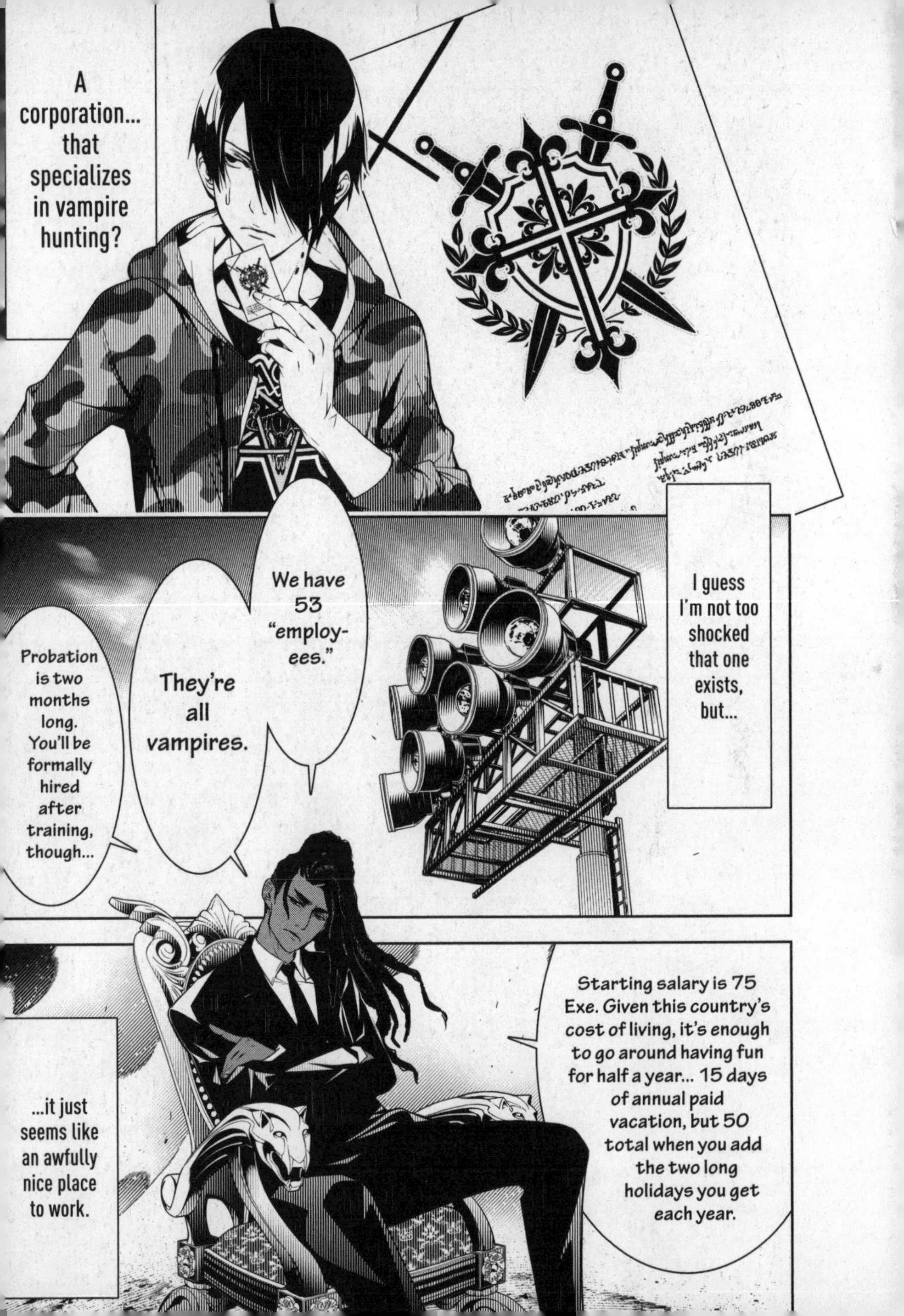
A corporation... that specializes in vampire hunting?
I guess I'm not too shocked that one exists, but...
We have 53 "employ-ees."
They're all vampires.
Probation is two months long. You'll be formally hired after training, though...
Starting salary is 75 Exe. Given this country's cost of living, it's enough to go around having fun for half a year... 15 days of annual paid vacation, but 50 total when you add the two long holidays you get each year.
...it just seems like an awfully nice place to work.

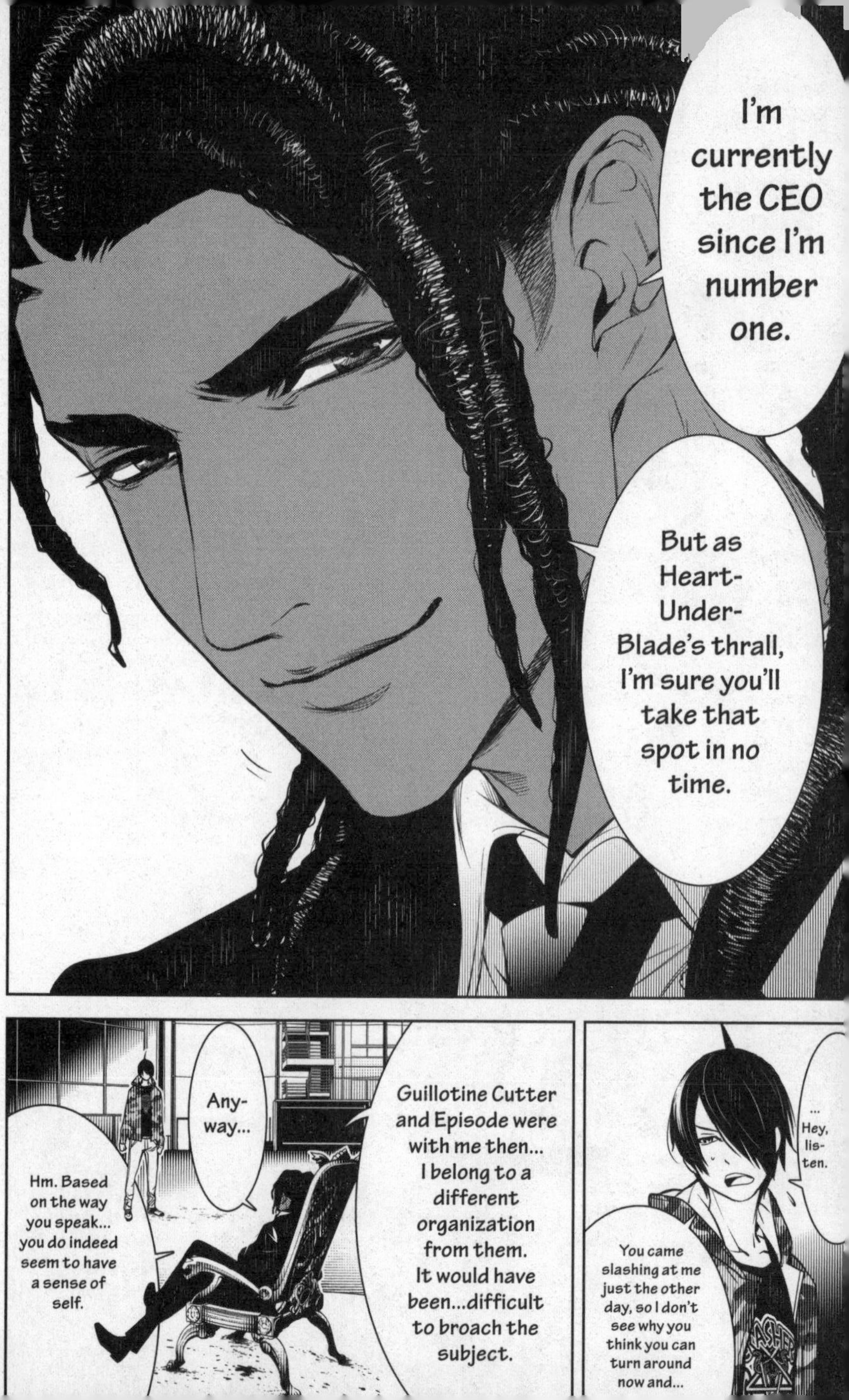
I'm currently the CEO since I'm number one.
But as Heart-Under-Blade's thrall, I'm sure you'll take that spot in no time.
... Hey, listen.
You came slashing at me just the other day, so I don't see why you think you can turn around now and...
Guillotine Cutter and Episode were with me then... I belong to a different organization from them. It would have been...difficult to broach the subject.
Any-way...
Hm. Based on the way you speak... you do indeed seem to have a sense of self.

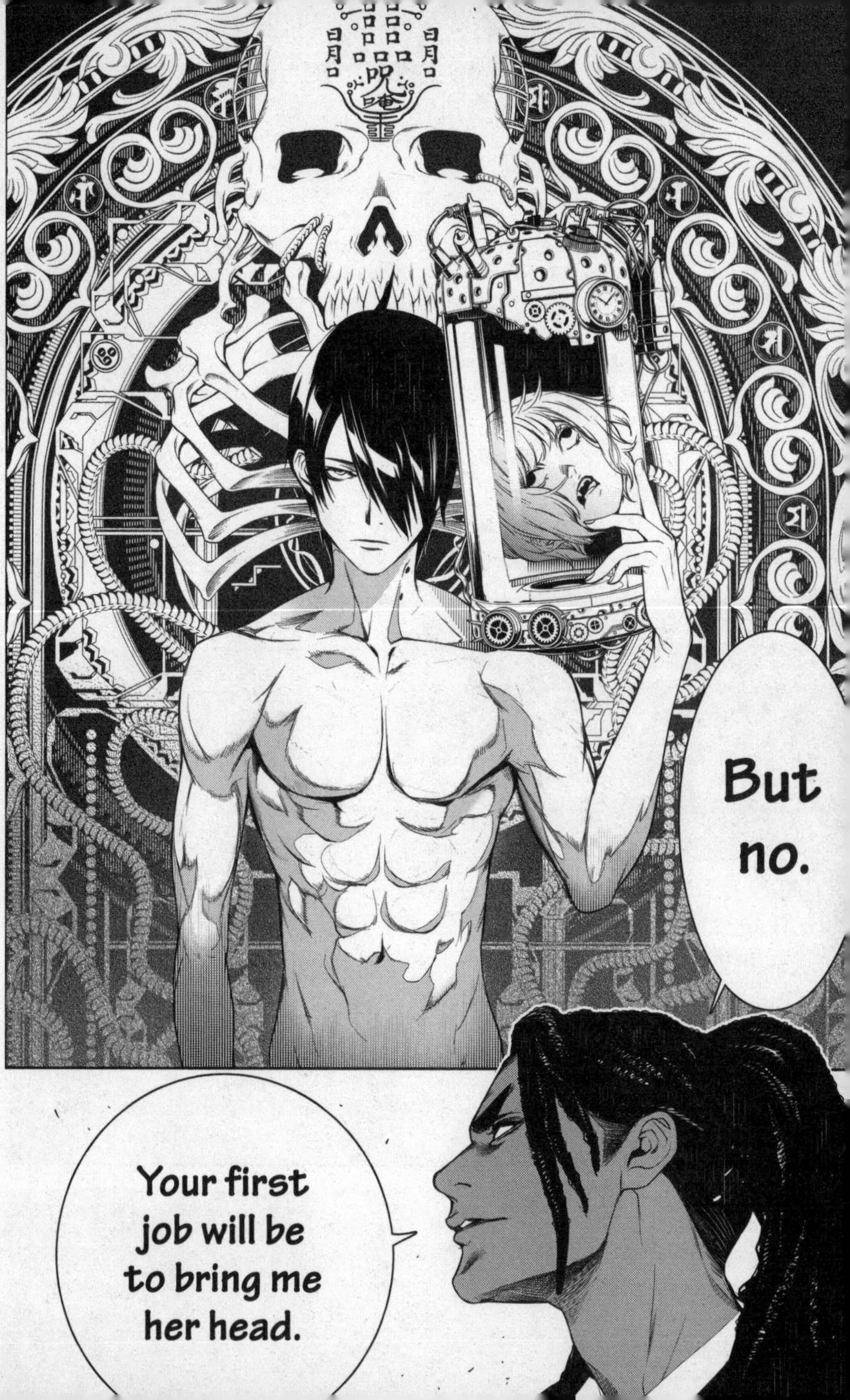
But no.
Your first job will be to bring me her head.

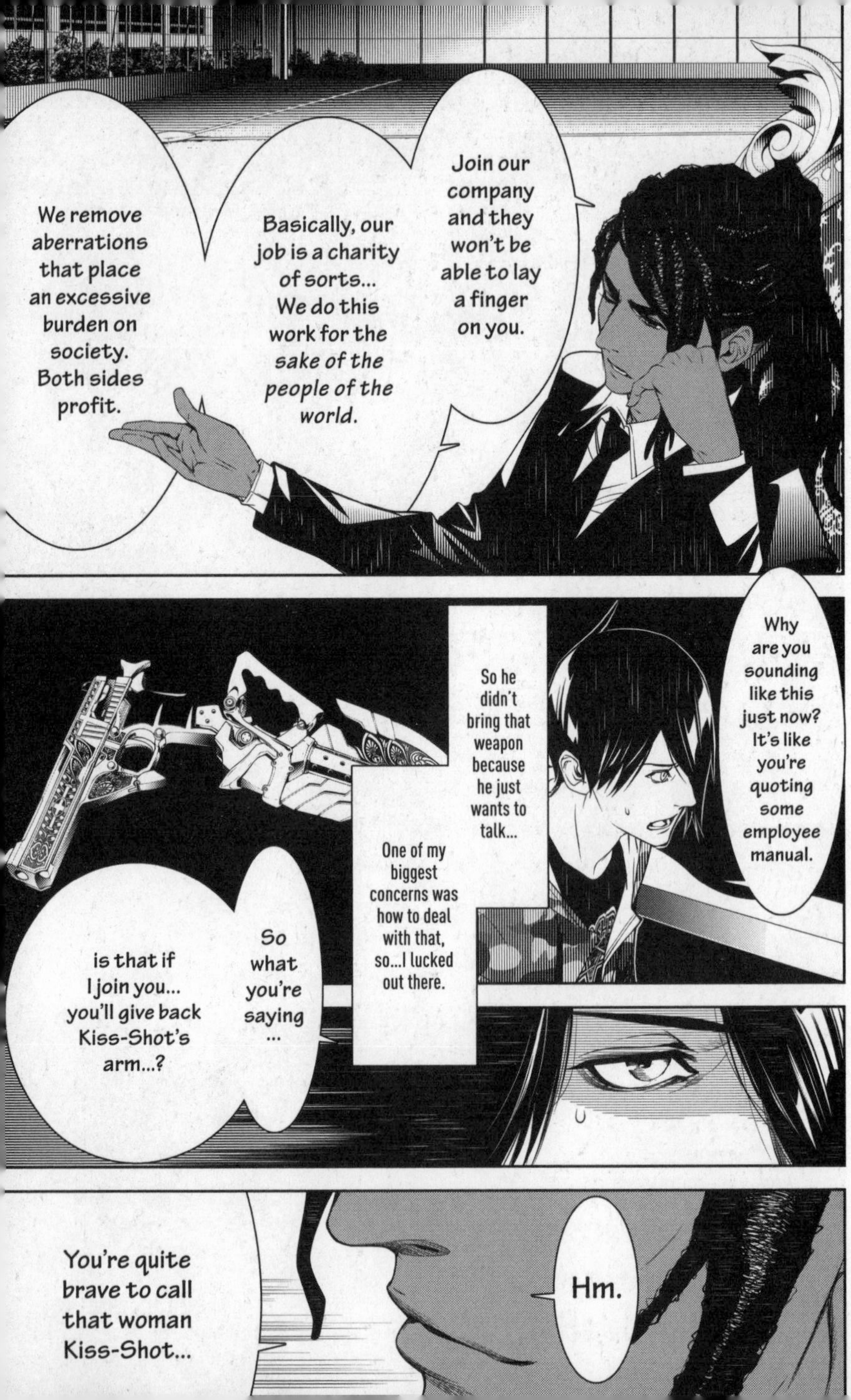
Join our company and they won't be able to lay a finger on you.
Basically, our job is a charity of sorts... We do this work for the *sake of the people of the world.*
We remove aberrations that place an excessive burden on society. Both sides profit.
Why are you sounding like this just now? It's like you're quoting some employee manual.
So he didn't bring that weapon because he just wants to talk...
One of my biggest concerns was how to deal with that, so...I lucked out there.
So what you're saying ...
is that if I join you... you'll give back Kiss-Shot's arm...?
Hm.
You're quite brave to call that woman Kiss-Shot...

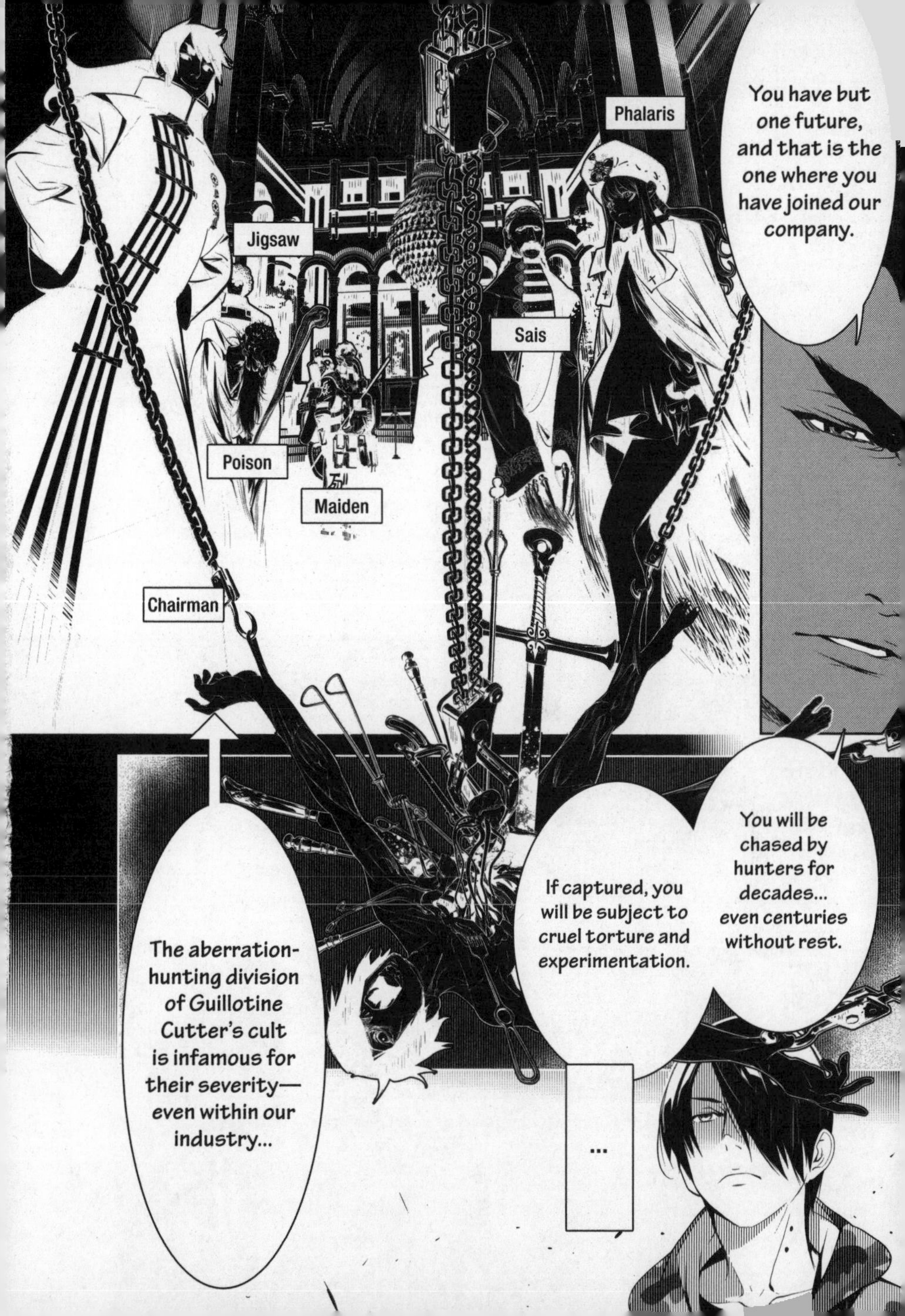
You have but one future, and that is the one where you have joined our company.
Phalaris
Sais
Jigsaw
Poison
Maiden
Chairman
You will be chased by hunters for decades... even centuries without rest.
If captured, you will be subject to cruel torture and experimentation.
...
The aberration-hunting division of Guillotine Cutter's cult is infamous for their severity—even within our industry...

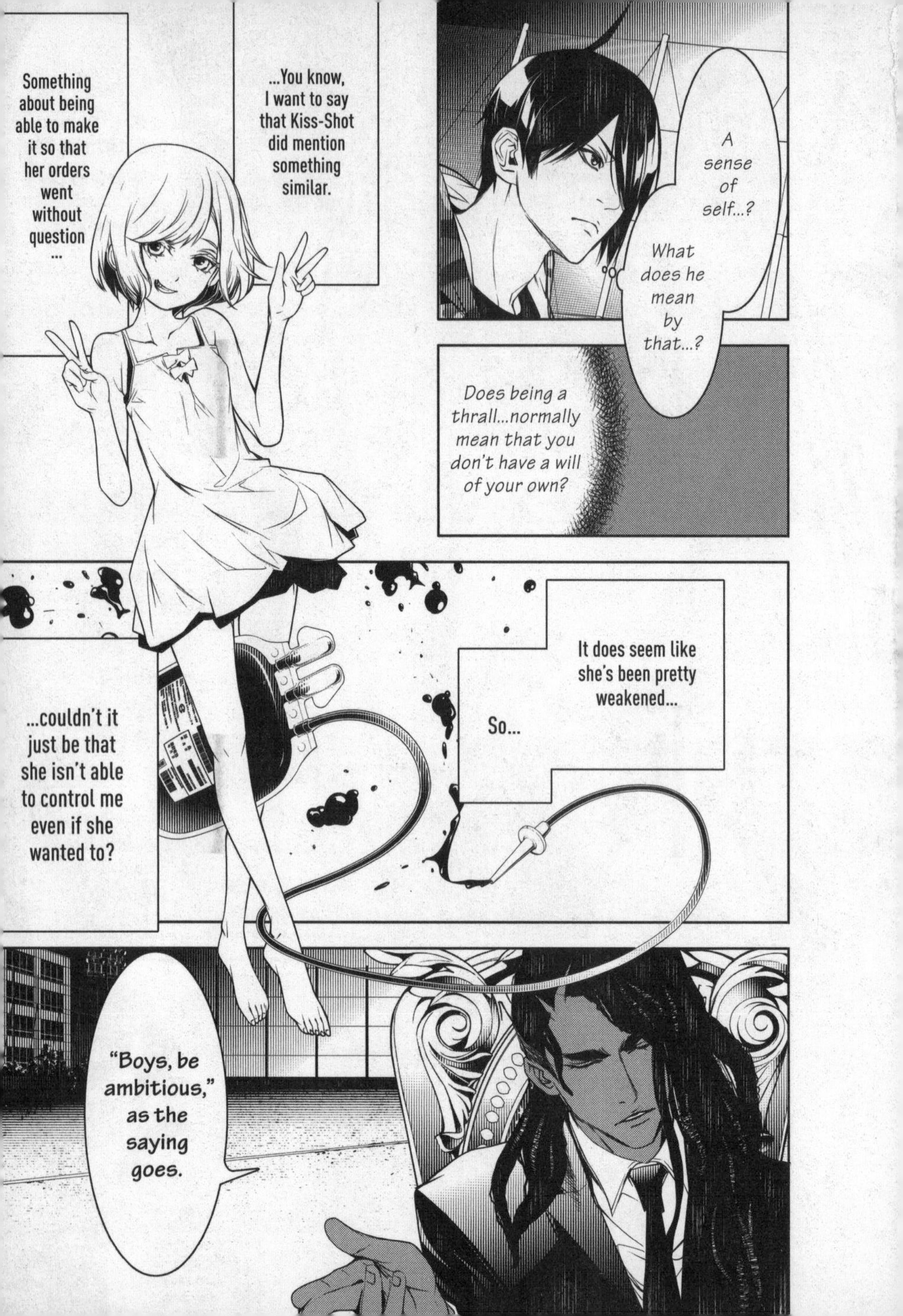
A sense of self...?
What does he mean by that...?
Does being a thrall...normally mean that you don't have a will of your own?
...You know, I want to say that Kiss-Shot did mention something similar.
Something about being able to make it so that her orders went without question...
It does seem like she's been pretty weakened...
So...
...couldn't it just be that she isn't able to control me even if she wanted to?
"Boys, be ambitious," as the saying goes.

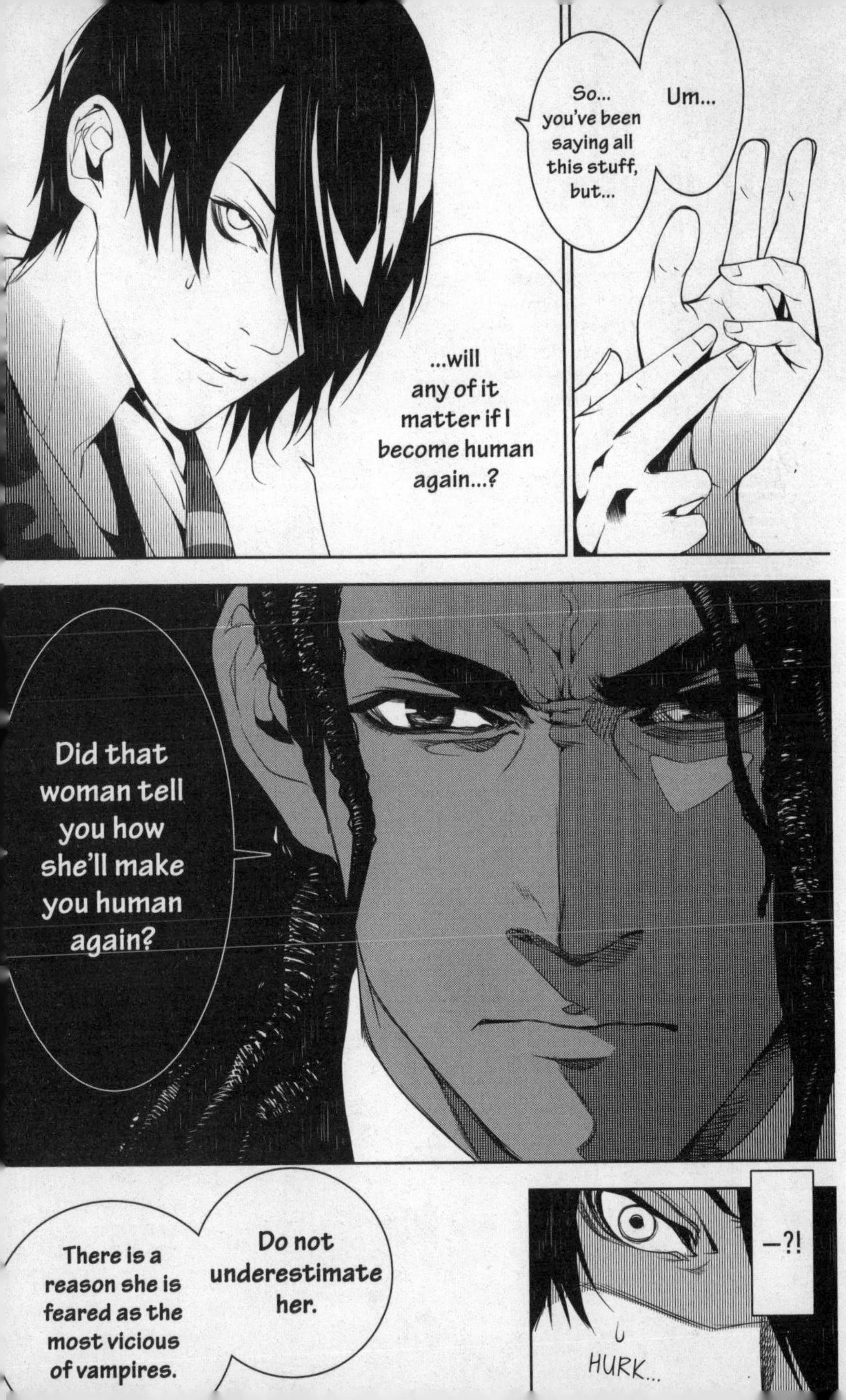
Um...
So... you've been saying all this stuff, but...
...will any of it matter if I become human again...?
Did that woman tell you how she'll make you human again?
—?!
HURK...
Do not underestimate her.
There is a reason she is feared as the most vicious of vampires.

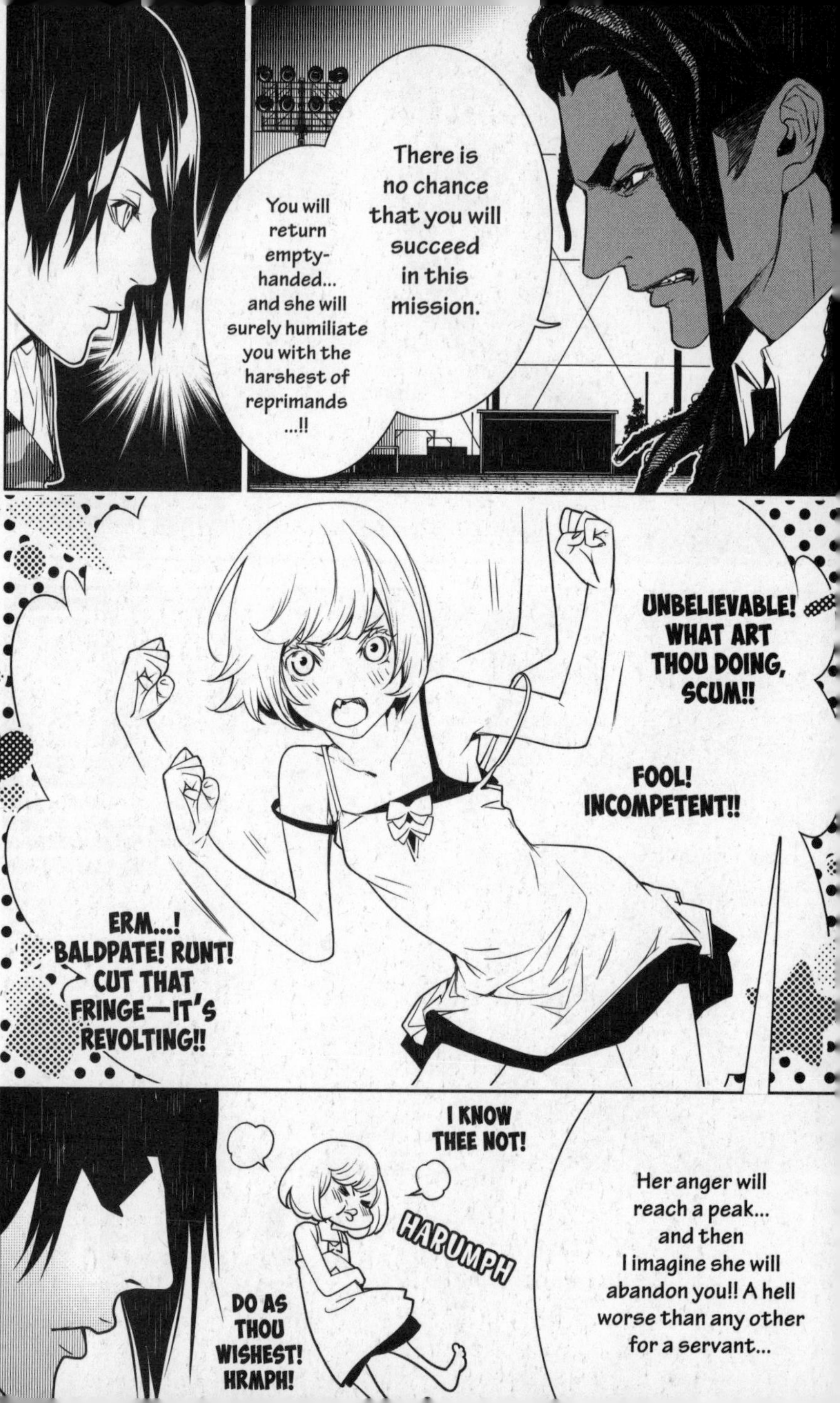
There is no chance that you will succeed in this mission.
You will return empty-handed... and she will surely humiliate you with the harshest of reprimands ...!!
UNBELIEVABLE! WHAT ART THOU DOING, SCUM!!
FOOL! INCOMPETENT!!
ERM...! BALDPATE! RUNT! CUT THAT FRINGE—IT'S REVOLTING!!
Her anger will reach a peak... and then I imagine she will abandon you!! A hell worse than any other for a servant...
I KNOW THEE NOT!
HARUMPH
DO AS THOU WISHEST! HRMPH!

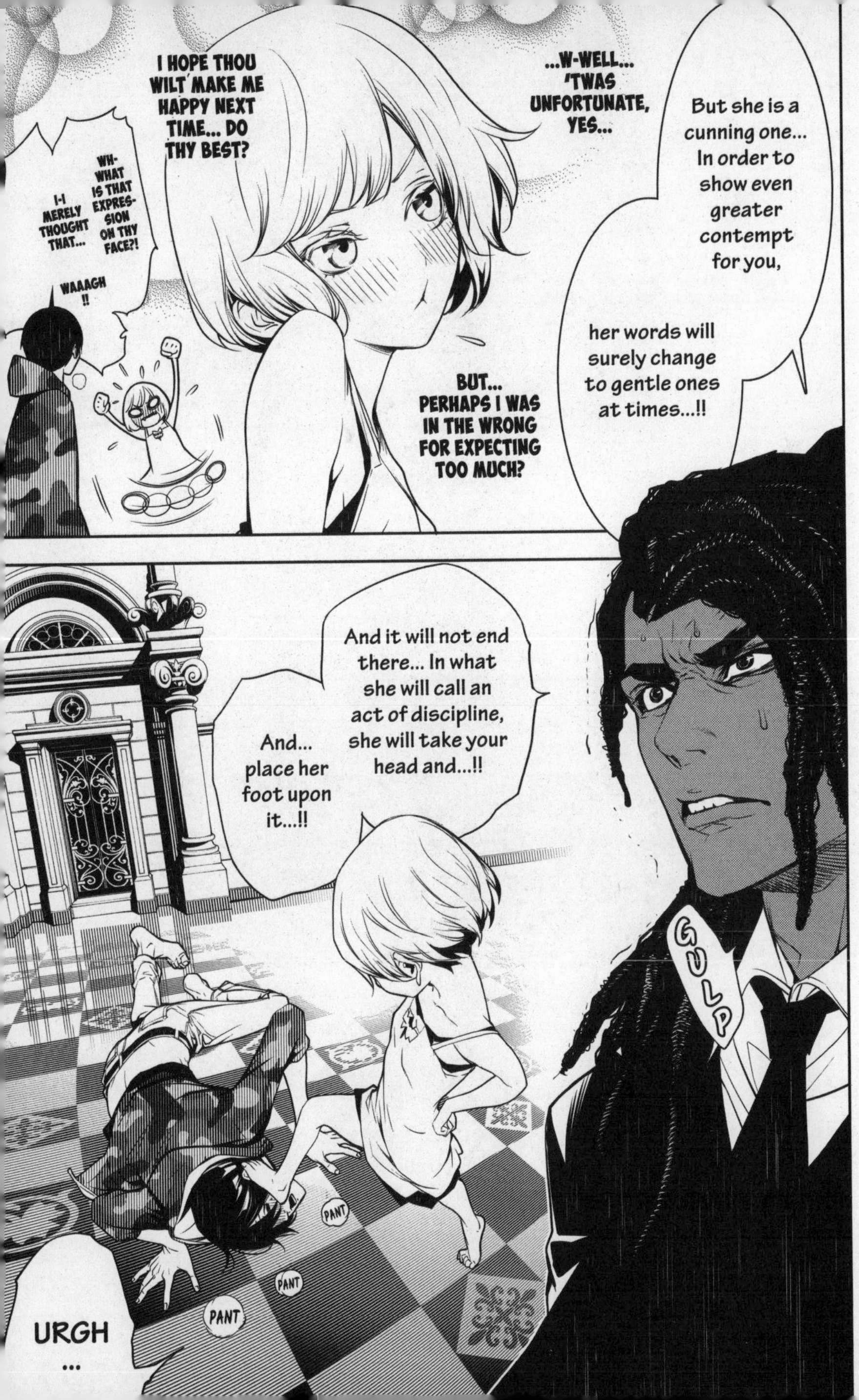
...W-WELL... 'TWAS UNFORTUNATE, YES...
I HOPE THOU WILT MAKE ME HAPPY NEXT TIME... DO THY BEST?
BUT... PERHAPS I WAS IN THE WRONG FOR EXPECTING TOO MUCH?
WH-WHAT IS THAT EXPRES-SION ON THY FACE?!
I-I MERELY THOUGHT THAT...
WAAAGH!!
But she is a cunning one... In order to show even greater contempt for you,
her words will surely change to gentle ones at times...!!
GULP
And it will not end there... In what she will call an act of discipline, she will take your head and...!!
And... place her foot upon it...!!
PANT
PANT
PANT
URGH...

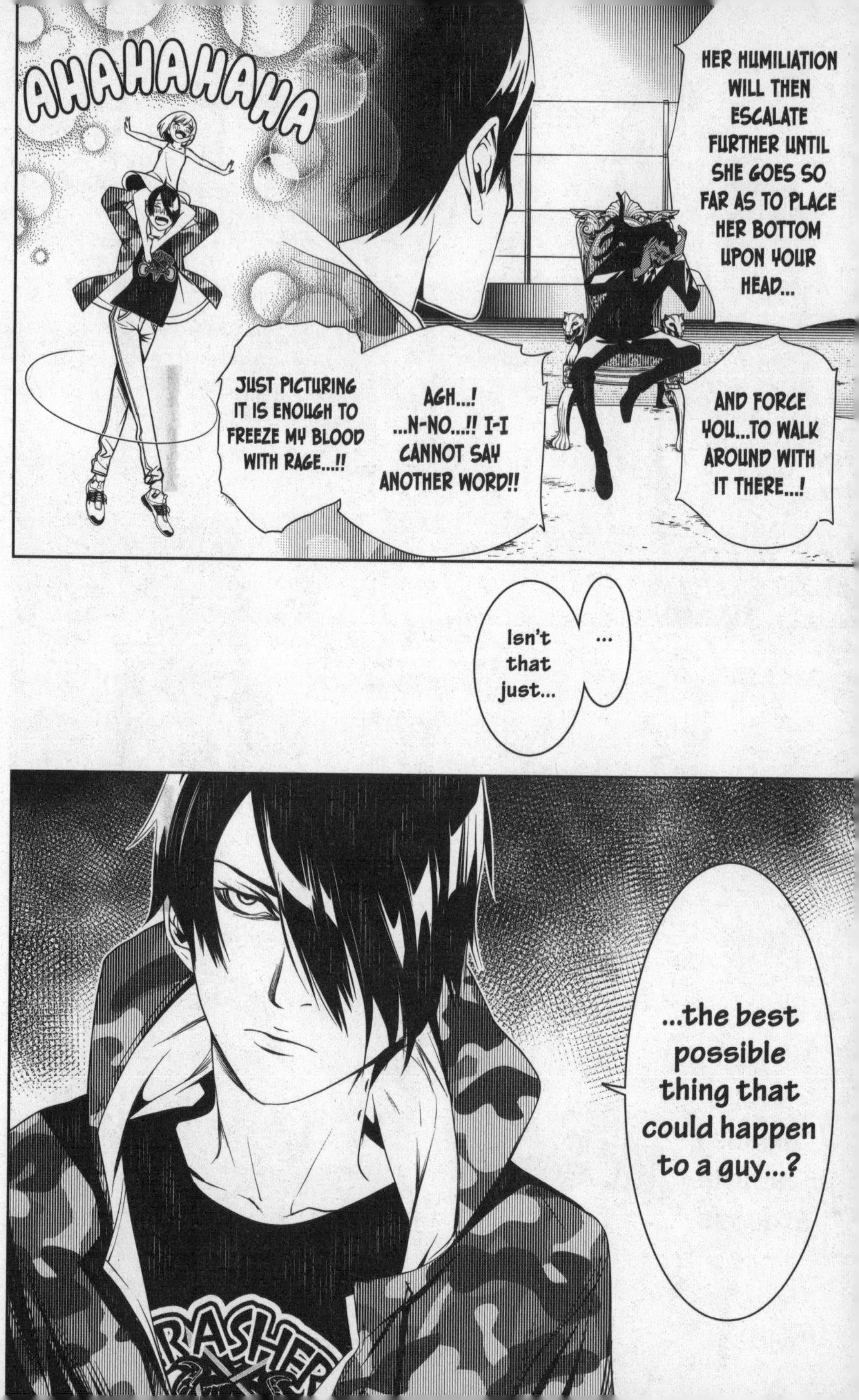
HER HUMILIATION WILL THEN ESCALATE FURTHER UNTIL SHE GOES SO FAR AS TO PLACE HER BOTTOM UPON YOUR HEAD...
AND FORCE YOU...TO WALK AROUND WITH IT THERE...!
AGH...! ...N-NO...!! I-I CANNOT SAY ANOTHER WORD!!
JUST PICTURING IT IS ENOUGH TO FREEZE MY BLOOD WITH RAGE...!!
AHAHAHAHAHA
...
Isn't that just...
...the best possible thing that could happen to a guy...?

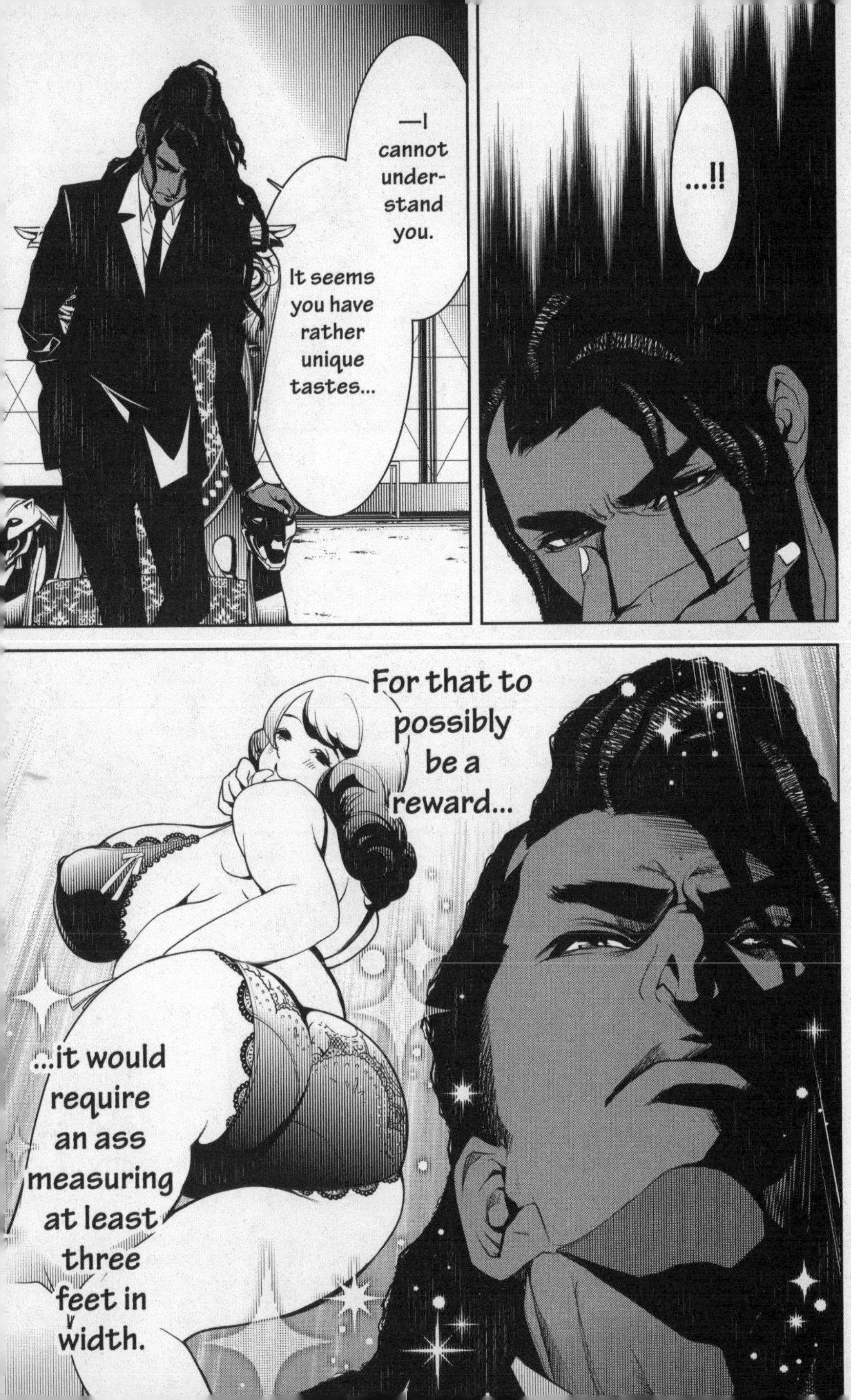
...!!
—I cannot under-stand you.
It seems you have rather unique tastes...
For that to possibly be a reward...
...it would require an ass measuring at least three feet in width.

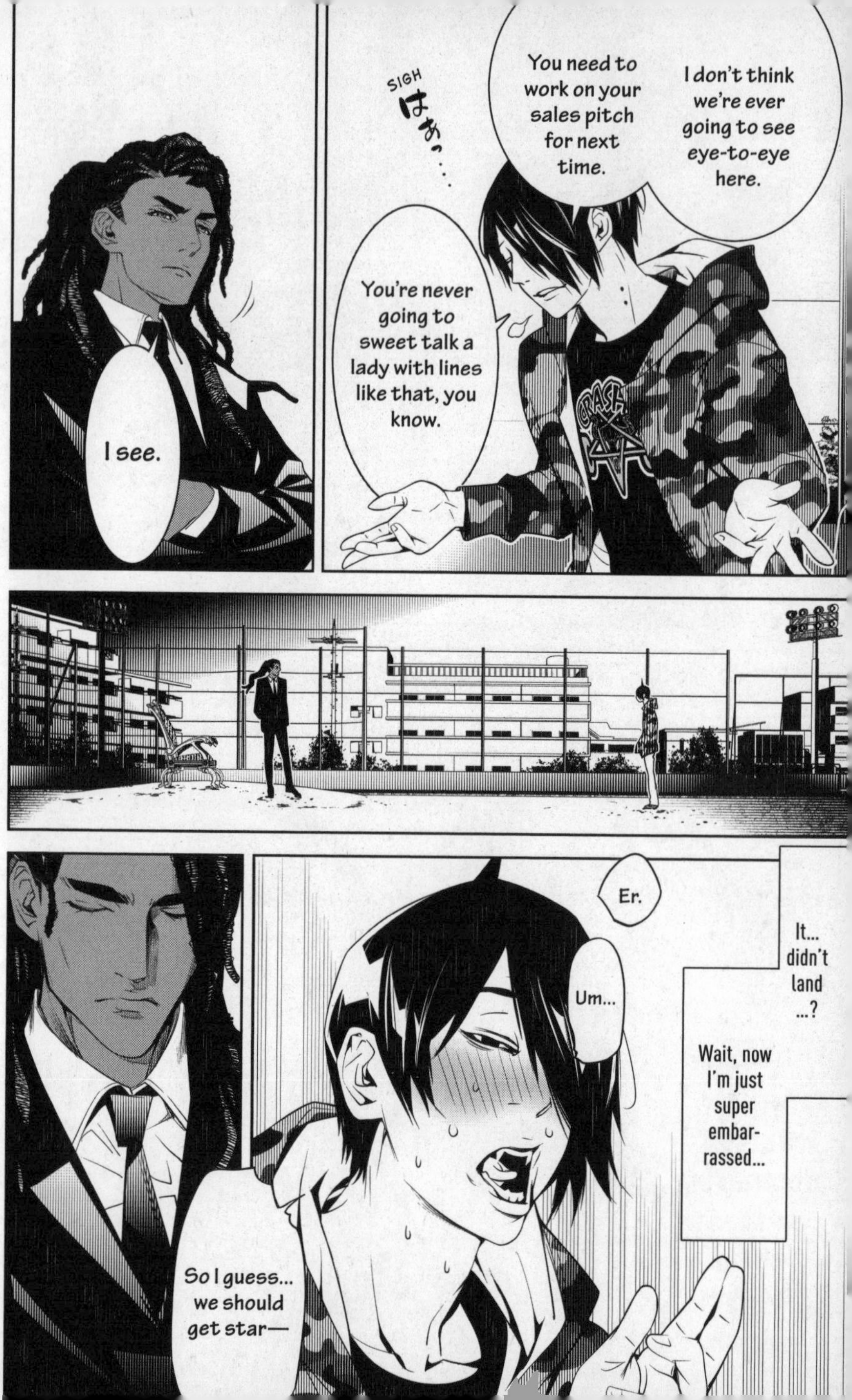
I don't think we're ever going to see eye-to-eye here.
You need to work on your sales pitch for next time.
SIGH
はあっ…
You're never going to sweet talk a lady with lines like that, you know.
I see.
Er.
It... didn't land ...?
Wait, now I'm just super embar-rassed...
Um...
So I guess... we should get star—

ZLURCH

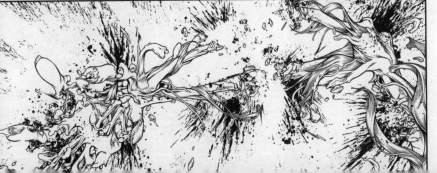

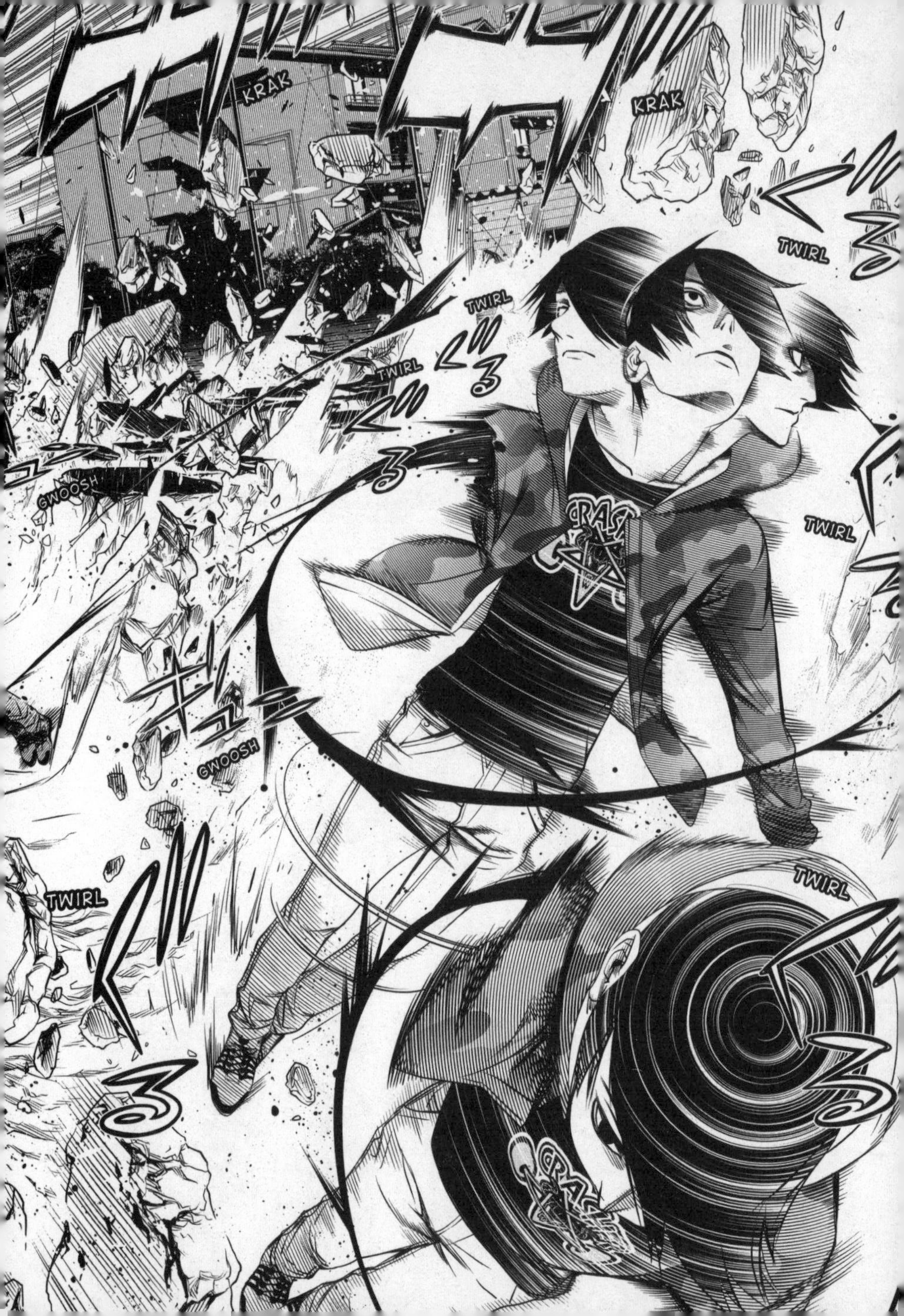
KRAK
KRAK
TWIRL
TWIRL
TWIRL
GWOOSH
TWIRL
GWOOSH
TWIRL
TWIRL

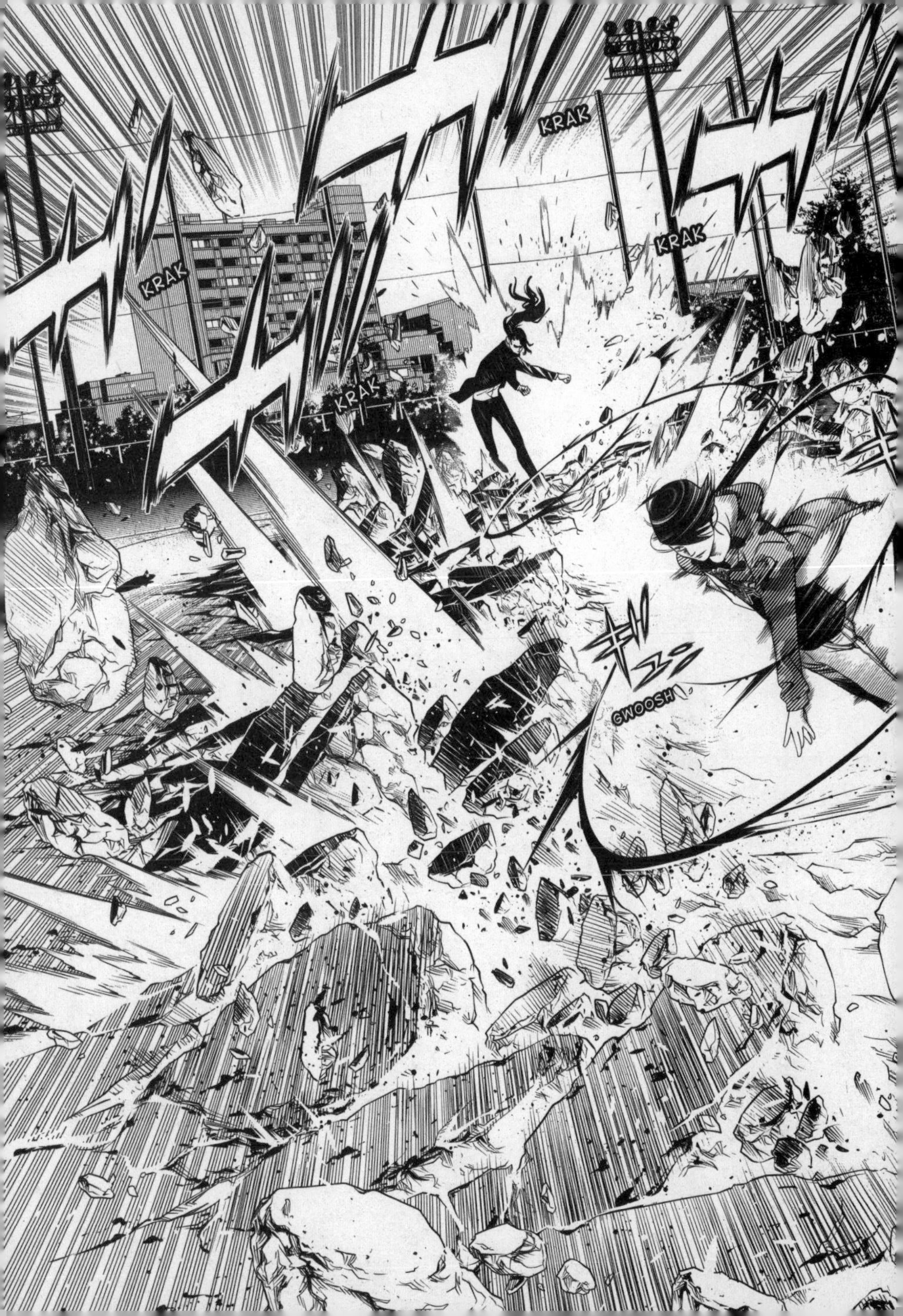
KRAK
KRAK
KRAK
KRAK
GWOOSH

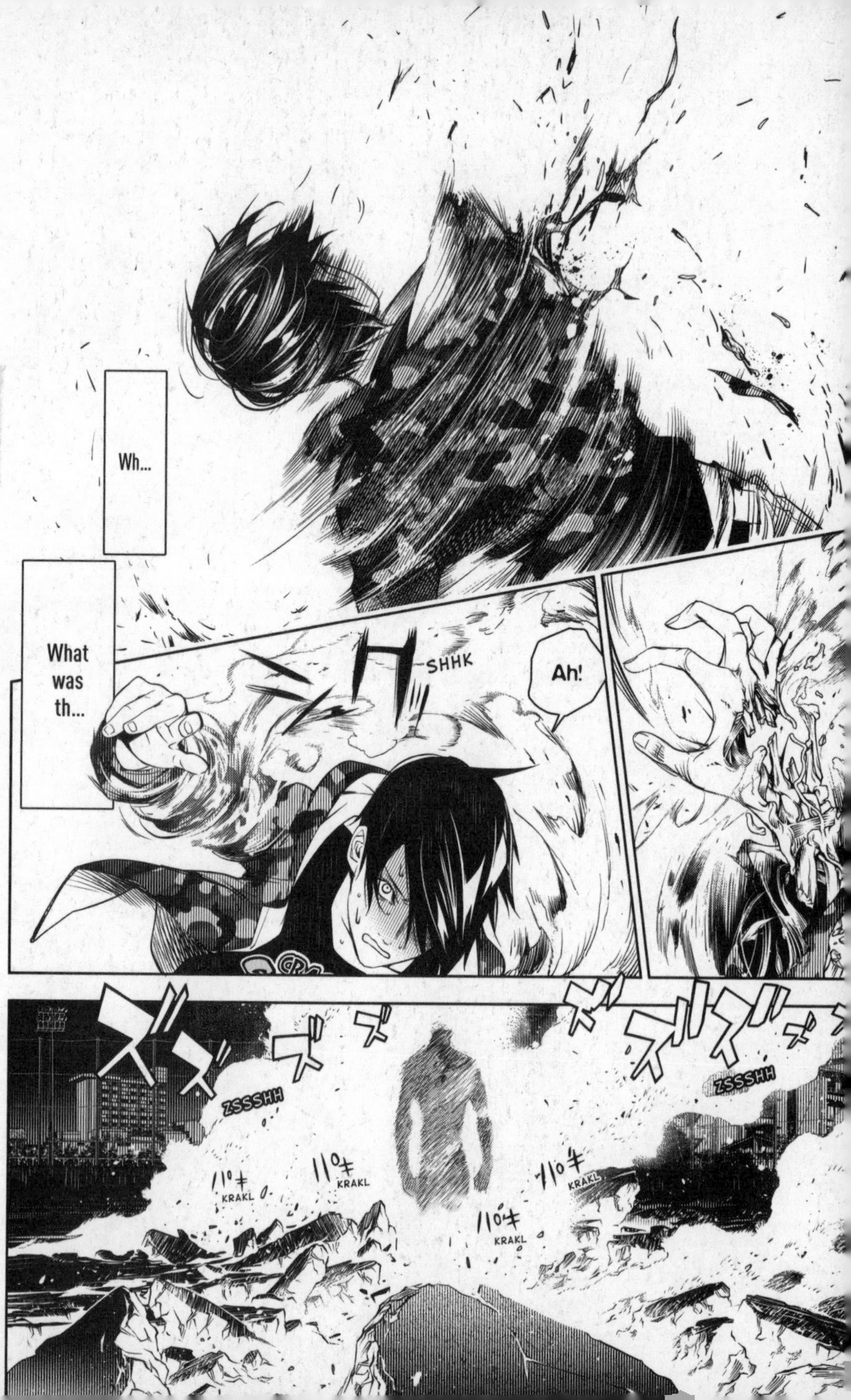

Wh...
What was th...
Ah!
SHHK
ZSSSHH
ZSSSHH
KRAKL
KRAKL
KRAKL
KRAKL

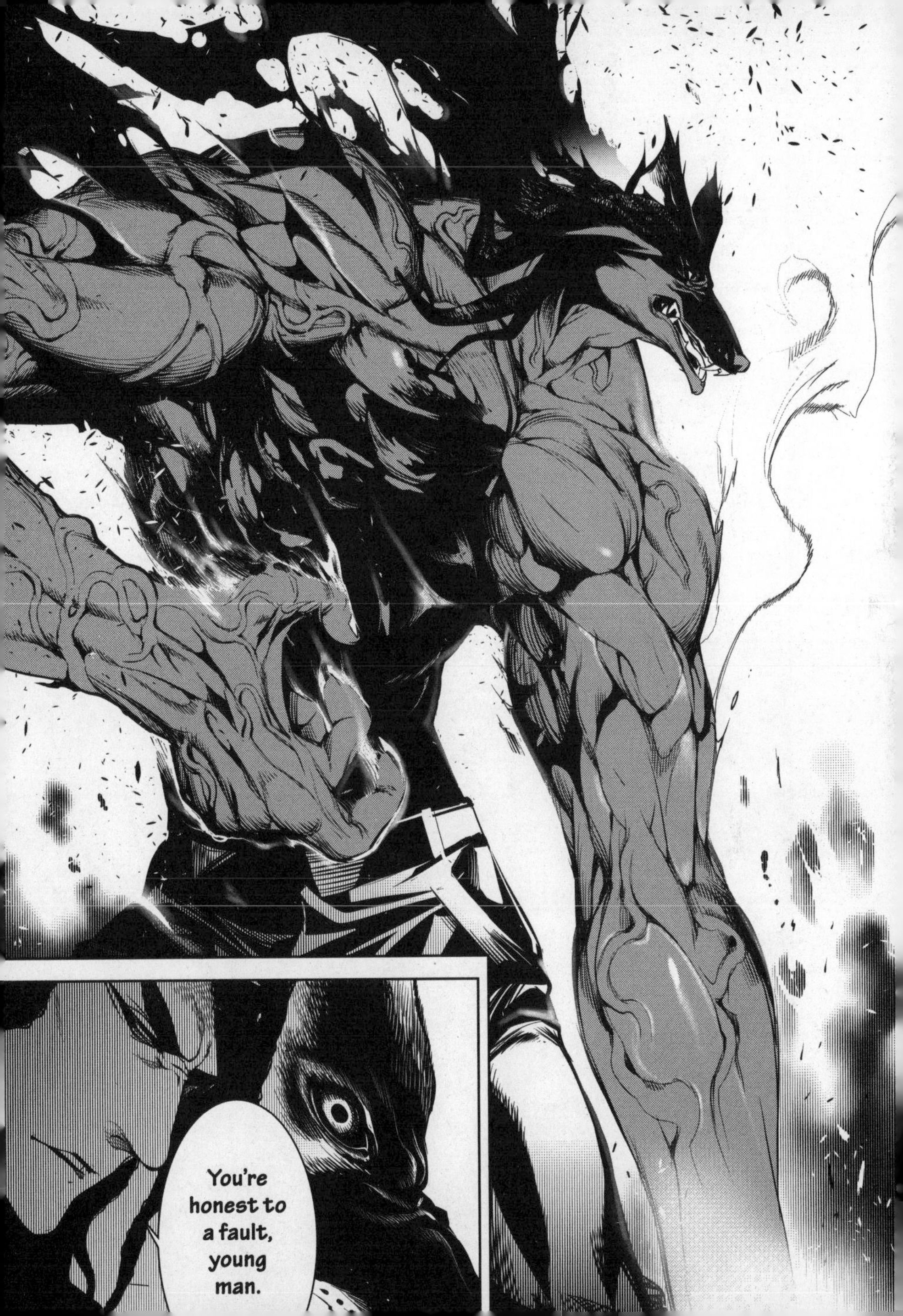
You're honest to a fault, young man.

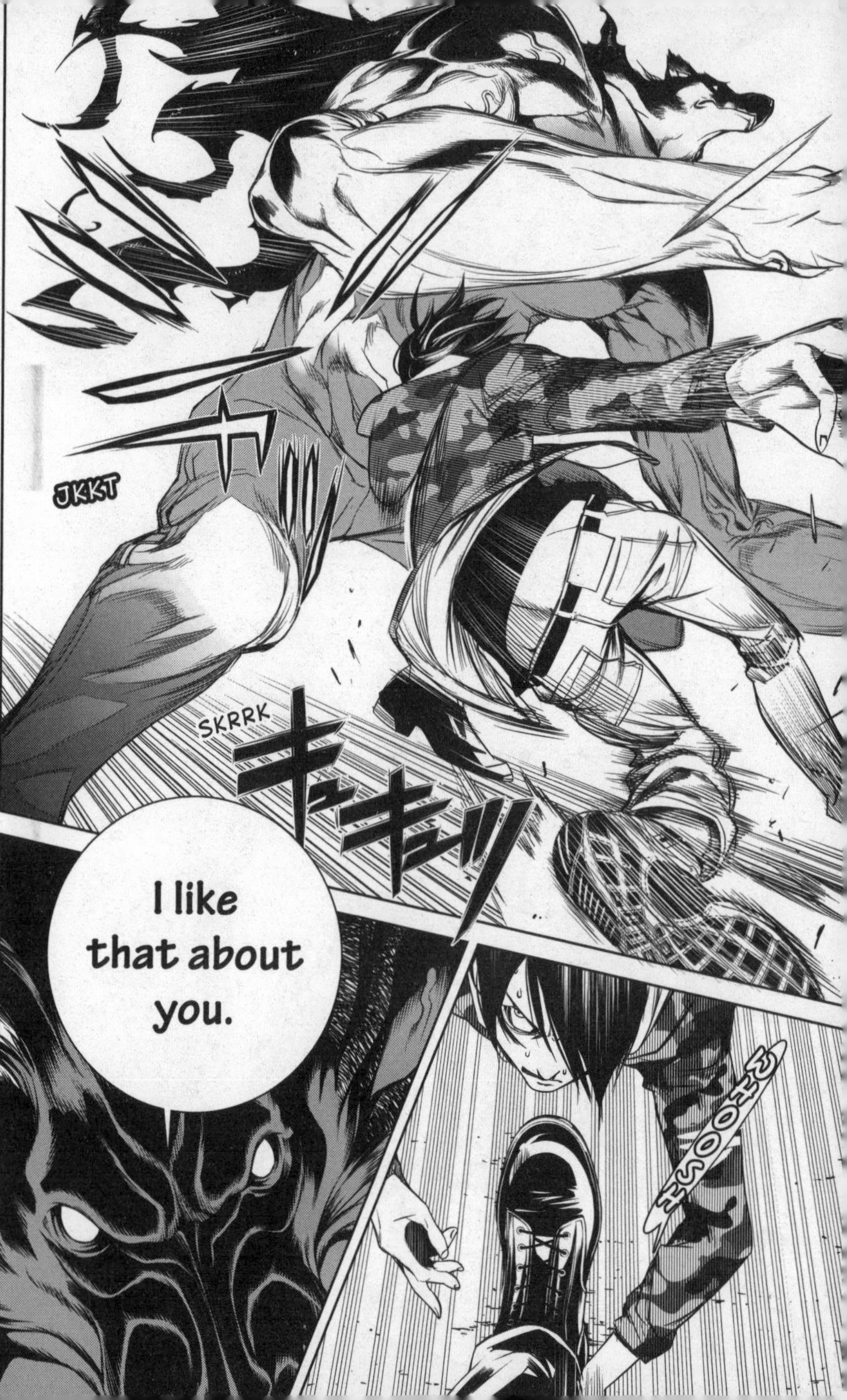
JKKT
SKRRK
WHOOSH
I like that about you.

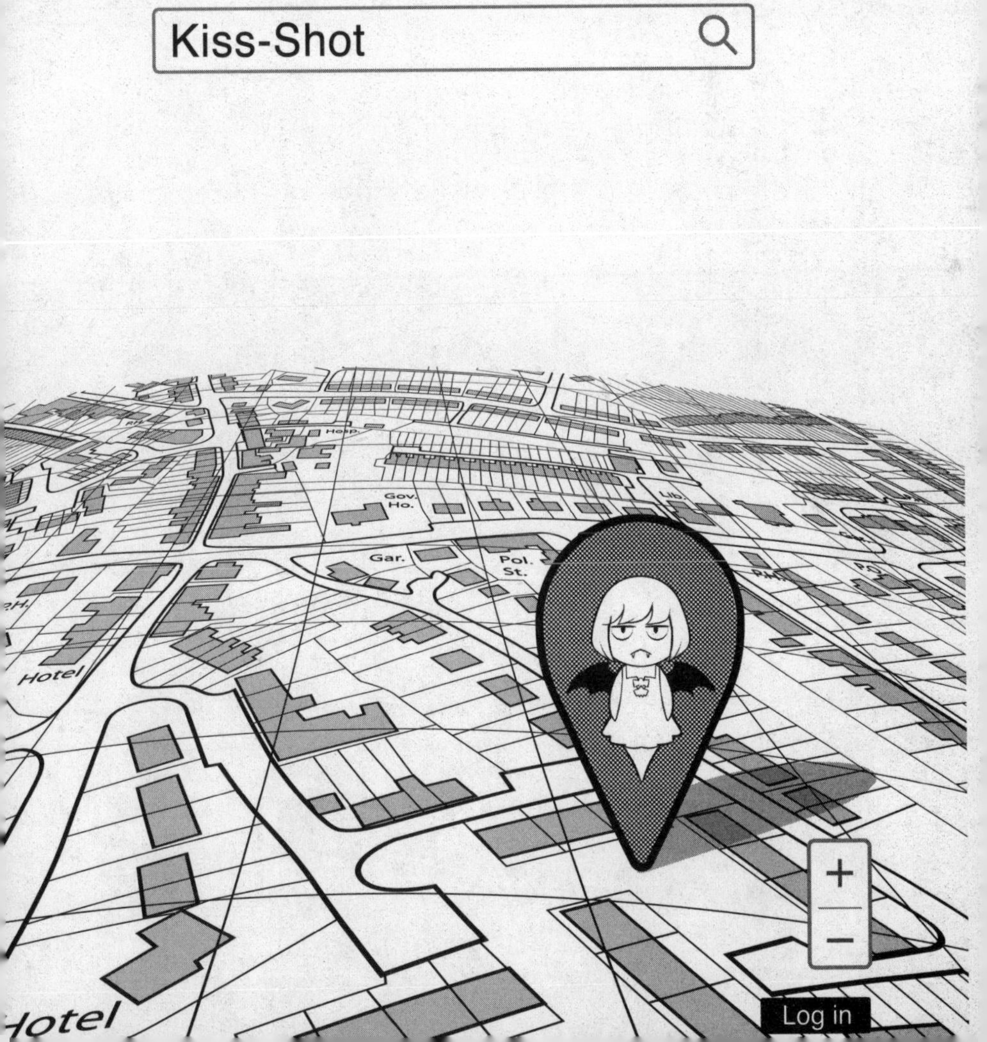
Kiss-Shot
Hosp.
Gov.
Ho.
Gar.
Pol.
St.
Hotel
Hotel
Log in

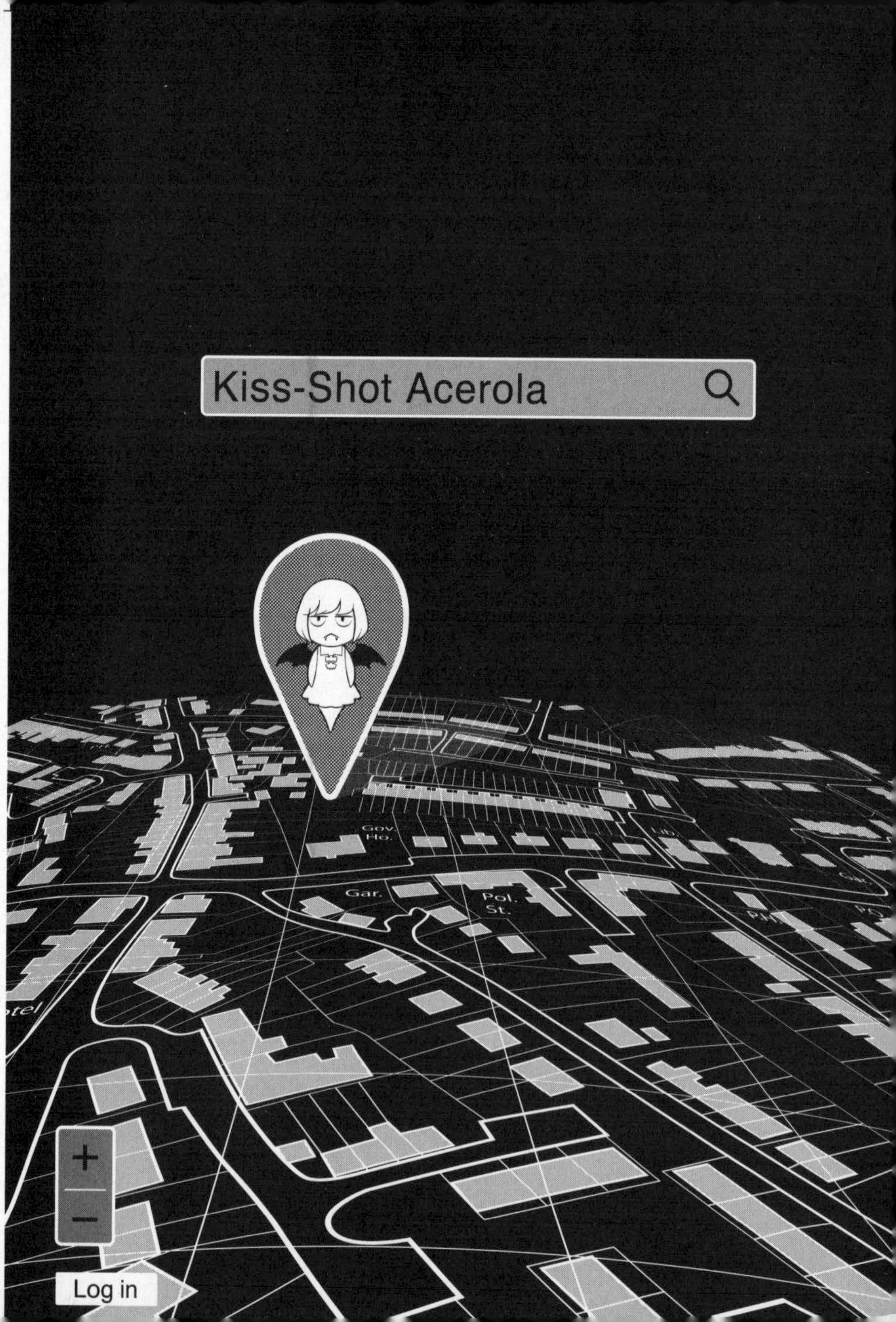
Kiss-Shot Acerola
Gov.
Ho.
Gar.
Pol.
St.
+
−
Log in

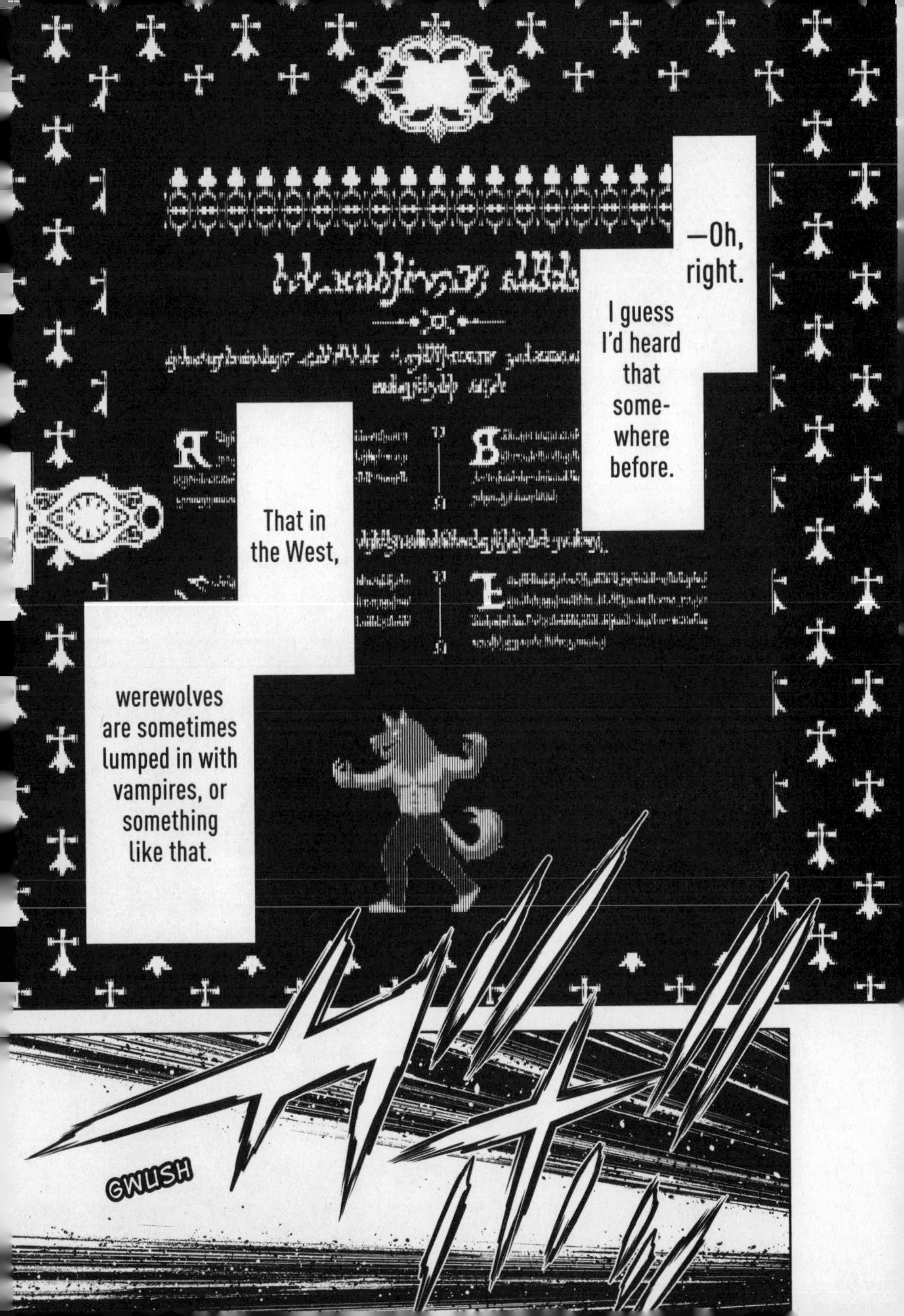
—Oh, right.
I guess I'd heard that some- where before.
That in the West,
werewolves are sometimes lumped in with vampires, or something like that.
GWUSH

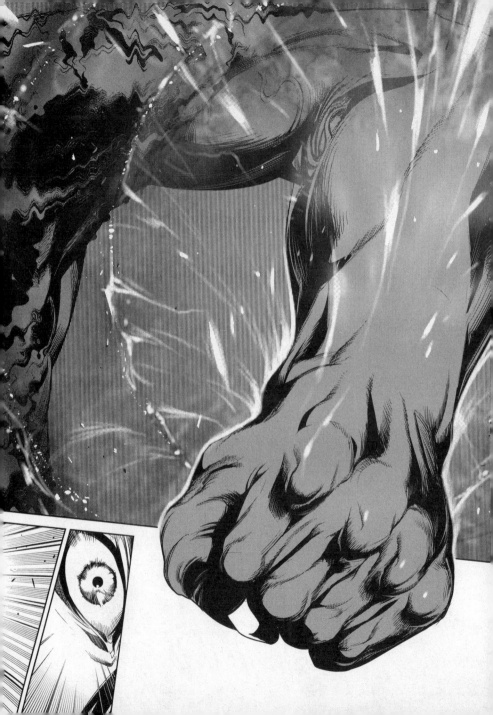

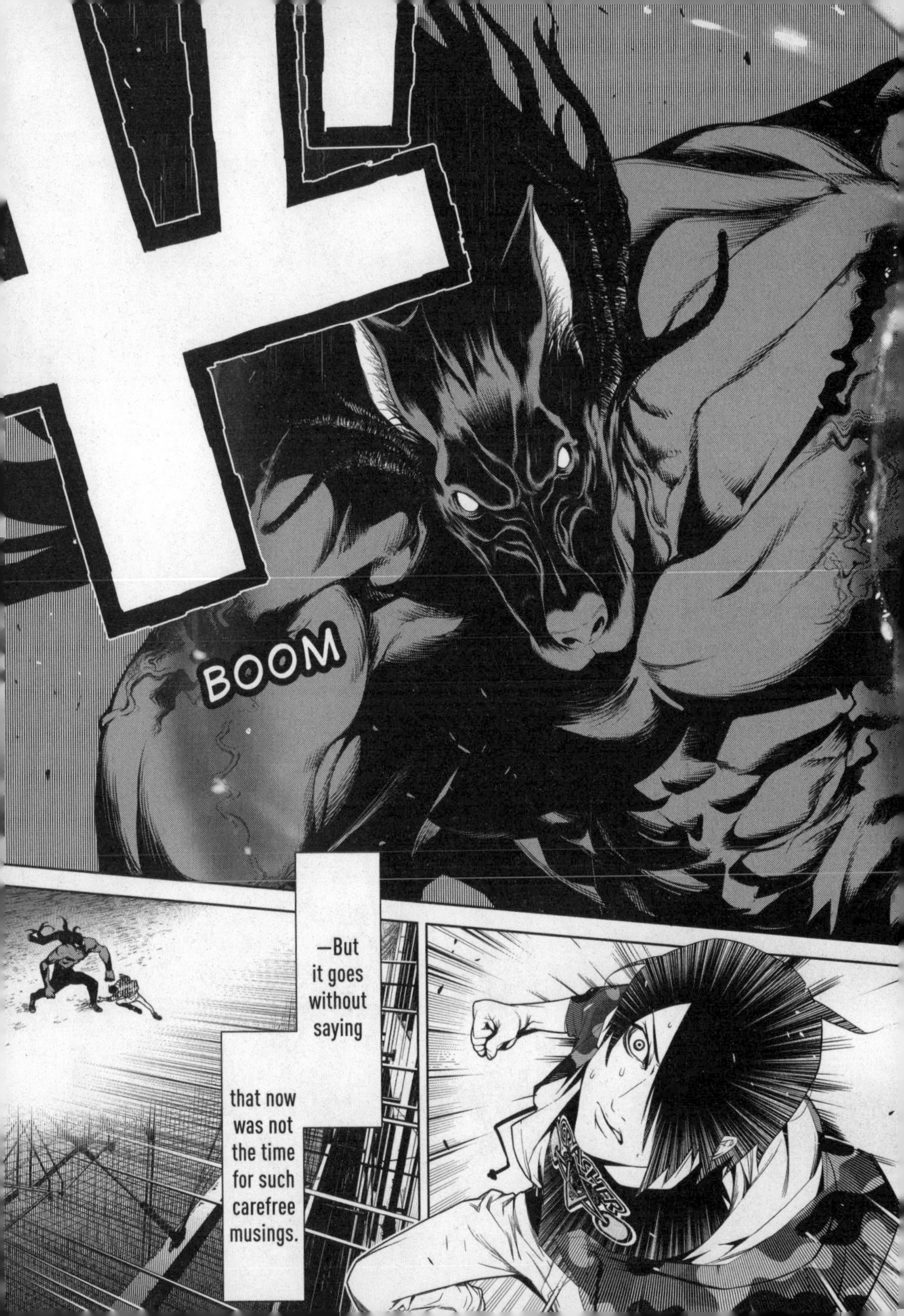
BOOM
—But it goes without saying
that now was not the time for such carefree musings.

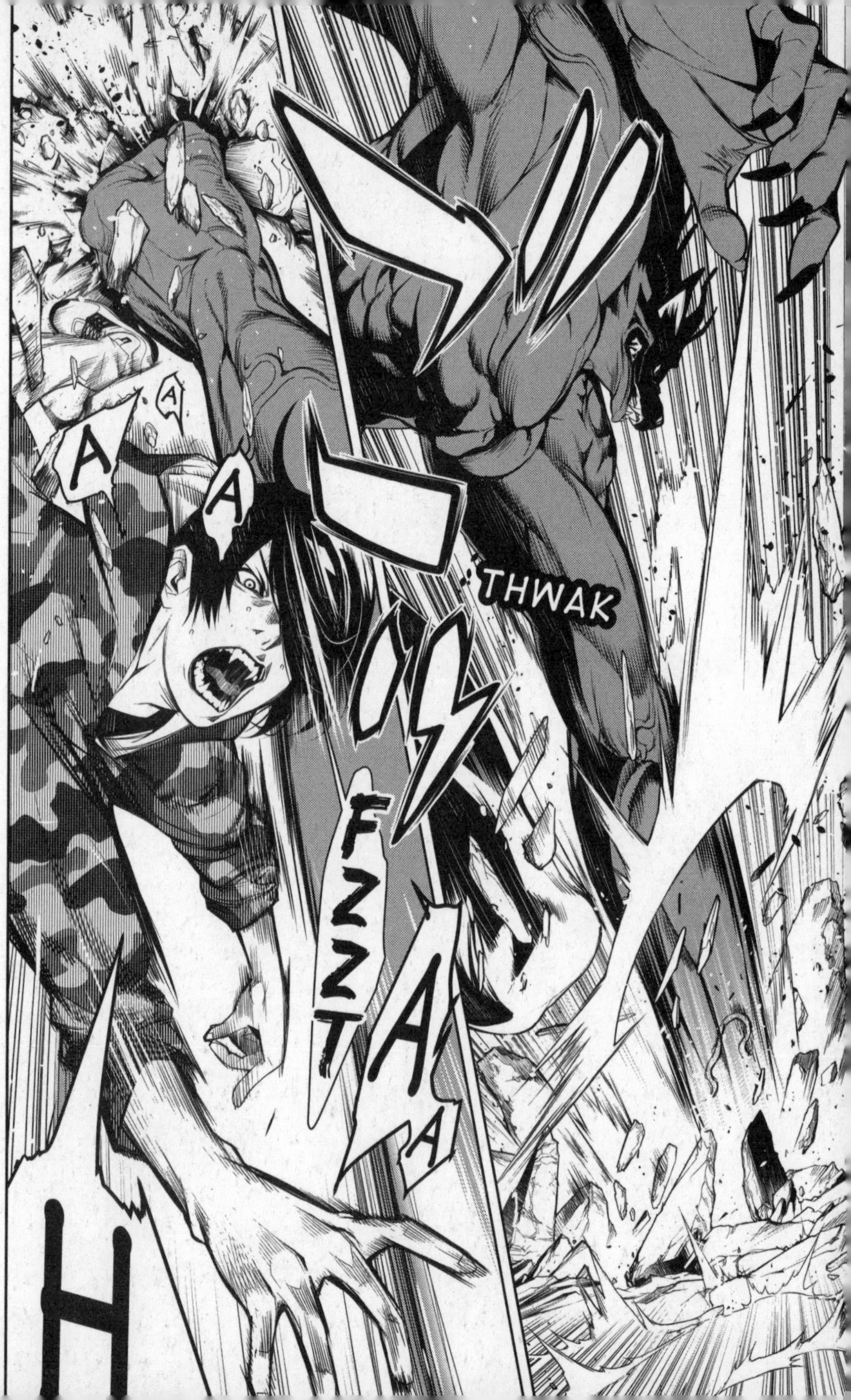
THWAK
A
A
A
A
FZZT
A
A
A
H

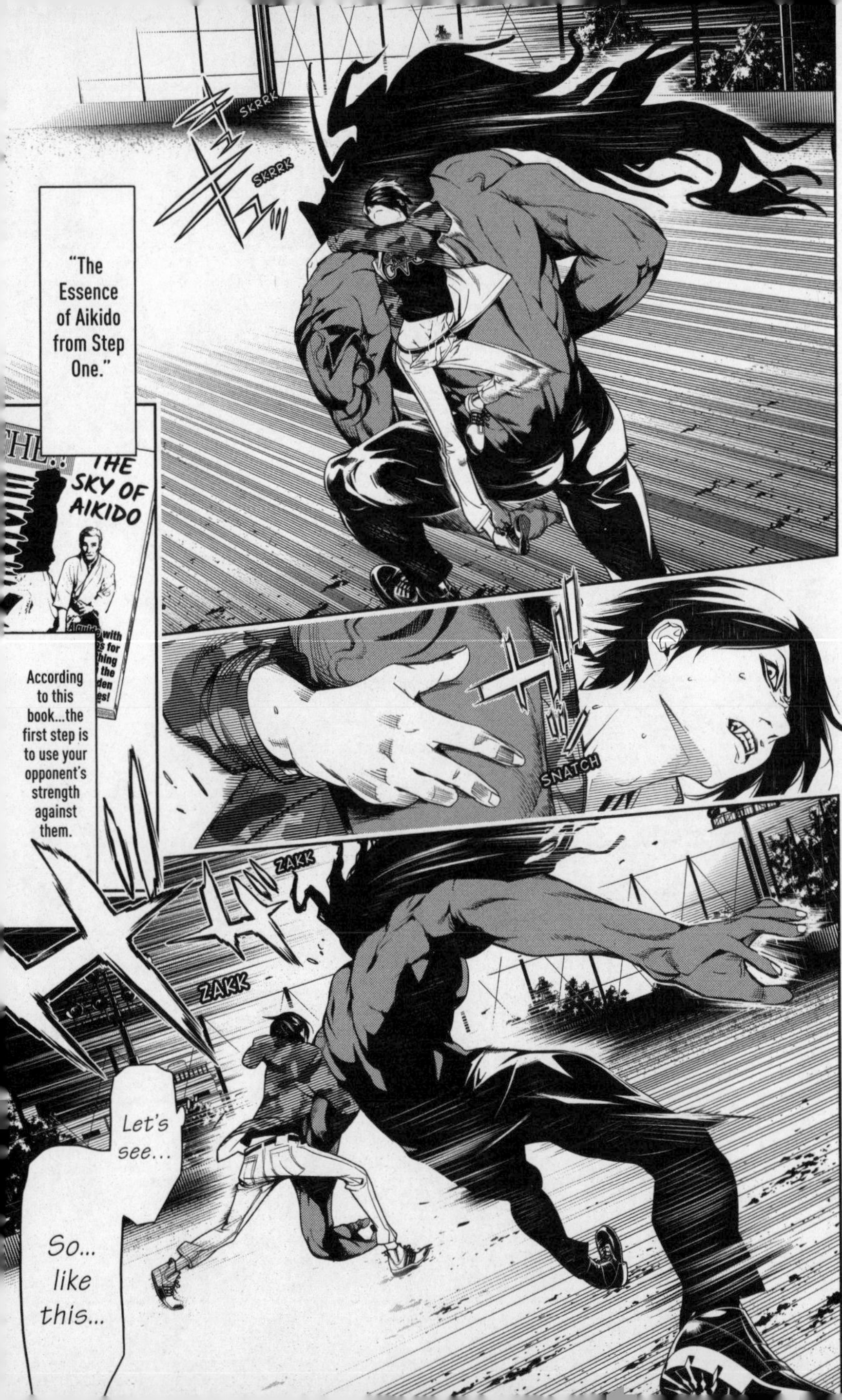
SKRRK
SKRRK
"The Essence of Aikido from Step One."
THE SKY OF AIKIDO
SNATCH
According to this book...the first step is to use your opponent's strength against them.
ZAKK
ZAKK
Let's see...
So... like this...

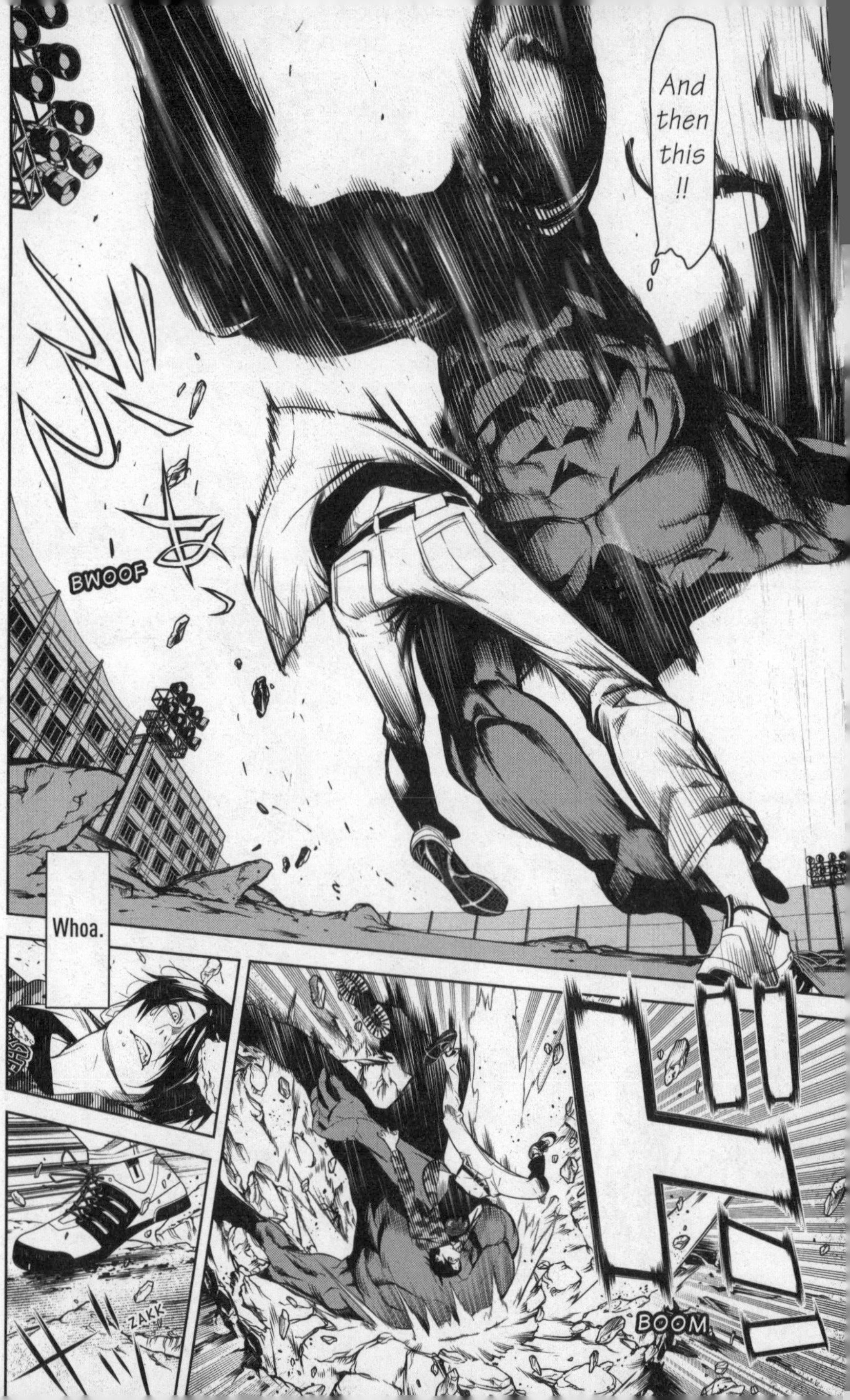
And then this!!
BWOOF
Whoa.
BOOM
ZAKK

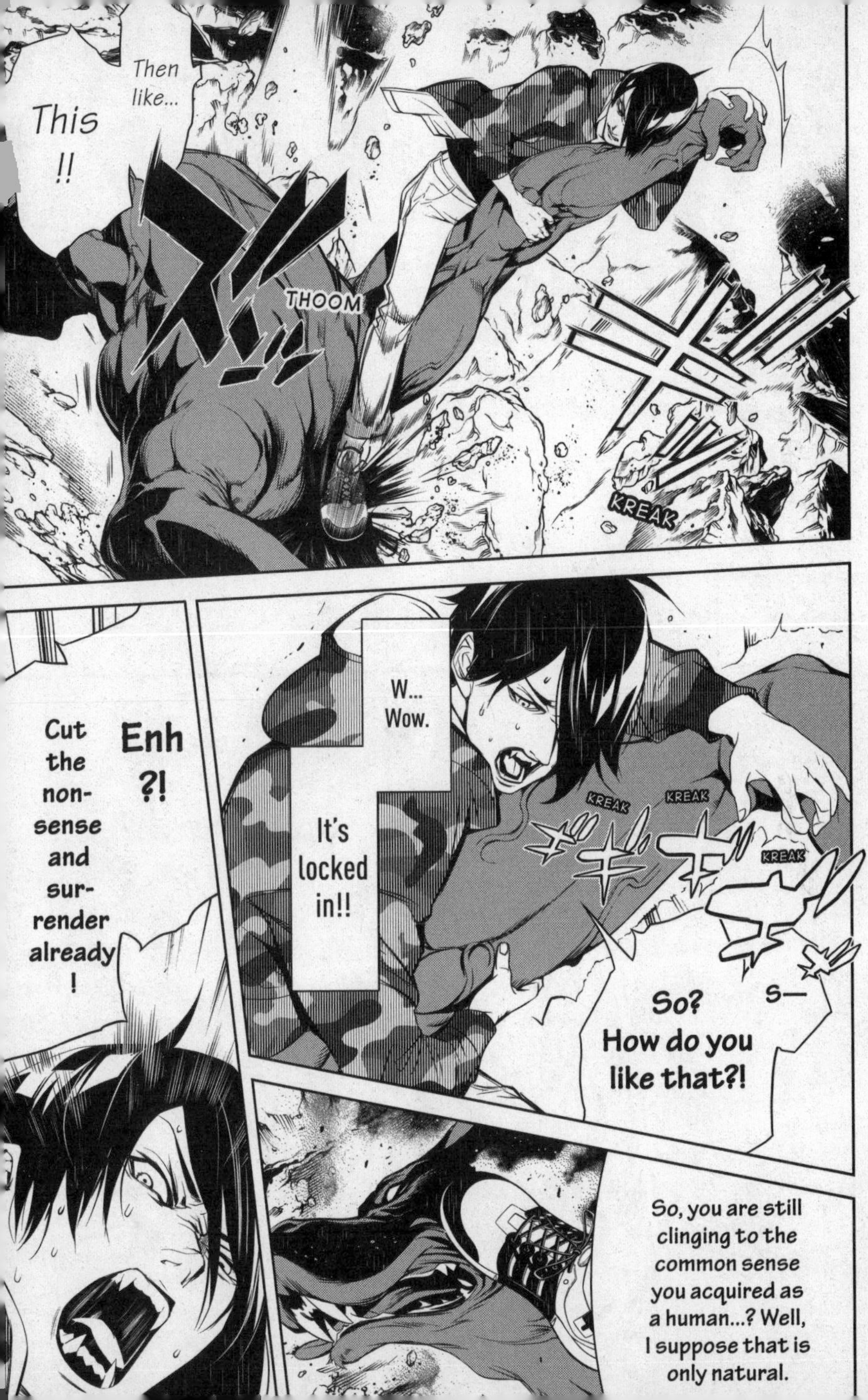
Then like...
This !!
THOOM
KREAK
KREAK
KREAK
KREAK
So? How do you like that?!
S—
W... Wow.
It's locked in!!
Enh ?!
Cut the non-sense and sur-render already !
So, you are still clinging to the common sense you acquired as a human...? Well, I suppose that is only natural.

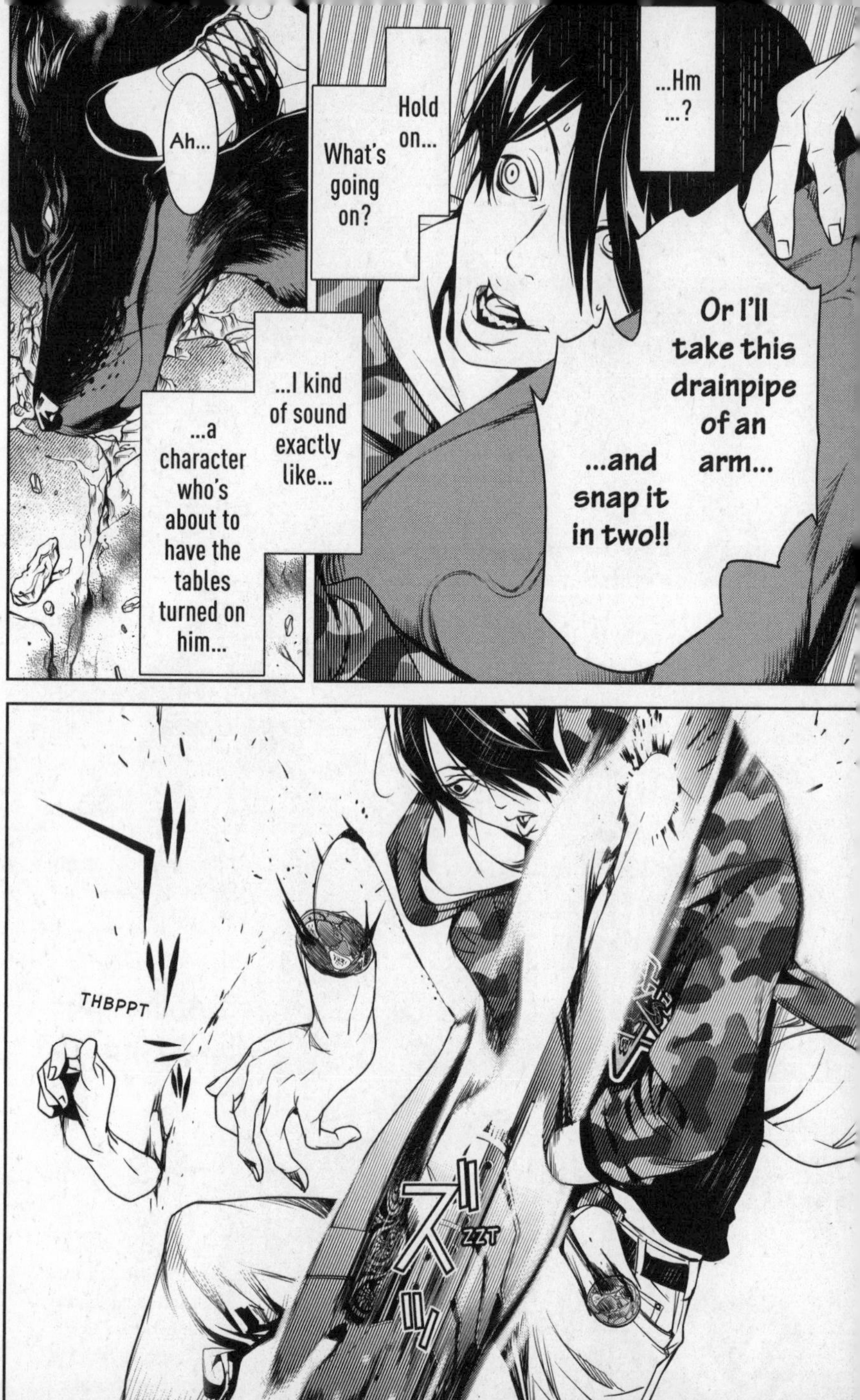
...Hm ...?
Or I'll take this drainpipe of an arm...
...and snap it in two!!
Hold on... What's going on?
...I kind of sound exactly like...
...a character who's about to have the tables turned on him...
Ah...
THBPPT
ZZT

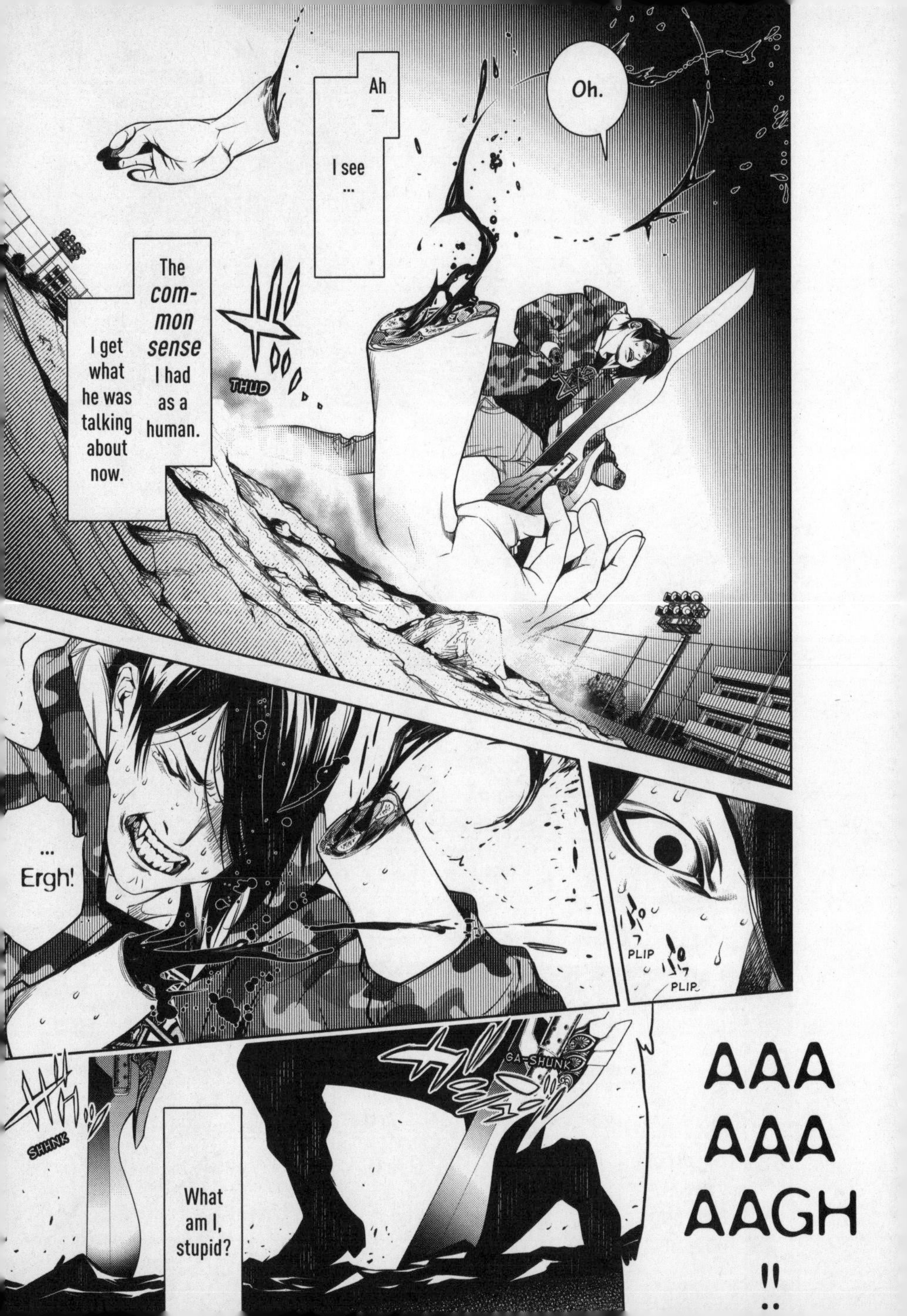
Oh.
Ah — I see ...
The common sense I had as a human.
I get what he was talking about now.
THUD
PLIP
PLIP
... Ergh!
AAA AAA AAGH !!
GA-SHUNK
What am I, stupid?
SHHNK

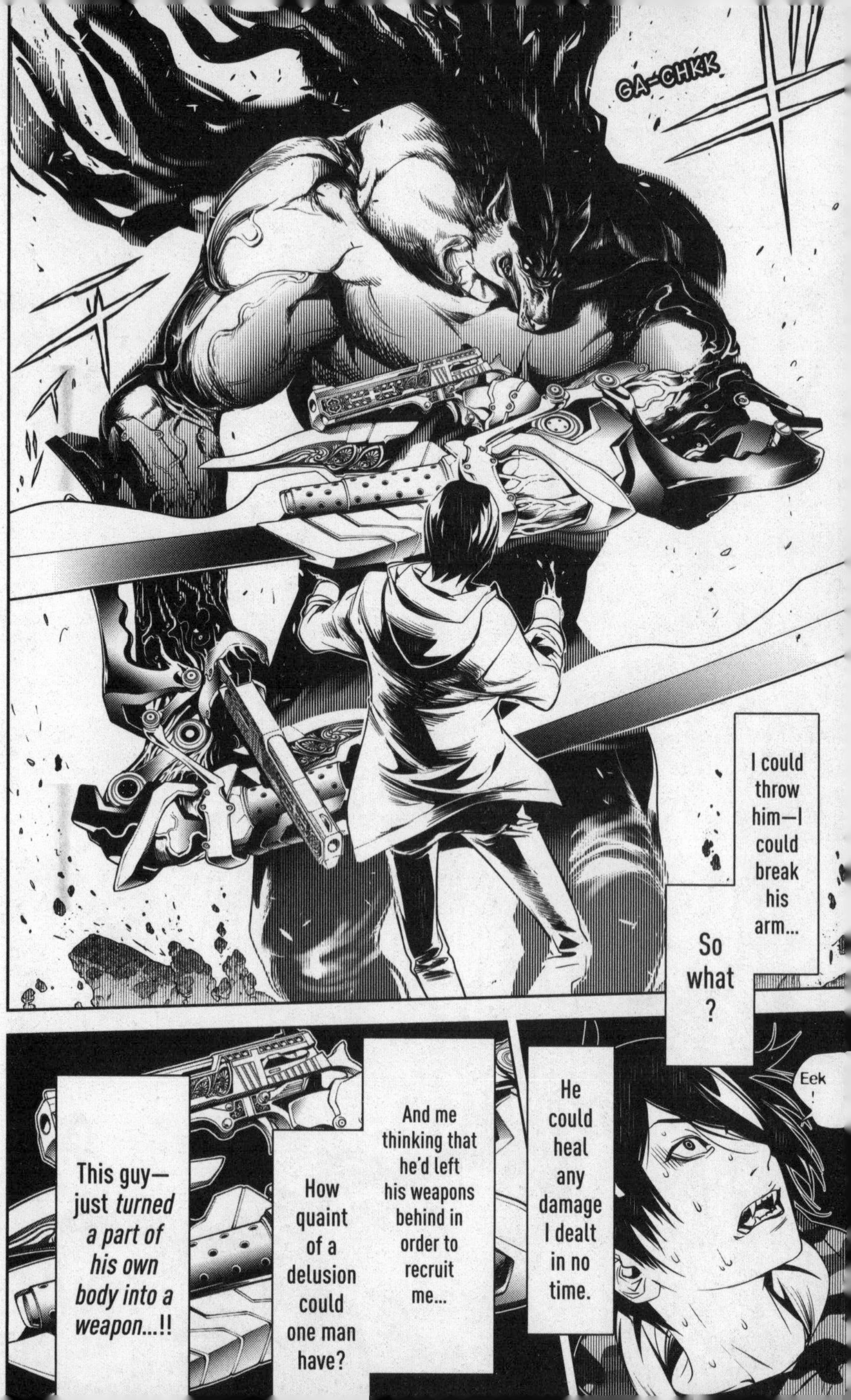
GA-CHKK
I could throw him—I could break his arm...
So what?
Eek!
He could heal any damage I dealt in no time.
And me thinking that he'd left his weapons behind in order to recruit me...
How quaint of a delusion could one man have?
This guy—just *turned a part of his own body into a weapon...!!*

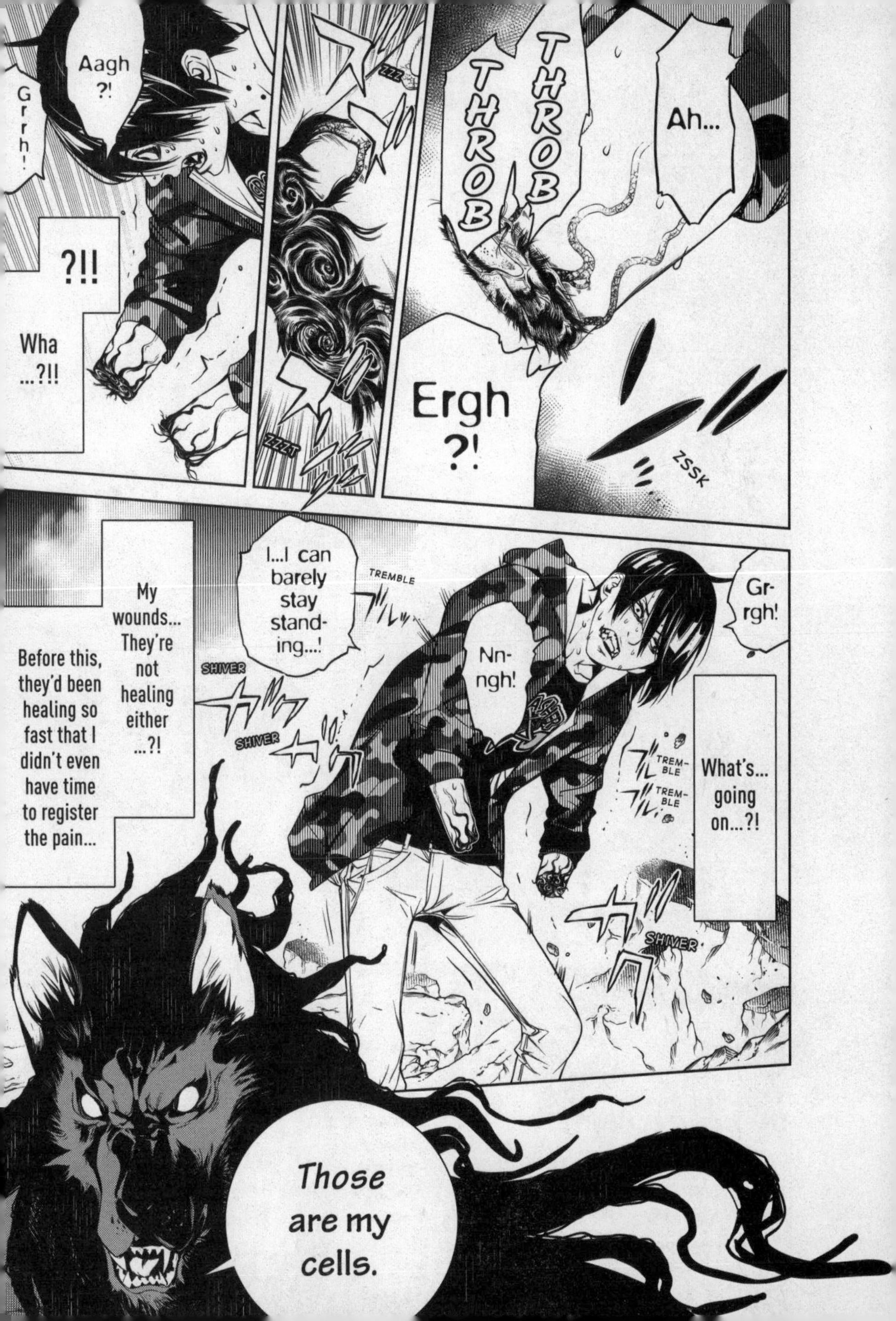
Ah...
THROB
THROB
Ergh ?!
ZSSK
Aagh ?!
Grrh!
?!!
Wha ...?!!
Gr-rgh!
What's... going on...?!
TREM-BLE
TREM-BLE
SHIVER
Nn-ngh!
I...I can barely stay stand-ing...!
TREMBLE
My wounds... They're not healing either ...?!
SHIVER
SHIVER
Before this, they'd been healing so fast that I didn't even have time to register the pain...
Those are my cells.

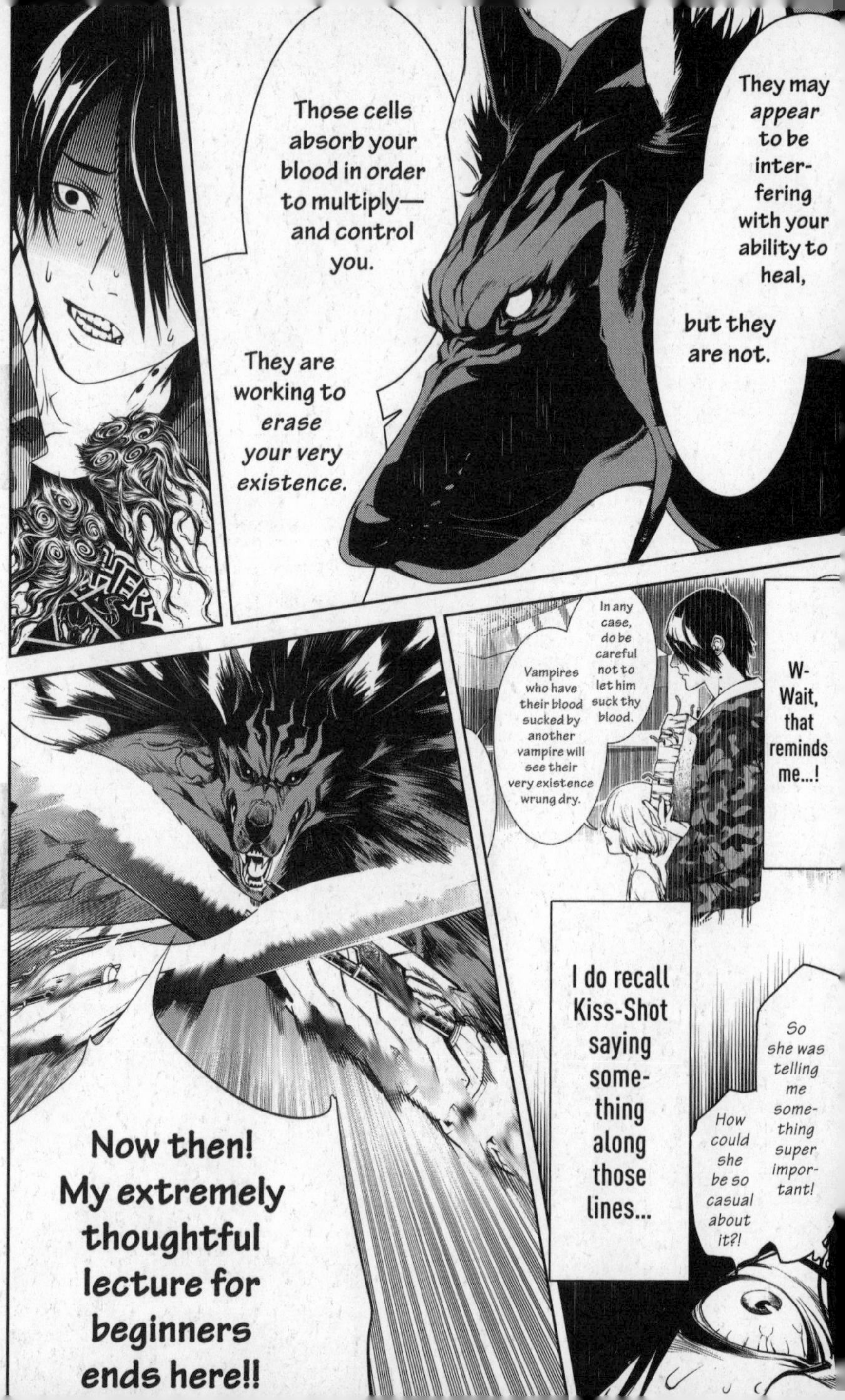
They may appear to be inter- fering with your ability to heal,
but they are not.
Those cells absorb your blood in order to multiply— and control you.
They are working to erase your very existence.
W- Wait, that reminds me...!
In any case, do be careful not to let him suck thy blood.
Vampires who have their blood sucked by another vampire will see their very existence wrung dry.
I do recall Kiss-Shot saying some- thing along those lines...
So she was telling me some- thing super impor- tant!
How could she be so casual about it?!
Now then! My extremely thoughtful lecture for beginners ends here!!

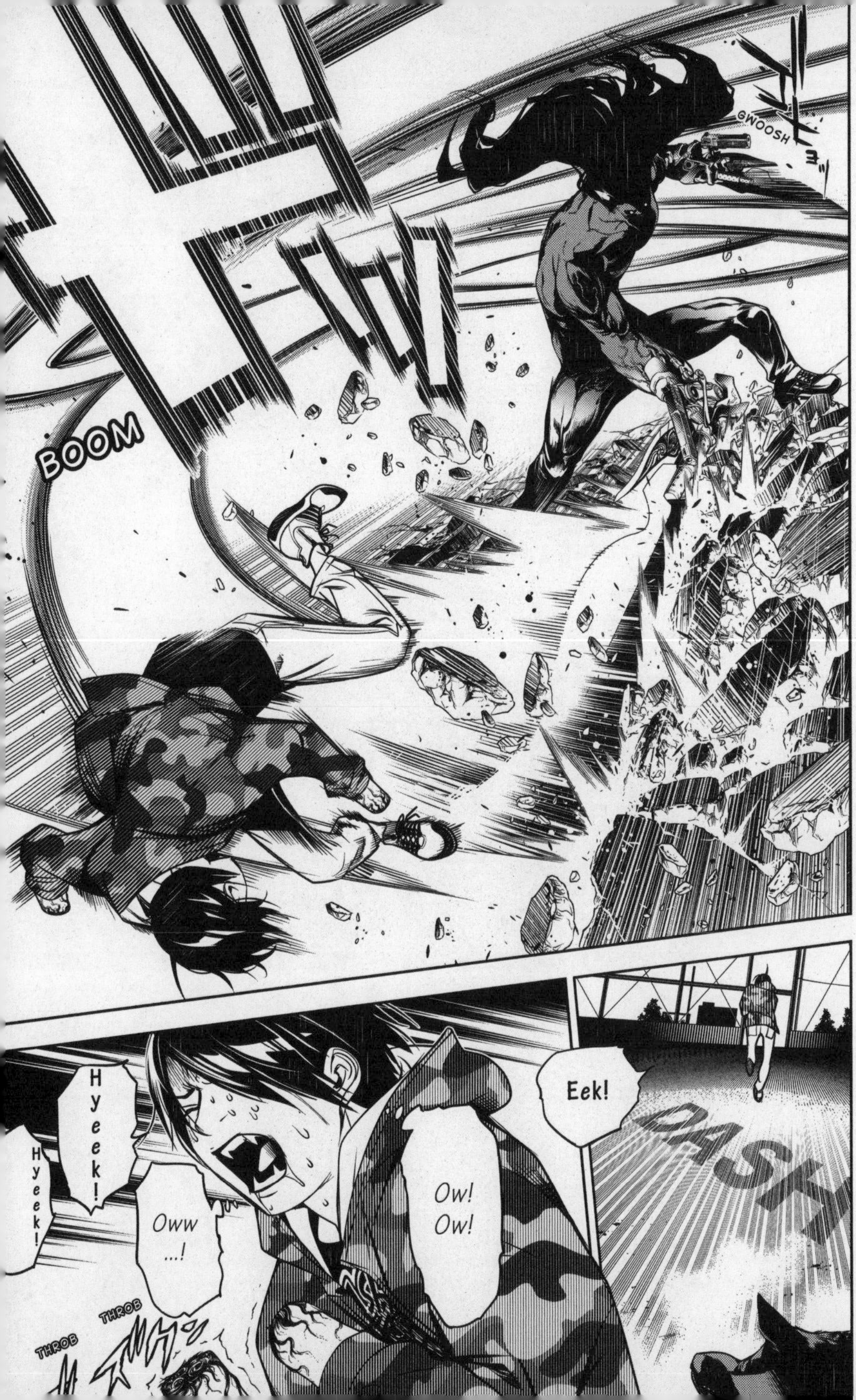
GWOOSH
BOOM
Eek!
DASH
Ow! Ow!
Hyeek!
Oww ...!
Hyeek!
THROB
THROB

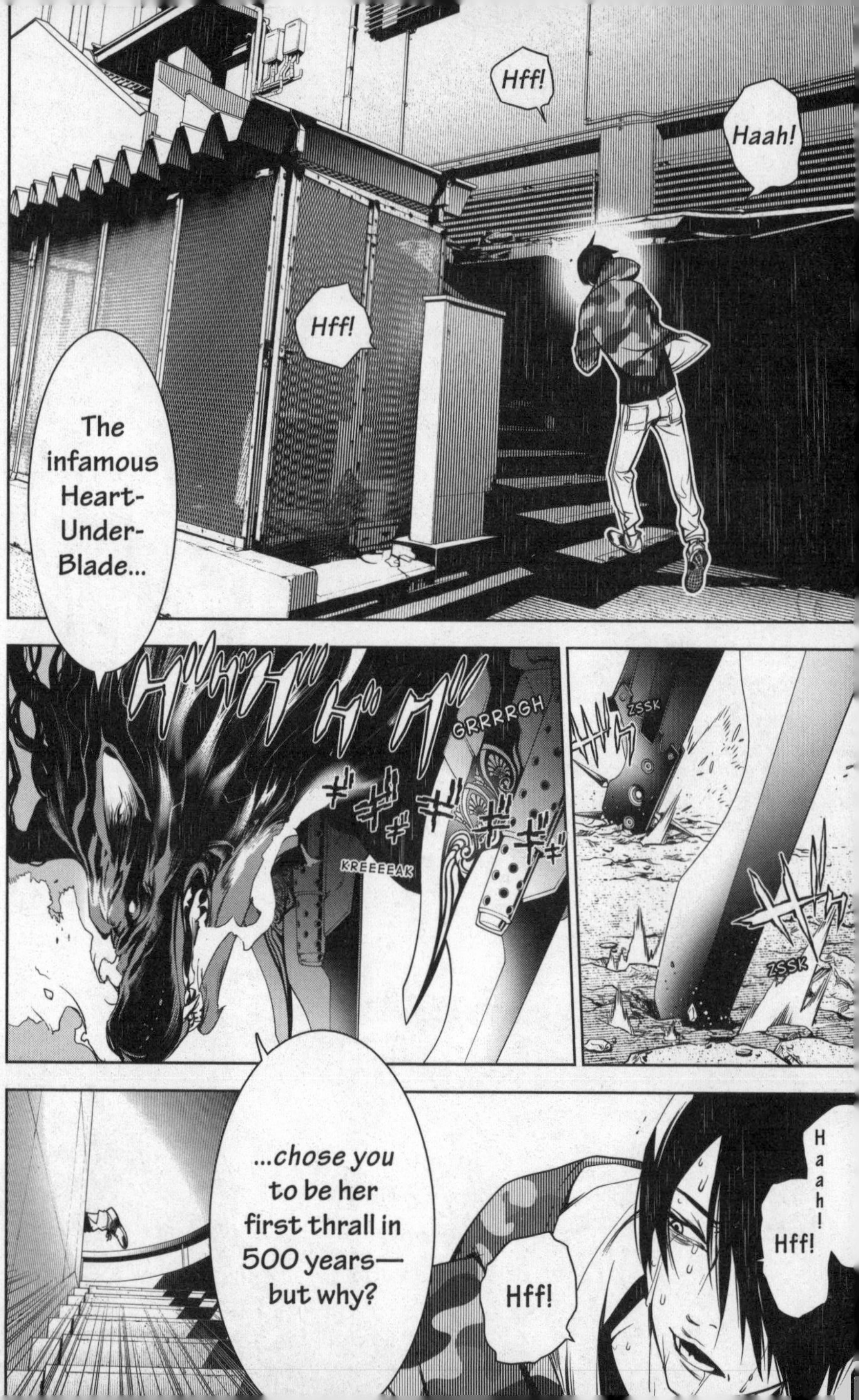
Hff!
Haah!
Hff!
The infamous Heart-Under-Blade...
ZSSK
ZSSK
GRRRRGH
KREEEEAK
Haah!
Hff!
Hff!
...chose you to be her first thrall in 500 years—but why?

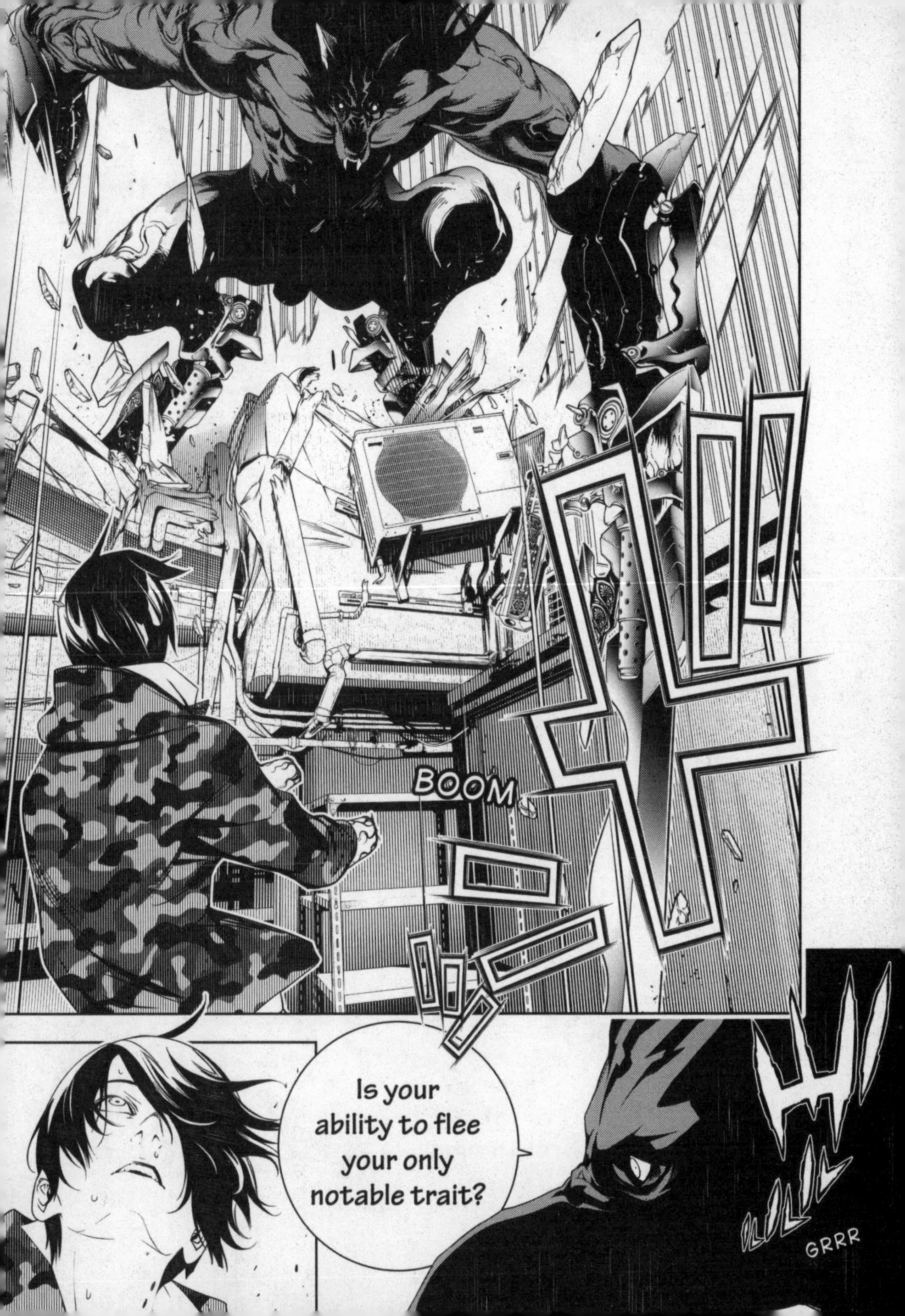
BOOM
Is your ability to flee your only notable trait?
GRRR

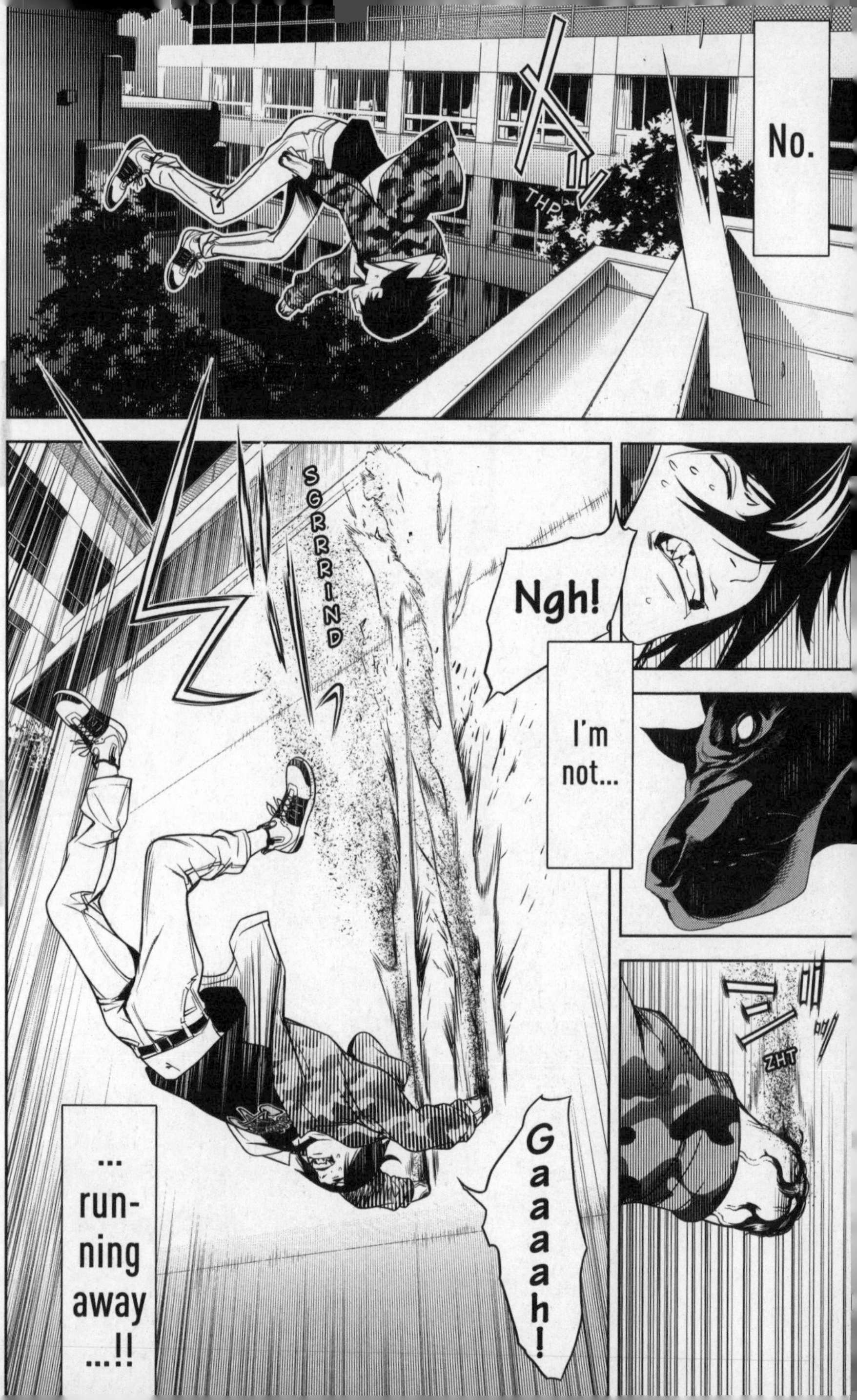
No.
THP
Ngh!
I'm not...
ZHT
SGRRRIND
Gaaaah!
...running away...!!

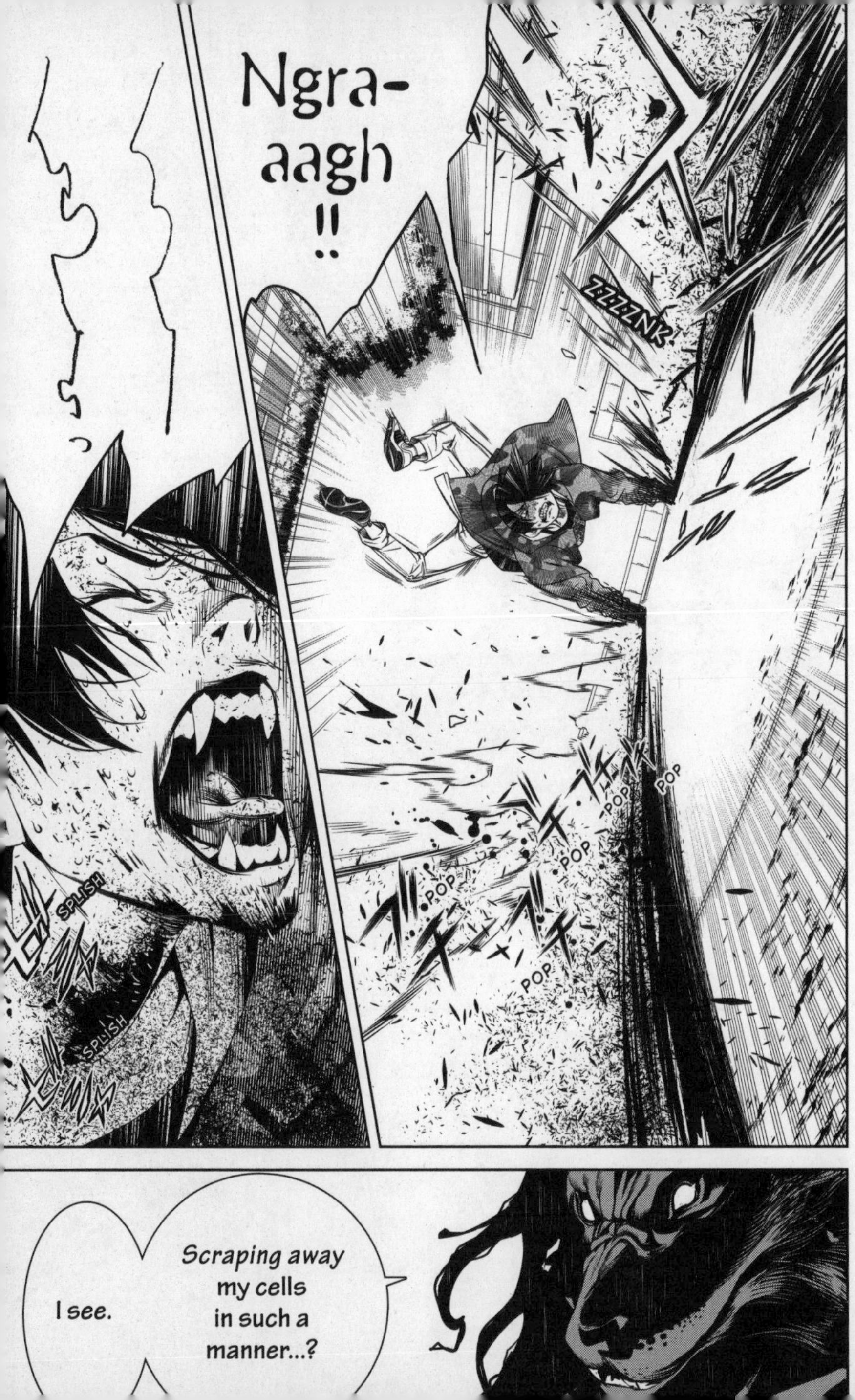
ZZZZZNK
POP
POP
POP
POP
POP
POP
Ngra-aagh!!
SPLISH
SPLISH
Scraping away my cells in such a manner...?
I see.

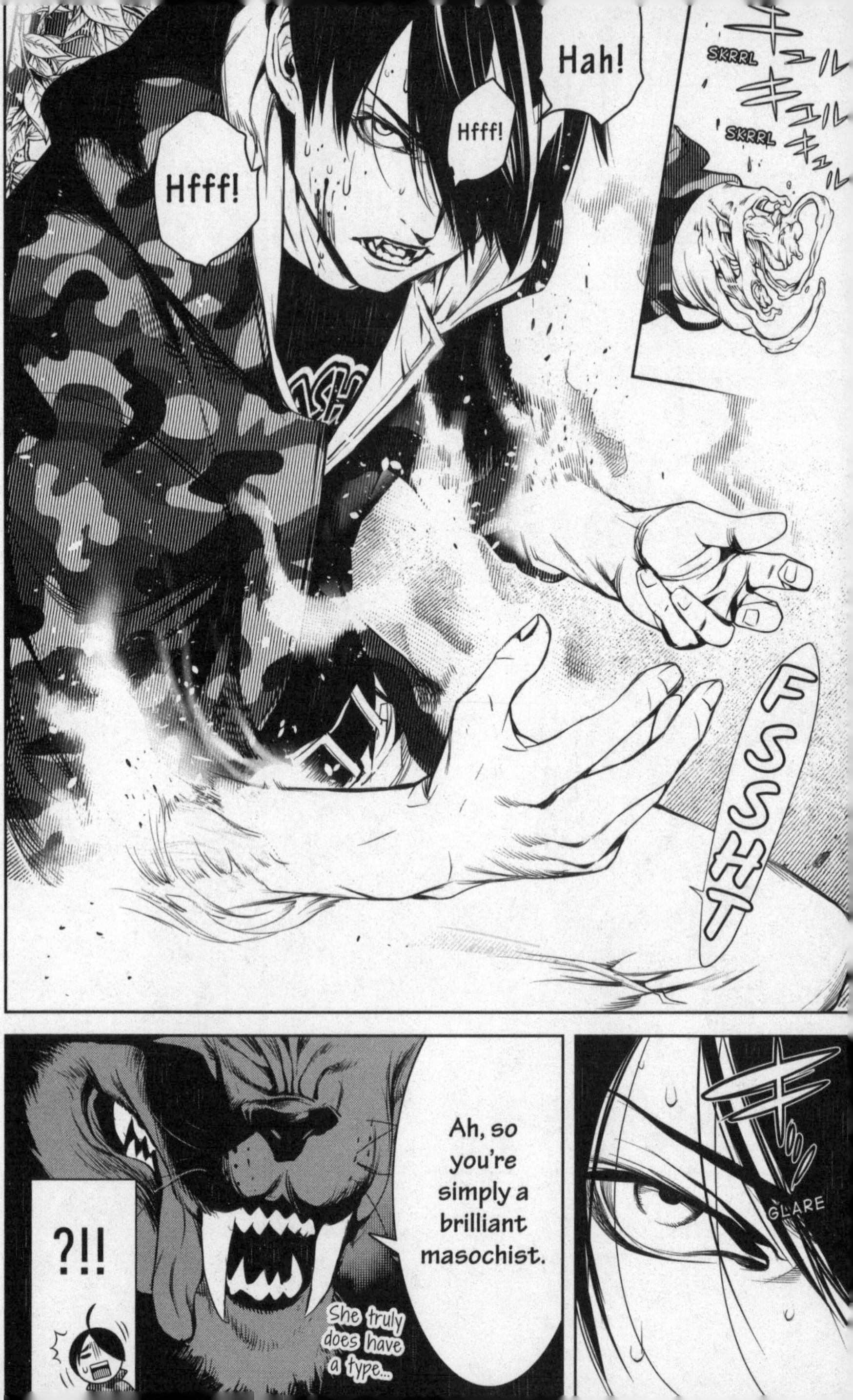
SKRRL
SKRRL
Hah!
Hfff!
Hfff!
FSSHT
GLARE
Ah, so you're simply a brilliant masochist.
?!!
She truly does have a type...

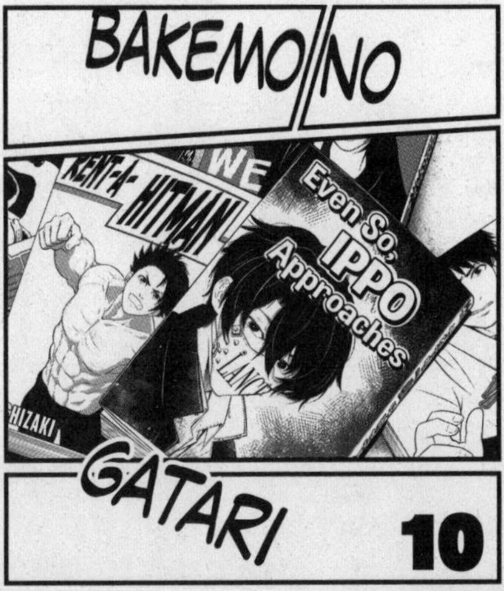
BAKEMONO
RENT-A-HITMAN
Even So, IPPO Approaches
GATARI
10

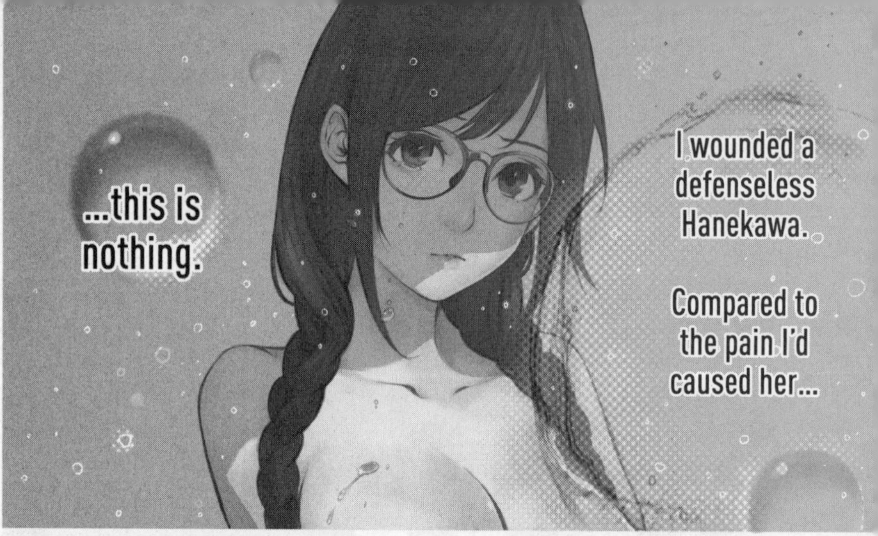
I wounded a defenseless Hanekawa.
Compared to the pain I'd caused her...
...this is nothing.
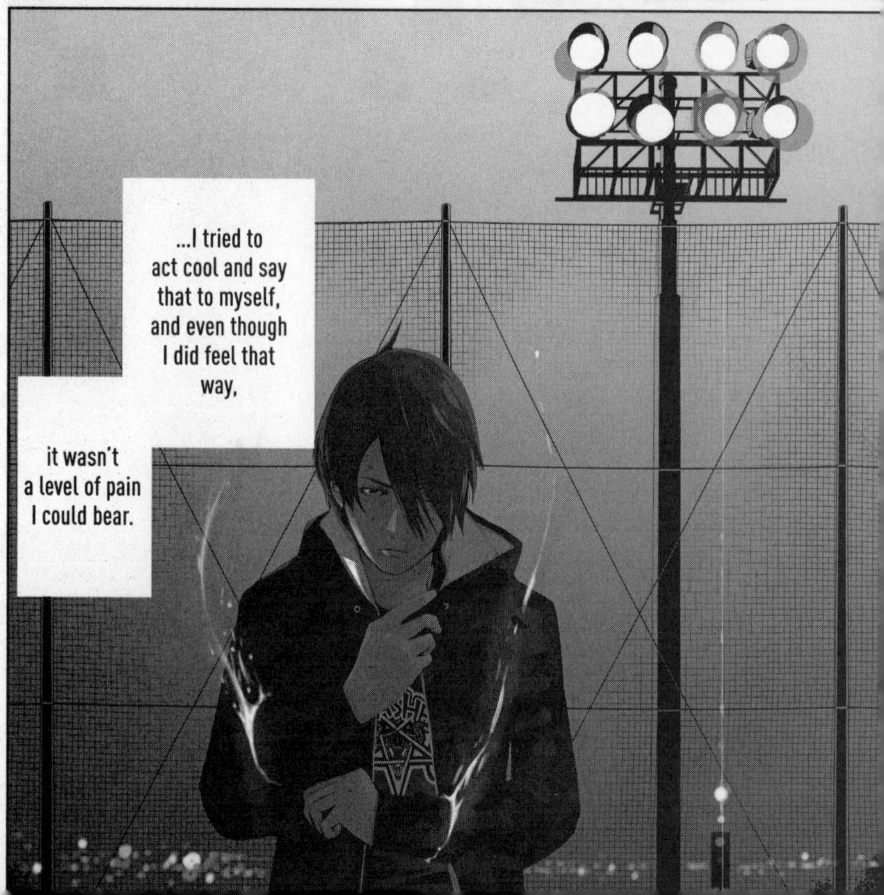
...I tried to act cool and say that to myself, and even though I did feel that way,
it wasn't a level of pain I could bear.

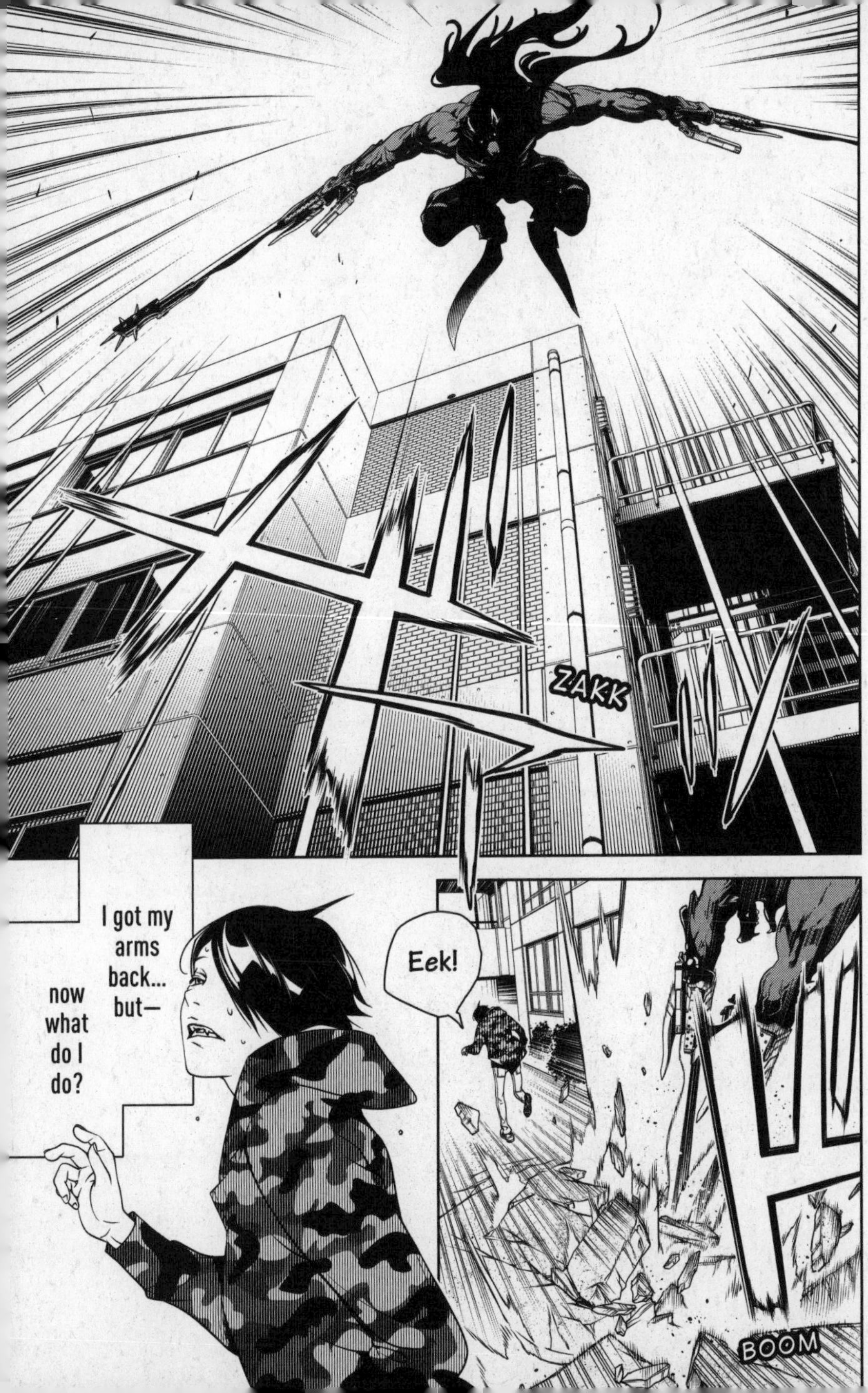
ZAKK
Eek!
BOOM
I got my arms back... but—
now what do I do?

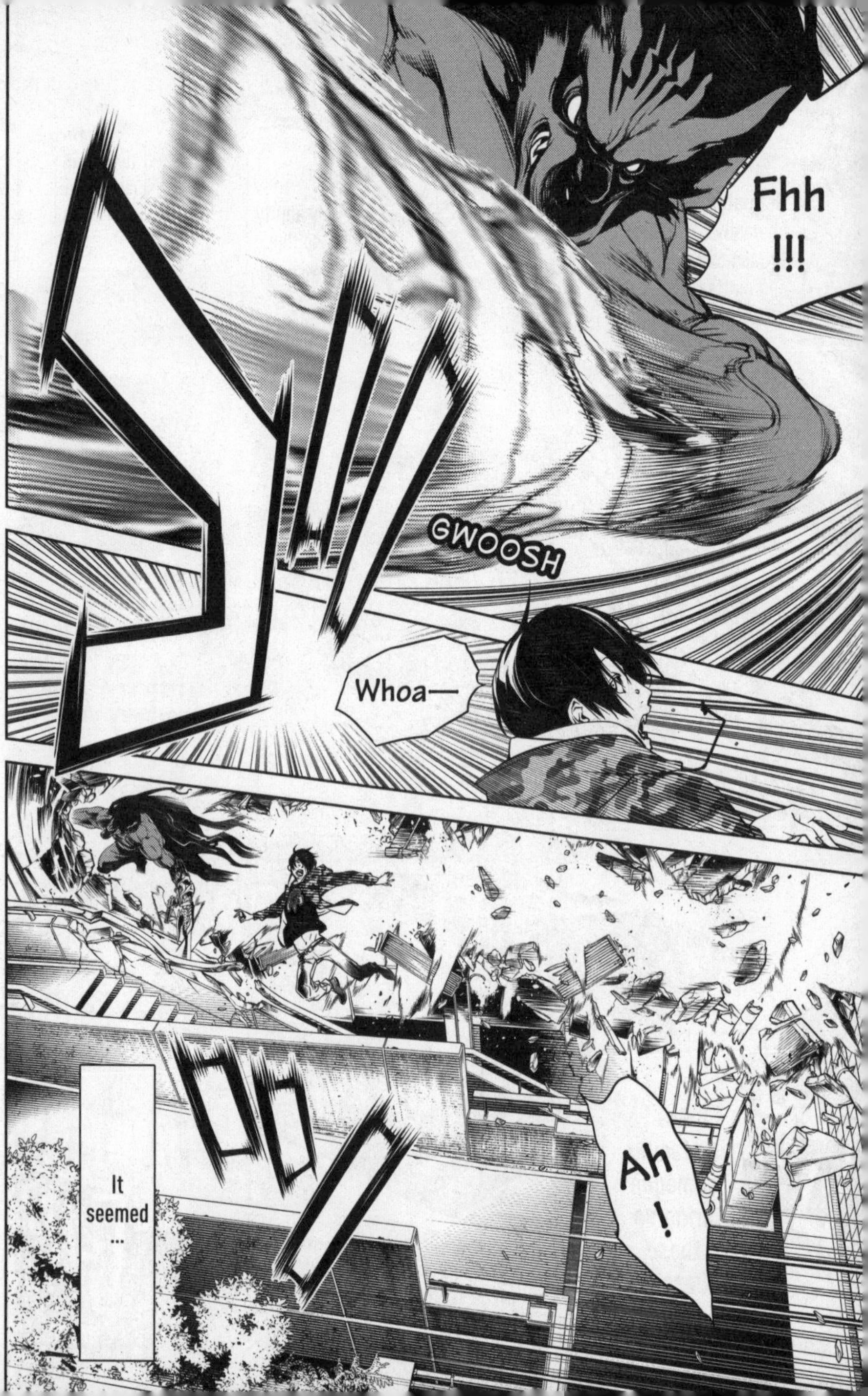
Fhh
!!!
GWOOSH
Whoa—
Ah
!
It
seemed
...

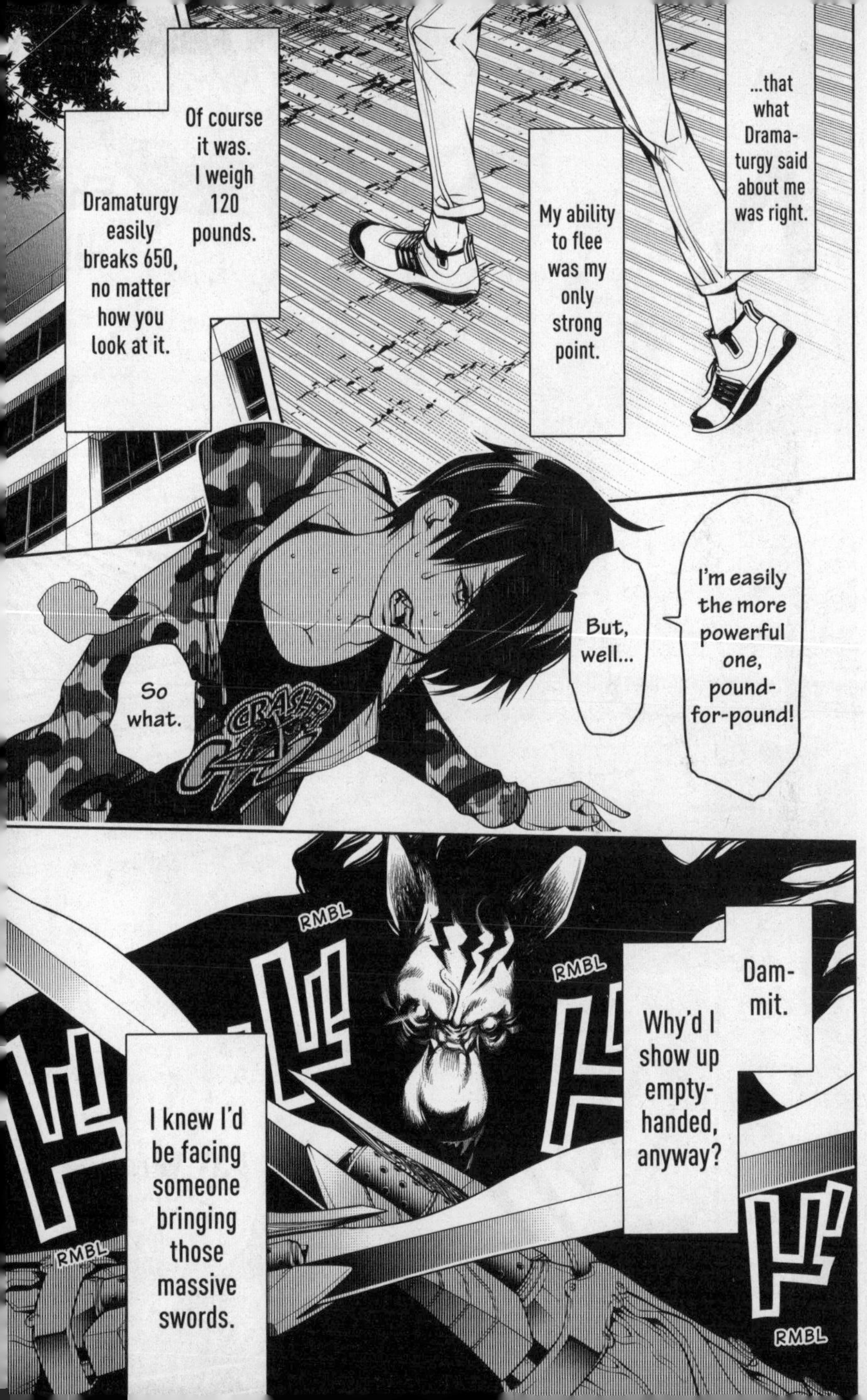
...that what Drama-turgy said about me was right.
My ability to flee was my only strong point.
Of course it was. I weigh 120 pounds.
Dramaturgy easily breaks 650, no matter how you look at it.
I'm easily the more powerful one, pound-for-pound!
But, well...
So what.
Dam-mit.
Why'd I show up empty-handed, anyway?
RMBL
RMBL
RMBL
I knew I'd be facing someone bringing those massive swords.
RMBL

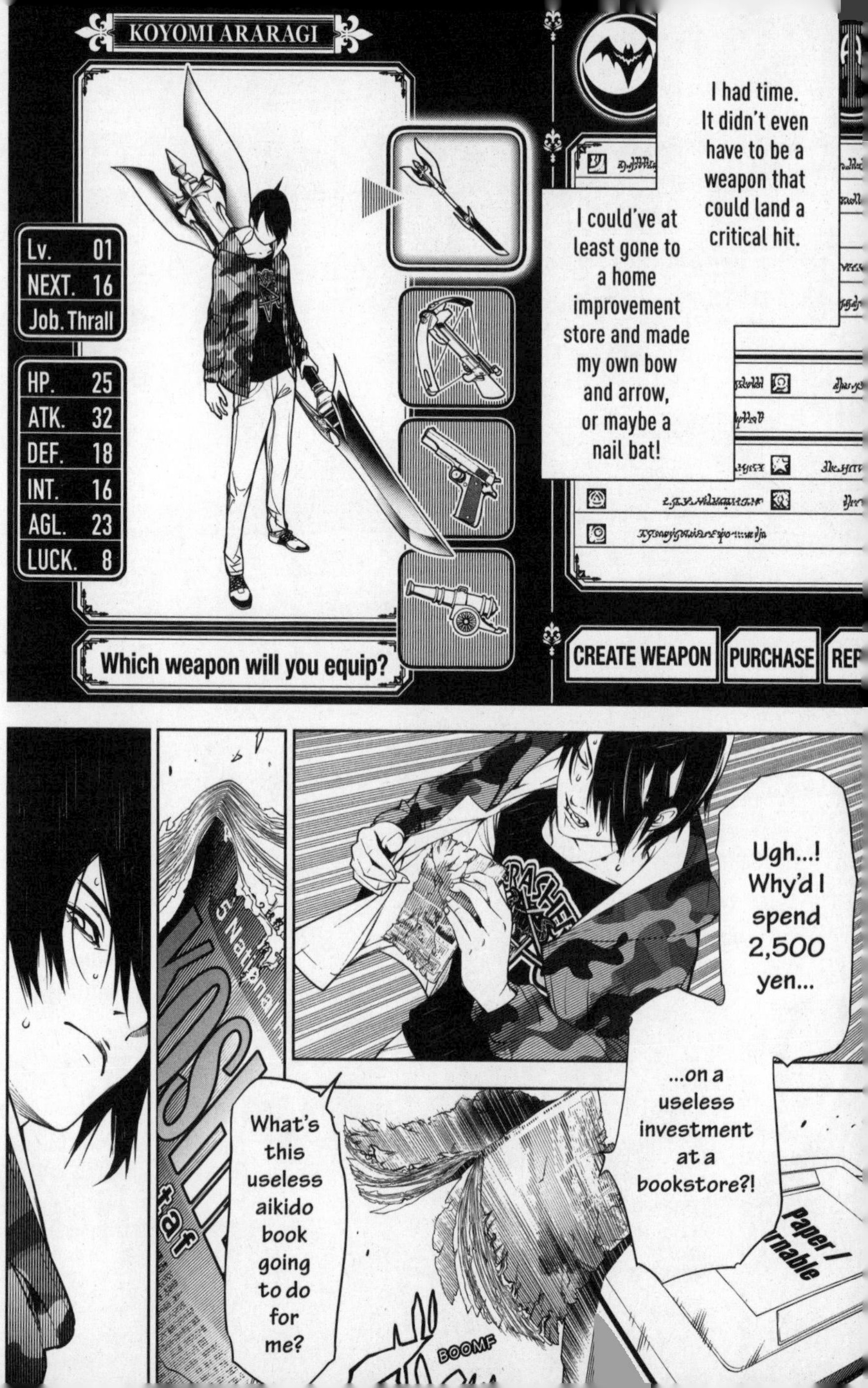
I had time. It didn't even have to be a weapon that could land a critical hit.
I could've at least gone to a home improvement store and made my own bow and arrow, or maybe a nail bat!
KOYOMI ARARAGI
Lv. 01
NEXT. 16
Job. Thrall
HP. 25
ATK. 32
DEF. 18
INT. 16
AGL. 23
LUCK. 8
Which weapon will you equip?
CREATE WEAPON
PURCHASE
REP
Ugh...! Why'd I spend 2,500 yen...
...on a useless investment at a bookstore?!
What's this useless aikido book going to do for me?
Paper /
BOOMF

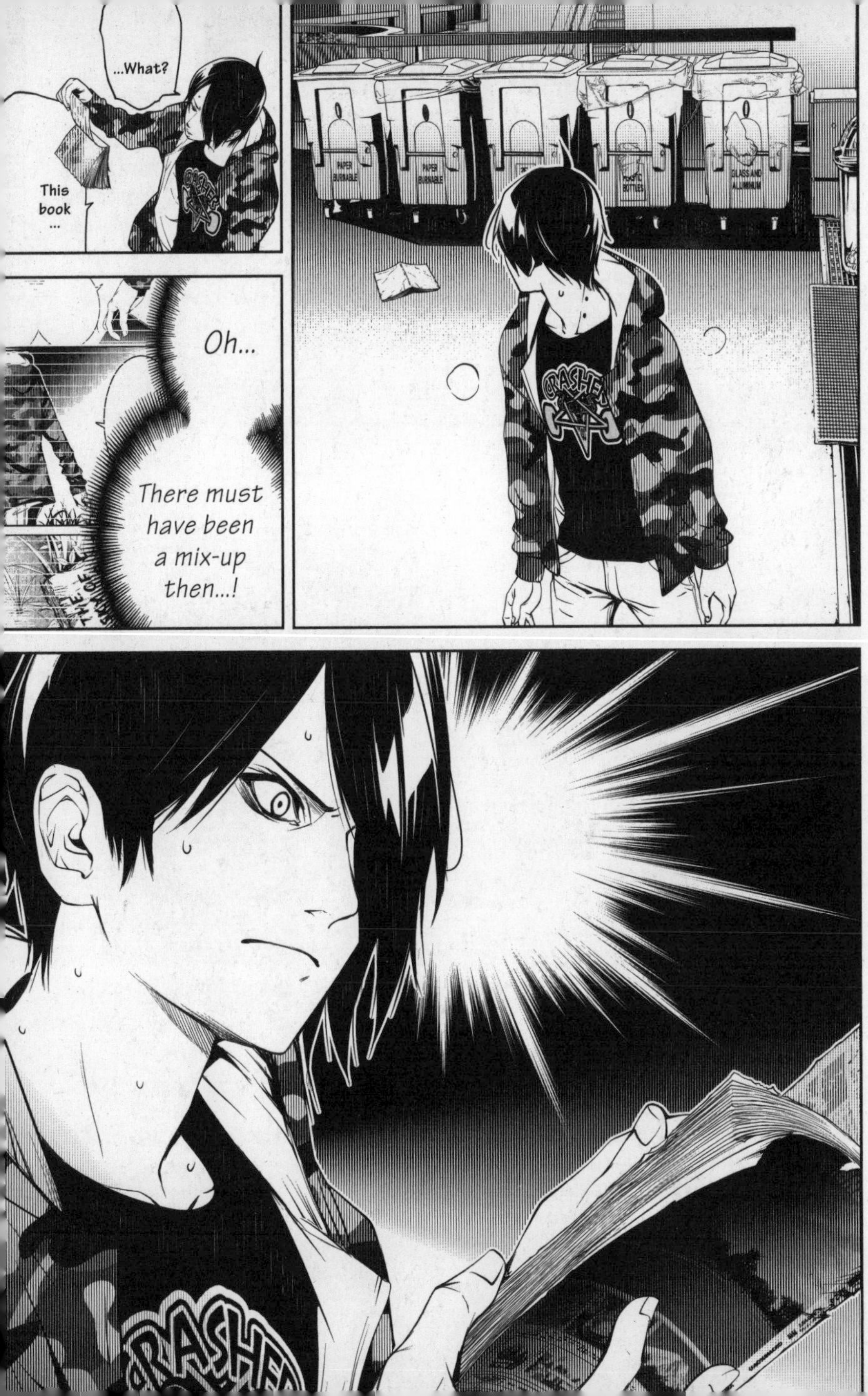
...What?
This book ...
Oh...
There must have been a mix-up then...!

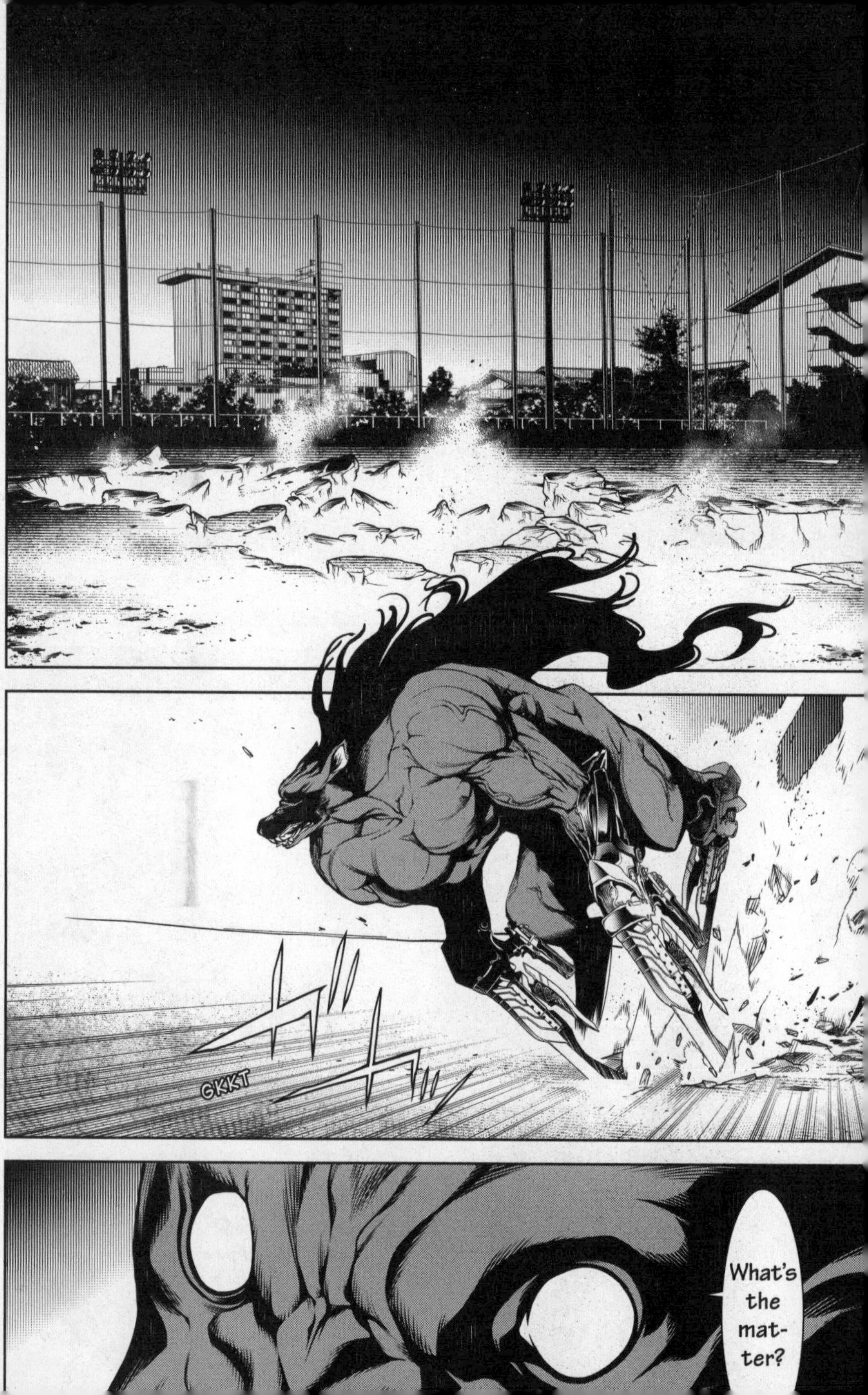
GKKT
What's the mat- ter?

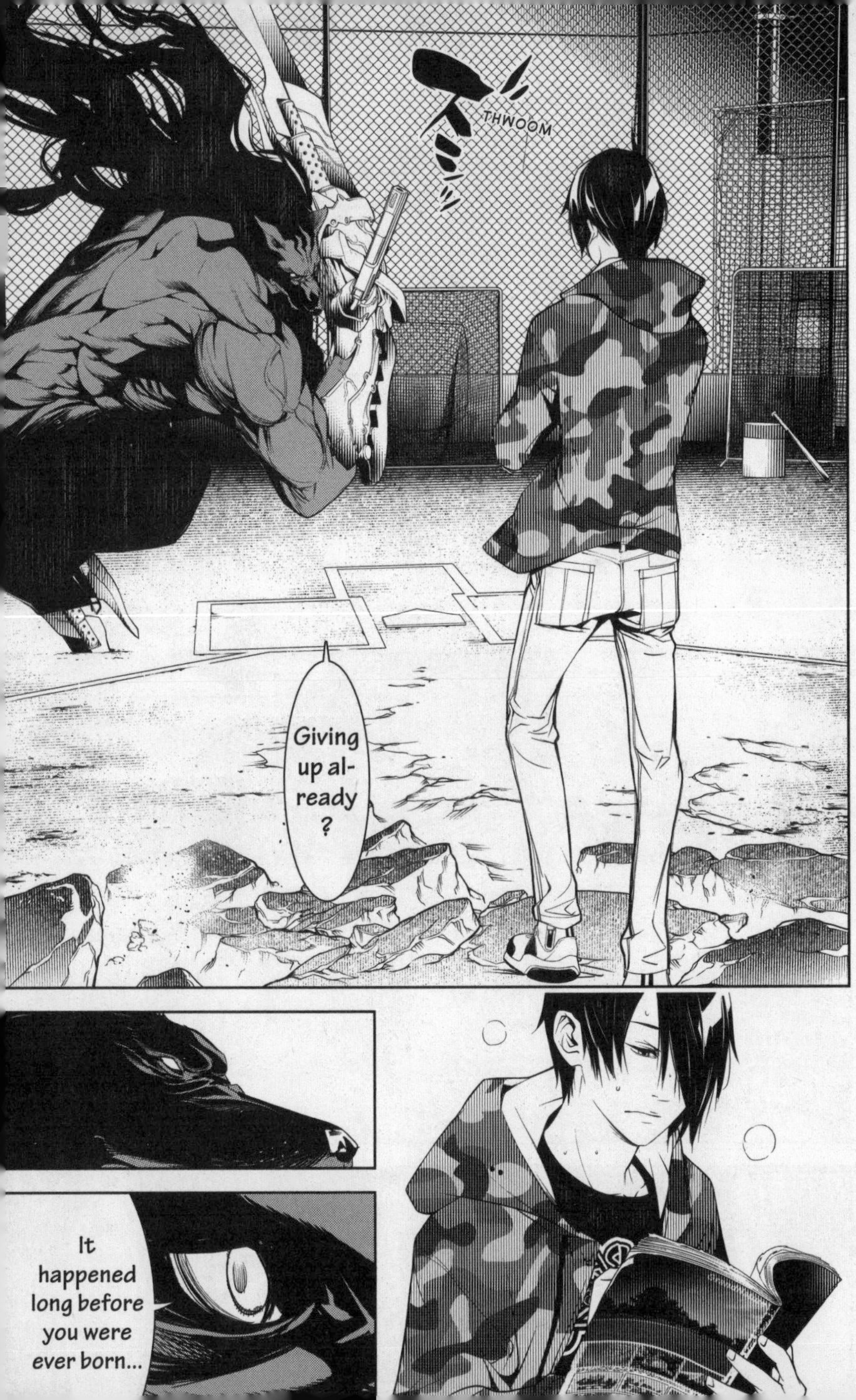
THWOOM
Giving up al-ready ?
It happened long before you were ever born...

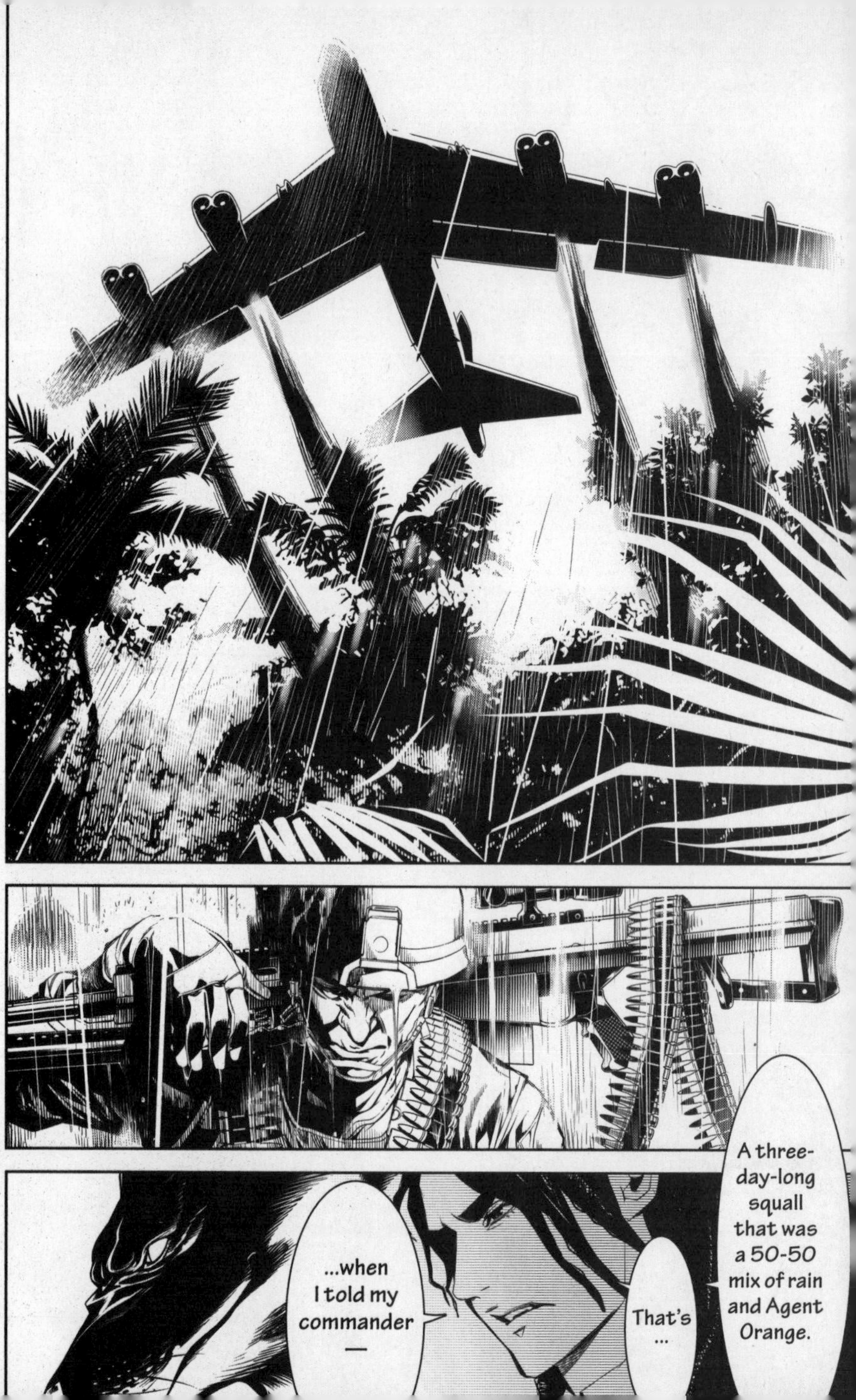
A three-day-long squall that was a 50-50 mix of rain and Agent Orange.
That's ...
...when I told my commander —

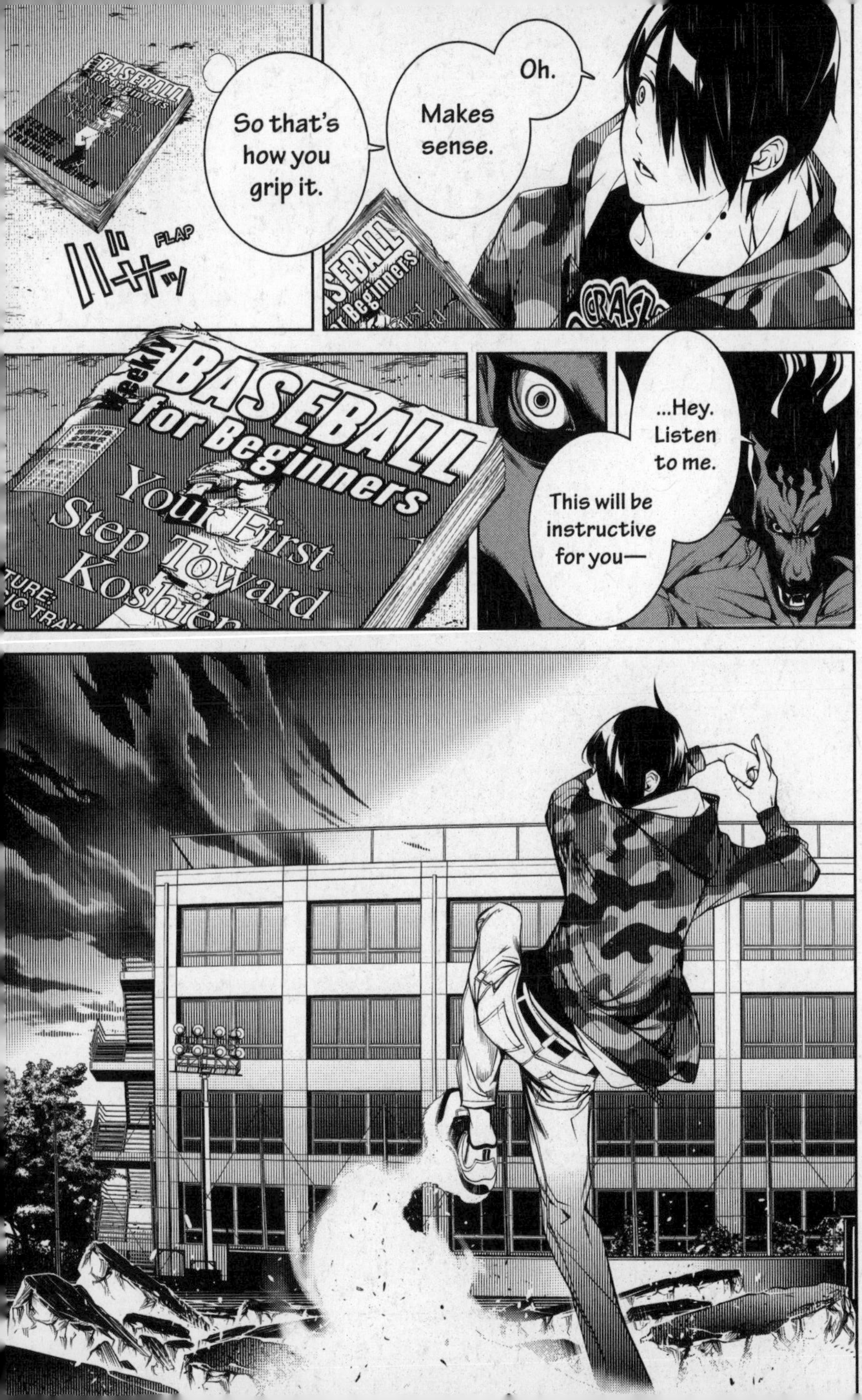

Oh.
Makes sense.
BASEBALL for Beginners
So that's how you grip it.
FLAP
...Hey. Listen to me.
This will be instructive for you—
Weekly BASEBALL for Beginners
Your First Step Toward Koshien

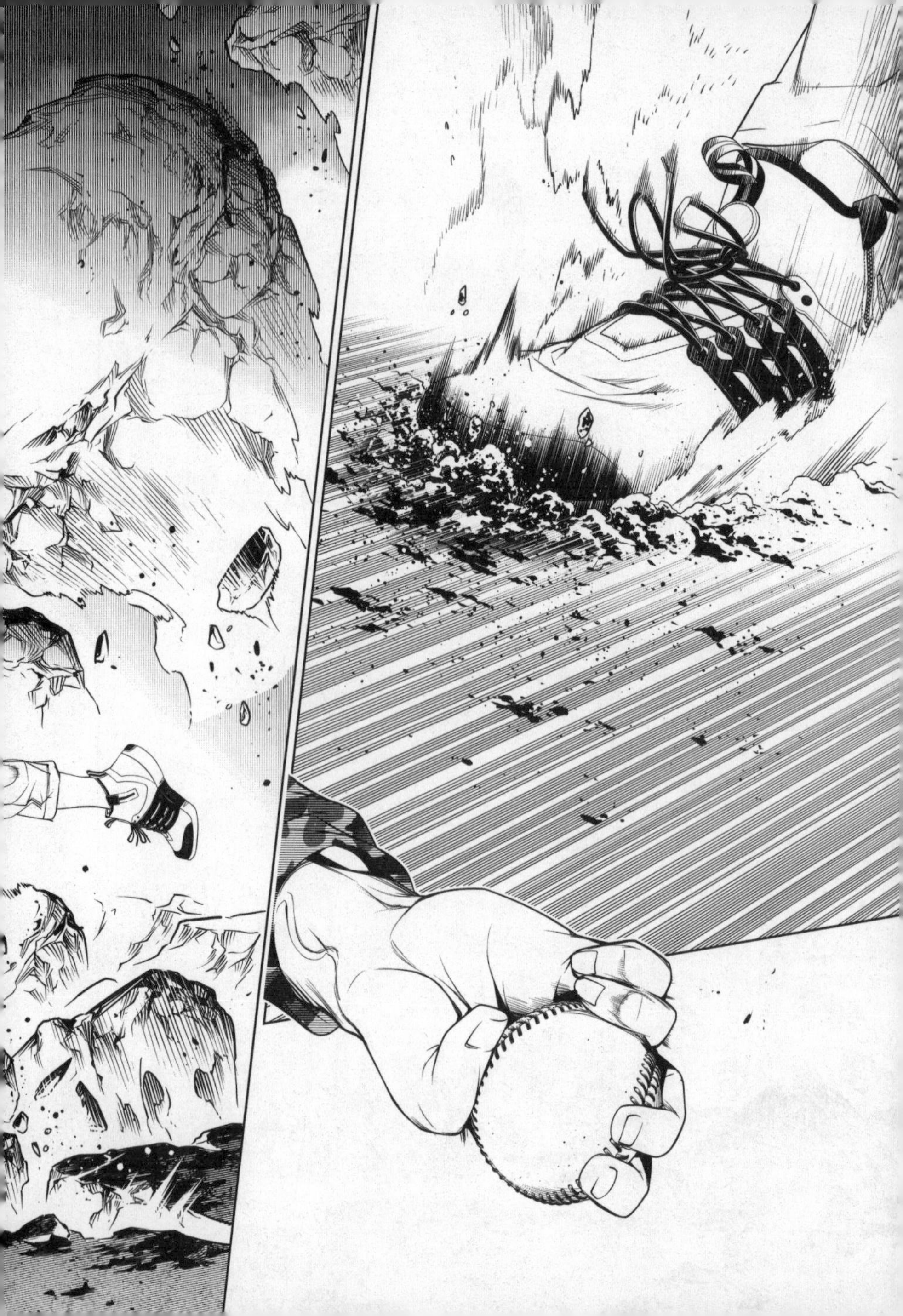

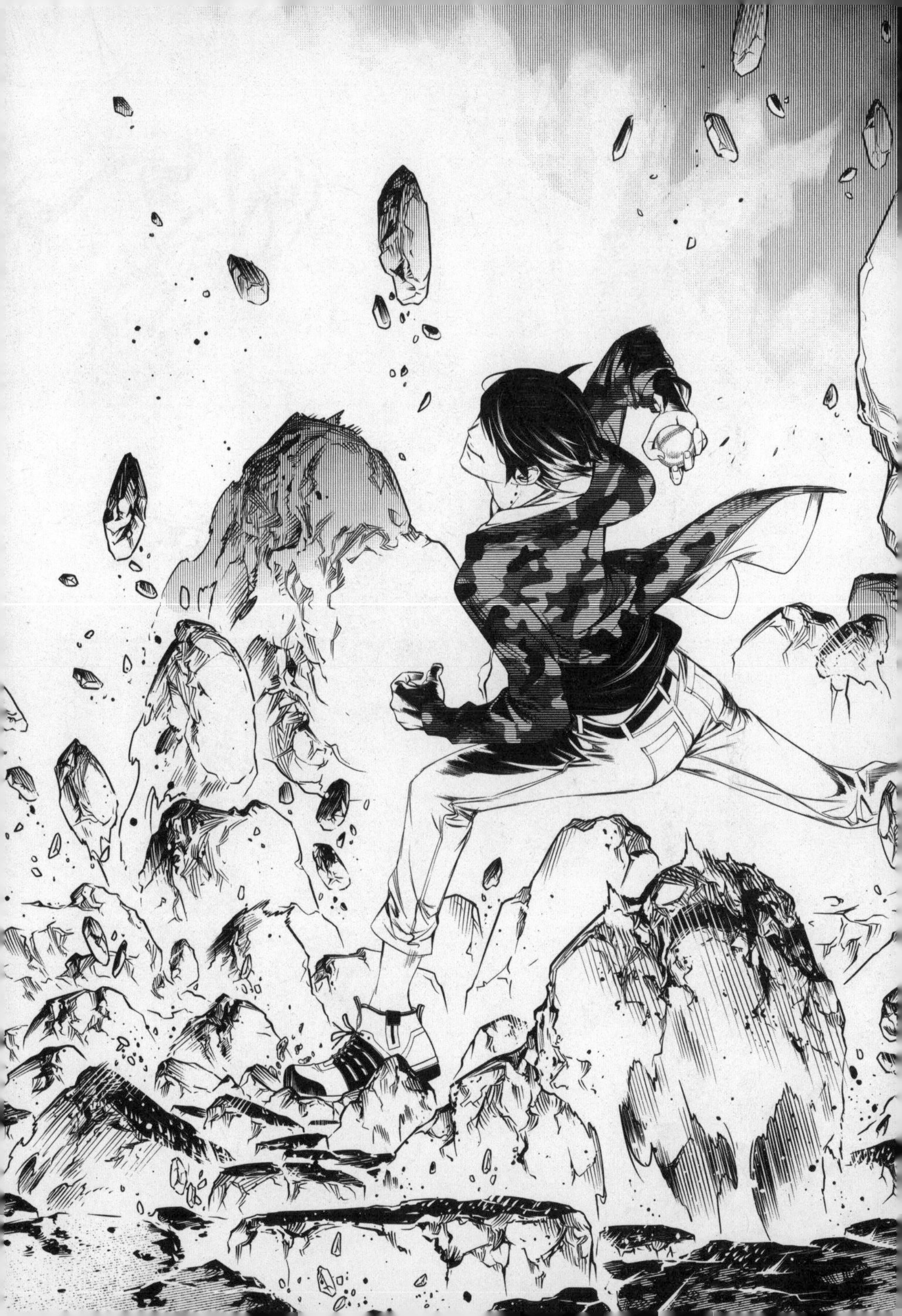

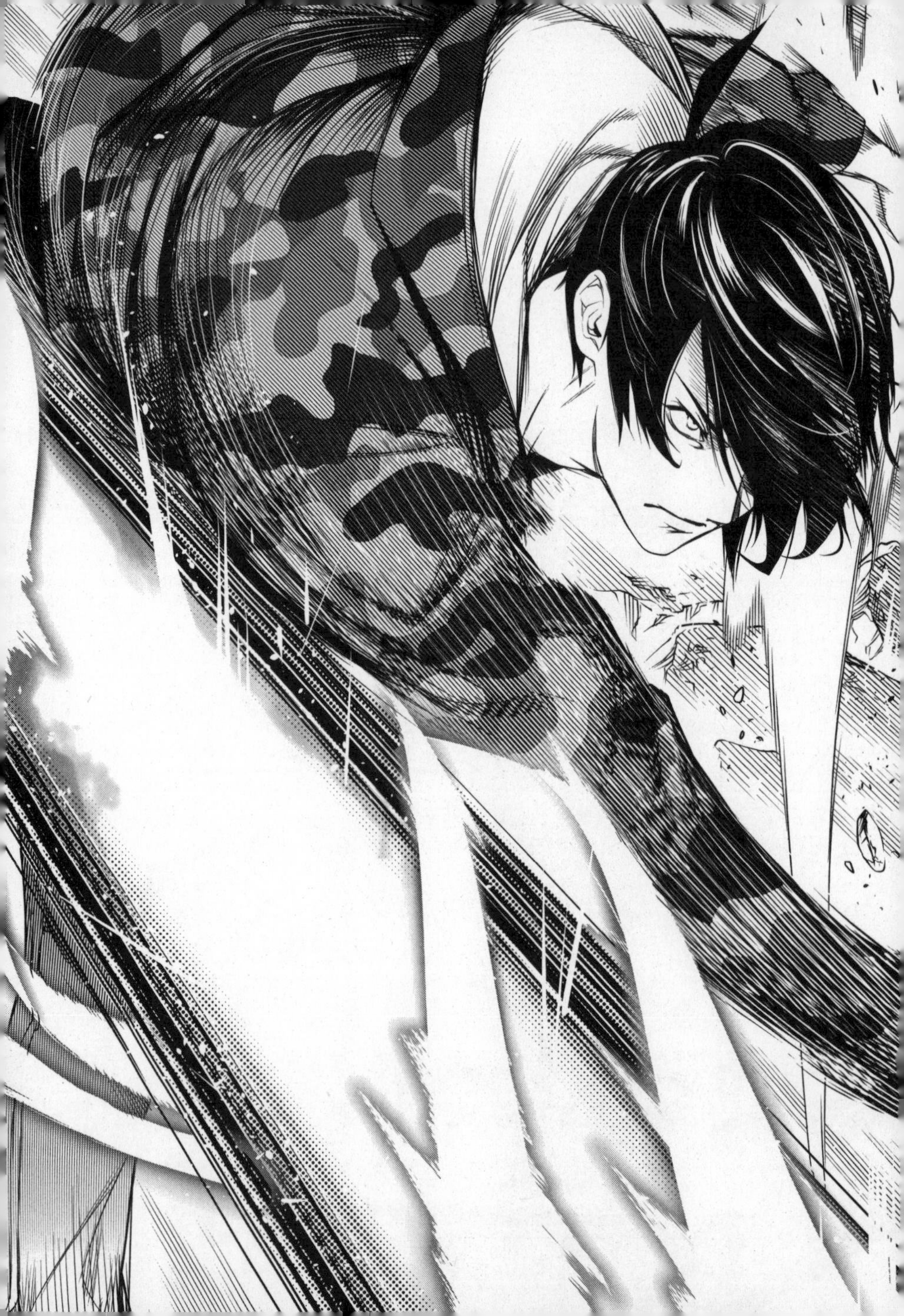

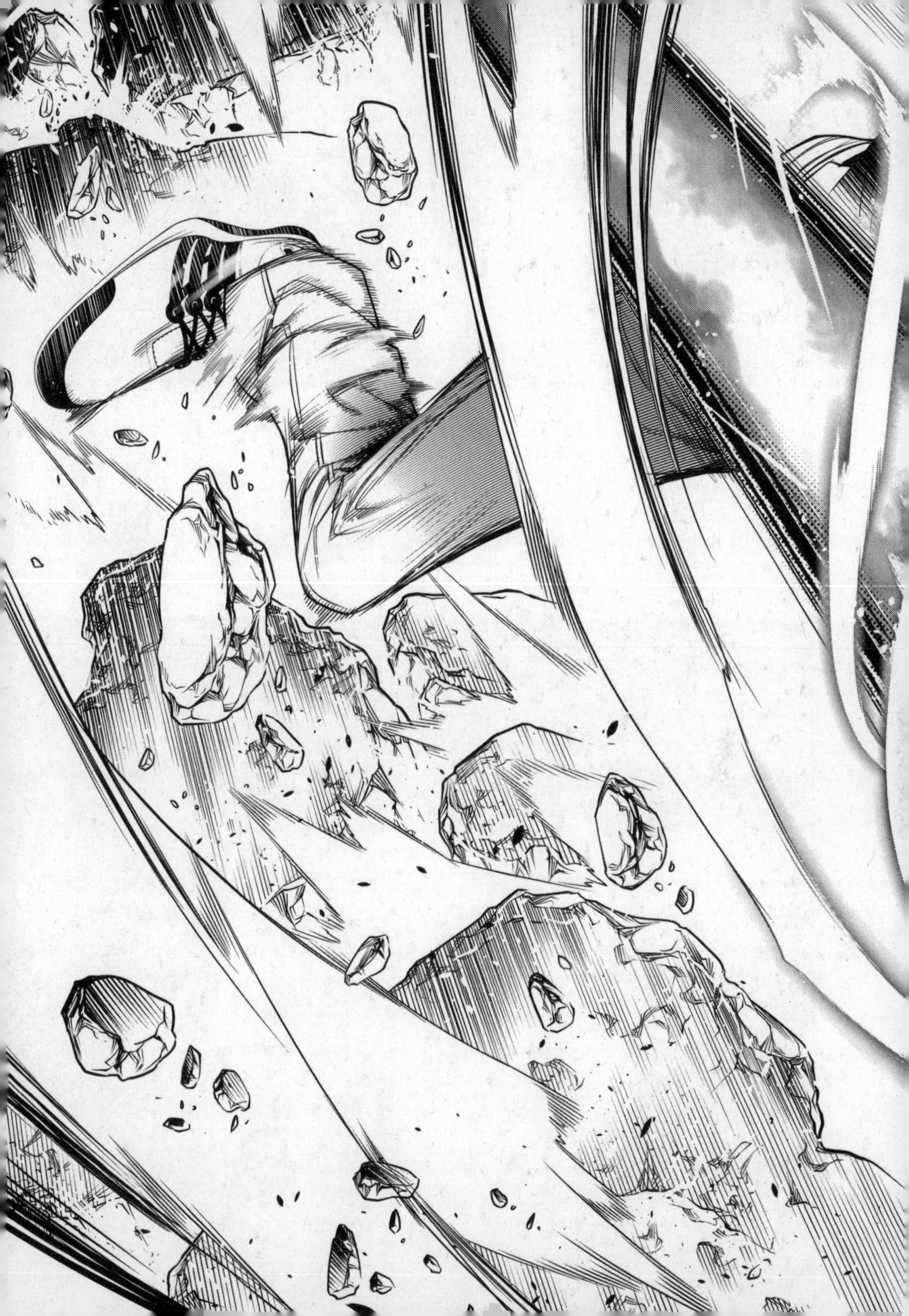

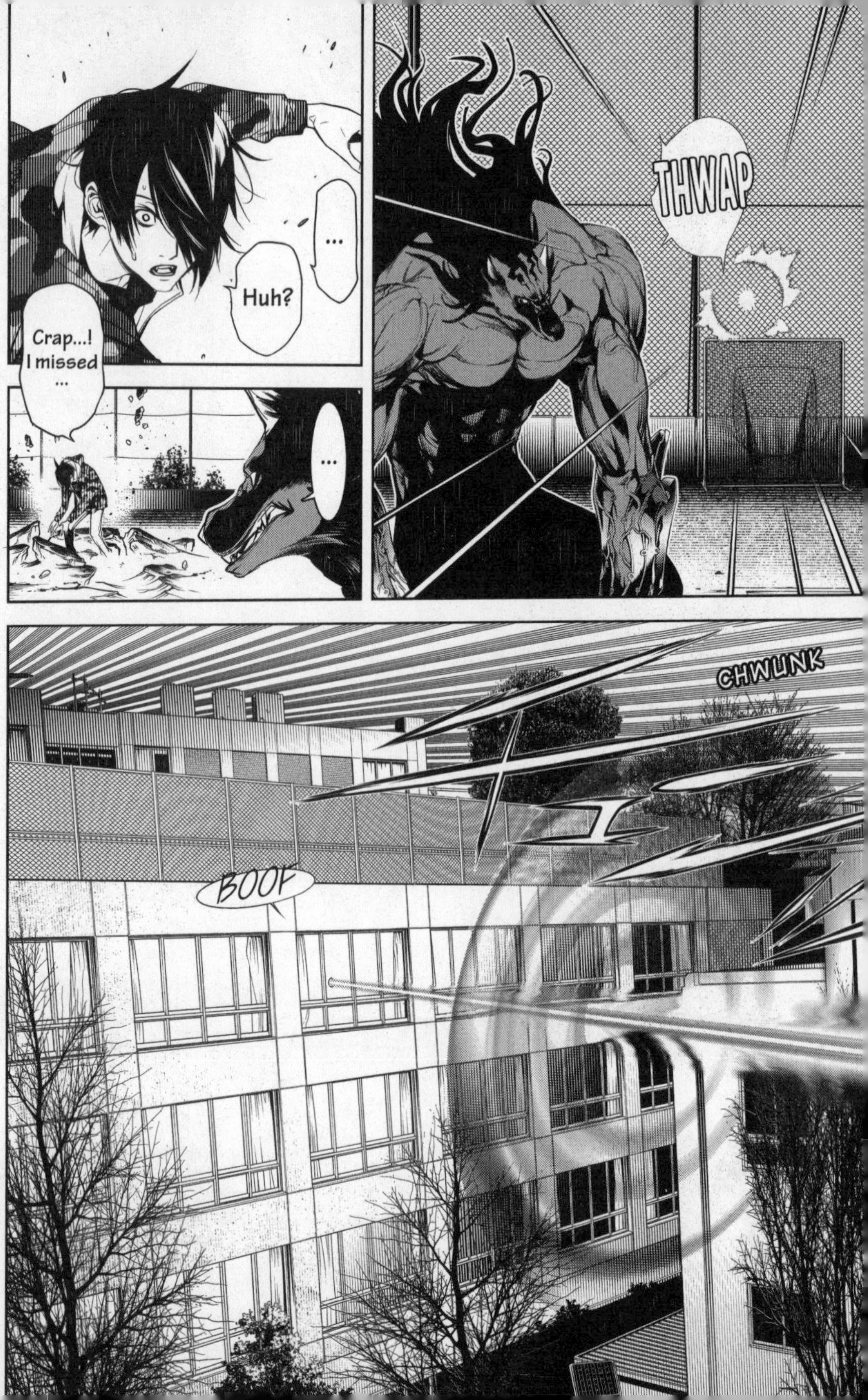
THWAP
...
Huh?
Crap...! I missed ...
...
CHWUNK
BOOF

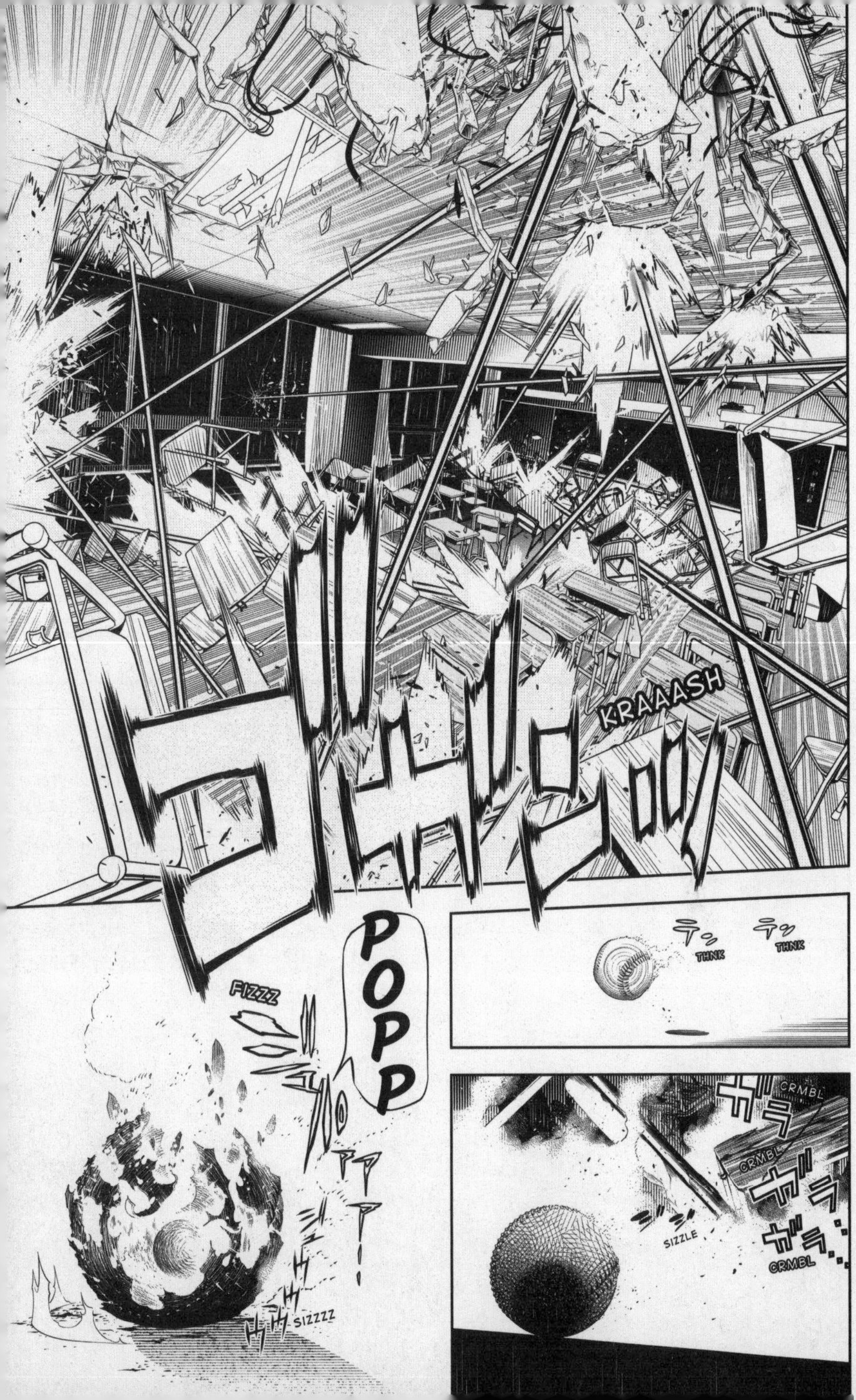
KRAAASH
THNK
THNK
CRMBL
CRMBL
SIZZLE
CRMBL
POPP
FIZZZ
SIZZZZ

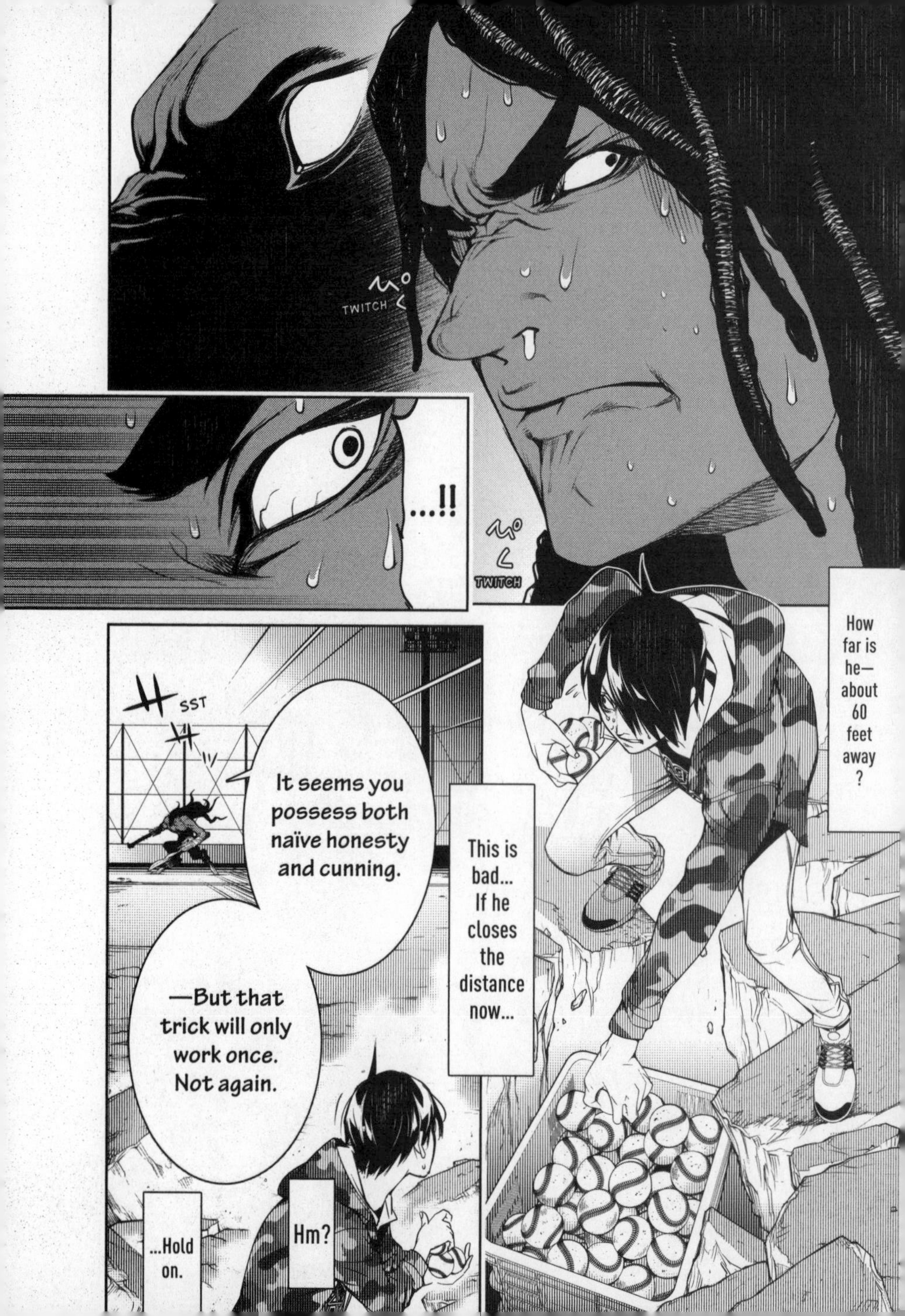
TWITCH
TWITCH
...!!
How far is he—about 60 feet away?
This is bad... If he closes the distance now...
SST
It seems you possess both naïve honesty and cunning.
—But that trick will only work once. Not again.
Hm?
...Hold on.

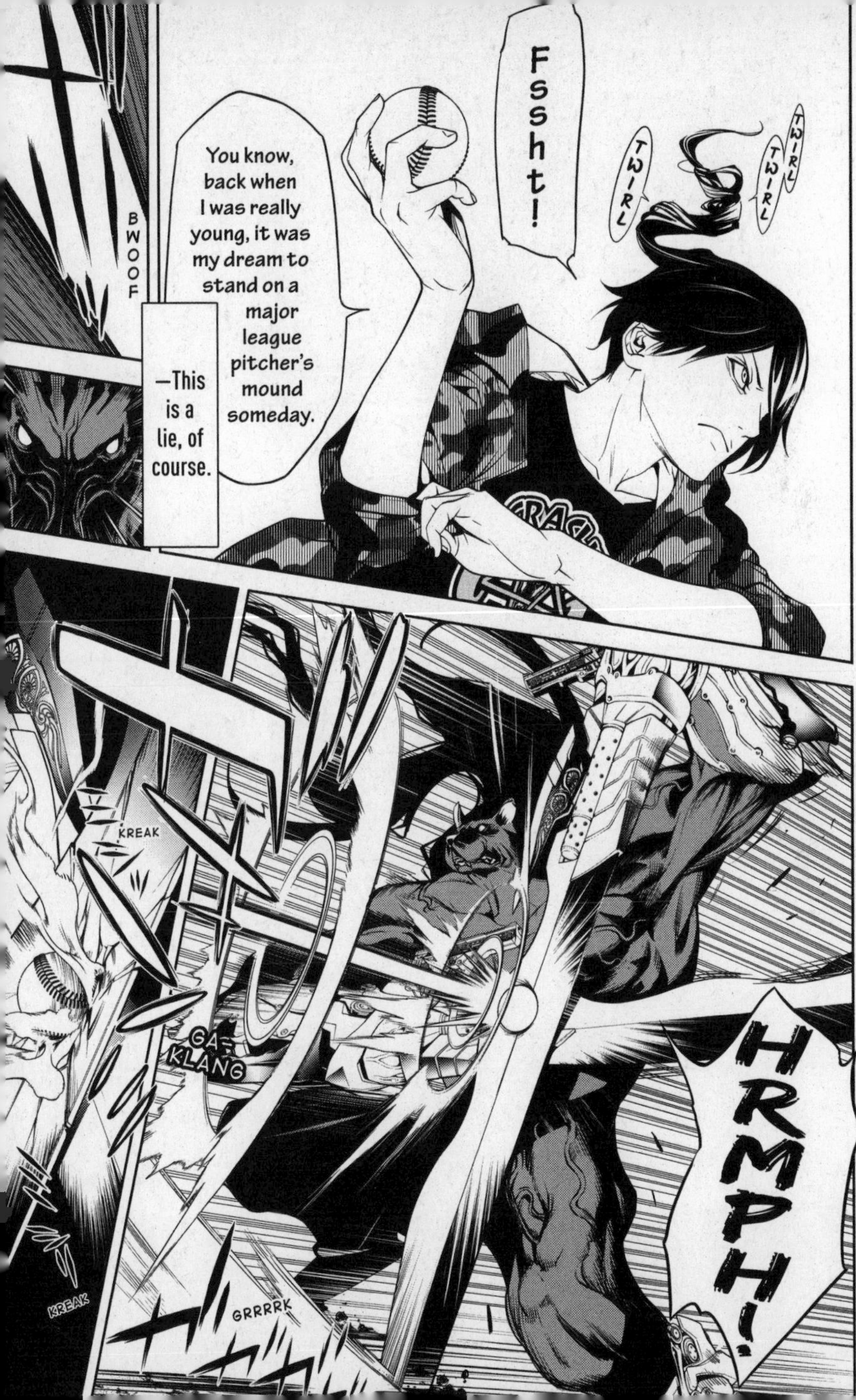
TWIRL
TWIRL
TWIRL
Fssht!
You know, back when I was really young, it was my dream to stand on a major league pitcher's mound someday.
—This is a lie, of course.
BWOOF
HRMPH!
GA-KLANG
KREAK
GRRRRK
KREAK

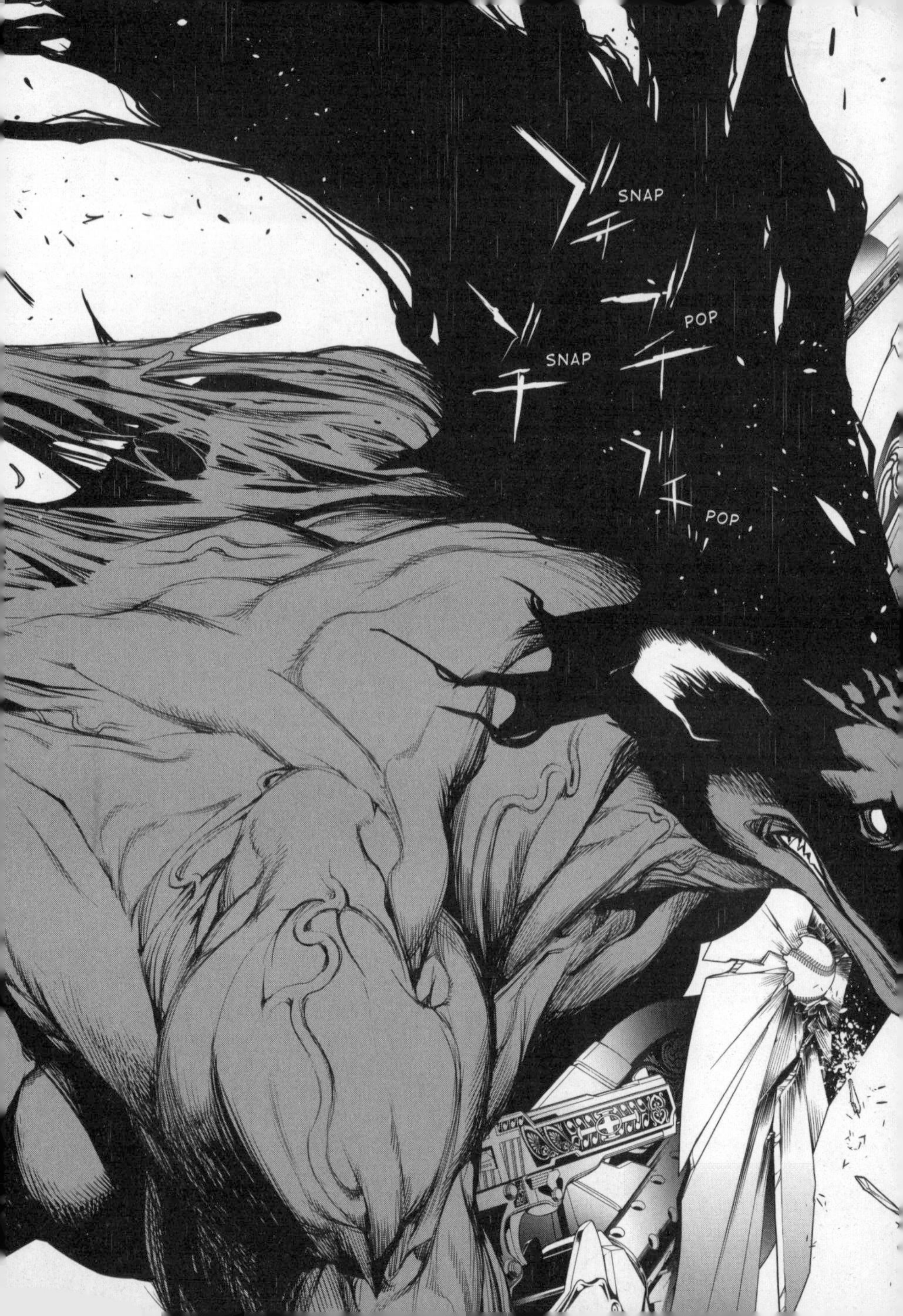
SNAP
POP
SNAP
POP

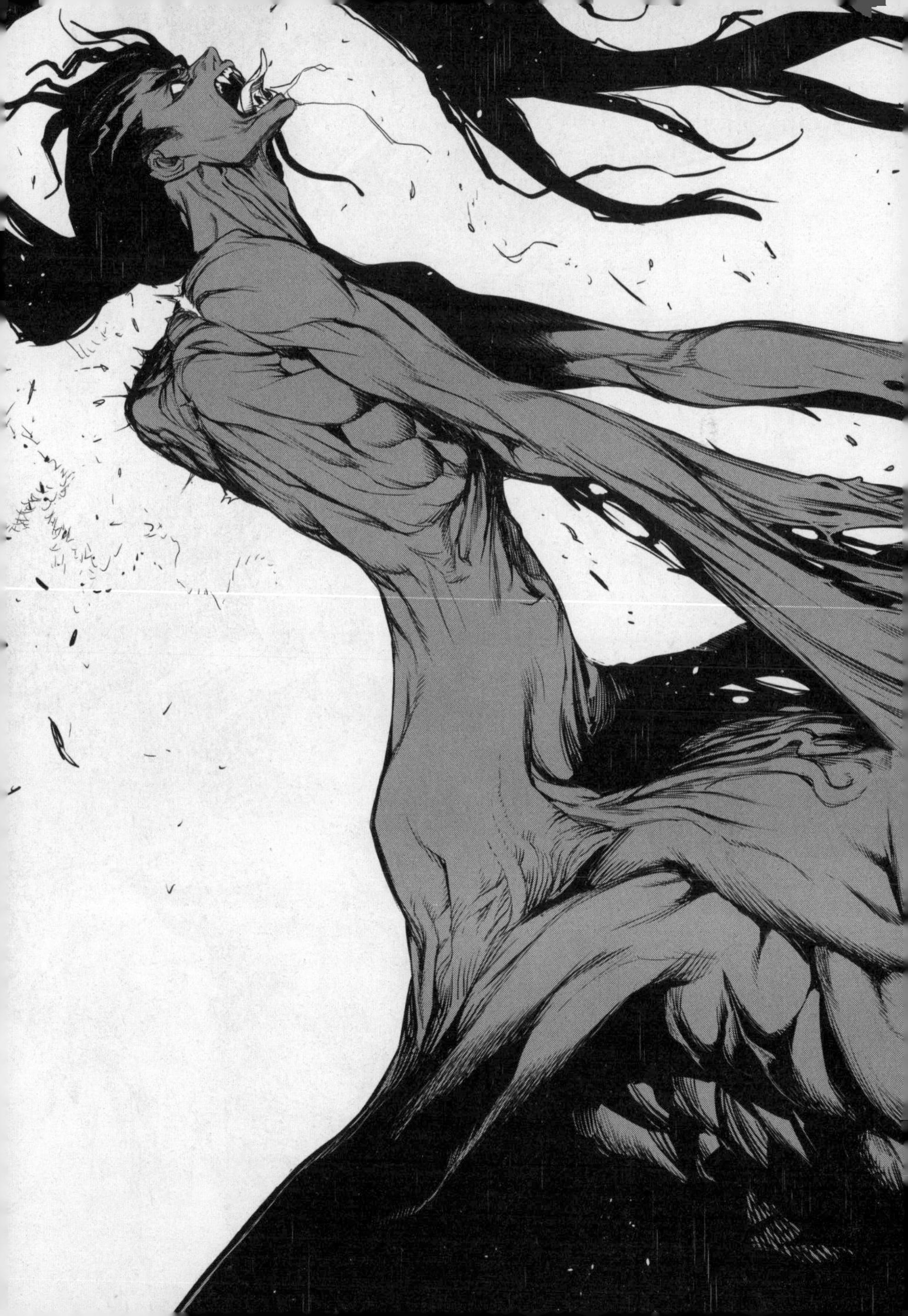

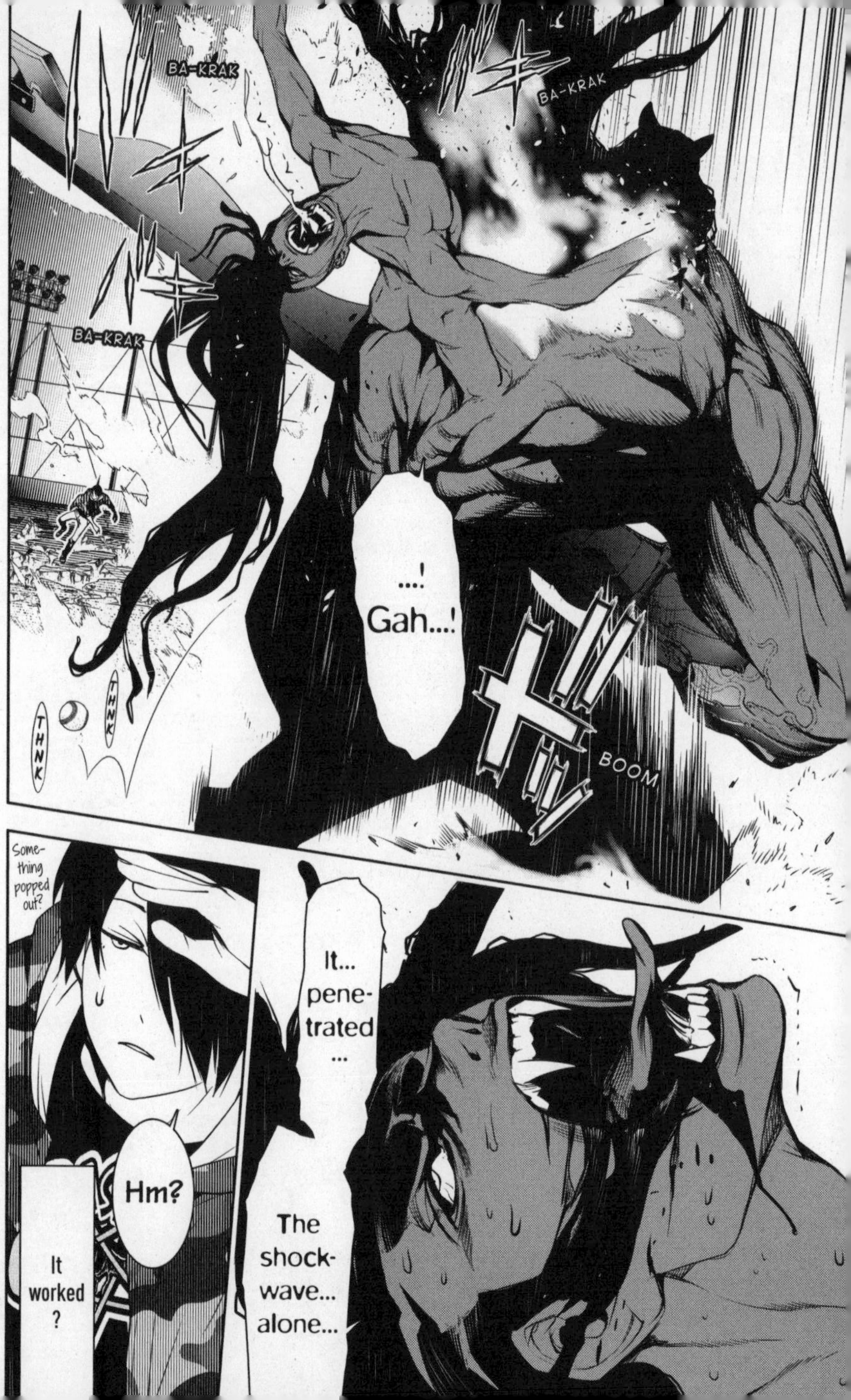
BA-KRAK
BA-KRAK
BA-KRAK
...! Gah...!
BOOM
THNK
THNK
It... pene-trated ...
The shock-wave... alone...
Some-thing popped out?
Hm?
It worked ?

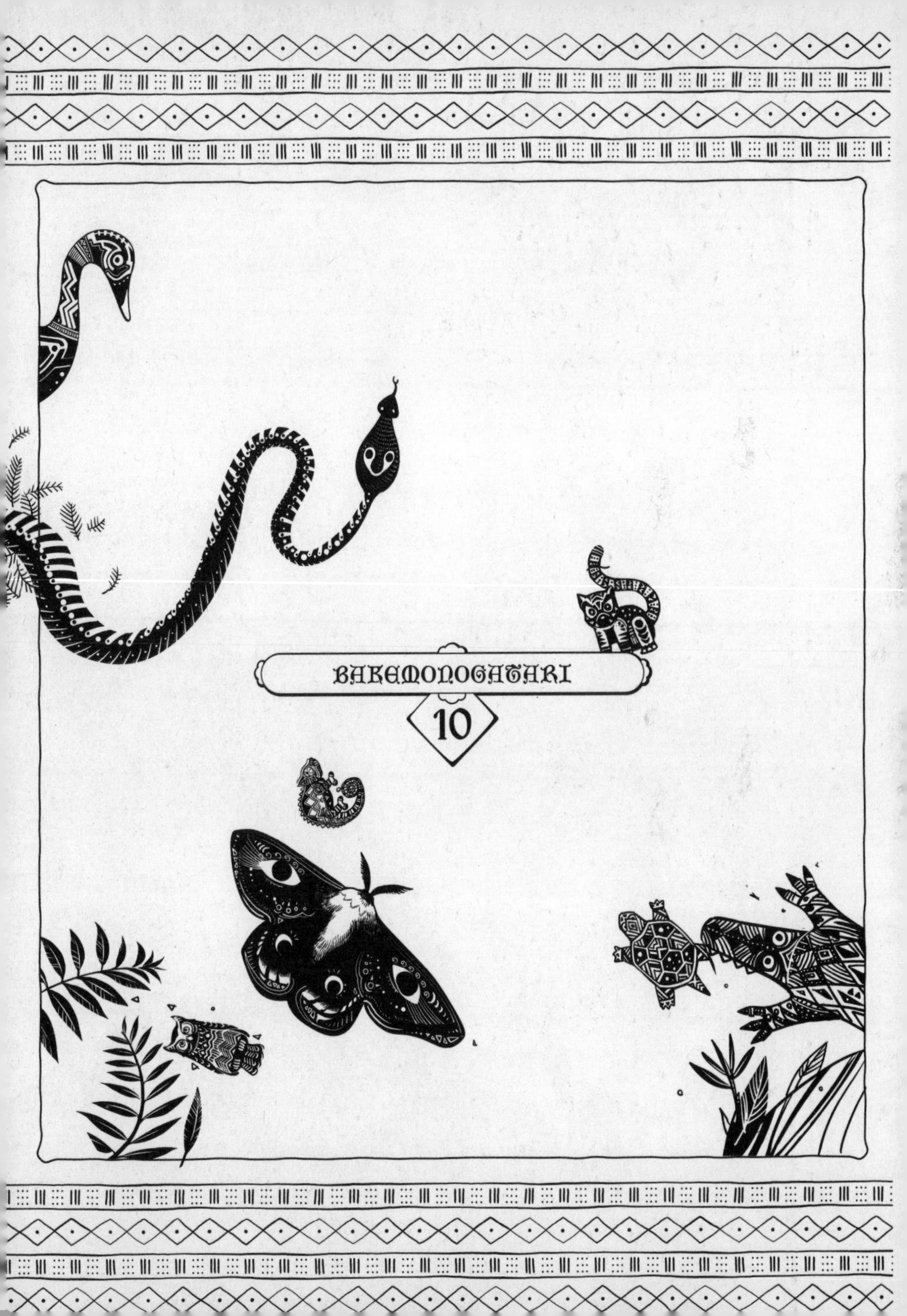
BAKEMONOGATARI
10

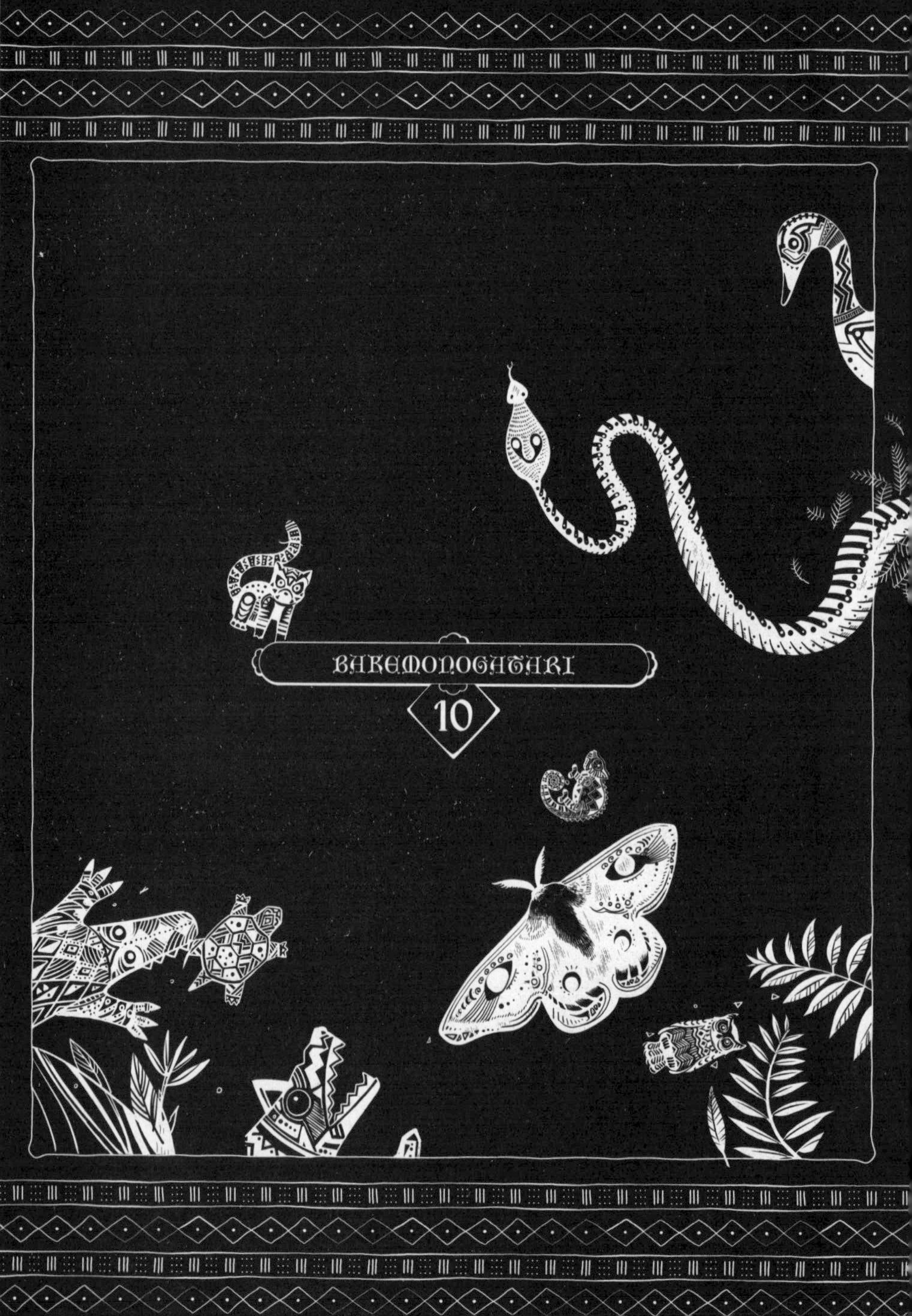
BAKEMONOGATARI
10

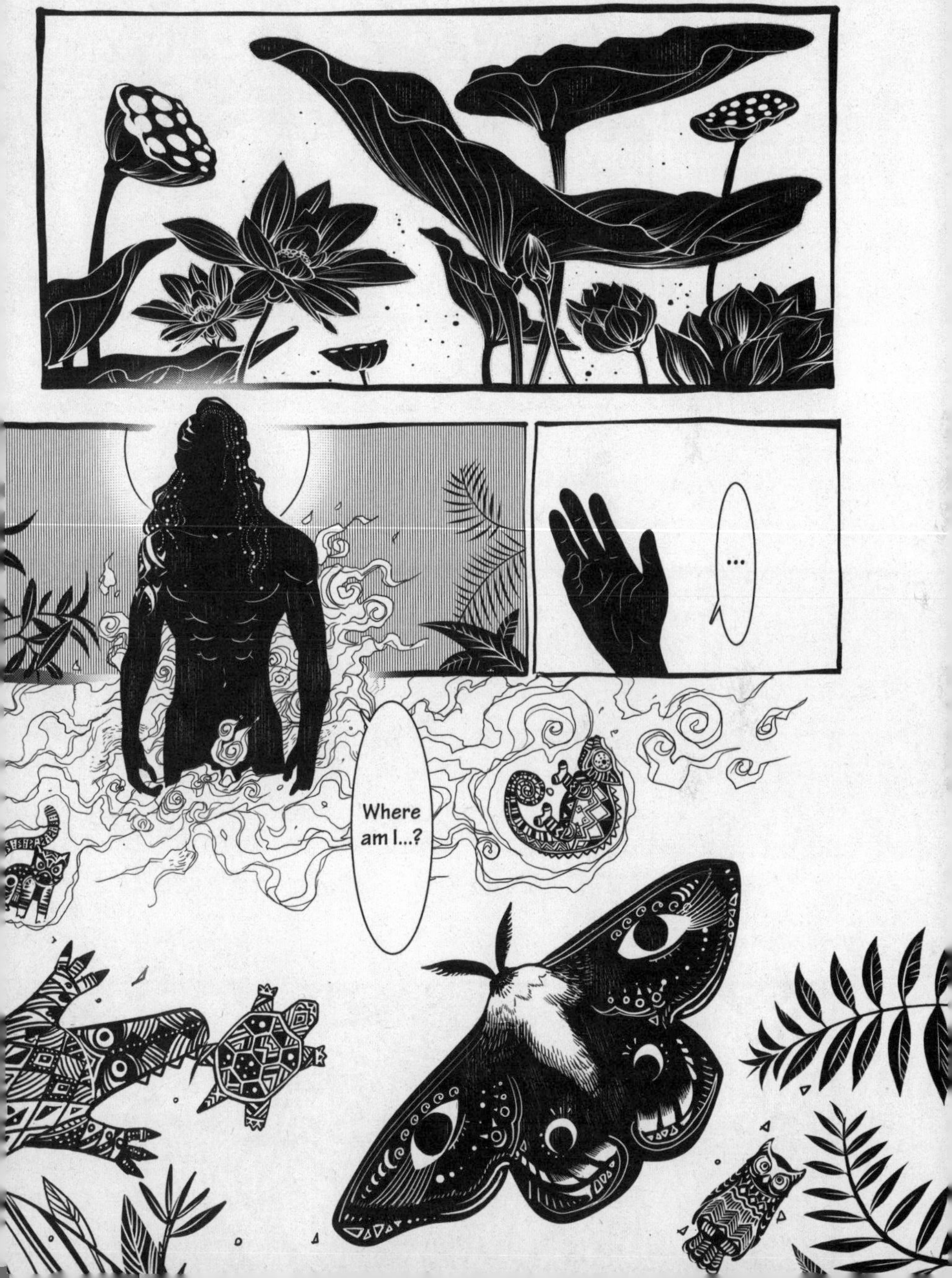
...
Where am I...?

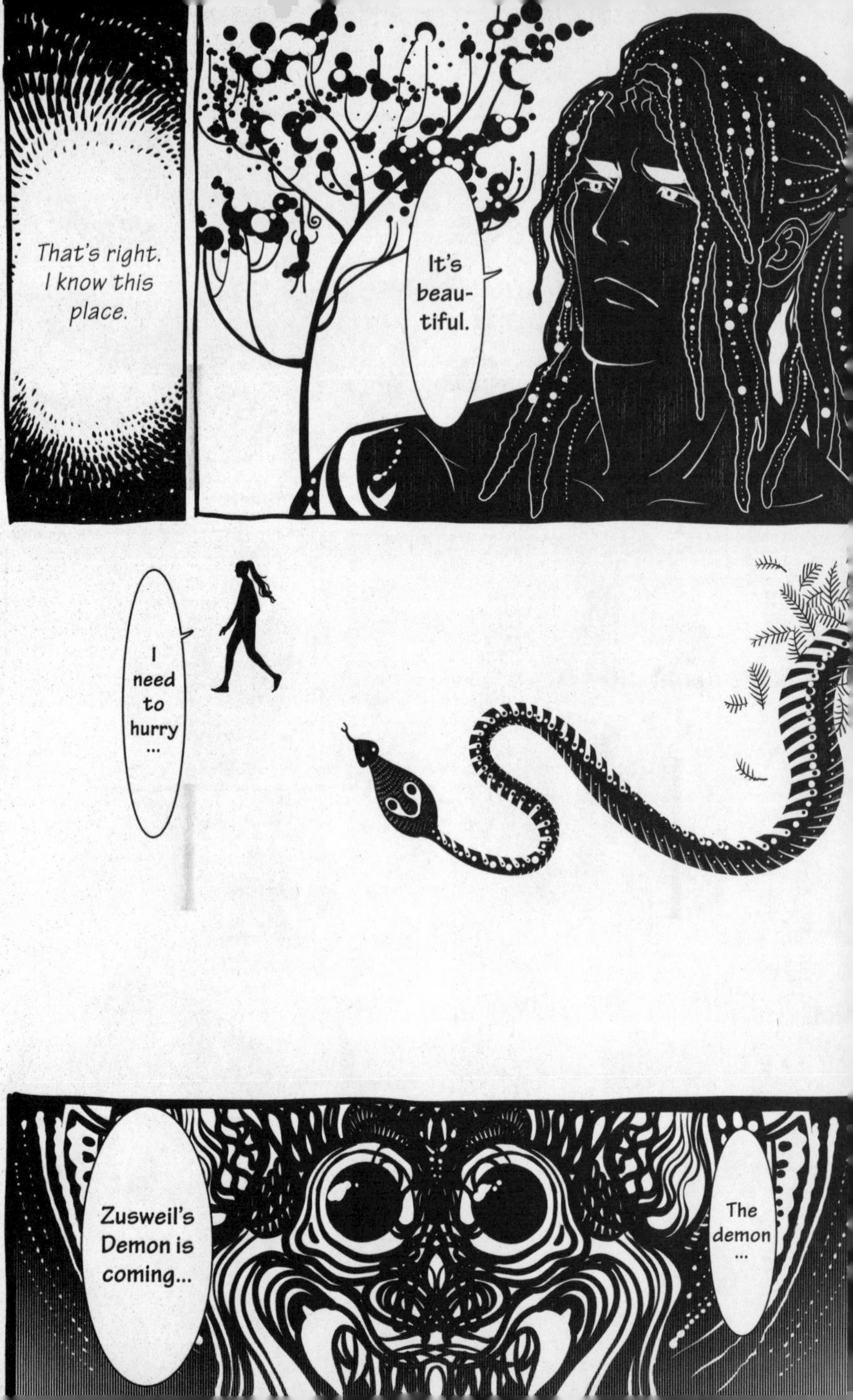
It's beau-tiful.
That's right. I know this place.
I need to hurry...
The demon...
Zusweil's Demon is coming...

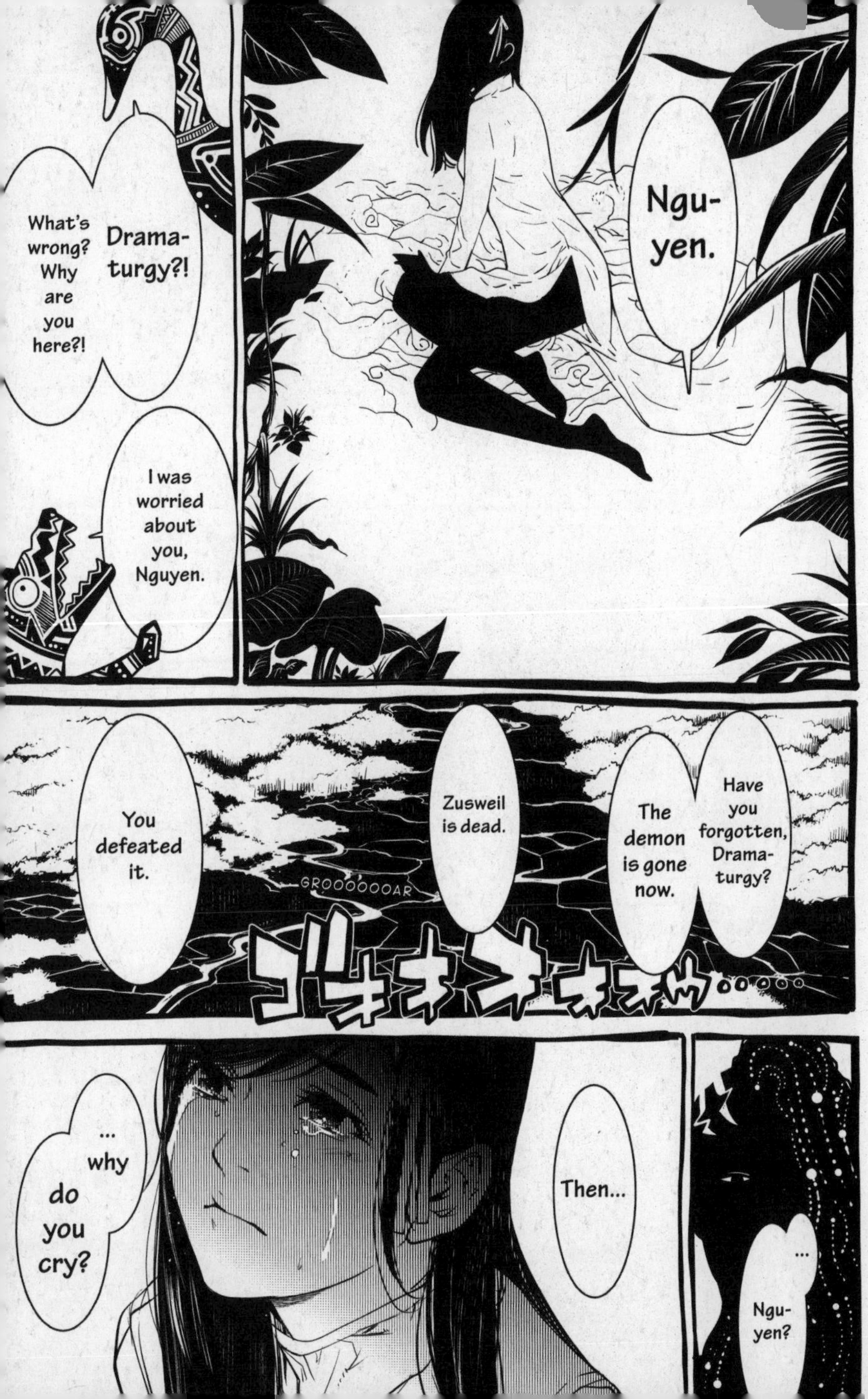
Ngu-yen.
Drama-turgy?!
What's wrong? Why are you here?!
I was worried about you, Nguyen.
Have you forgotten, Drama-turgy?
The demon is gone now.
Zusweil is dead.
GROOOOOOAR
You defeated it.
...
Ngu-yen?
Then...
...why do you cry?

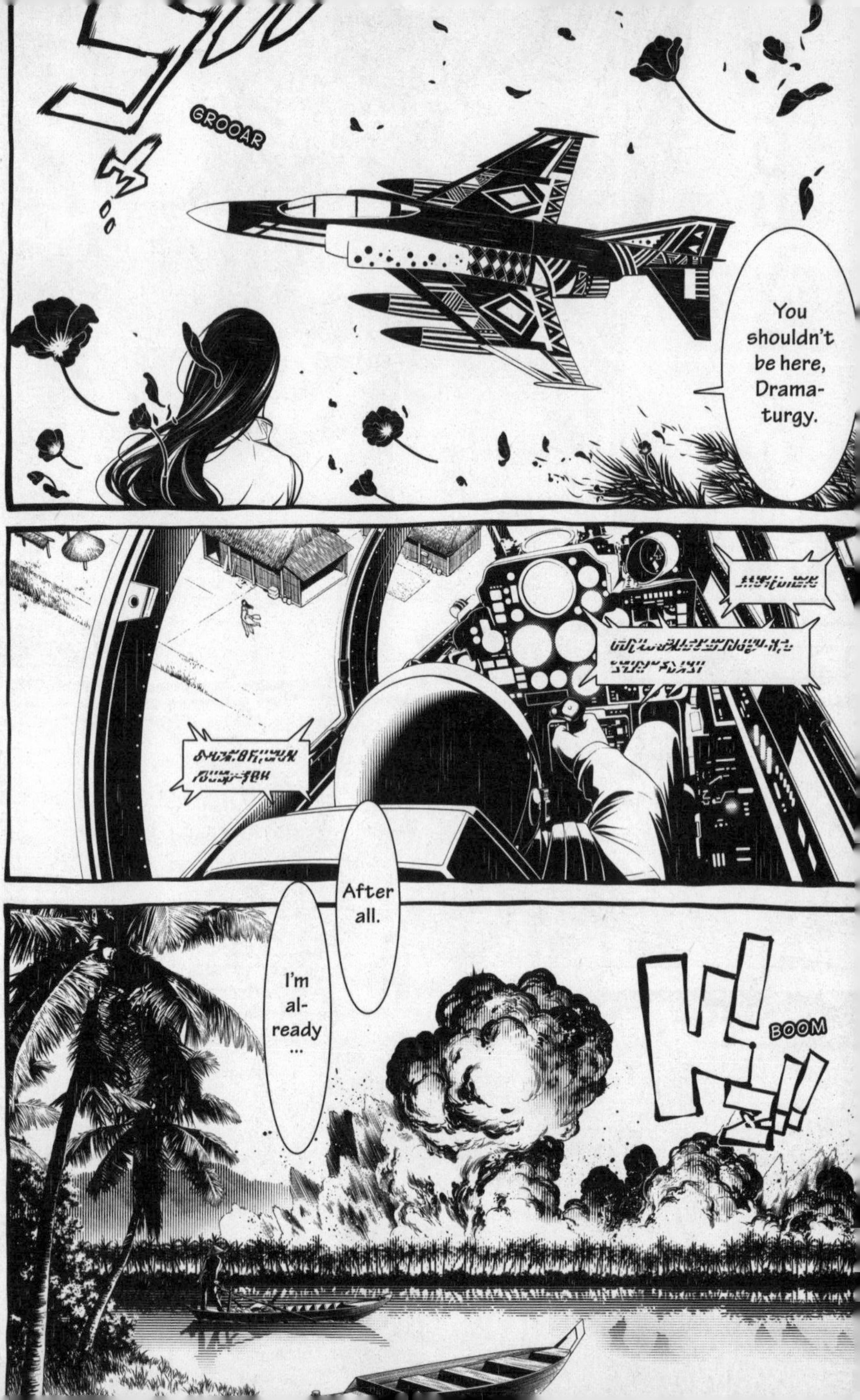
GROOAR
You shouldn't be here, Drama-turgy.
After all.
I'm al-ready ...
BOOM

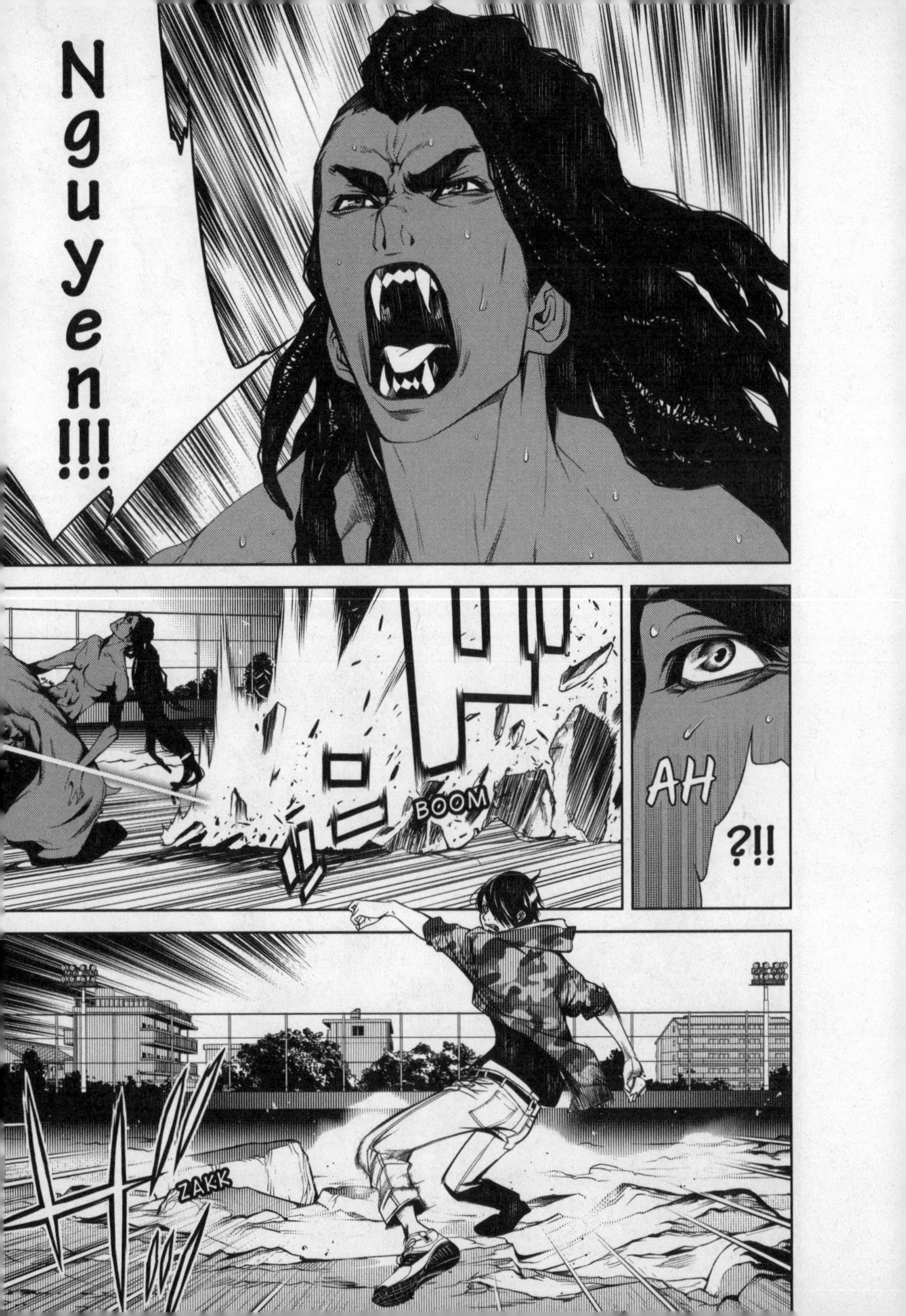
Nguyen!!!
AH
?!!
BOOM
ZAKK

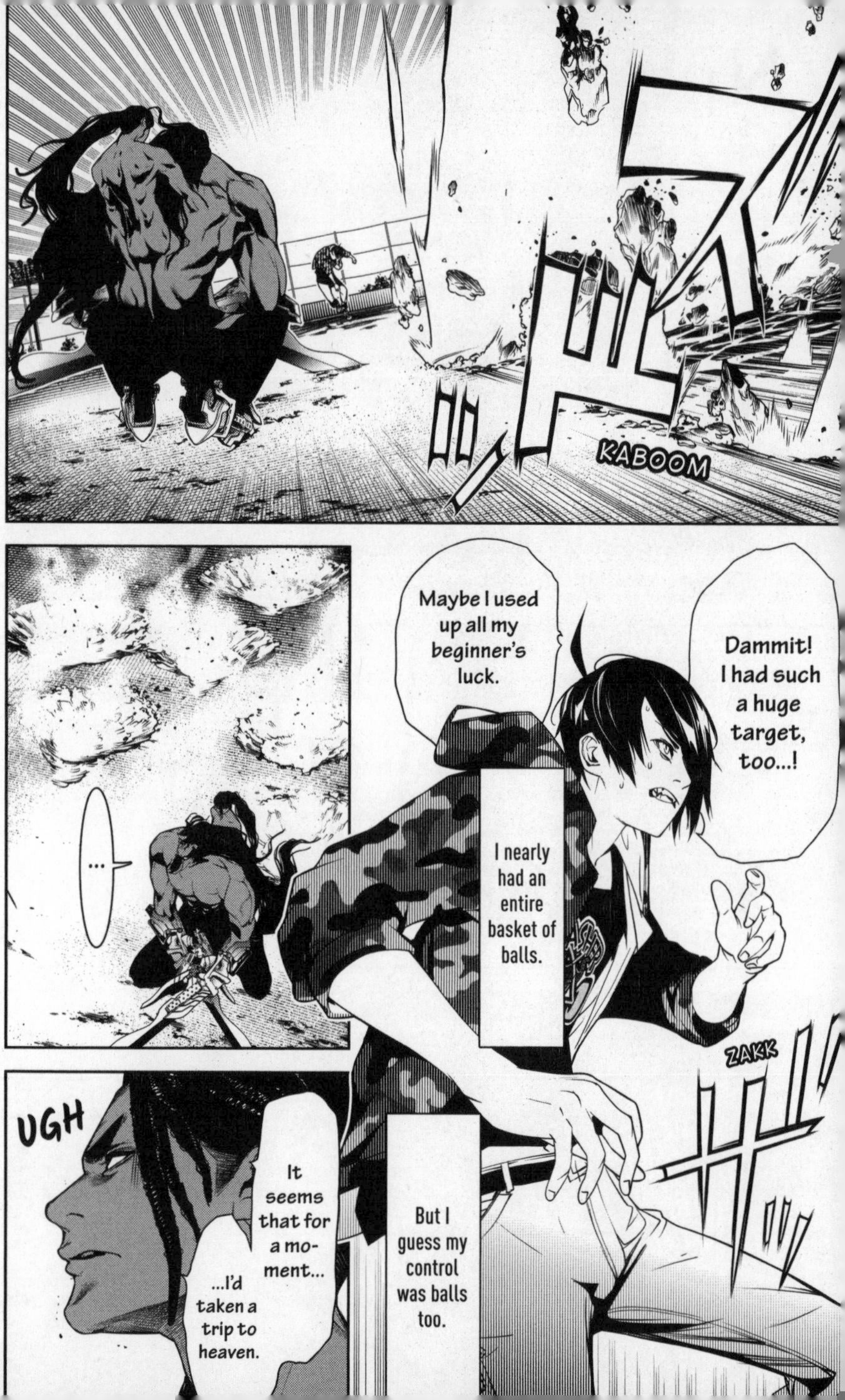
KABOOM
Dammit! I had such a huge target, too...!
Maybe I used up all my beginner's luck.
I nearly had an entire basket of balls.
...
ZAKK
But I guess my control was balls too.
UGH
It seems that for a moment...
...I'd taken a trip to heaven.

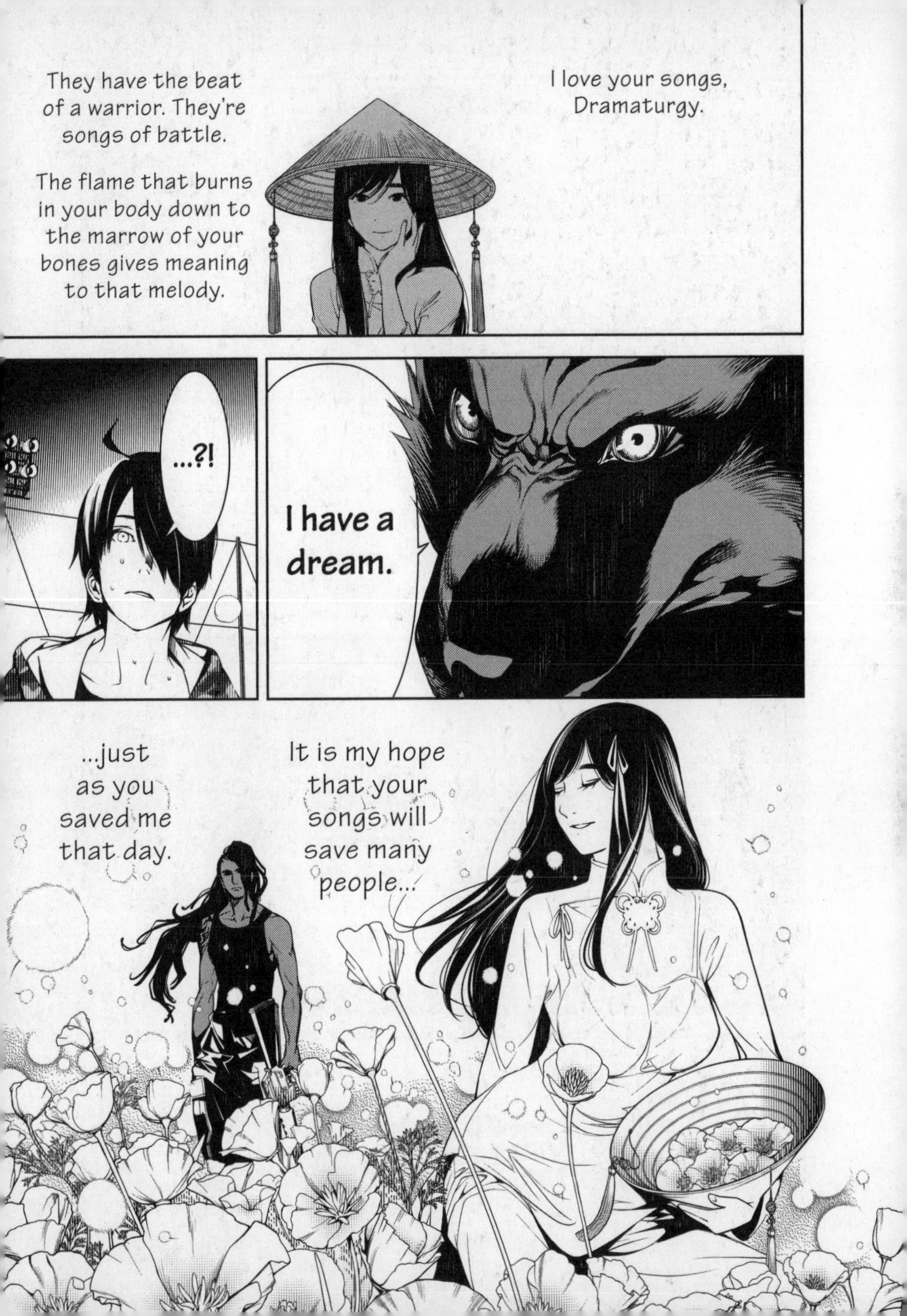
I love your songs, Dramaturgy.
They have the beat of a warrior. They're songs of battle.
The flame that burns in your body down to the marrow of your bones gives meaning to that melody.
I have a dream.
...?!
It is my hope that your songs will save many people...
...just as you saved me that day.

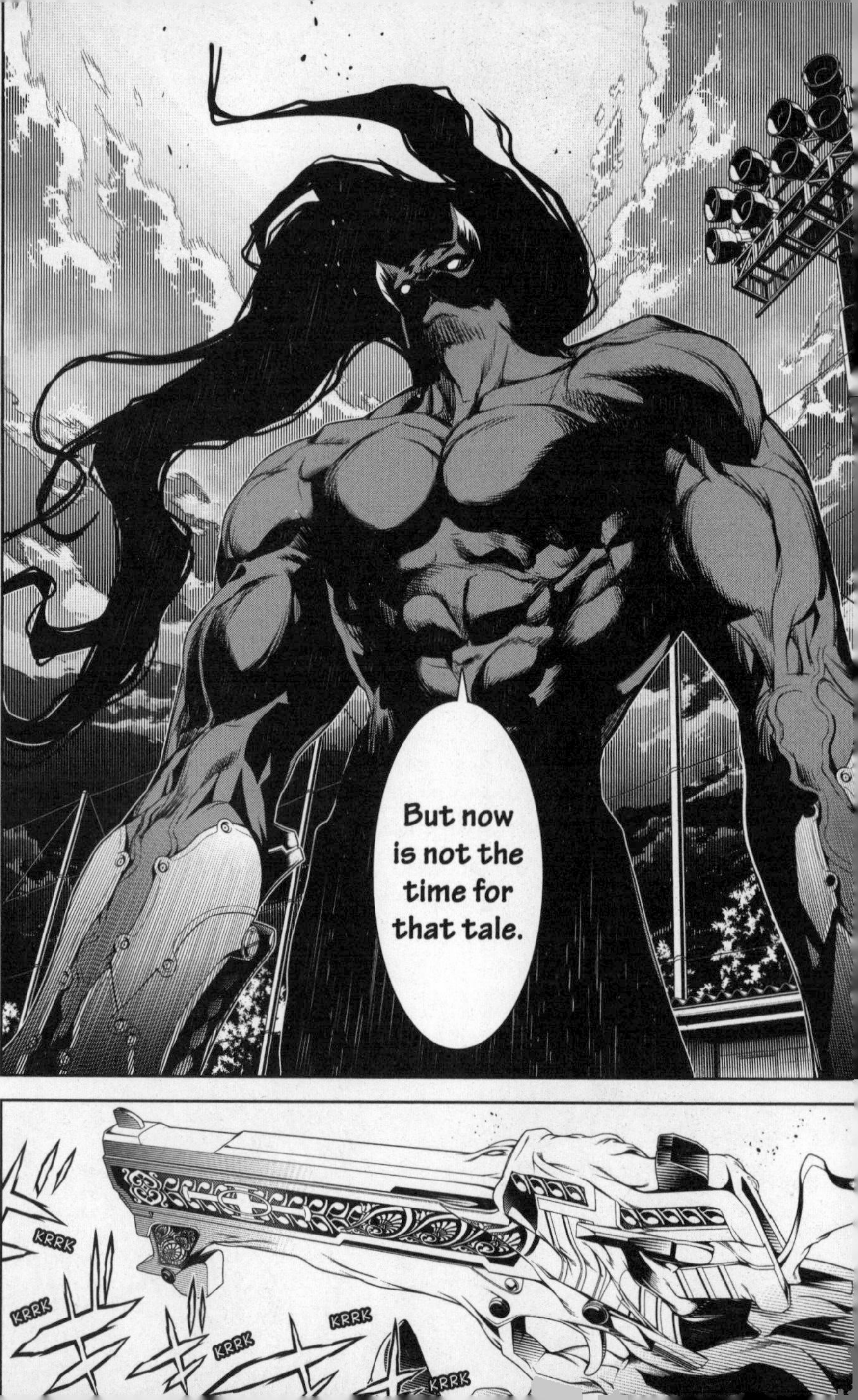
But now is not the time for that tale.
KRRK
KRRK
KRRK
KRRK
KRRK

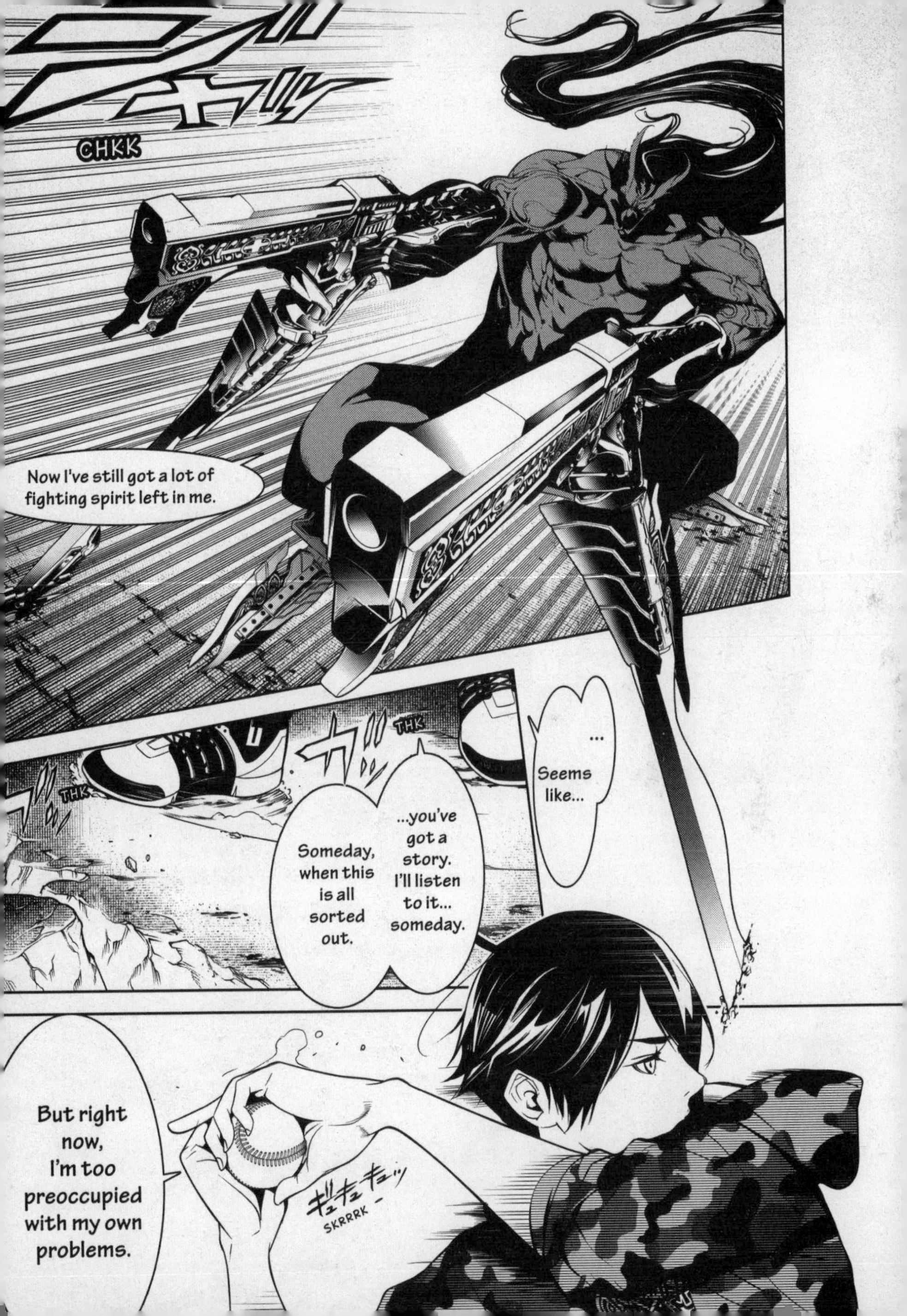
CHKK
Now I've still got a lot of fighting spirit left in me.
...
Seems like...
...you've got a story. I'll listen to it... someday.
THK
Someday, when this is all sorted out.
THK
But right now, I'm too preoccupied with my own problems.
SKRRRK

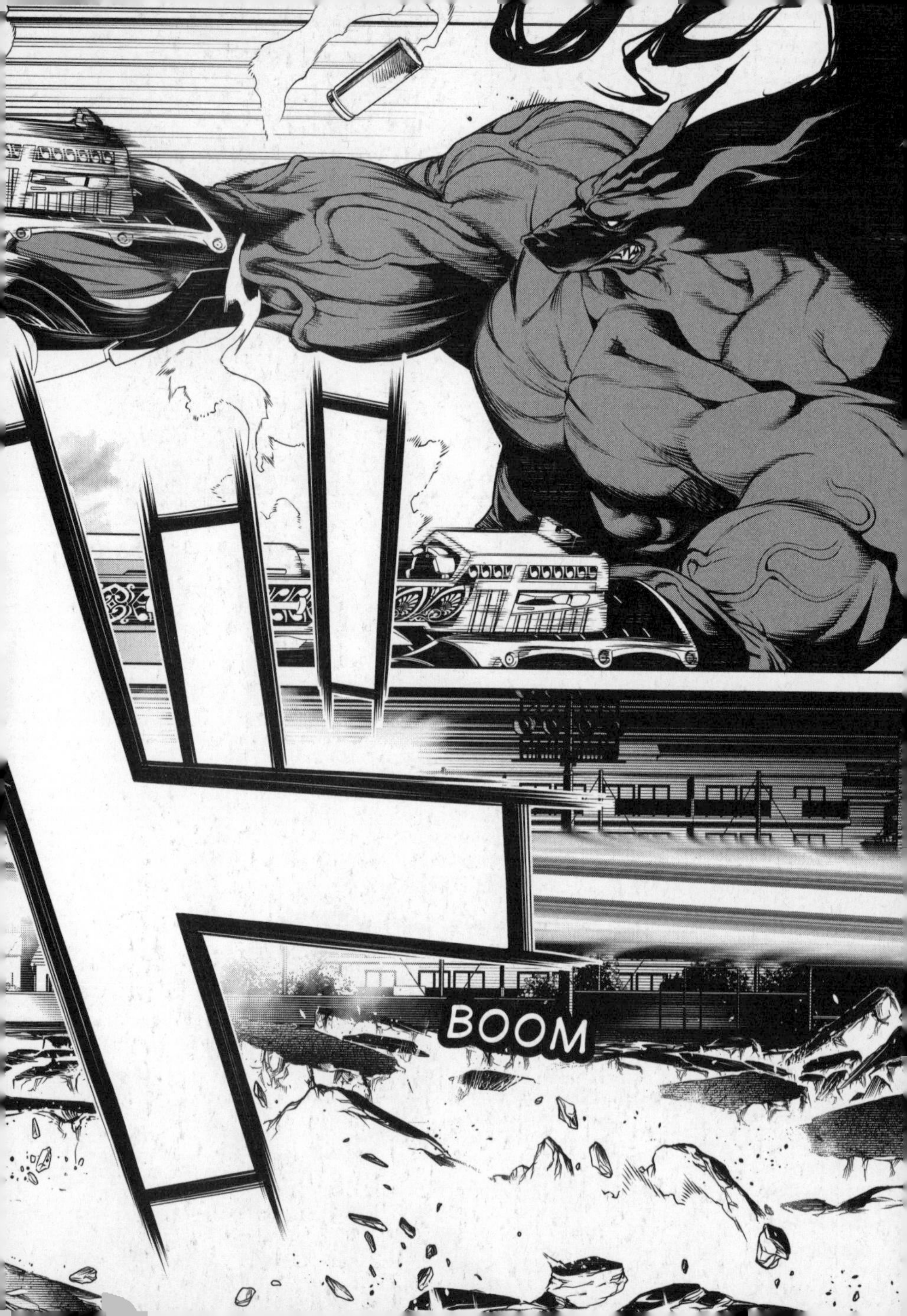
BOOM

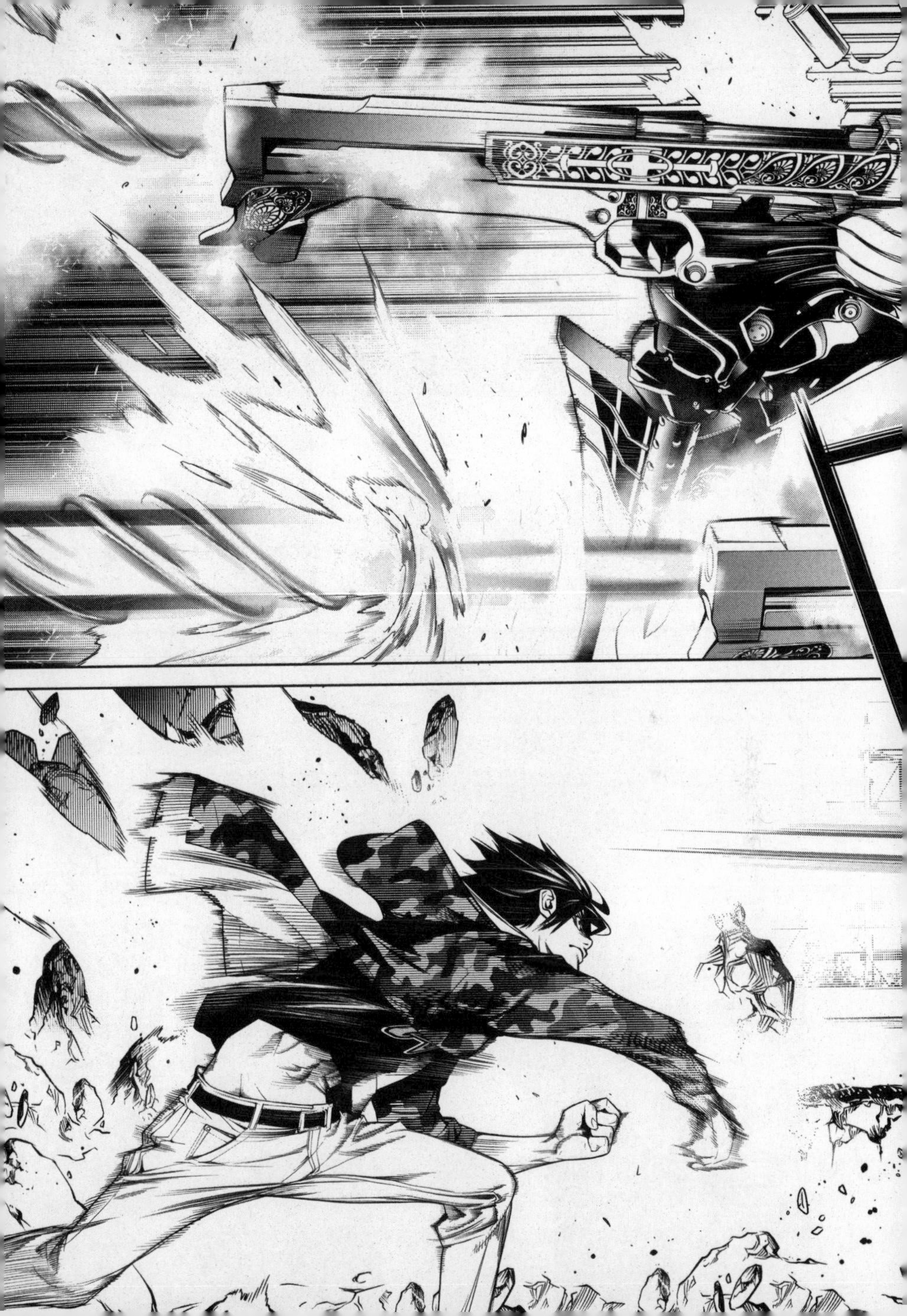

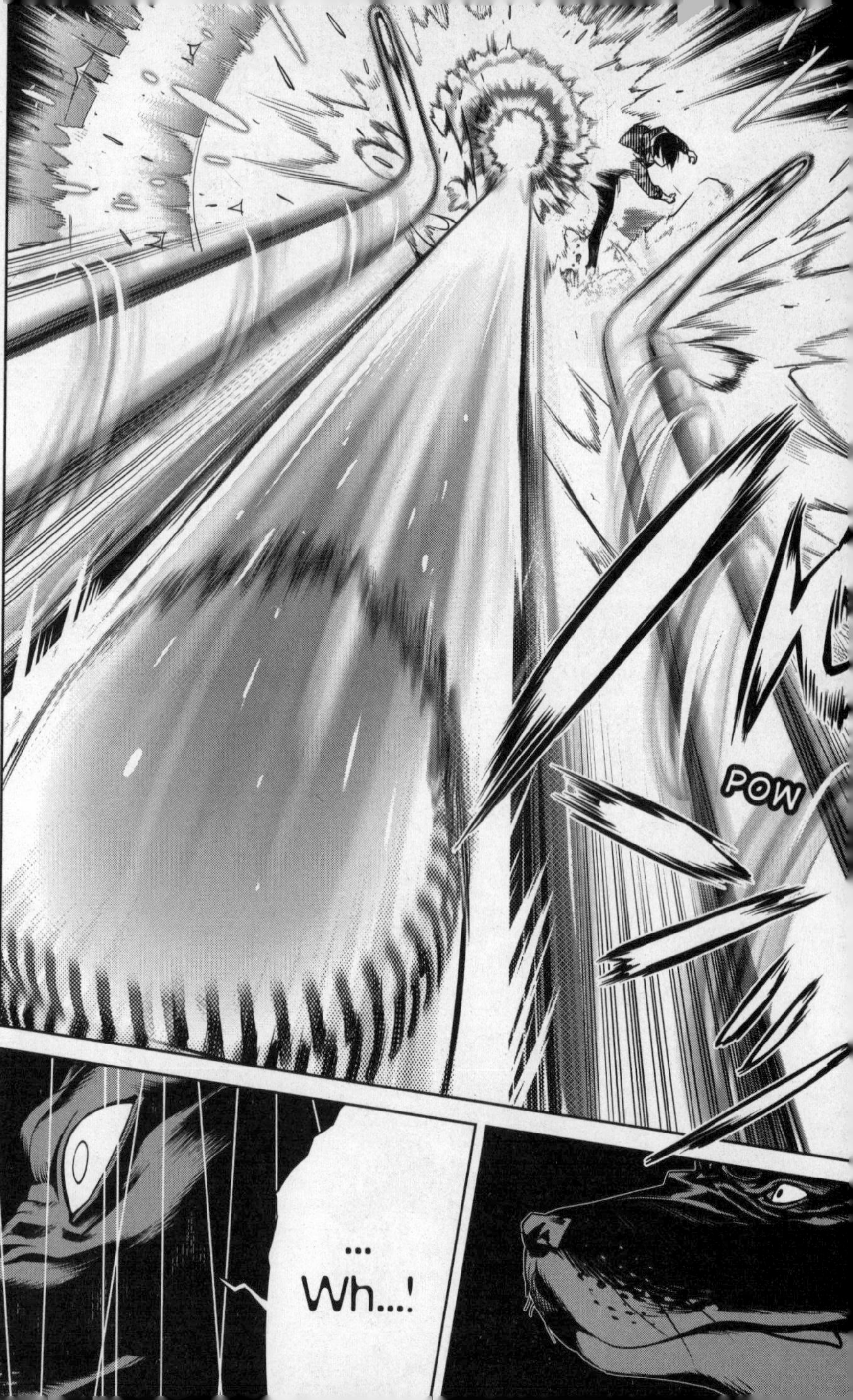
POW
... Wh...!

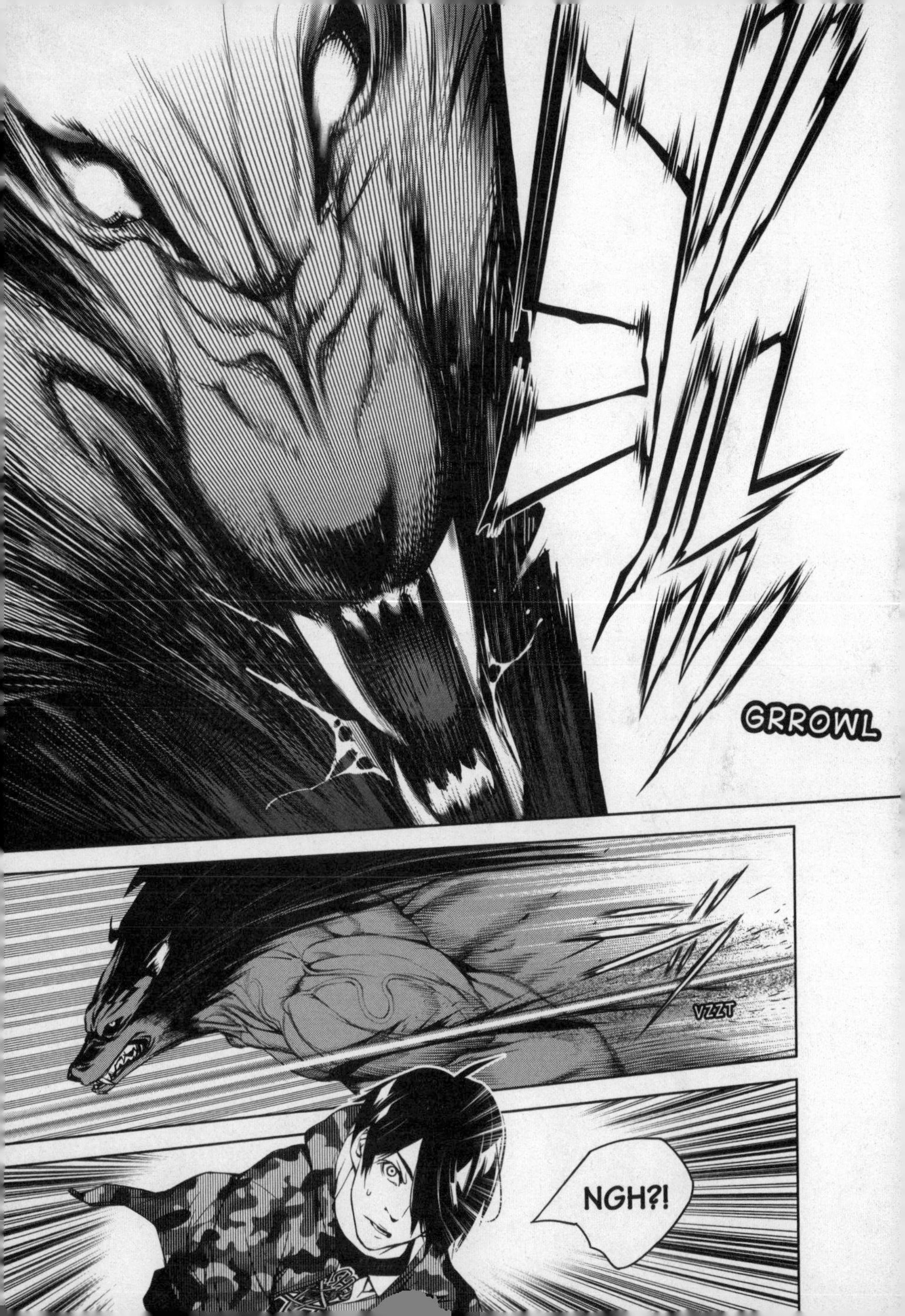
GRROWL
VZZT
NGH?!

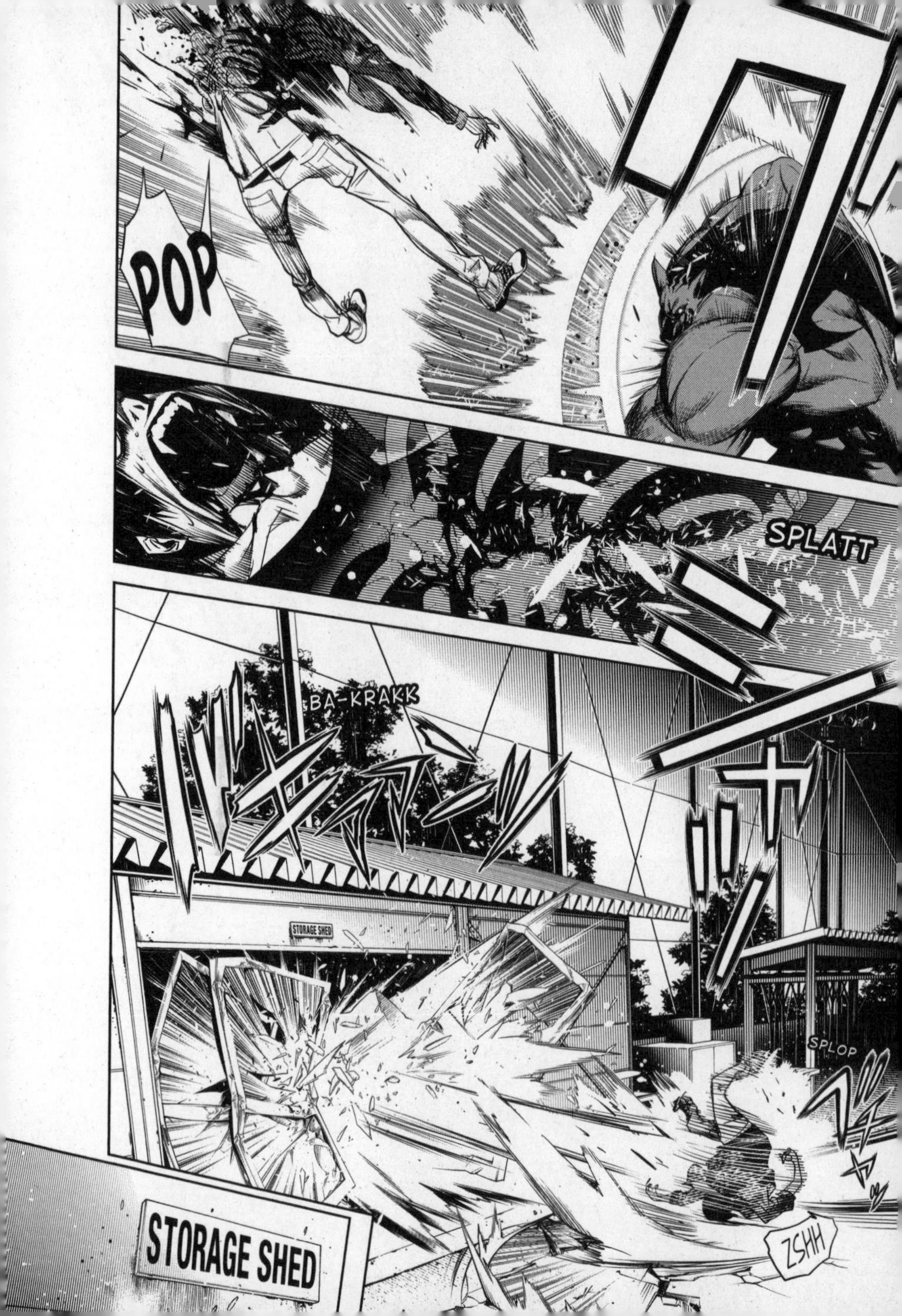
POP
SPLATT
BA-KRAKK
STORAGE SHED
SPLOP
ZSHH
STORAGE SHED

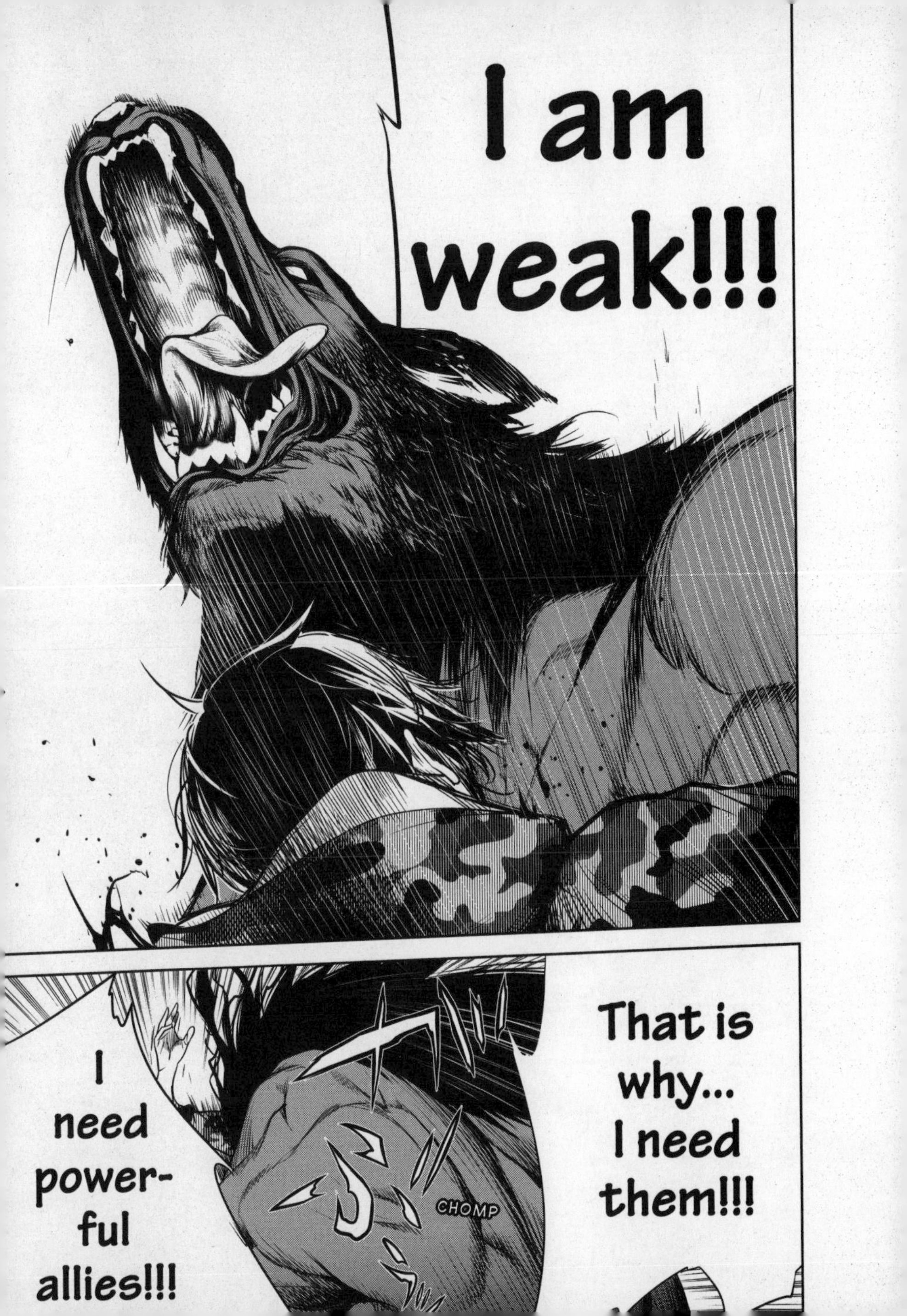
I am weak!!!
That is why... I need them!!!
CHOMP
I need power-ful allies!!!

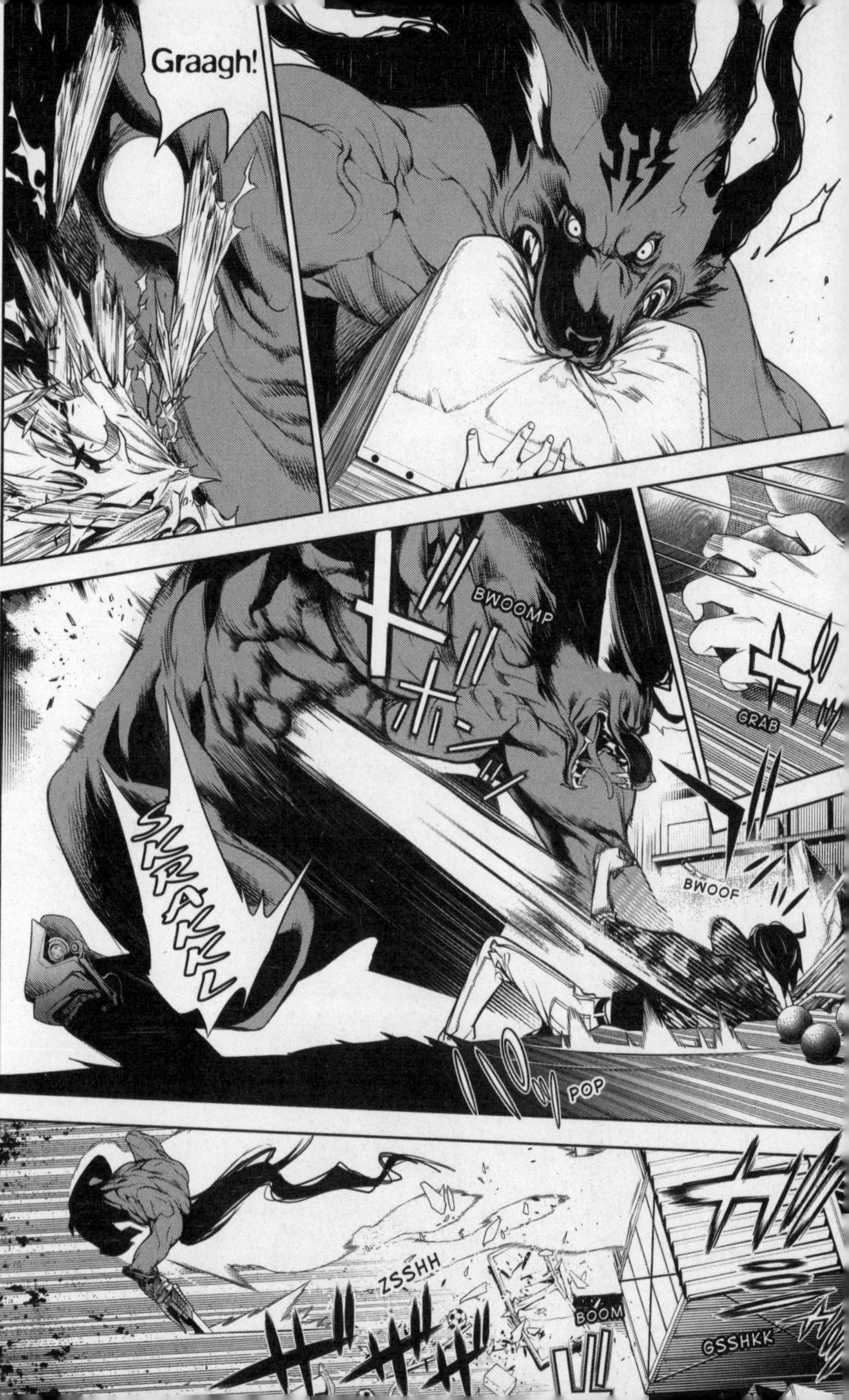
Graagh!
GRAB
BWOOMP
BWOOF
SKRAKKK
POP
GSSHKK
BOOM
ZSSHH

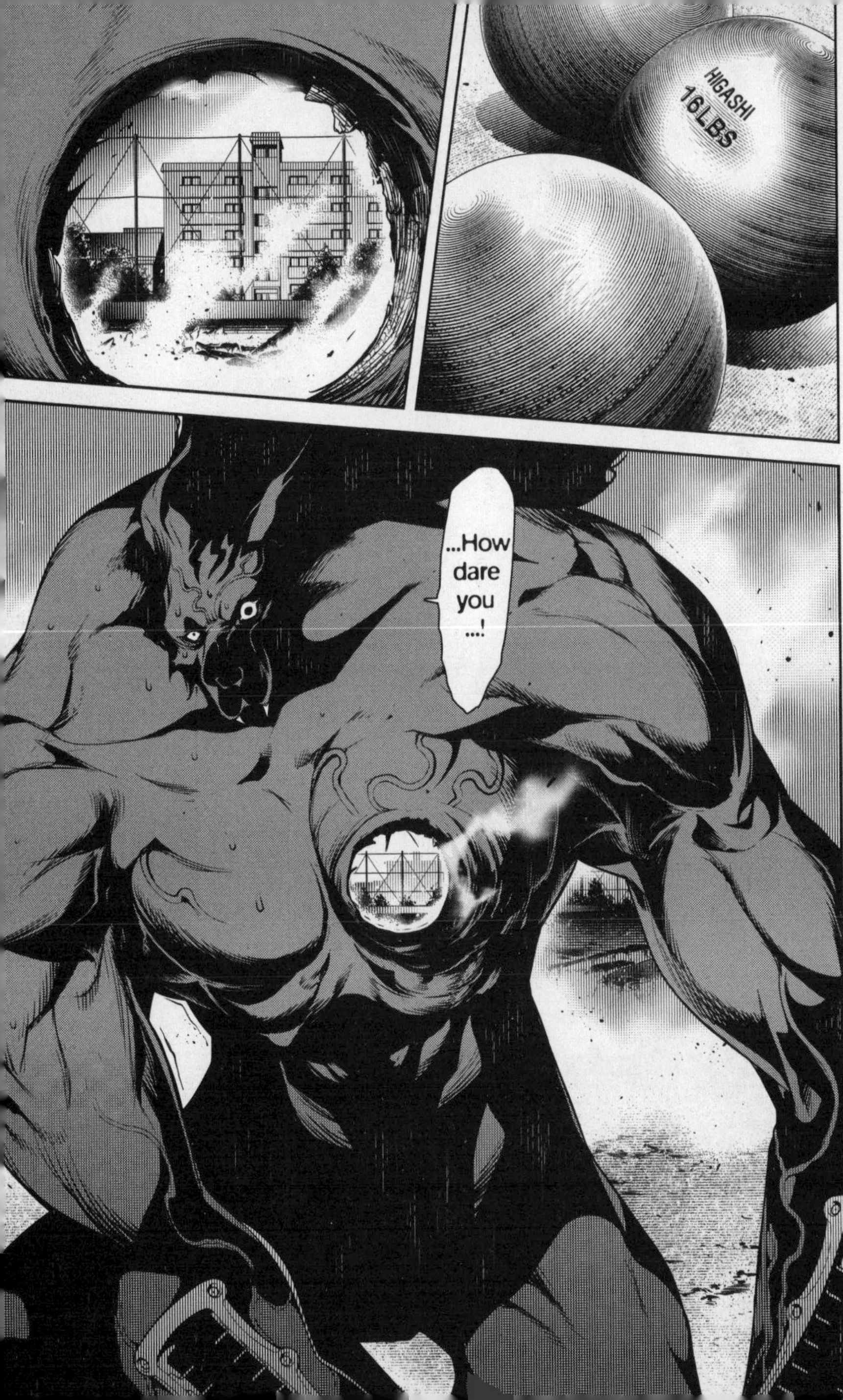
HIGASHI
16LBS
...How dare you ...!

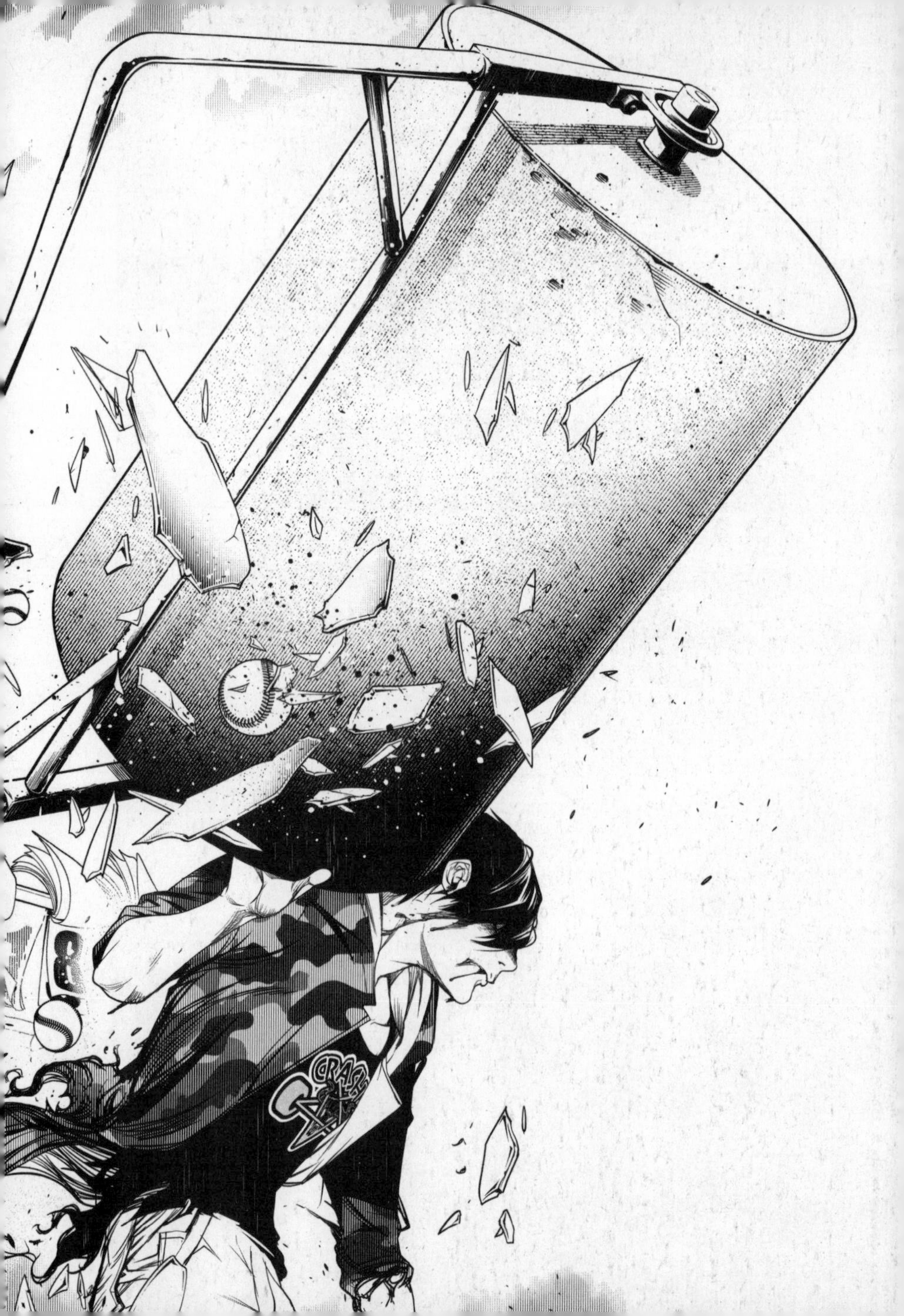

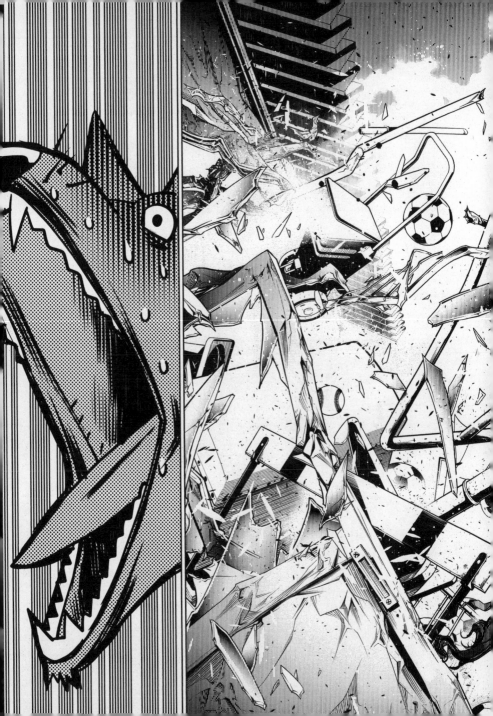

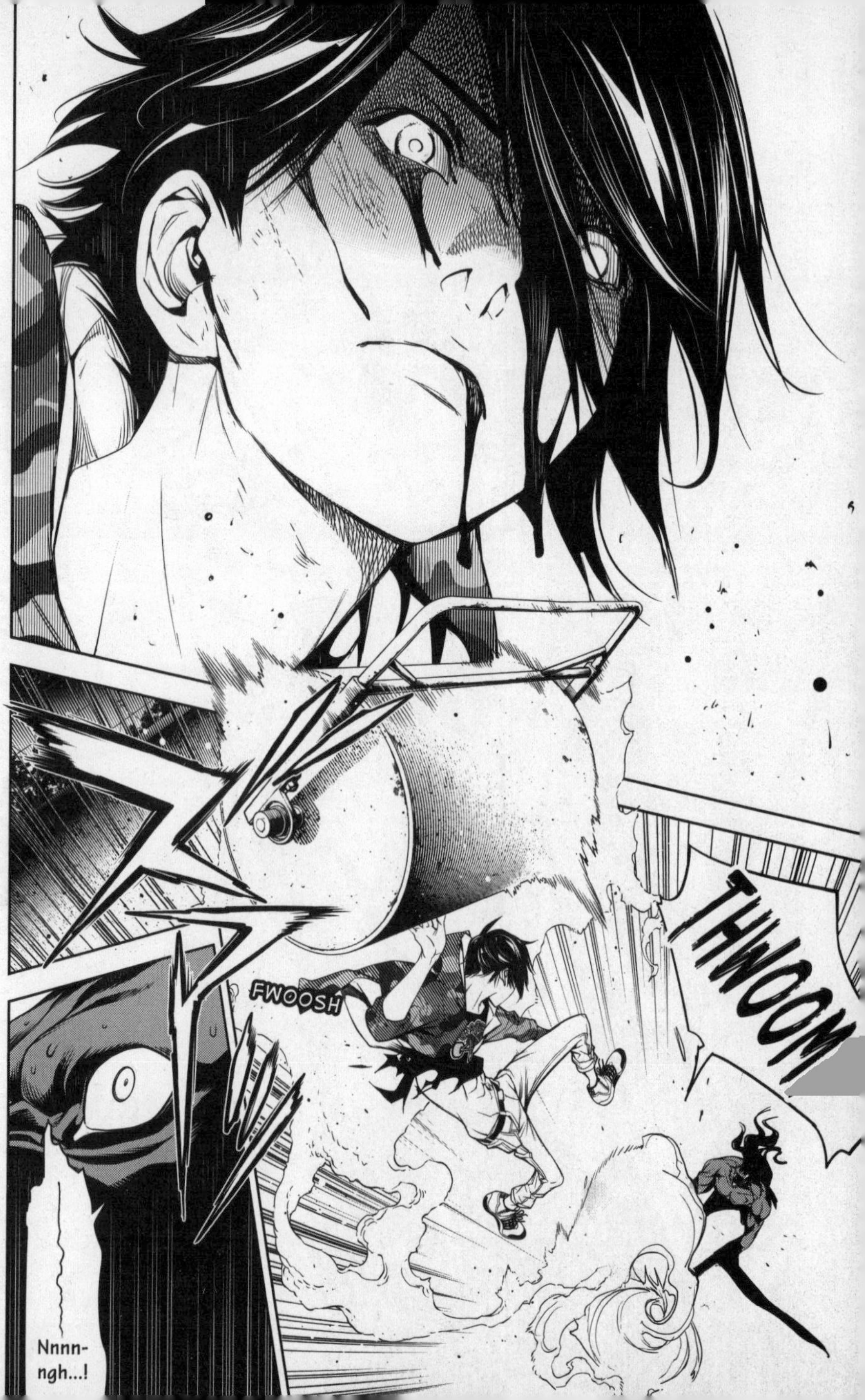
THWOOM
FWOOSH
Nnnn-
ngh...!

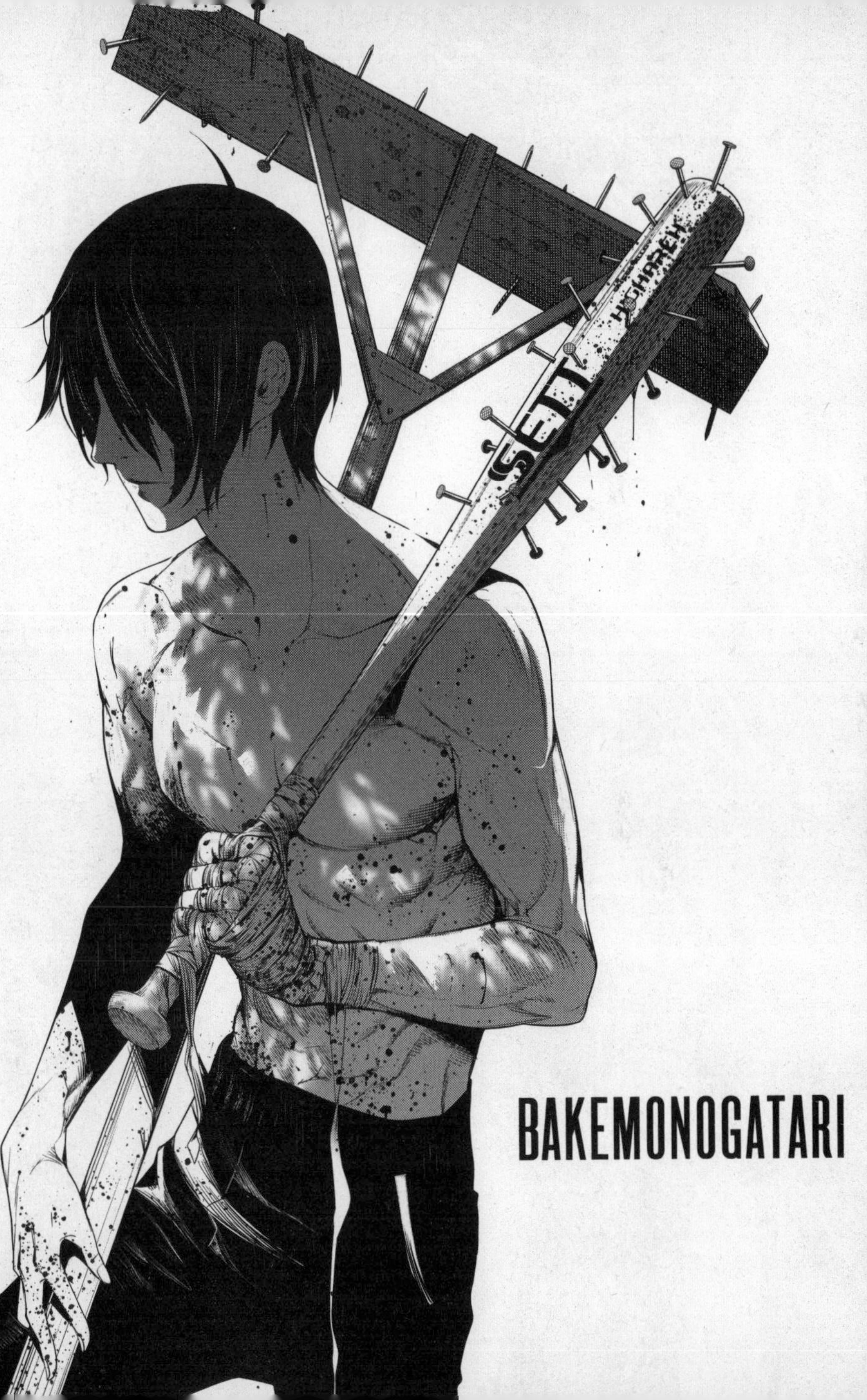

BAKEMONOGATARI

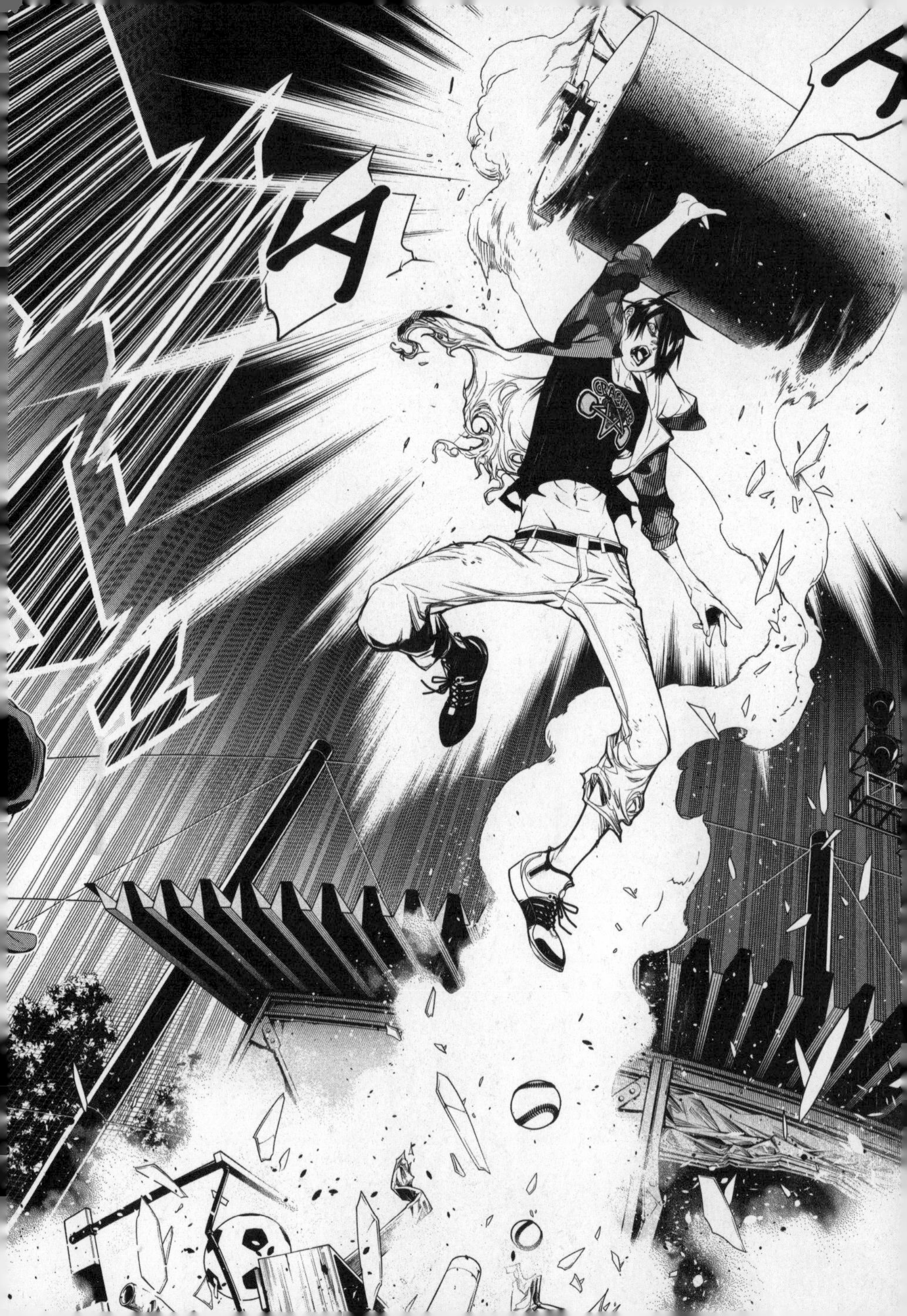
A

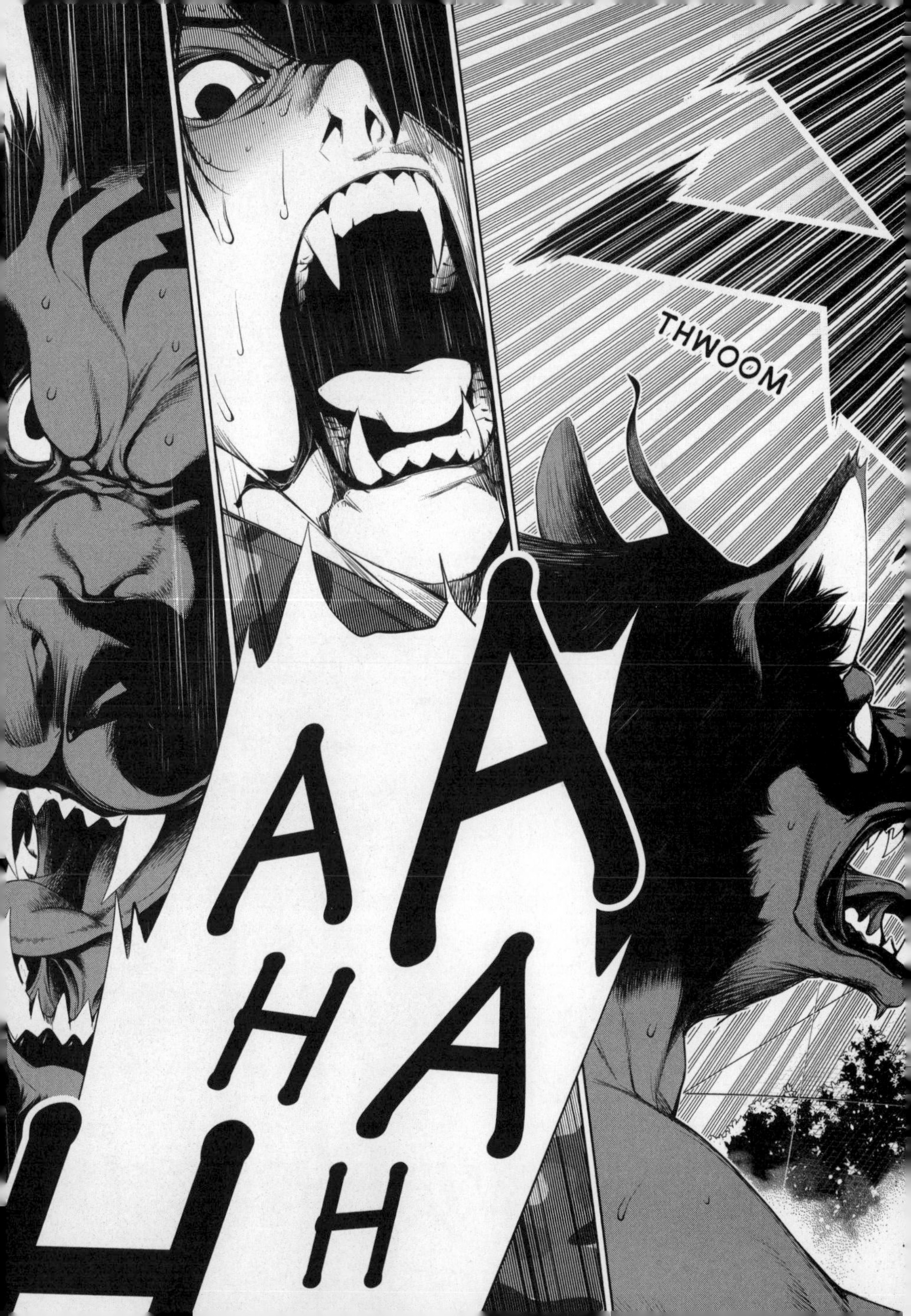
THWOOM
AAHAHH

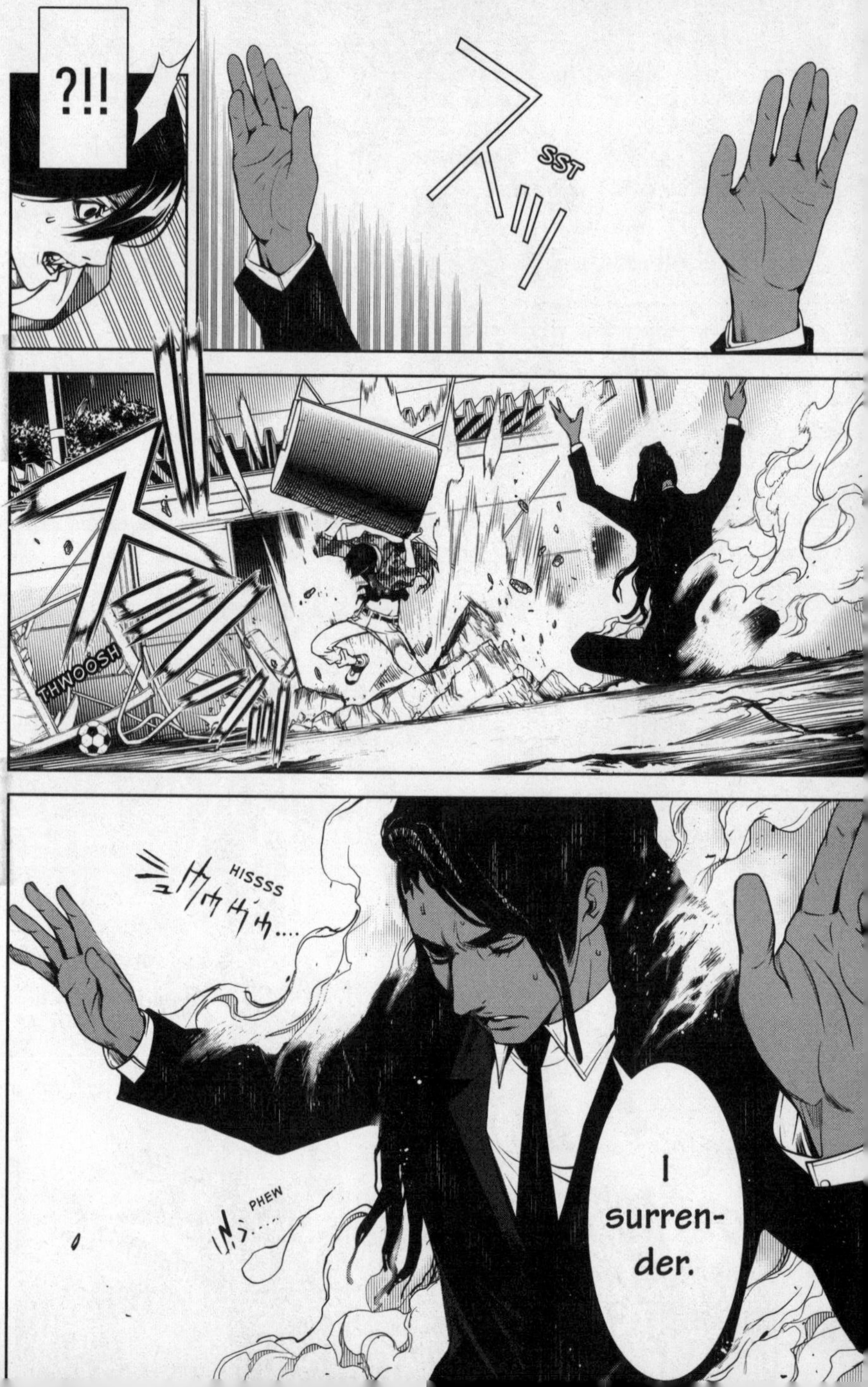
SST
?!!
THWOOSH
HISSSS
PHEW
I surren-der.

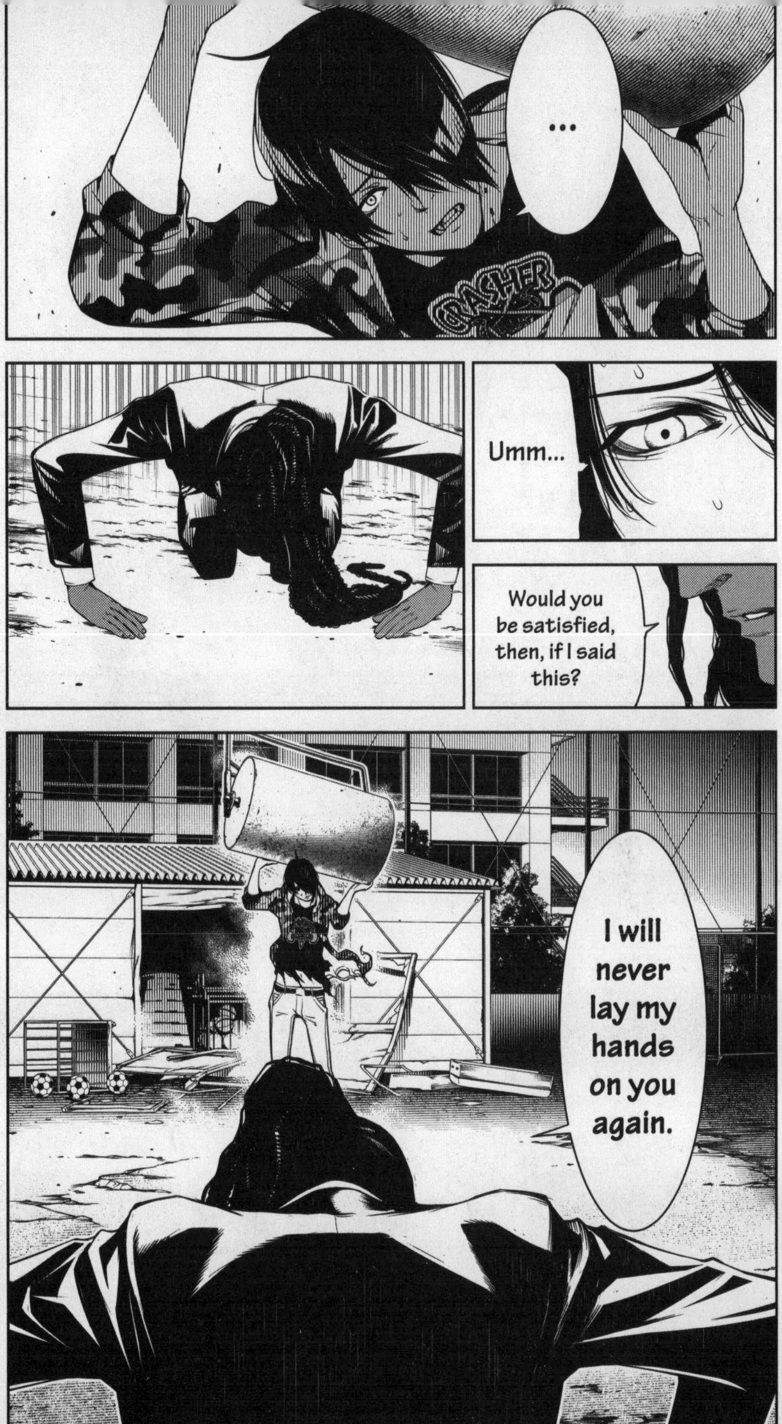
...
Umm...
Would you be satisfied, then, if I said this?
I will never lay my hands on you again.

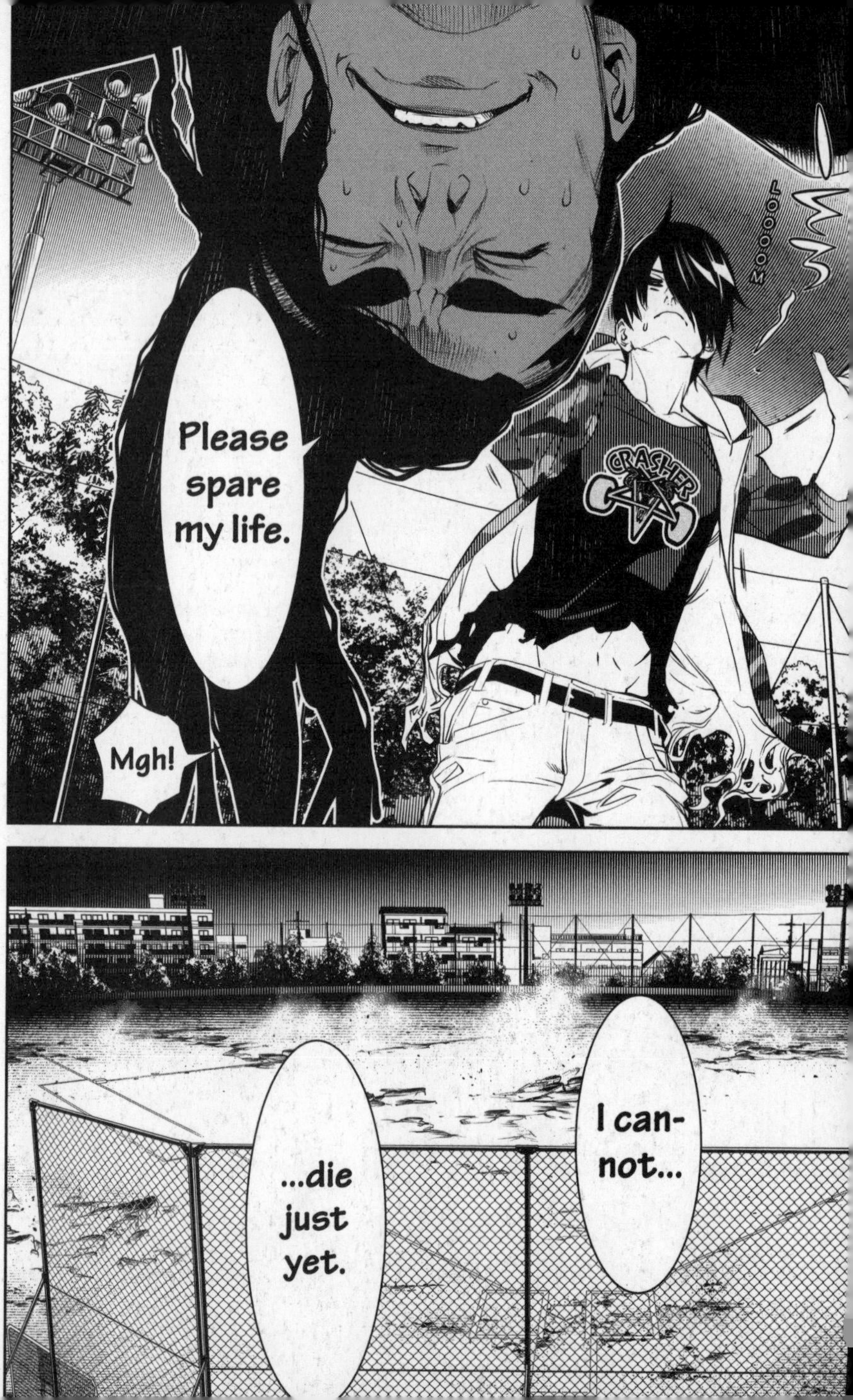
LOOOOOM
Please spare my life.
Mgh!
I cannot...
...die just yet.

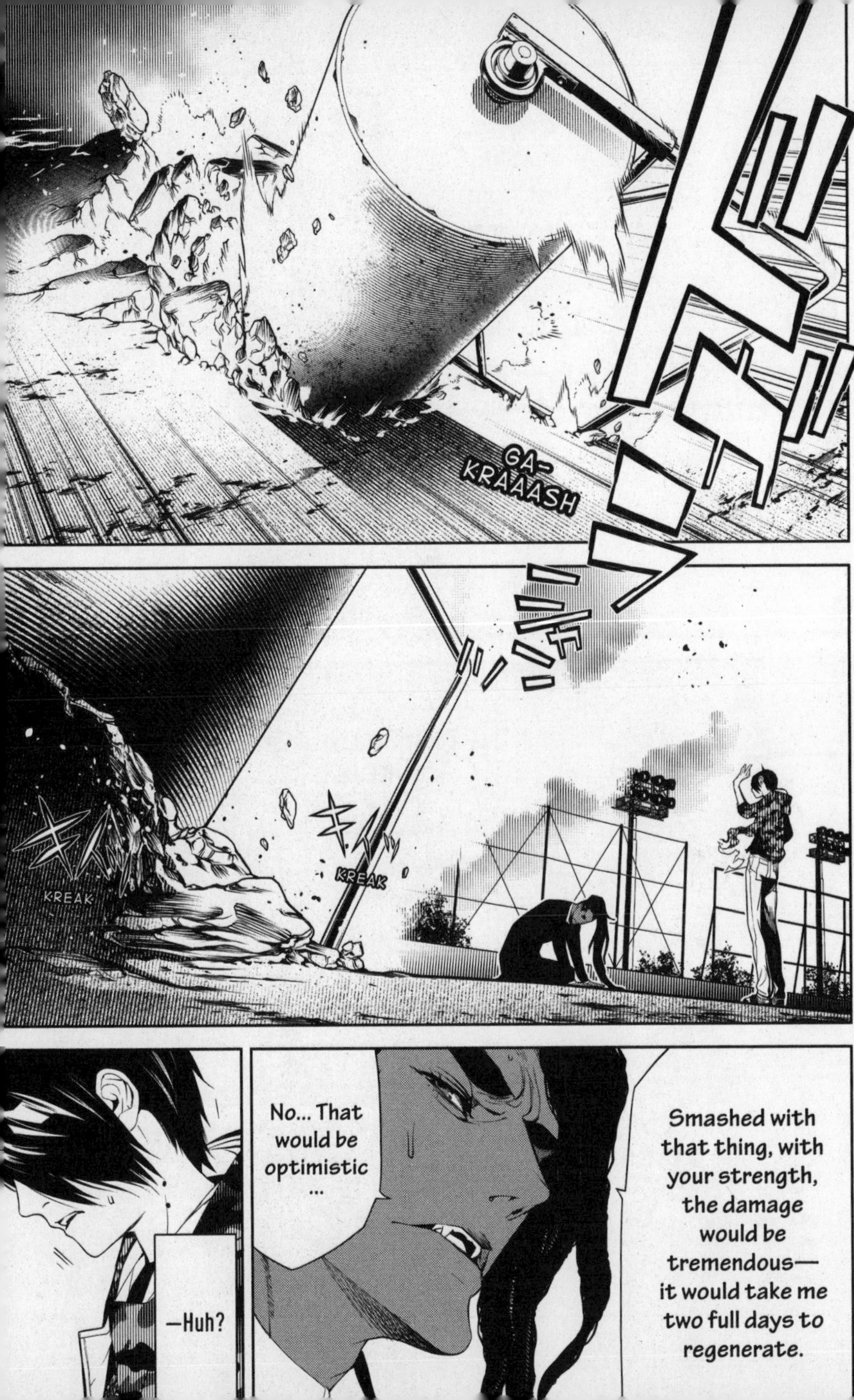
GA-
KRAAASH
KREAK
KREAK
Smashed with that thing, with your strength, the damage would be tremendous—it would take me two full days to regenerate.
No... That would be optimistic ...
—Huh?

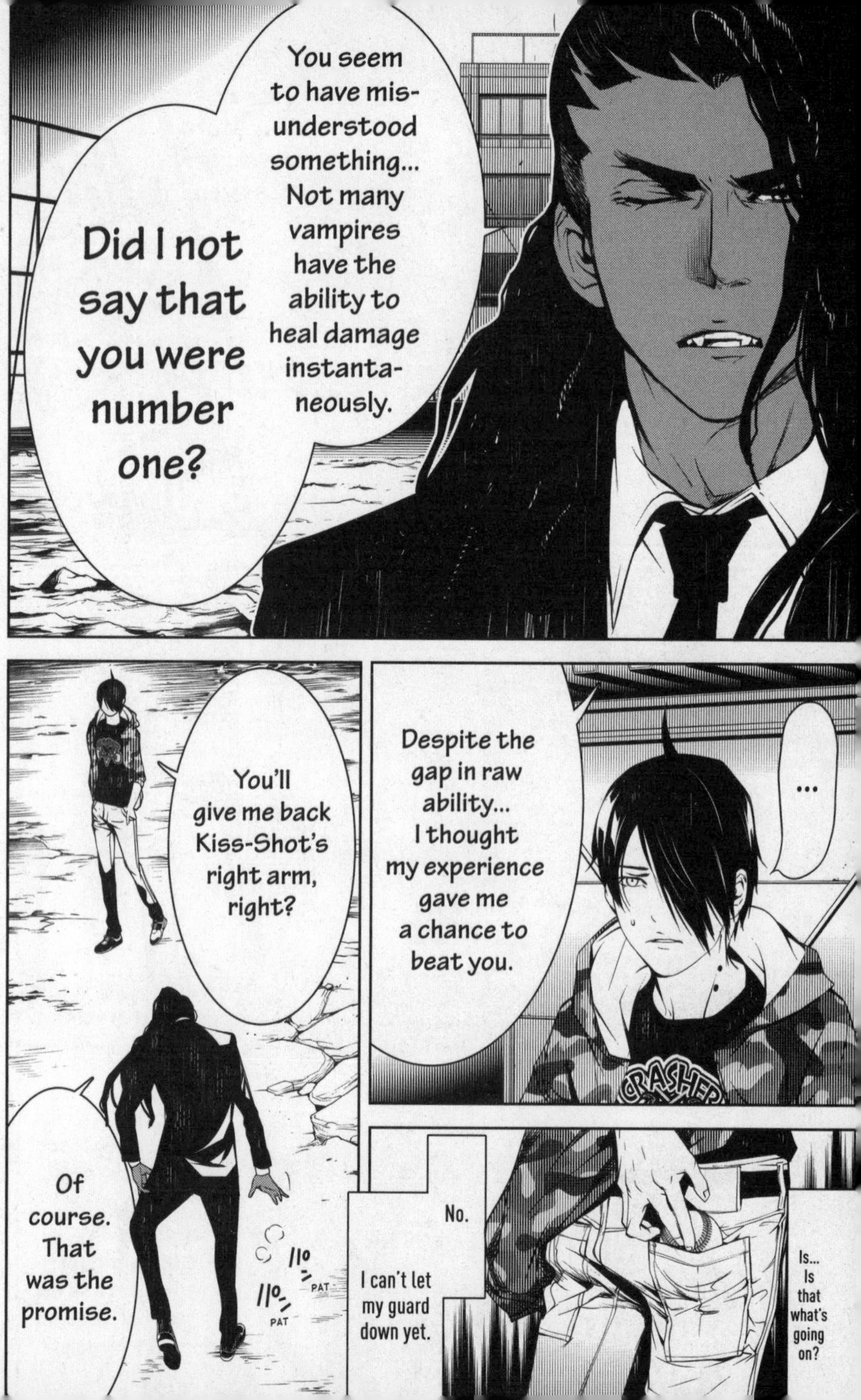
You seem to have mis-understood something... Not many vampires have the ability to heal damage instantaneously.
Did I not say that you were number one?
...
Despite the gap in raw ability... I thought my experience gave me a chance to beat you.
Is... Is that what's going on?
No.
I can't let my guard down yet.
You'll give me back Kiss-Shot's right arm, right?
Of course. That was the promise.
PAT
PAT

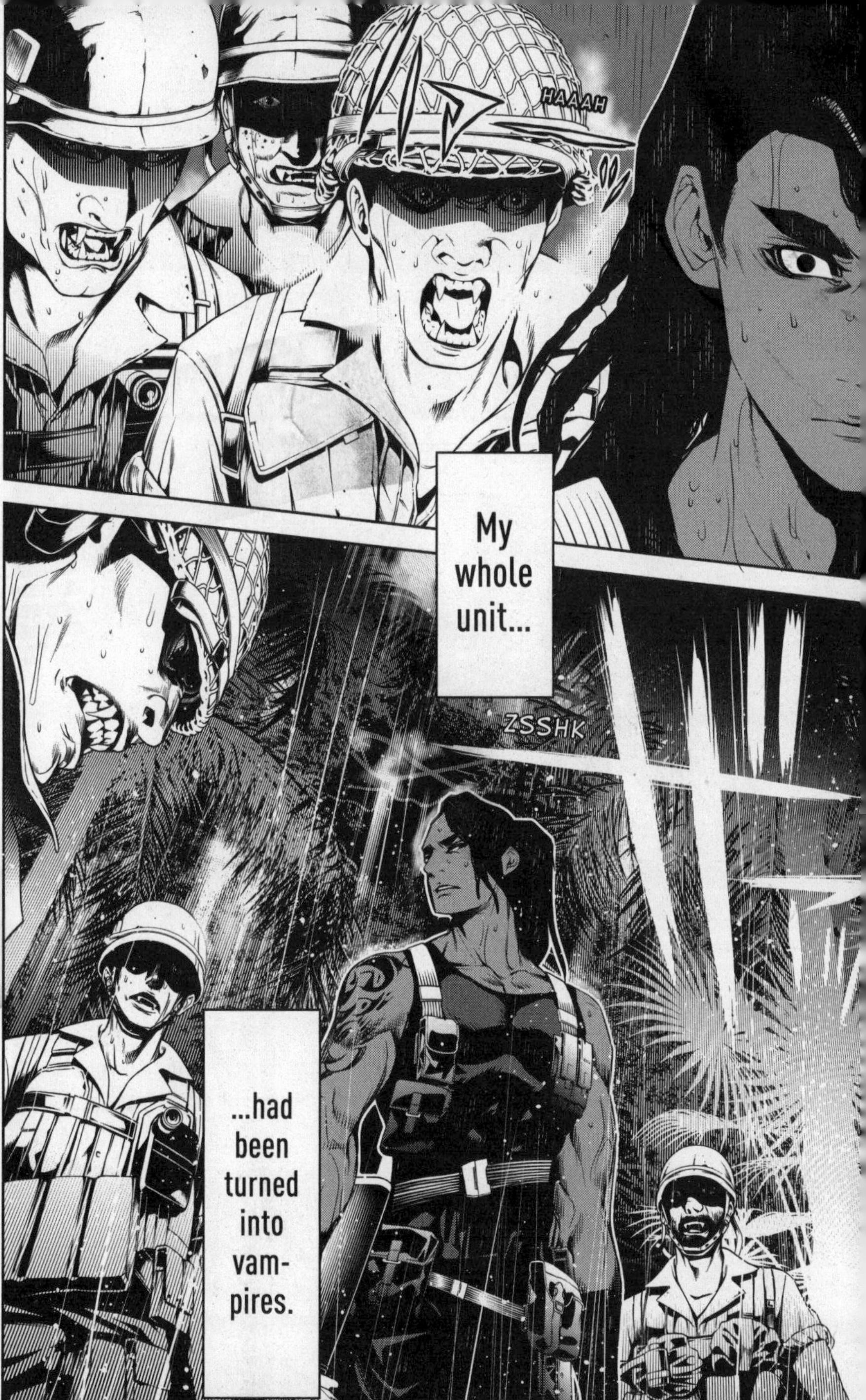
HAAAH
My whole unit...
ZSSHK
...had been turned into vam-pires.

Sir.
...Your back.
It's burning-ing.
FZZT
SPLUTTER SPLUTTER
It was as dark as night in the jungle as the squall fell...
Still, the sun's weak beams found their way in from time to time.
Thanks to that, I finally realized that something was wrong.
HAAAAH

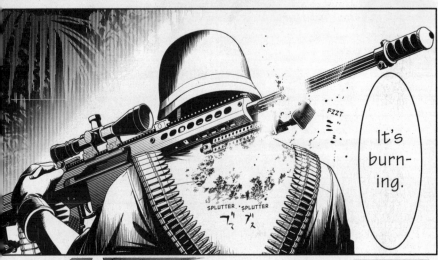

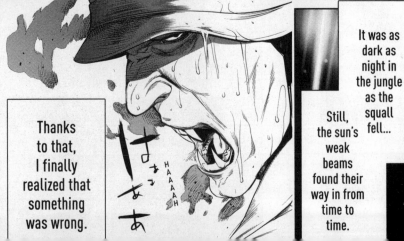

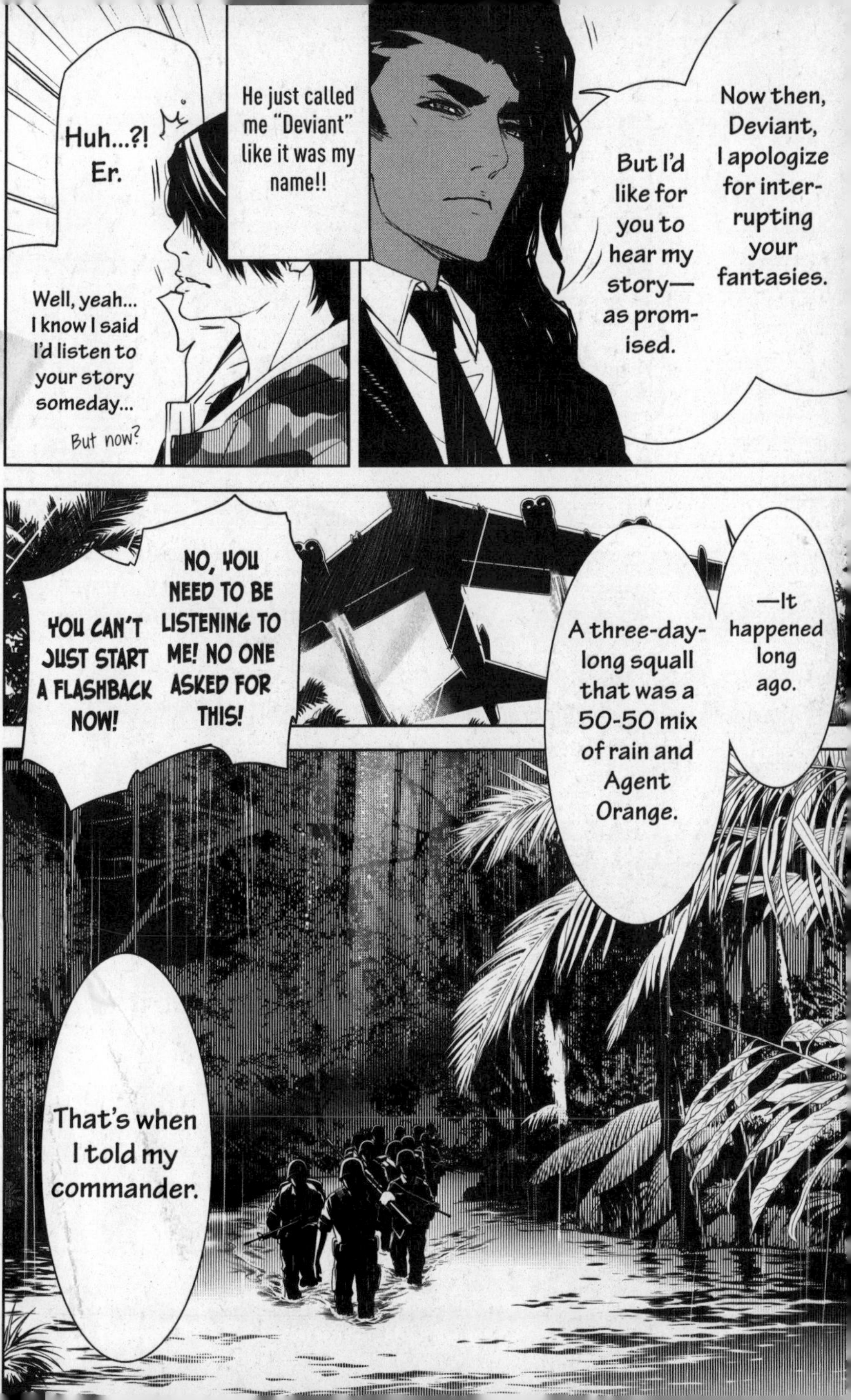
Now then, Deviant, I apologize for interrupting your fantasies.
But I'd like for you to hear my story—as promised.
He just called me "Deviant" like it was my name!!
Huh...?! Er.
Well, yeah... I know I said I'd listen to your story someday...
But now?
—It happened long ago.
A three-day-long squall that was a 50-50 mix of rain and Agent Orange.
NO, YOU NEED TO BE LISTENING TO ME! NO ONE ASKED FOR THIS!
YOU CAN'T JUST START A FLASHBACK NOW!
That's when I told my commander.

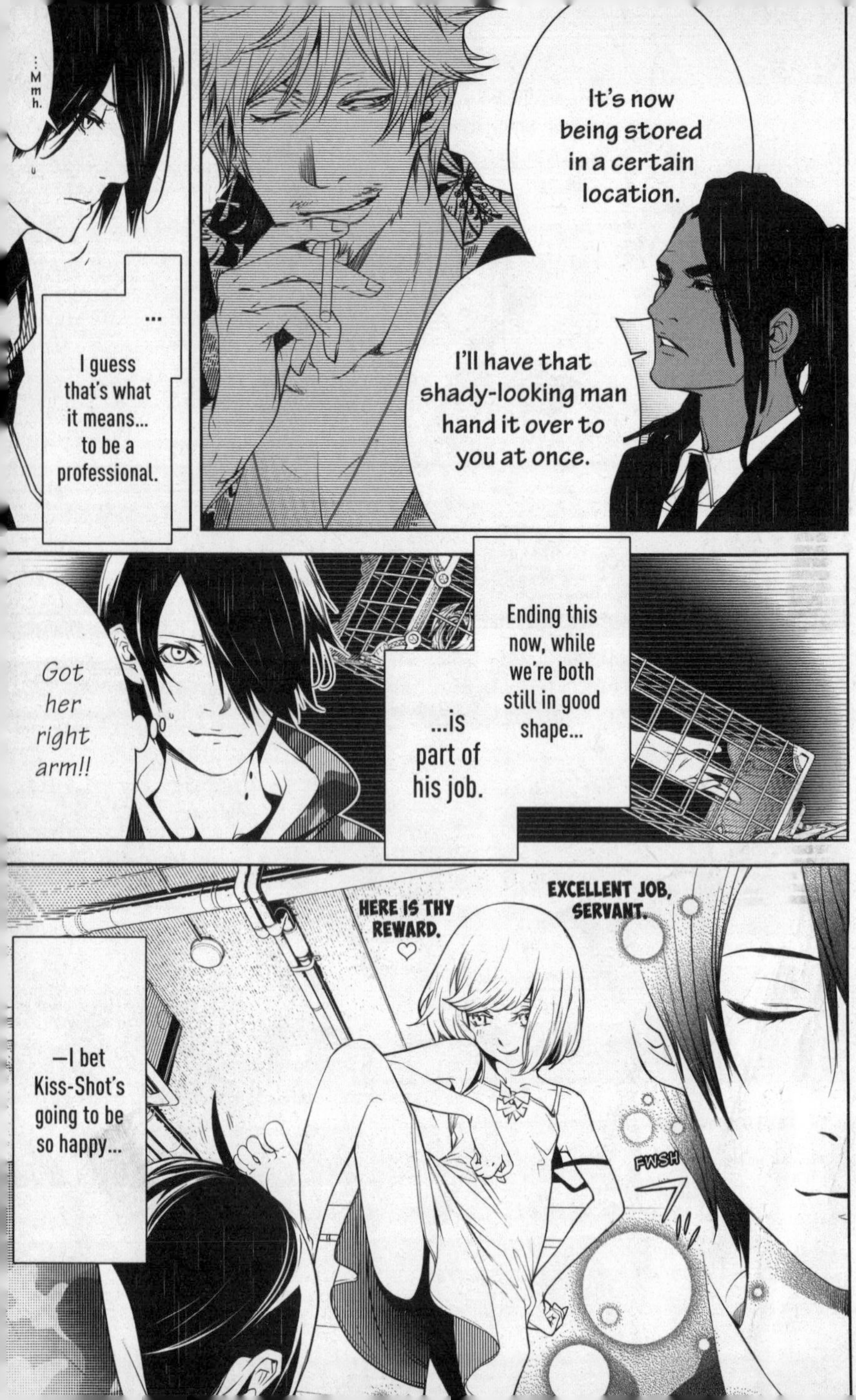
It's now being stored in a certain location.
I'll have that shady-looking man hand it over to you at once.
...Mmh.
...
I guess that's what it means... to be a professional.
Ending this now, while we're both still in good shape...
...is part of his job.
Got her right arm!!
EXCELLENT JOB, SERVANT.
HERE IS THY REWARD. ♡
FWSH
—I bet Kiss-Shot's going to be so happy...

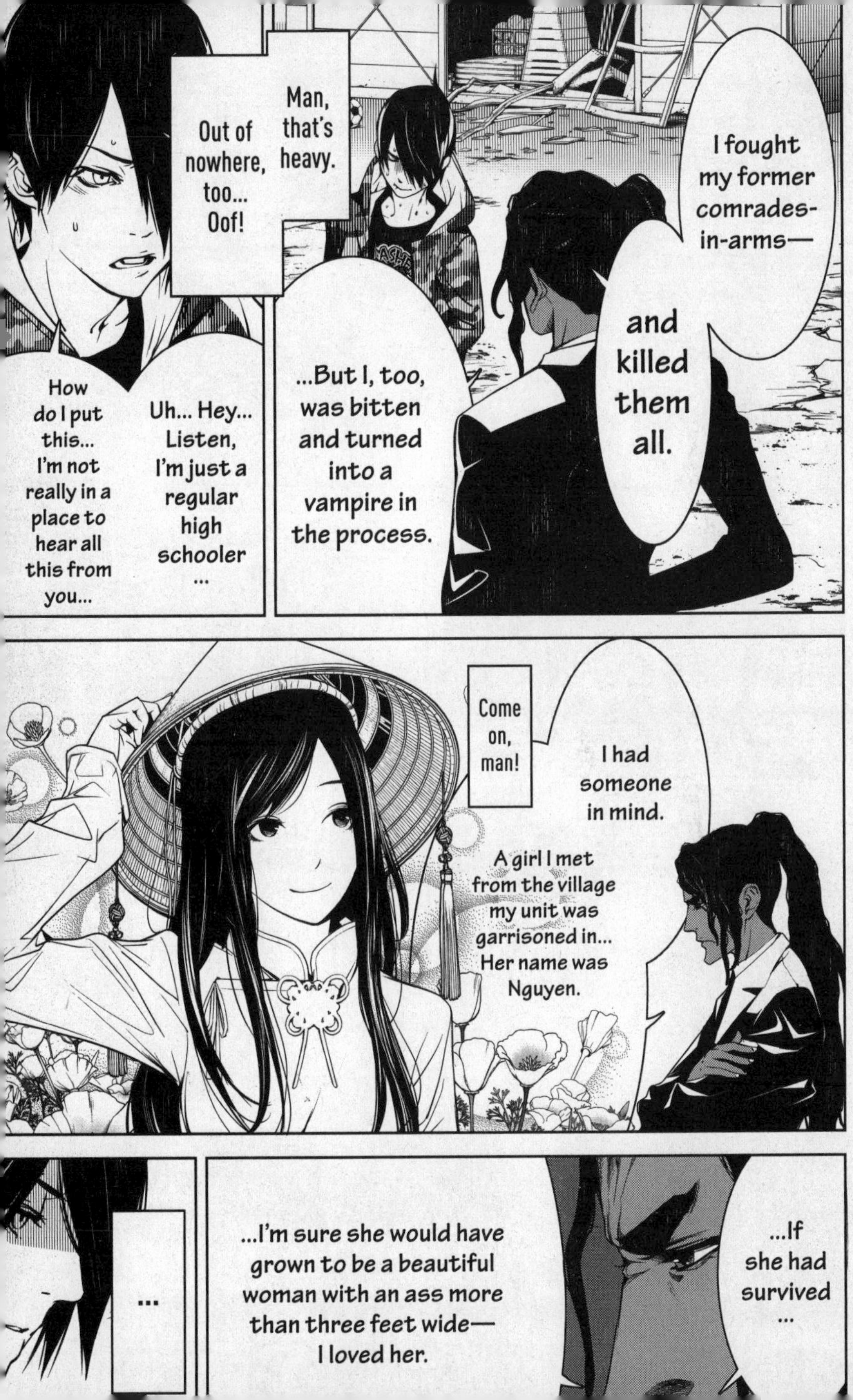
I fought my former comrades-in-arms—
and killed them all.
...But I, too, was bitten and turned into a vampire in the process.
Man, that's heavy.
Out of nowhere, too... Oof!
Uh... Hey... Listen, I'm just a regular high schooler ...
How do I put this... I'm not really in a place to hear all this from you...
I had someone in mind.
Come on, man!
A girl I met from the village my unit was garrisoned in... Her name was Nguyen.
...If she had survived ...
...I'm sure she would have grown to be a beautiful woman with an ass more than three feet wide— I loved her.
...

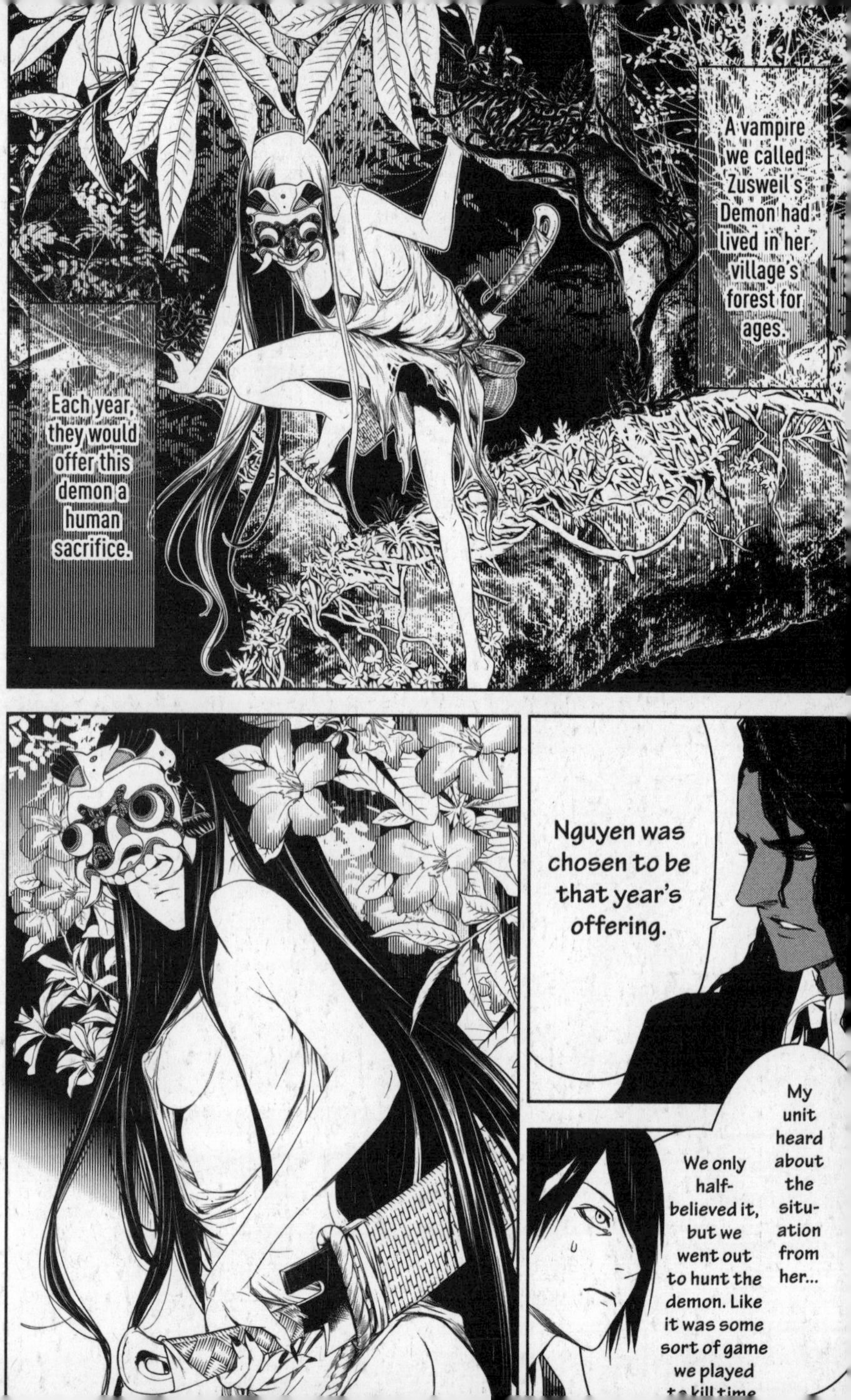
A vampire we called Zusweil's Demon had lived in her village's forest for ages.
Each year, they would offer this demon a human sacrifice.
Nguyen was chosen to be that year's offering.
My unit heard about the situation from her...
We only half-believed it, but we went out to hunt the demon. Like it was some sort of game we played to kill time

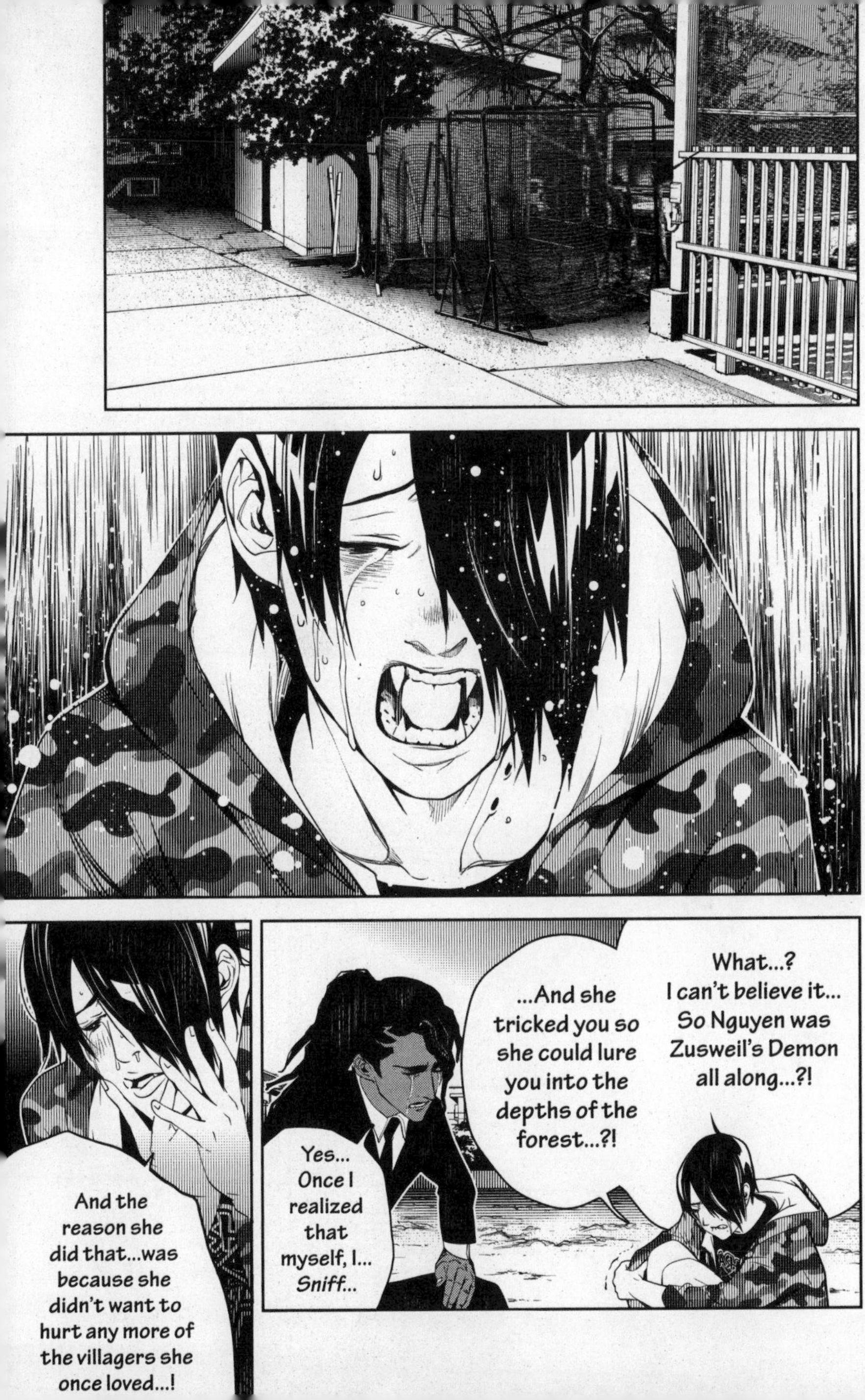
What...? I can't believe it... So Nguyen was Zusweil's Demon all along...?!
...And she tricked you so she could lure you into the depths of the forest...?!
Yes... Once I realized that myself, I... *Sniff*...
And the reason she did that...was because she didn't want to hurt any more of the villagers she once loved...!

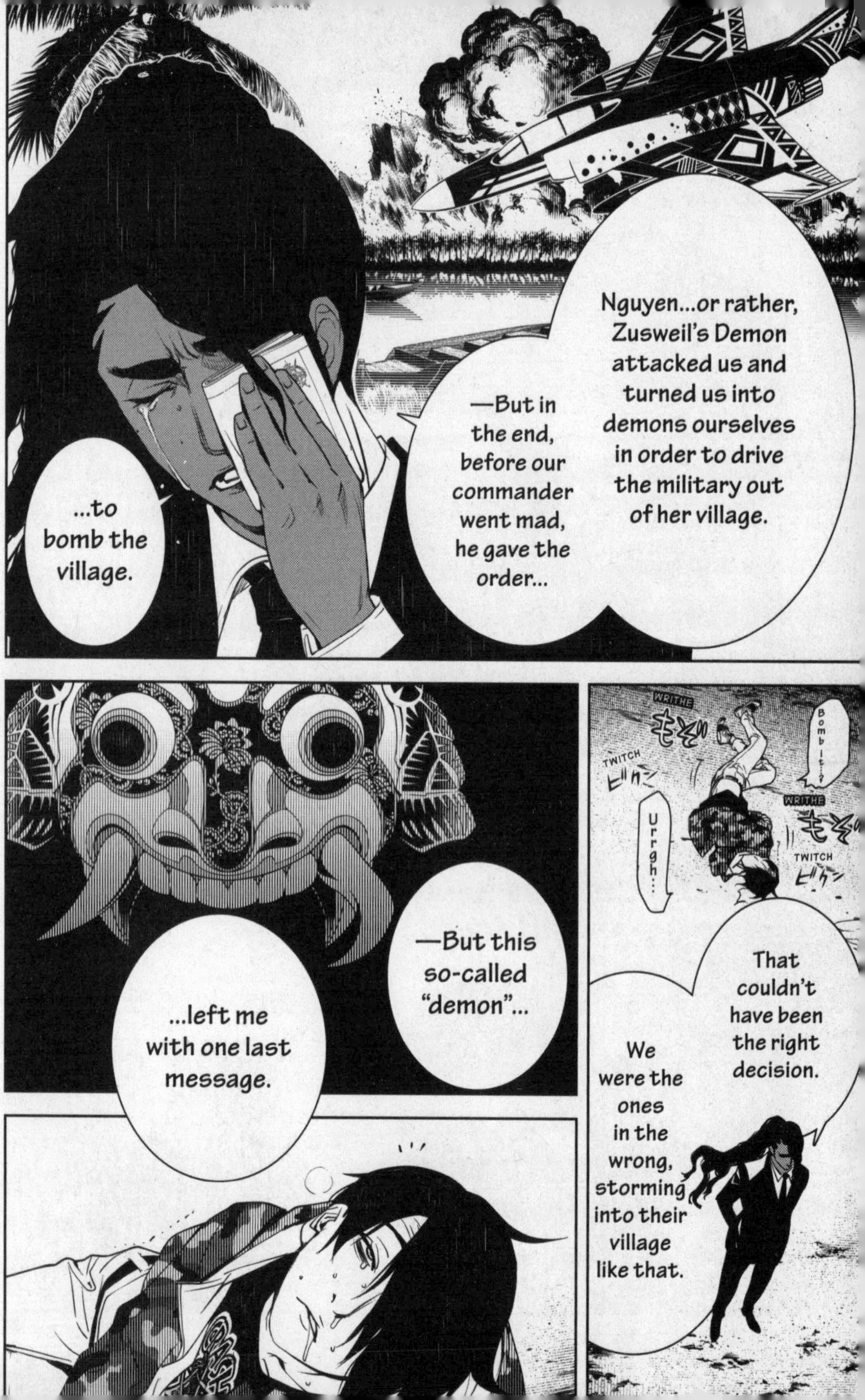
Nguyen...or rather, Zusweil's Demon attacked us and turned us into demons ourselves in order to drive the military out of her village.
—But in the end, before our commander went mad, he gave the order...
...to bomb the village.
WRITHE
Bomb it...?
TWITCH
WRITHE
TWITCH
Urrgh...
That couldn't have been the right decision.
We were the ones in the wrong, storming into their village like that.
—But this so-called "demon"...
...left me with one last message.

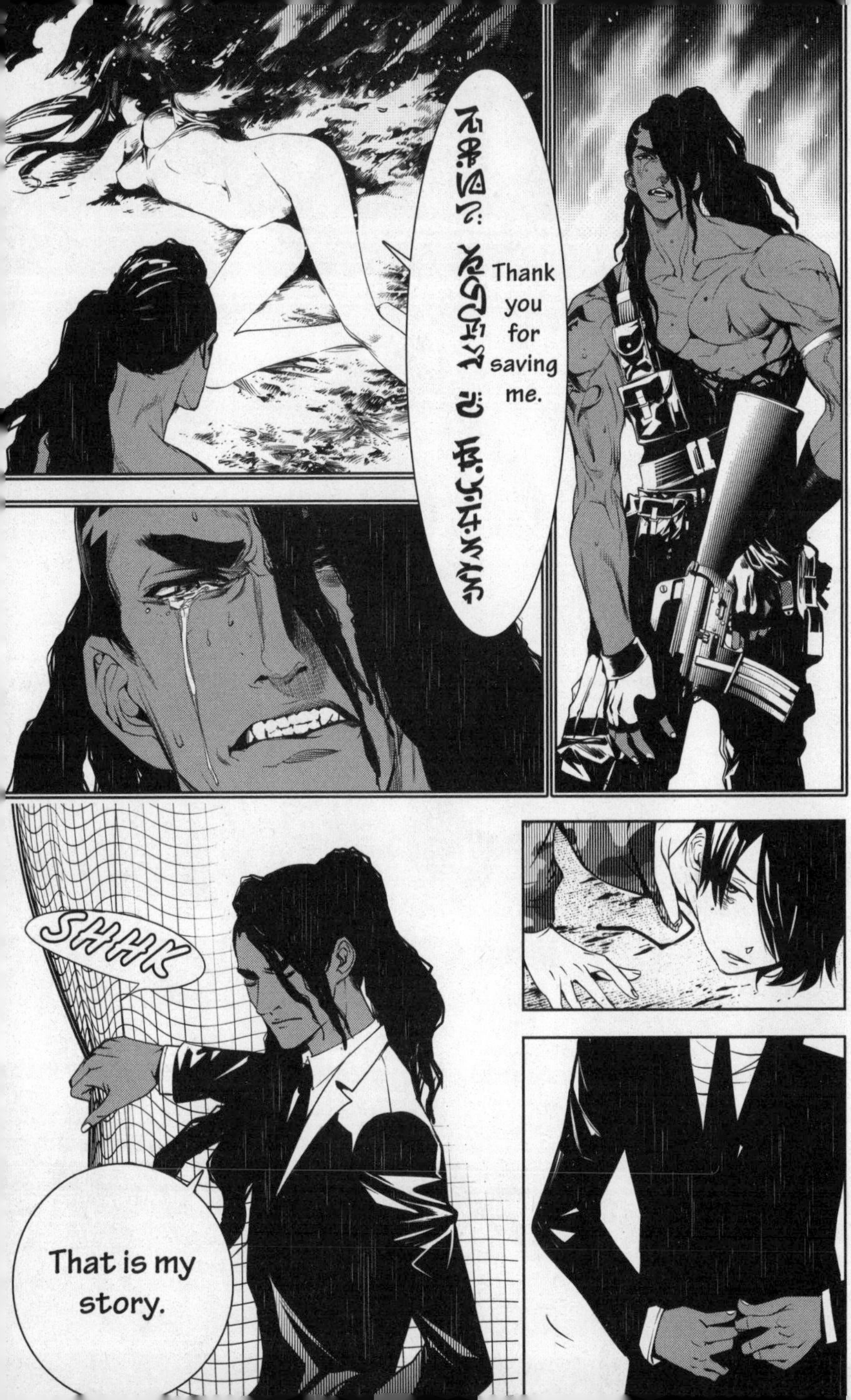
Thank you for saving me.
SHHK
That is my story.

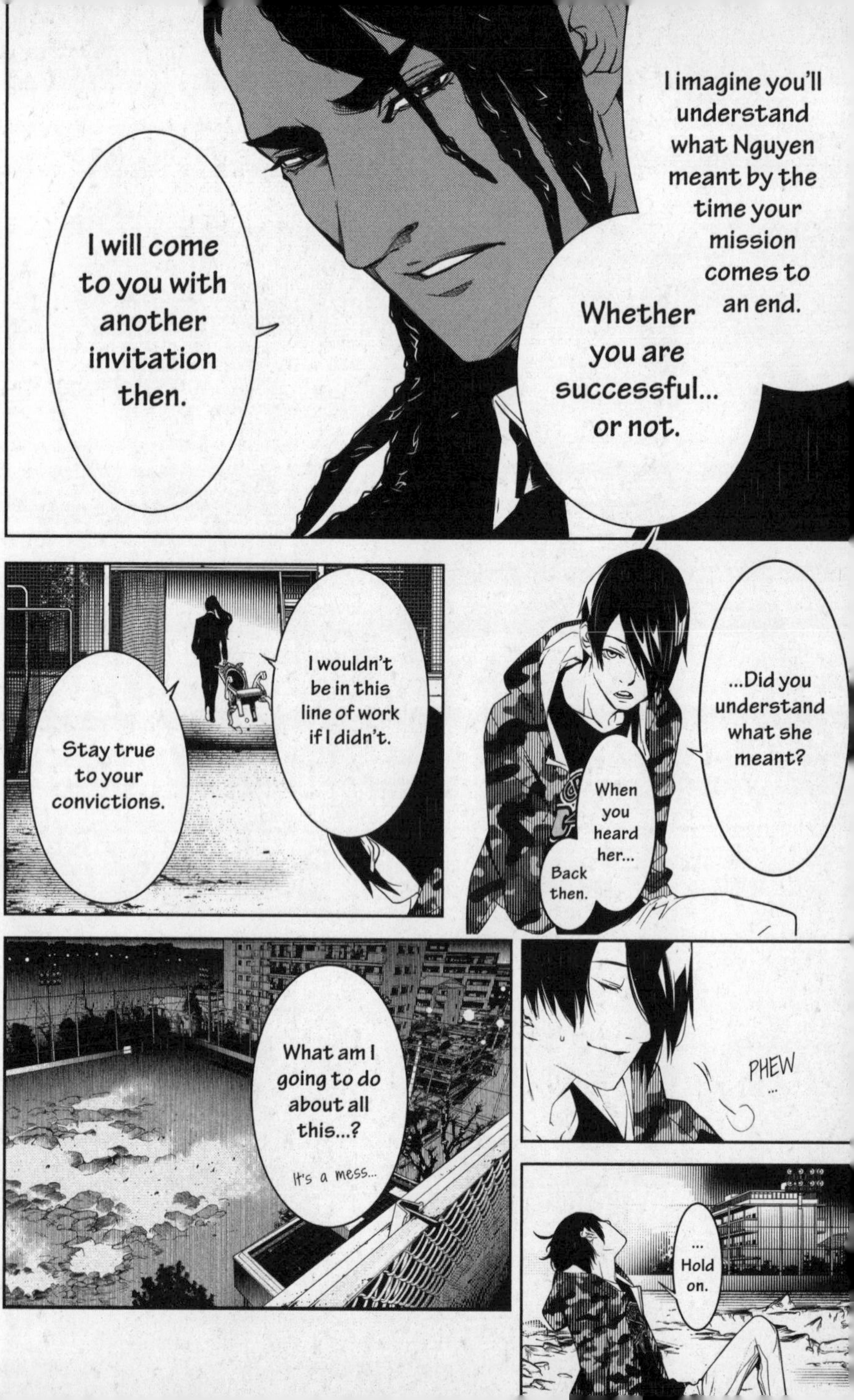
I imagine you'll understand what Nguyen meant by the time your mission comes to an end.
Whether you are successful... or not.
I will come to you with another invitation then.
...Did you understand what she meant?
When you heard her...
Back then.
I wouldn't be in this line of work if I didn't.
Stay true to your convictions.
PHEW...
... Hold on.
What am I going to do about all this...?
It's a mess...

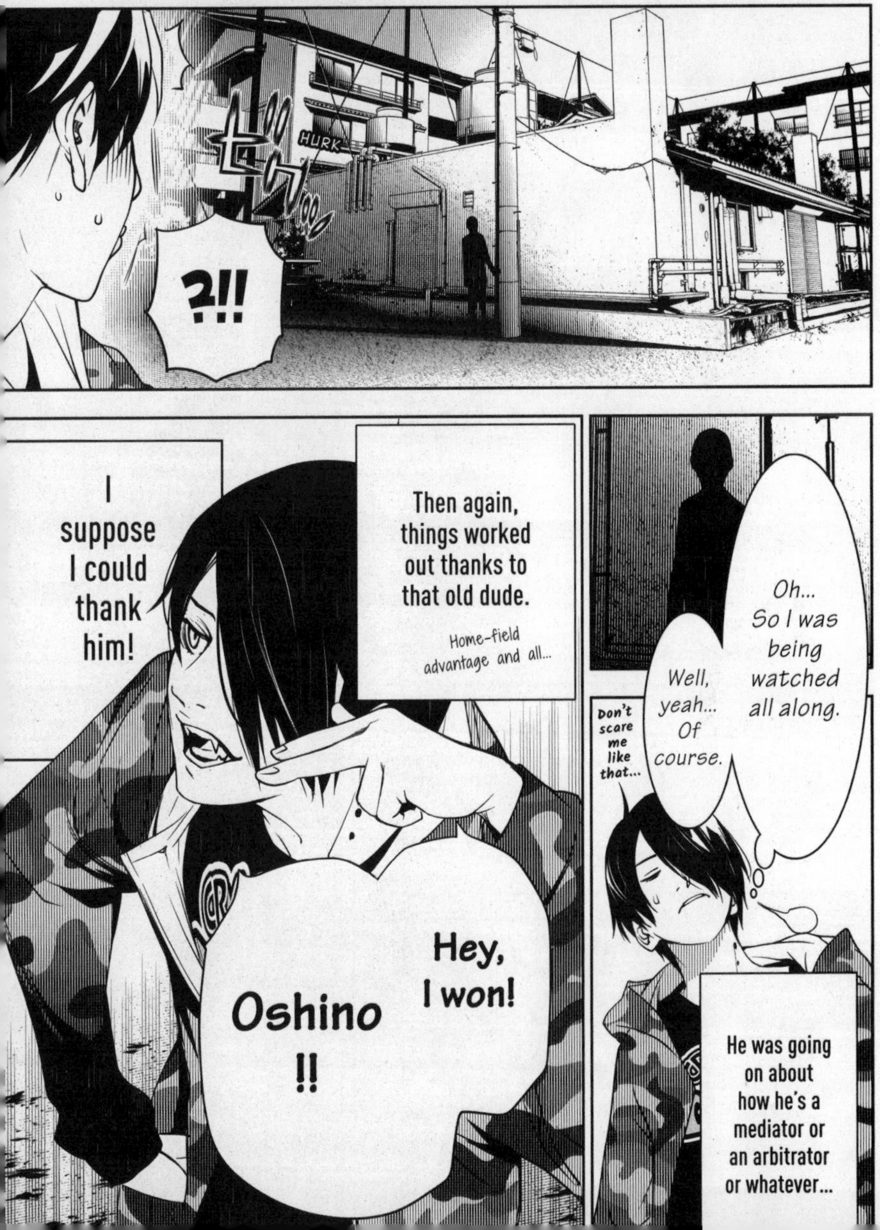
HURK
?!!
Oh... So I was being watched all along.
Well, yeah... Of course.
Don't scare me like that...
He was going on about how he's a mediator or an arbitrator or whatever...
Then again, things worked out thanks to that old dude.
Home-field advantage and all...
I suppose I could thank him!
Hey, I won!
Oshino!!

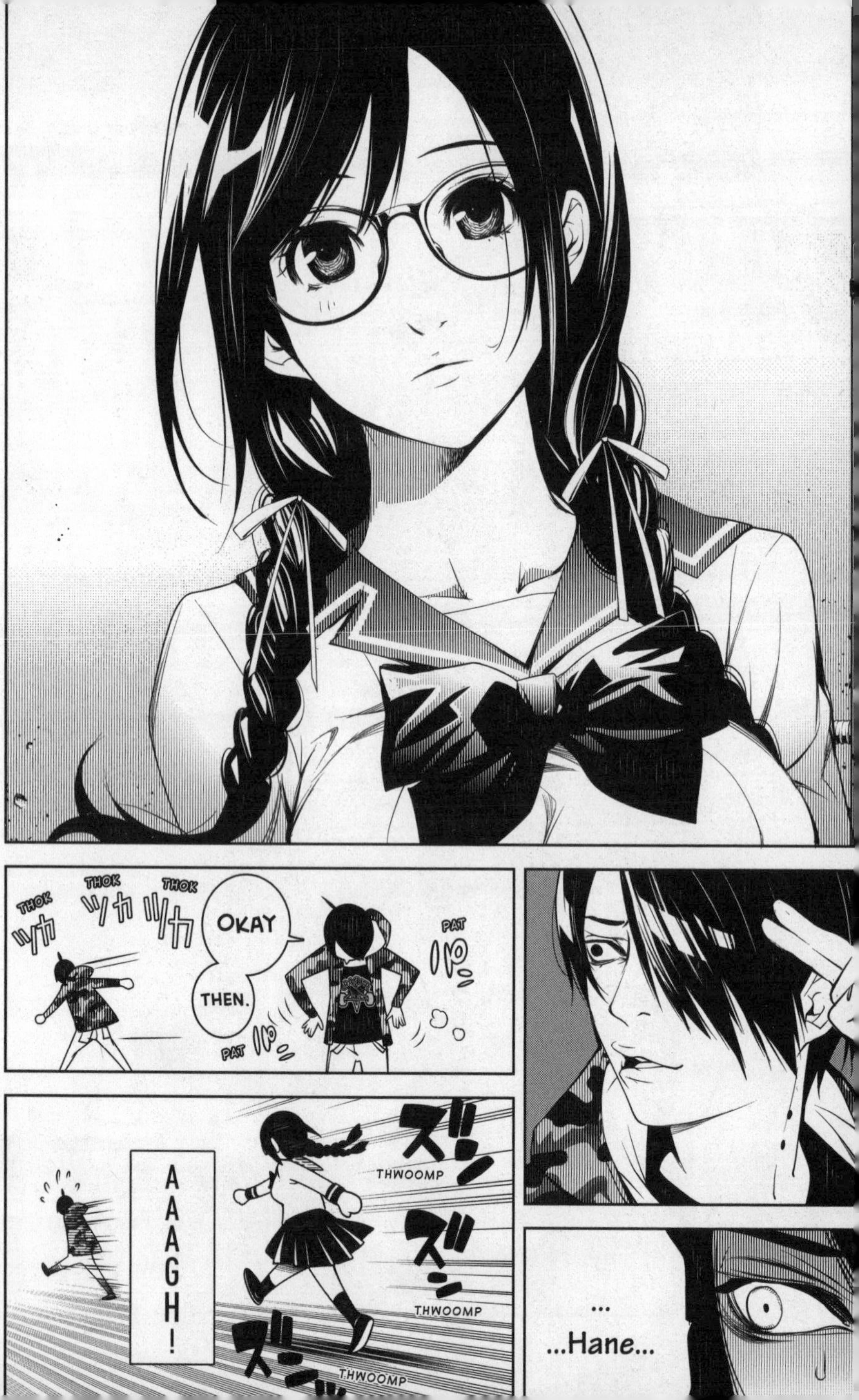
PAT
OKAY
THEN.
PAT
THOK
THOK
THOK
...
...Hane...
THWOOMP
THWOOMP
THWOOMP
AAAGH!

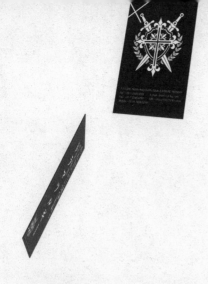

Glow Balls
Every Vampire
Annihilating
Organization

Headhunter

Dramaturgy

BAKEMONOGATARI 10

Glow-Balls
Every Vampire
Annihilating
Organization

Headhunter

Dramaturgy

BAKEMONOGATARI 10

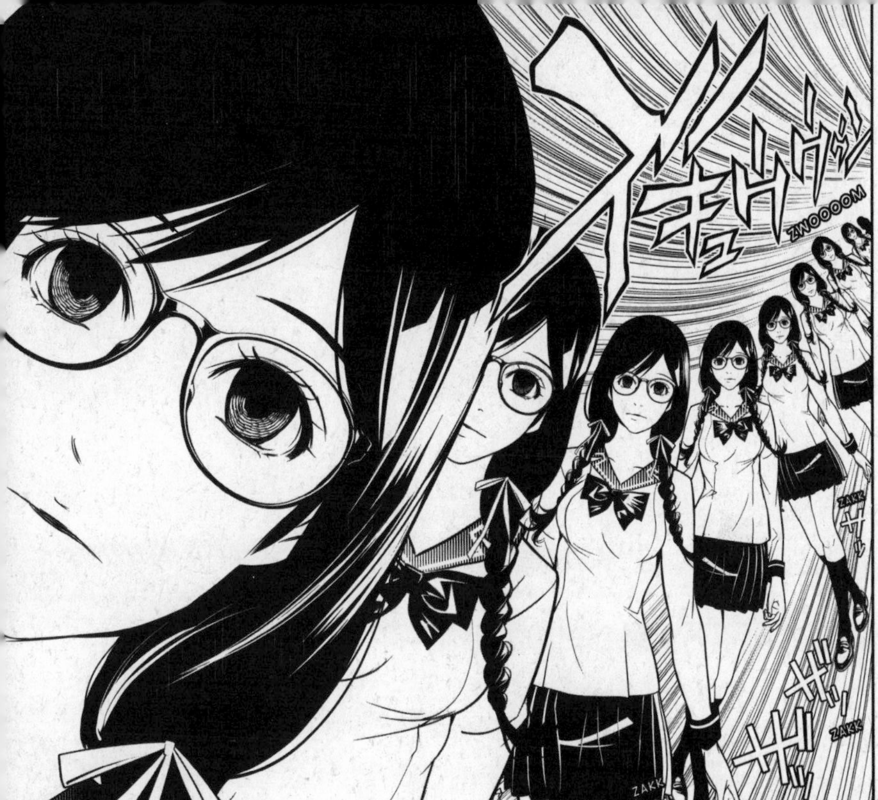
ZNOOOOM
ZAKK
ZAKK
ZAKK
ZAKK

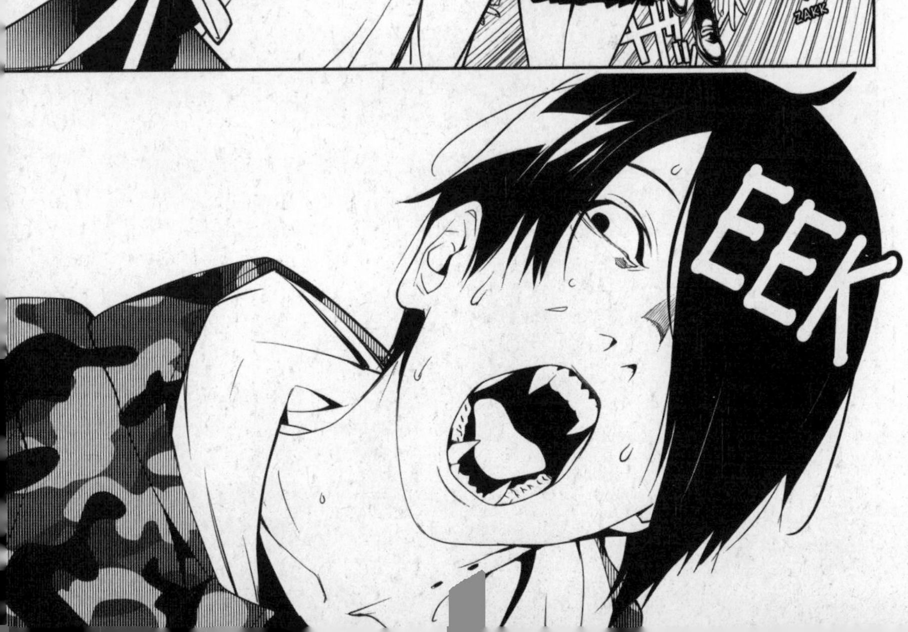
EEK

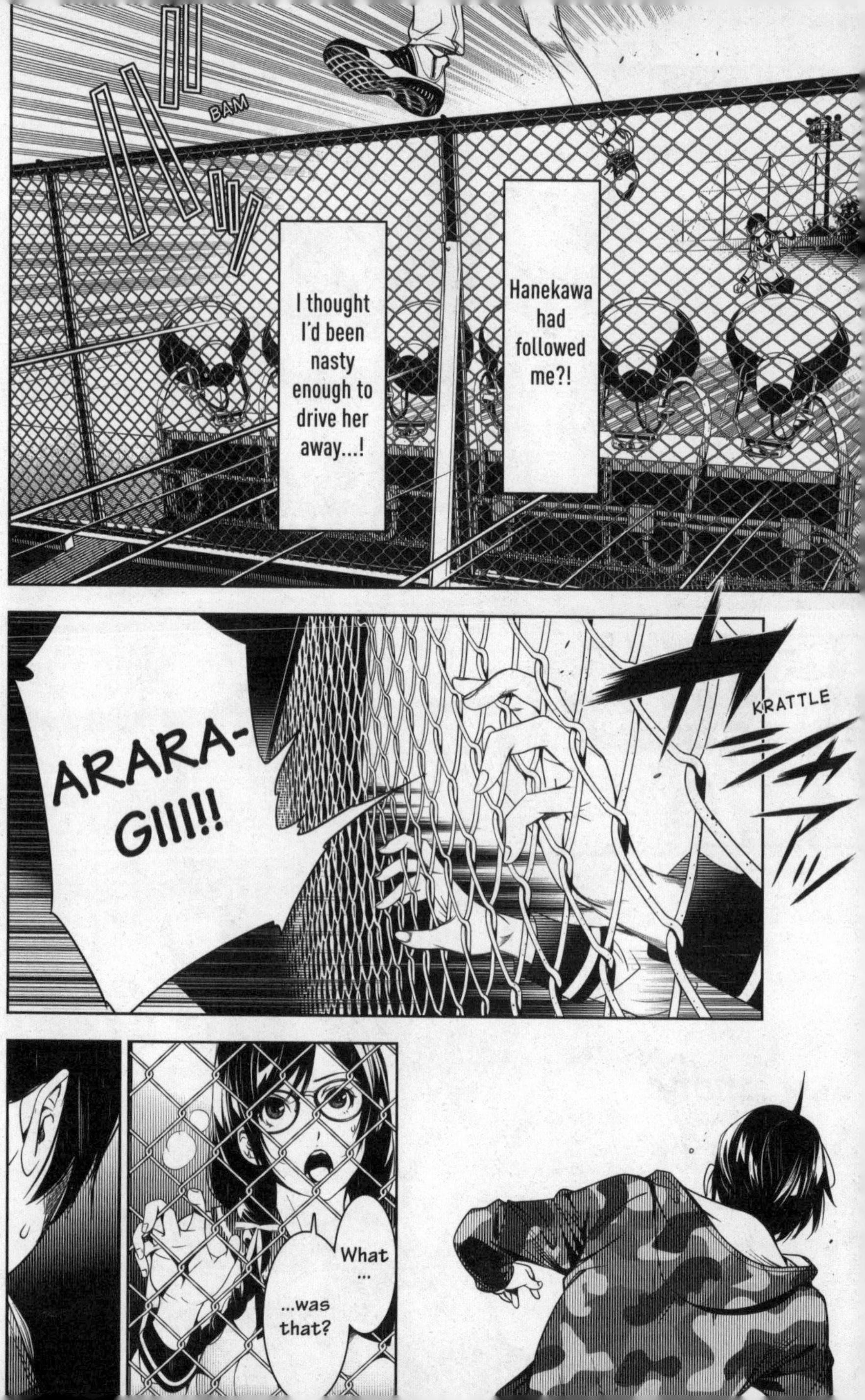
BAM
Hanekawa had followed me?!
I thought I'd been nasty enough to drive her away...!
KRATTLE
ARARA-GIIII!!
What ...
...was that?

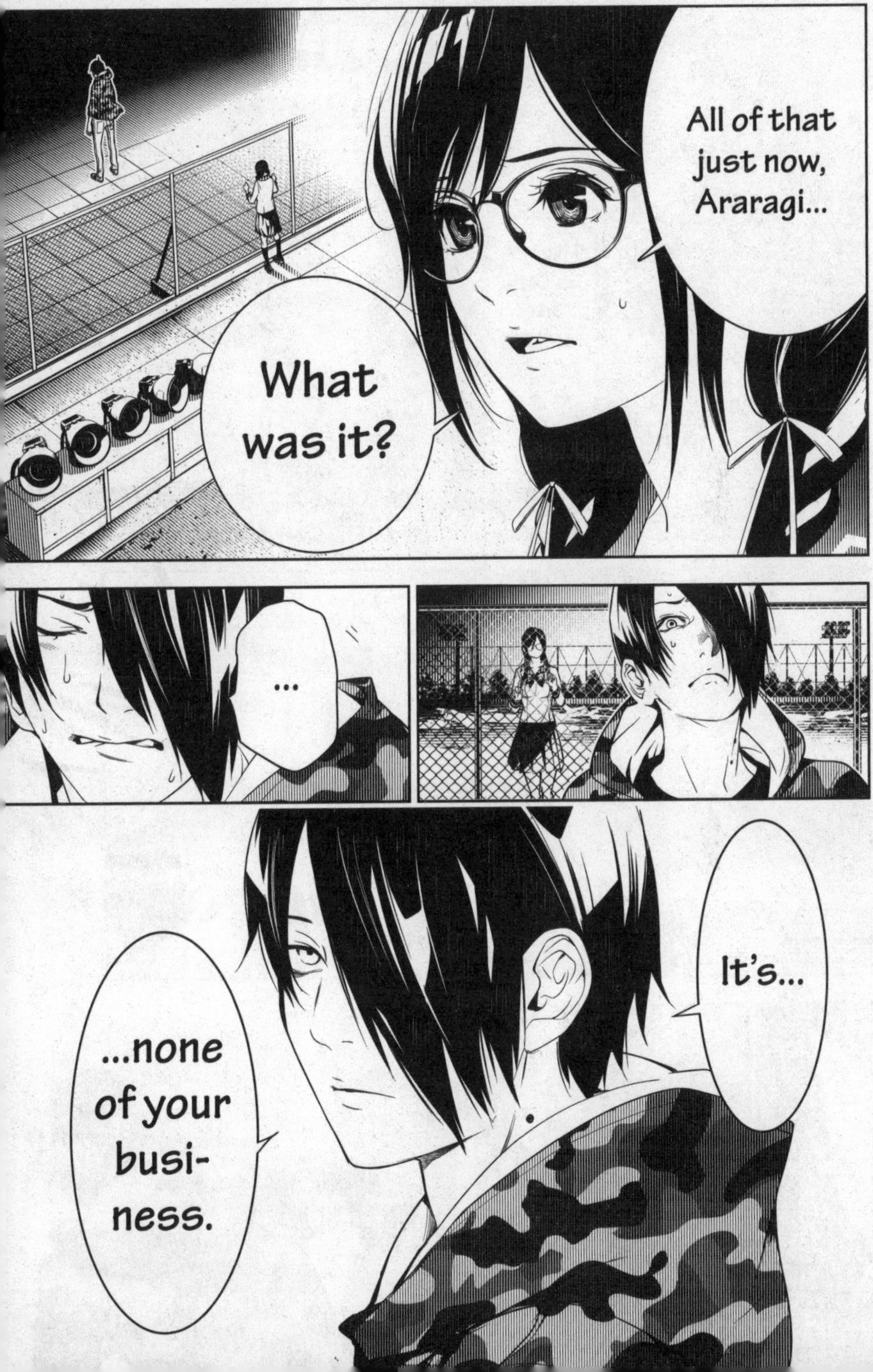
All of that just now, Araragi...
What was it?
...
It's...
...none of your busi-ness.

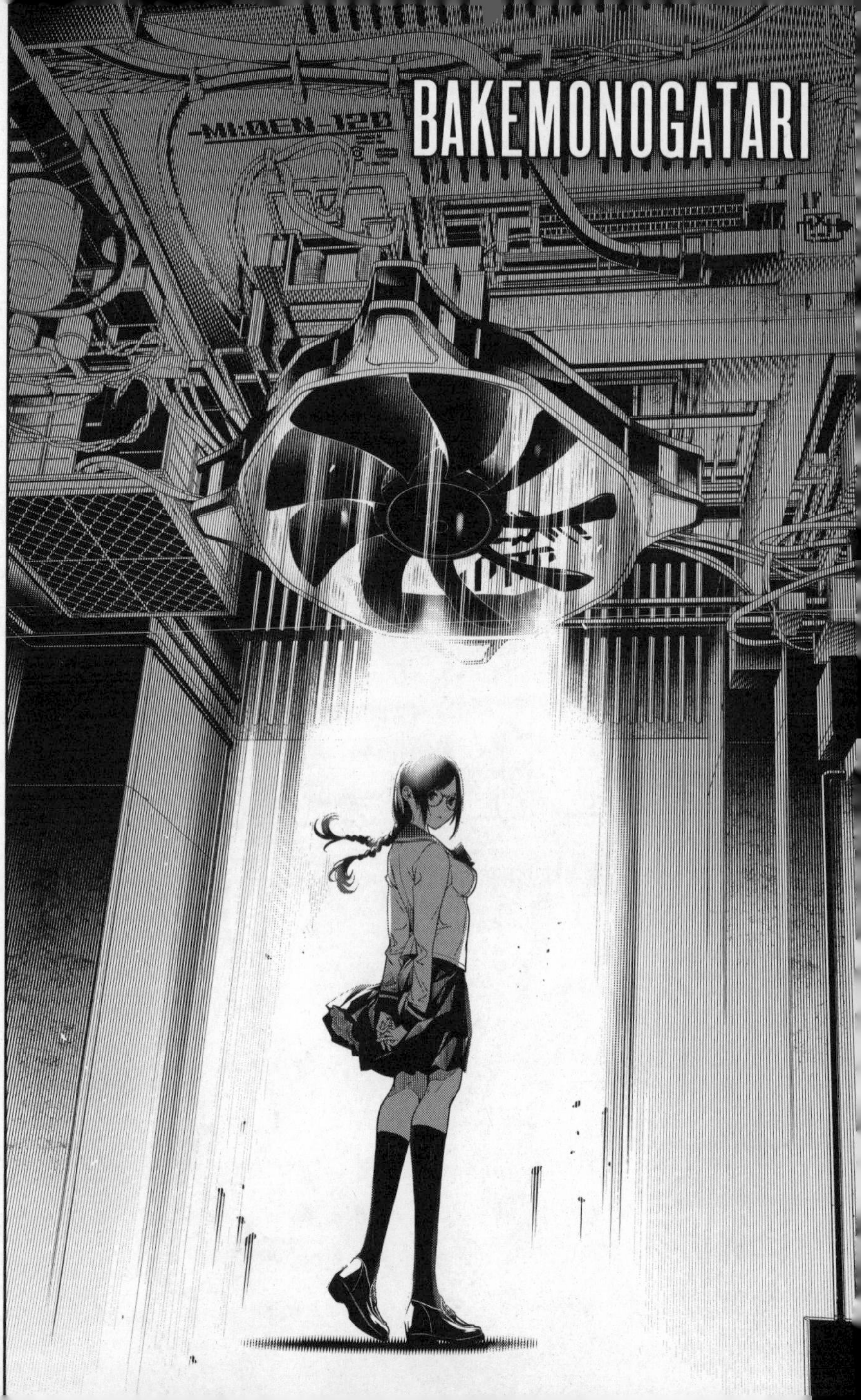
BAKEMONOGATARI
-MI-DEN-120

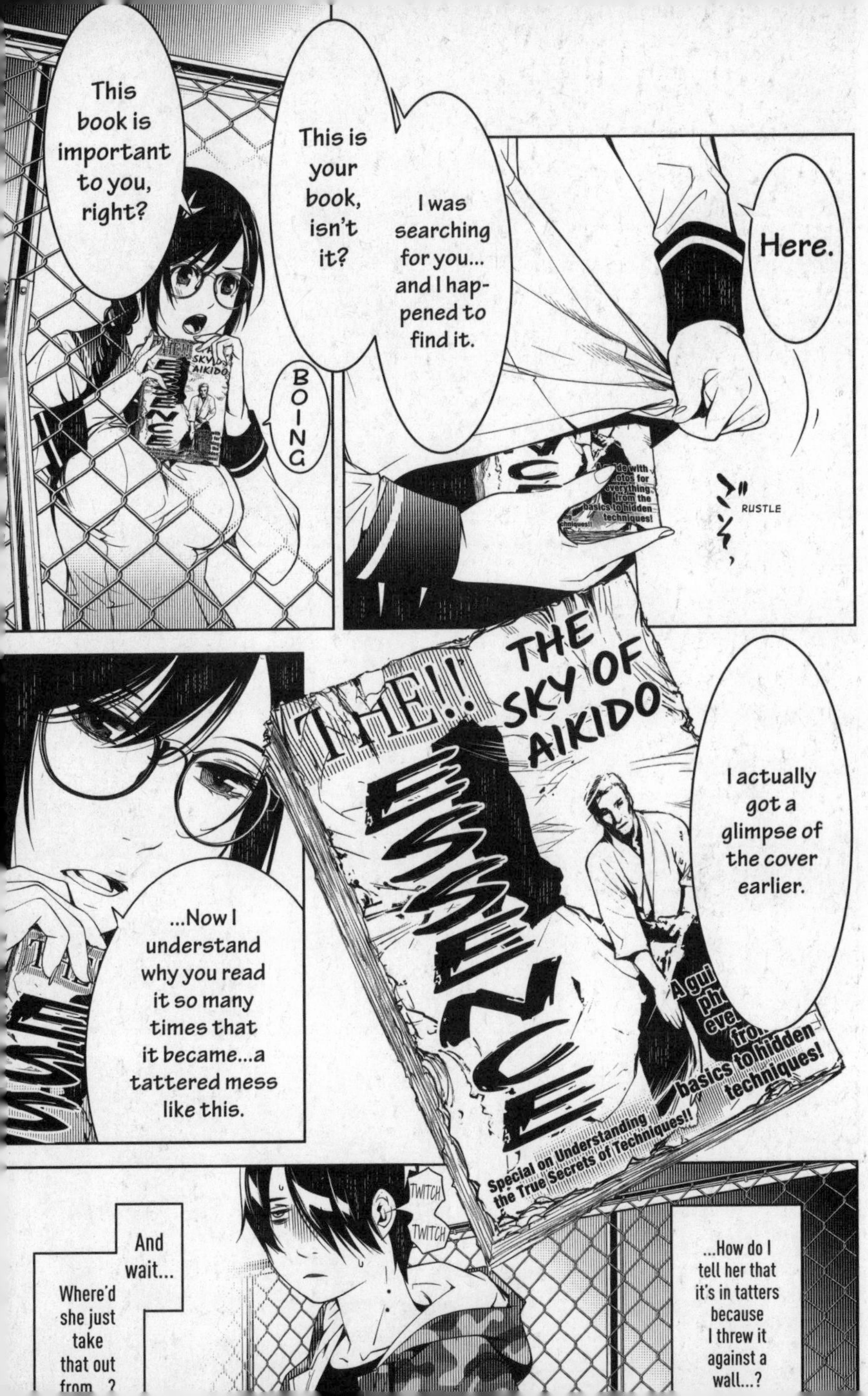
Here.
RUSTLE
This is your book, isn't it?
I was searching for you... and I happened to find it.
BOING
This book is important to you, right?
I actually got a glimpse of the cover earlier.
THE!!
THE SKY OF AIKIDO
basics to hidden techniques!
Special on Understanding the True Secrets of Techniques!!
...Now I understand why you read it so many times that it became...a tattered mess like this.
...How do I tell her that it's in tatters because I threw it against a wall...?
TWITCH
TWITCH
And wait...
Where'd she just take that out from...?

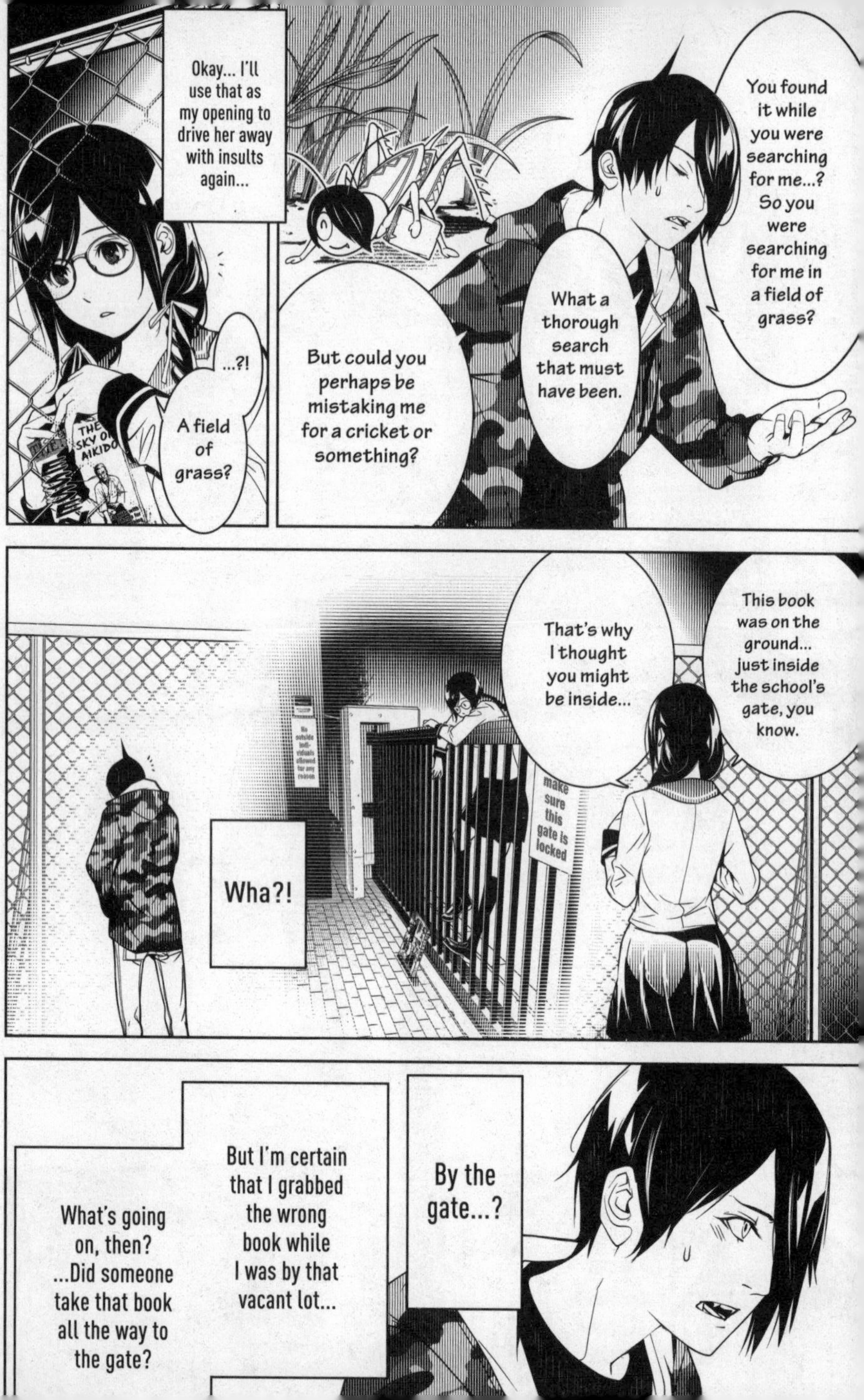
You found it while you were searching for me...? So you were searching for me in a field of grass?
What a thorough search that must have been.
But could you perhaps be mistaking me for a cricket or something?
Okay... I'll use that as my opening to drive her away with insults again...
...?!
A field of grass?
This book was on the ground... just inside the school's gate, you know.
That's why I thought you might be inside...
make sure this gate is locked
Wha?!
By the gate...?
But I'm certain that I grabbed the wrong book while I was by that vacant lot...
What's going on, then? ...Did someone take that book all the way to the gate?

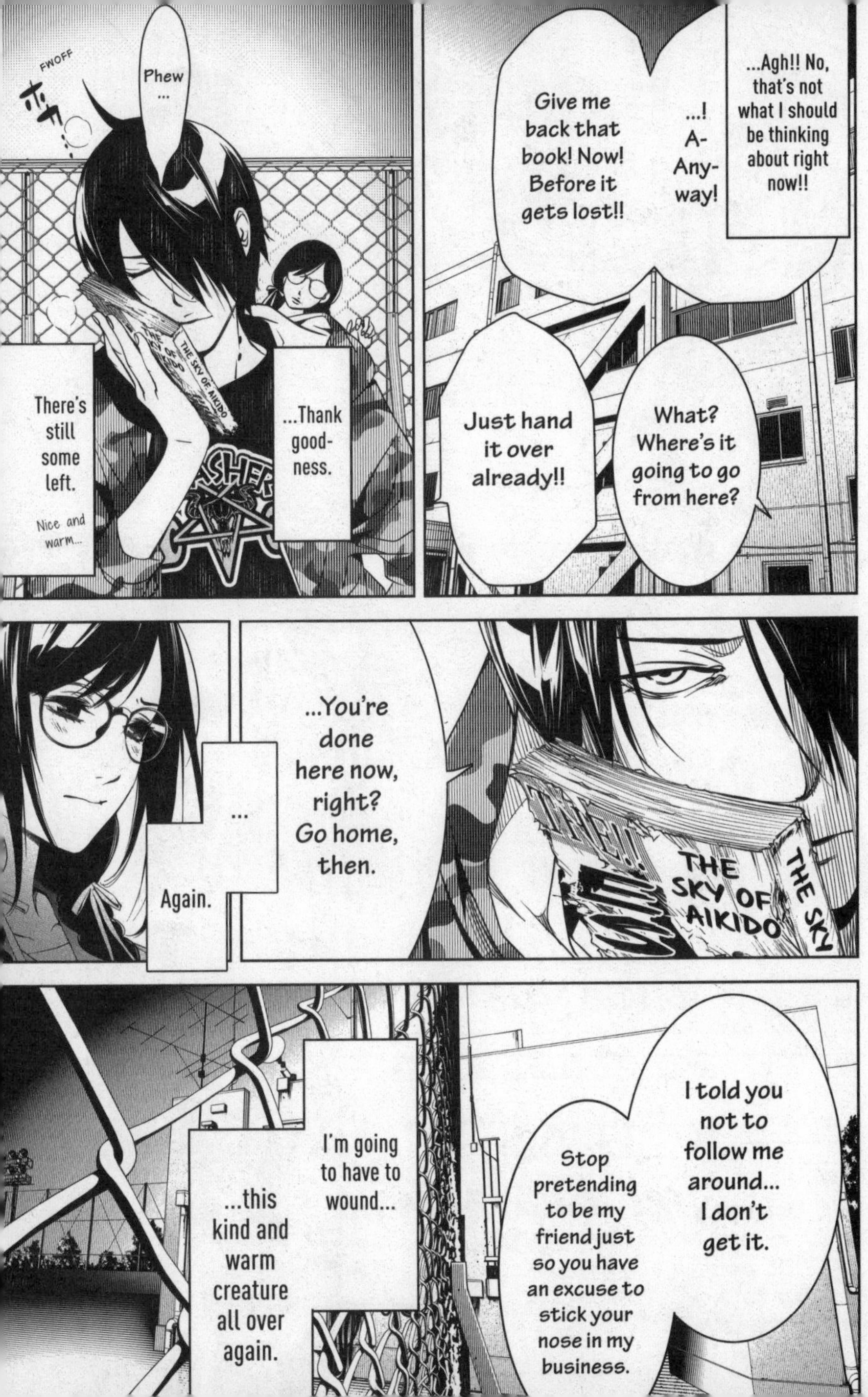
...Agh!! No, that's not what I should be thinking about right now!!
...! A- Any- way!
Give me back that book! Now! Before it gets lost!!
What? Where's it going to go from here?
Just hand it over already!!
Phew ...
FWOFF
...Thank goodness.
There's still some left.
Nice and warm...
THE SKY OF AIKIDO
...You're done here now, right? Go home, then.
THE SKY OF AIKIDO
THE SKY
...
Again.
I told you not to follow me around... I don't get it.
Stop pretending to be my friend just so you have an excuse to stick your nose in my business.
I'm going to have to wound...
...this kind and warm creature all over again.

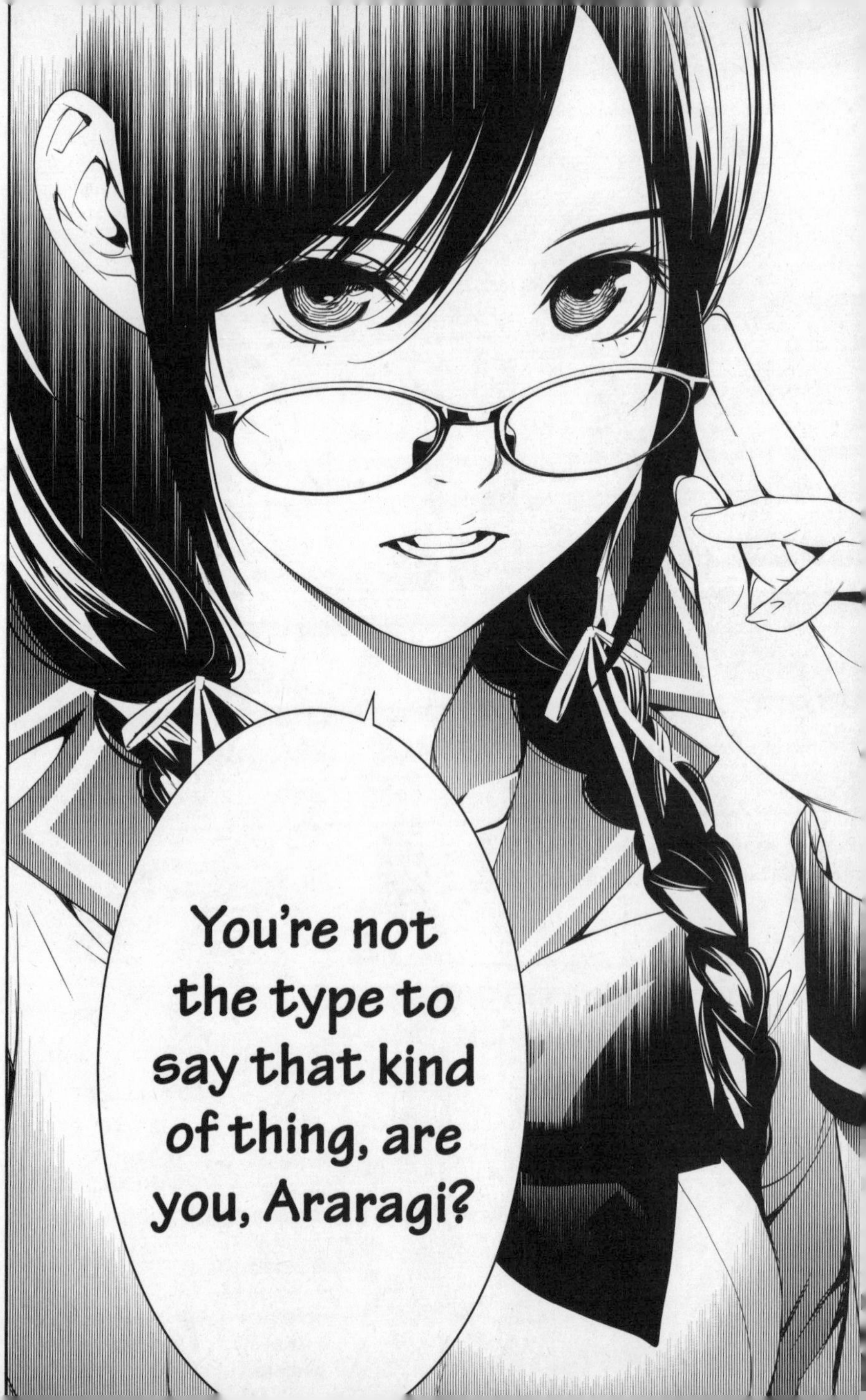
You're not the type to say that kind of thing, are you, Araragi?

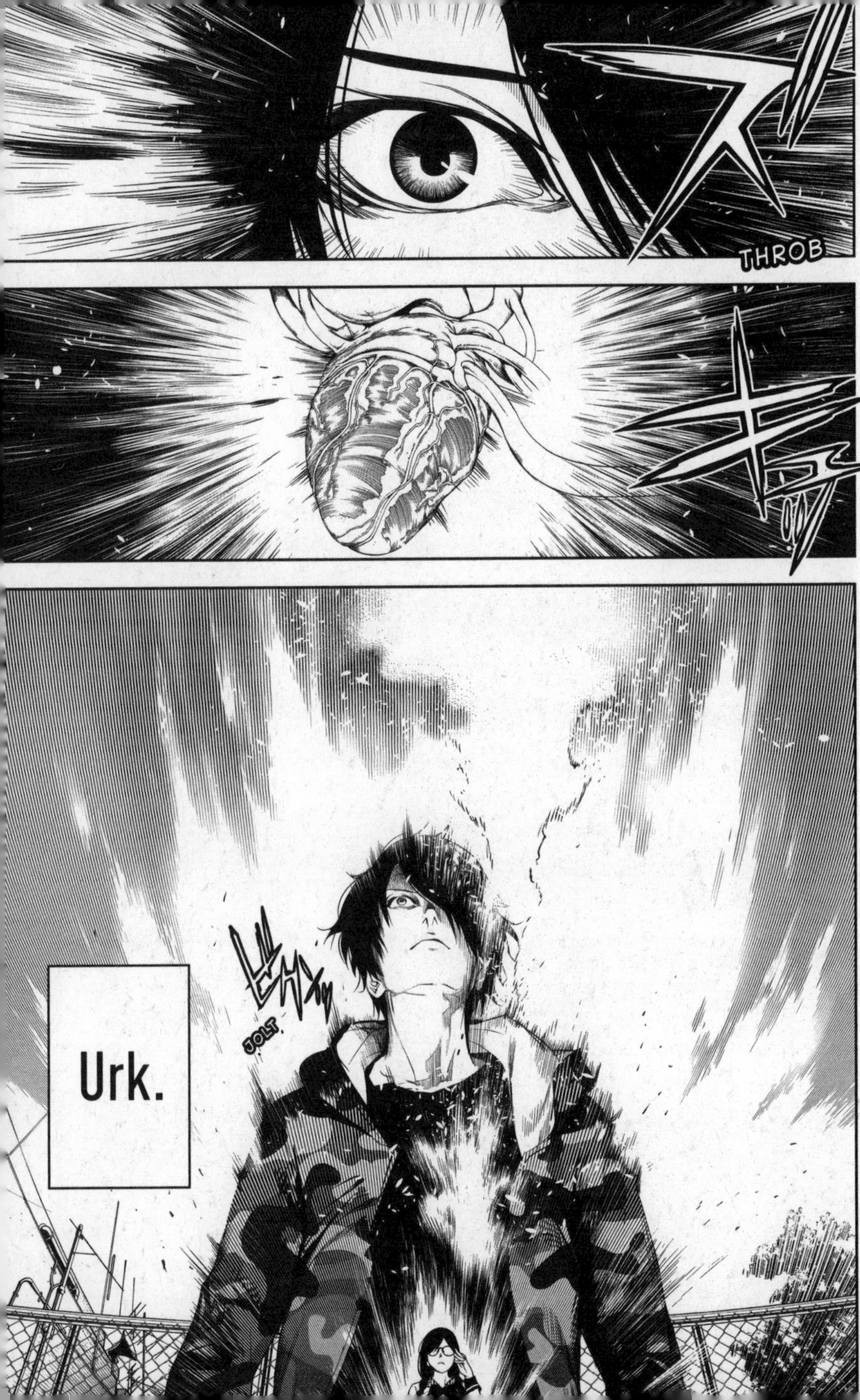
THROB
JOLT
Urk.

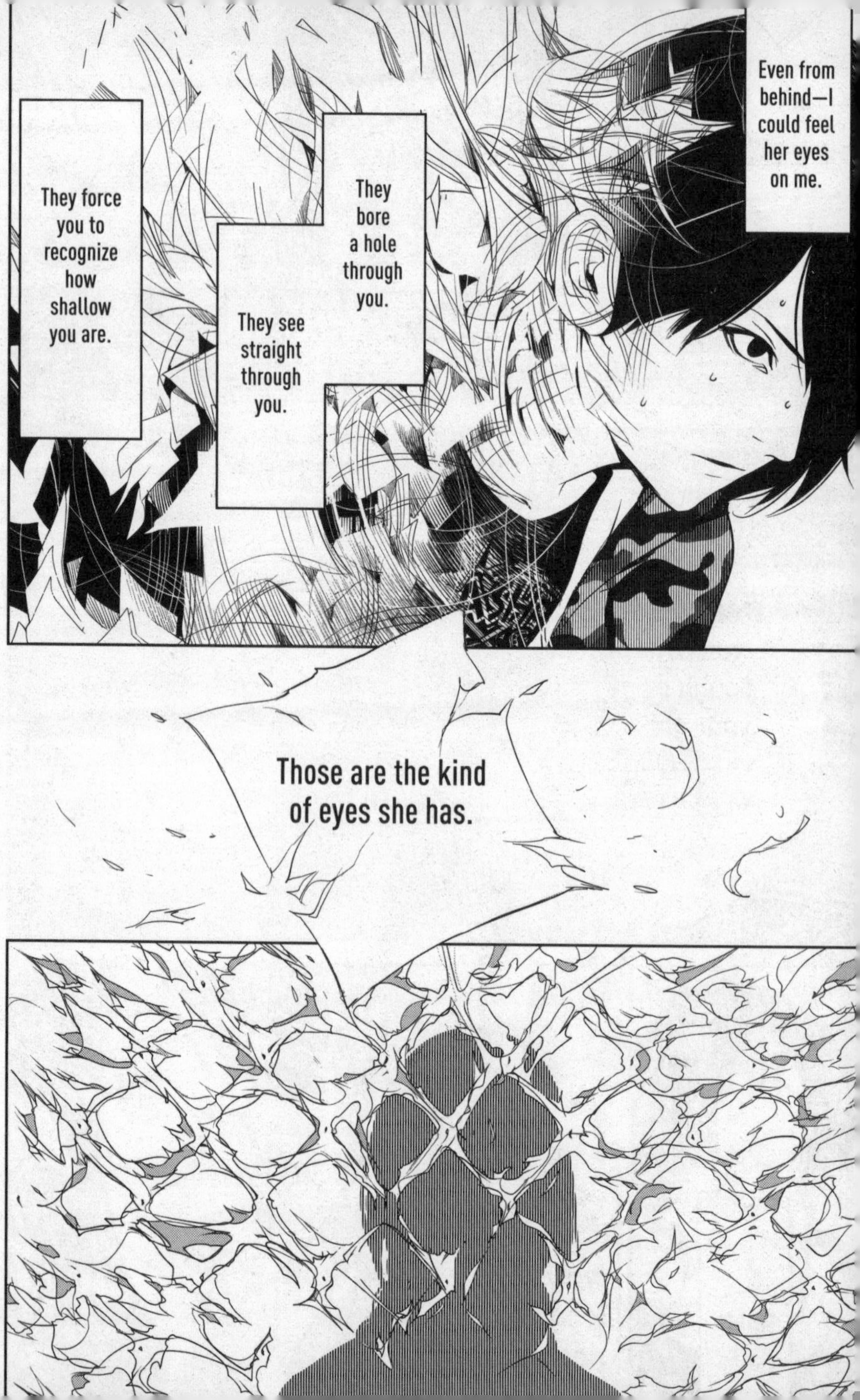
Even from behind—I could feel her eyes on me.
They bore a hole through you.
They see straight through you.
They force you to recognize how shallow you are.
Those are the kind of eyes she has.

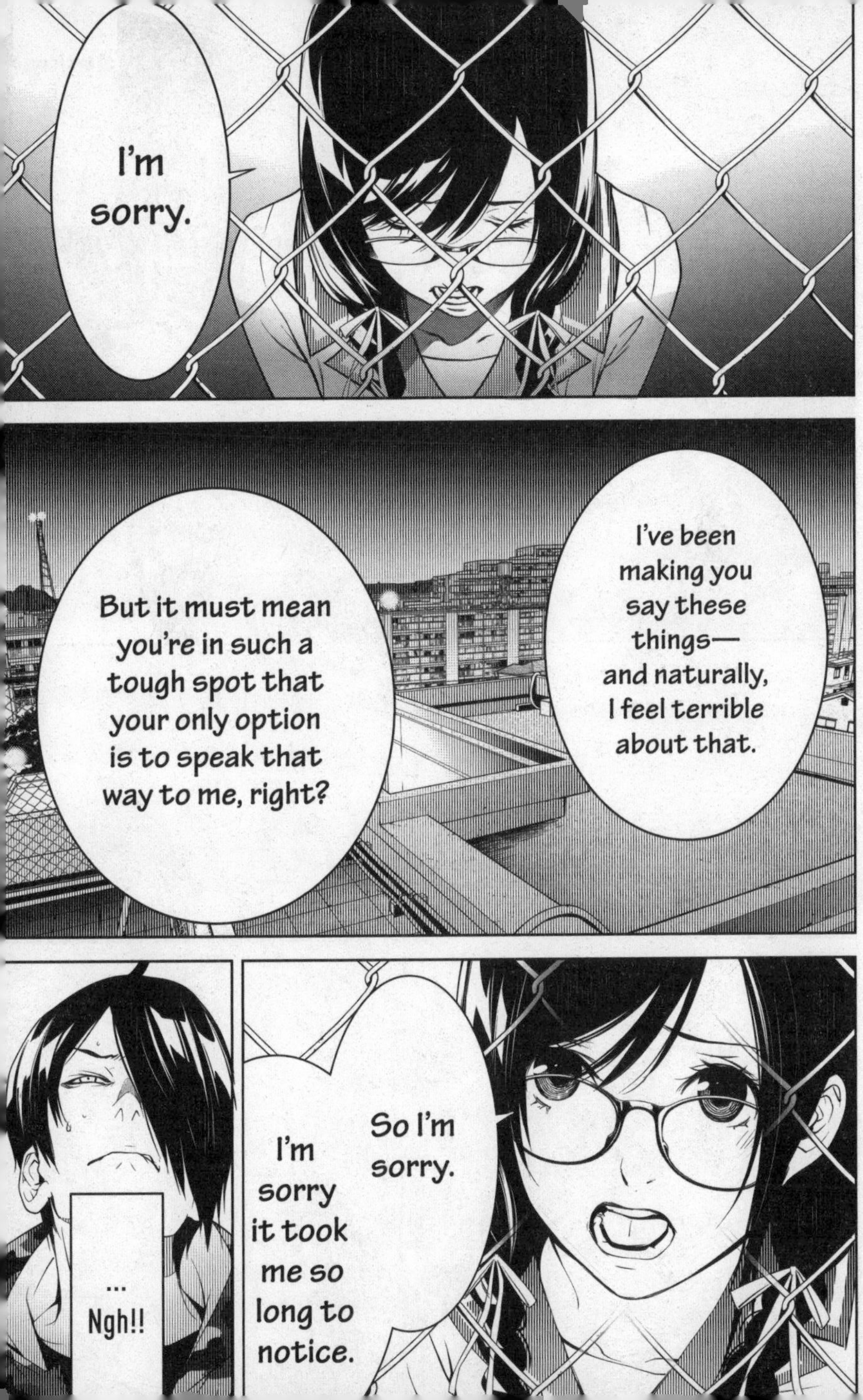
I'm sorry.
I've been making you say these things— and naturally, I feel terrible about that.
But it must mean you're in such a tough spot that your only option is to speak that way to me, right?
So I'm sorry.
I'm sorry it took me so long to notice.
... Ngh!!

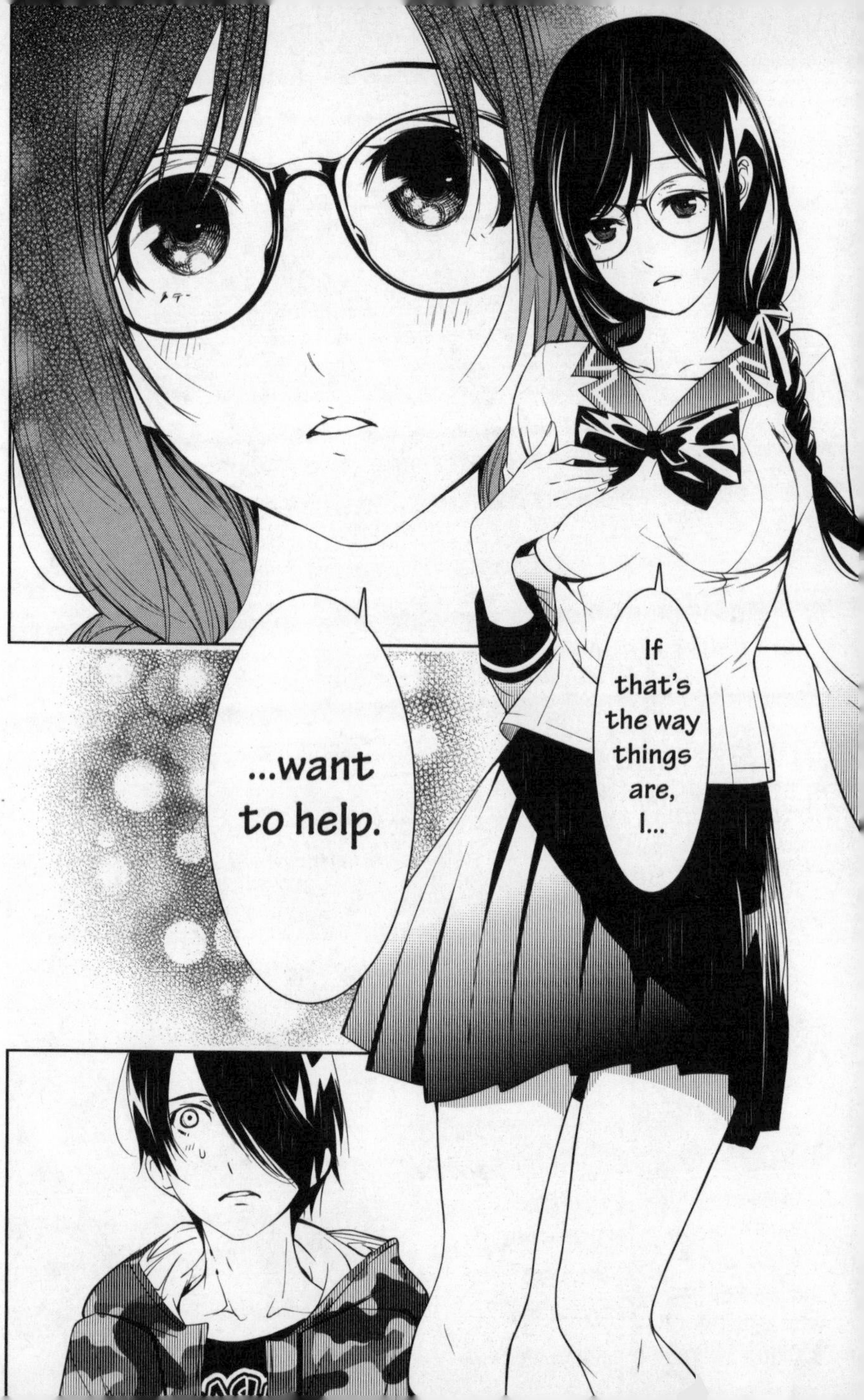
If that's the way things are, I...
...want to help.

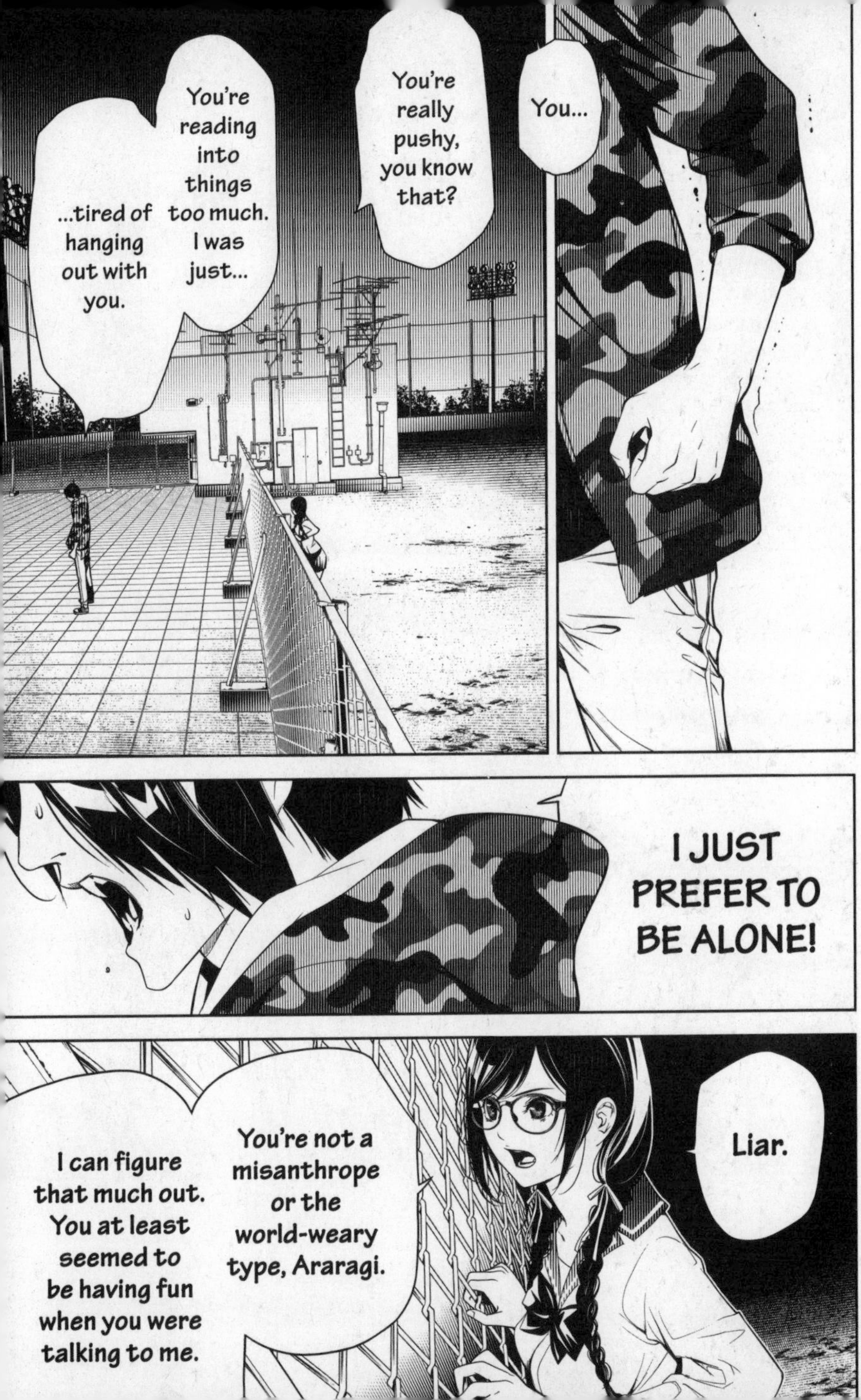
You...
You're really pushy, you know that?
You're reading into things too much. I was just...
...tired of hanging out with you.
I JUST PREFER TO BE ALONE!
Liar.
You're not a misanthrope or the world-weary type, Araragi.
I can figure that much out. You at least seemed to be having fun when you were talking to me.

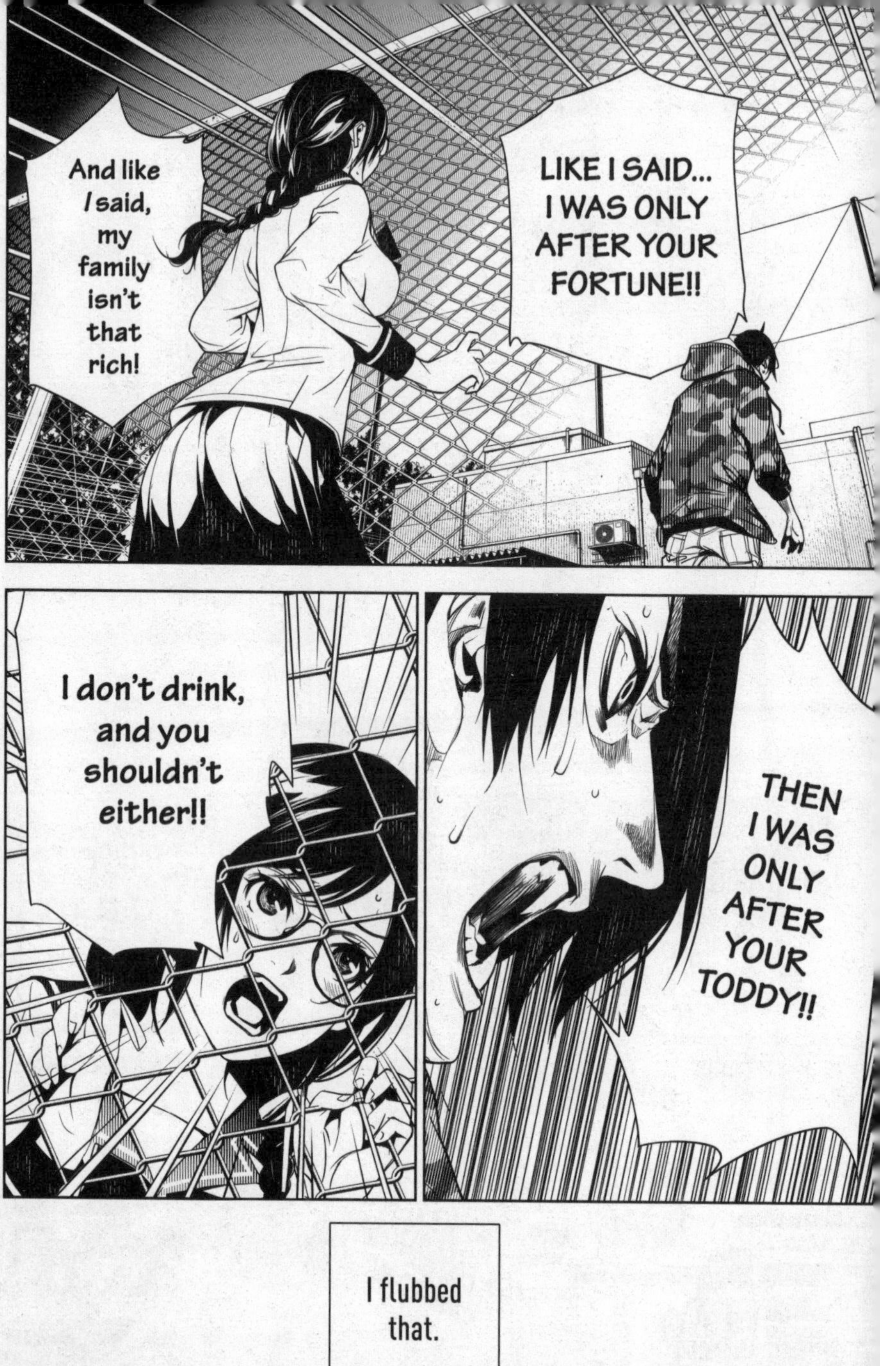
LIKE I SAID... I WAS ONLY AFTER YOUR FORTUNE!!
And like I said, my family isn't that rich!
THEN I WAS ONLY AFTER YOUR TODDY!!
I don't drink, and you shouldn't either!!
I flubbed that.

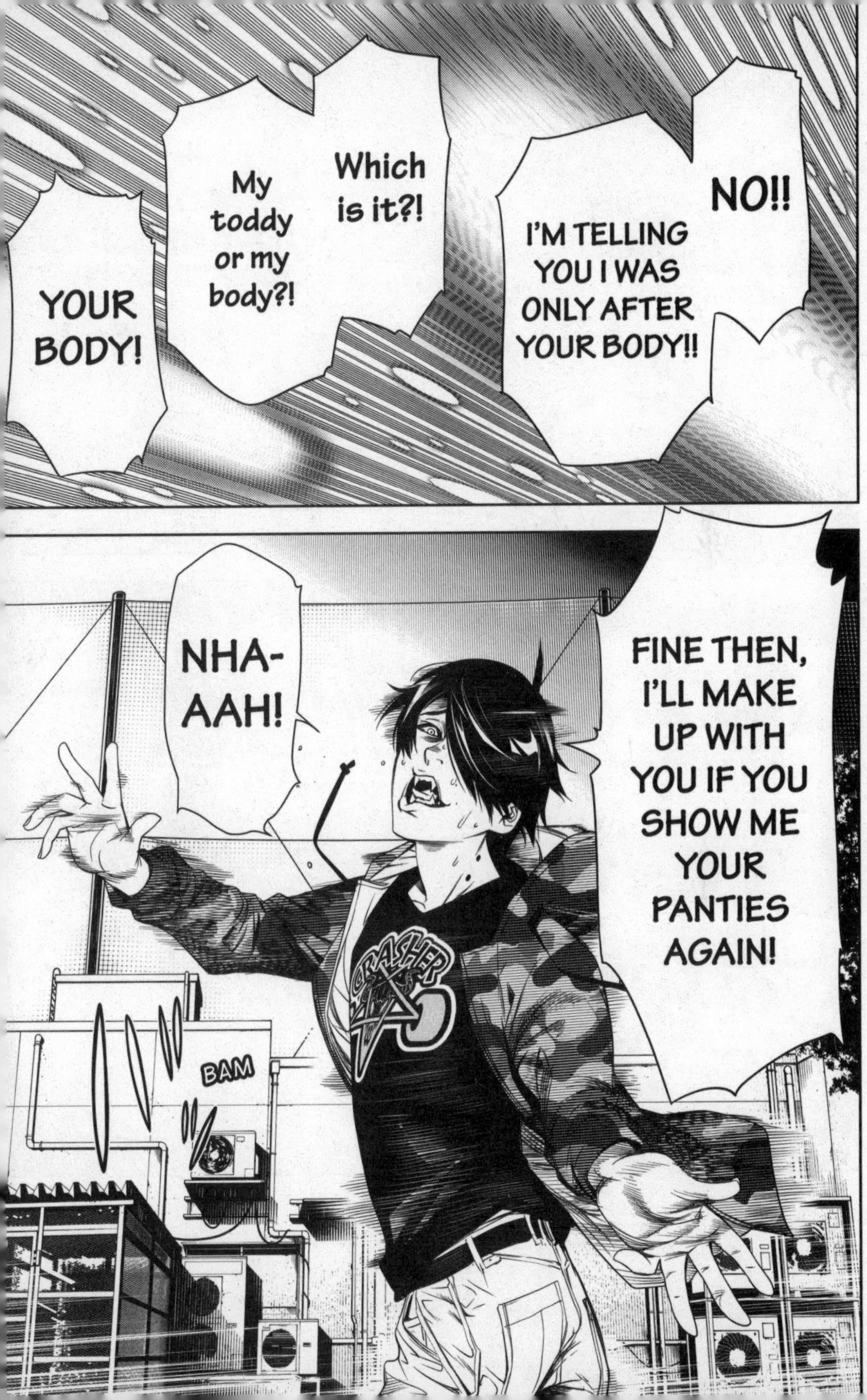
NO!!
I'M TELLING YOU I WAS ONLY AFTER YOUR BODY!!
Which is it?!
My toddy or my body?!
YOUR BODY!
FINE THEN, I'LL MAKE UP WITH YOU IF YOU SHOW ME YOUR PANTIES AGAIN!
NHA-AAH!
BAM
CRASHER

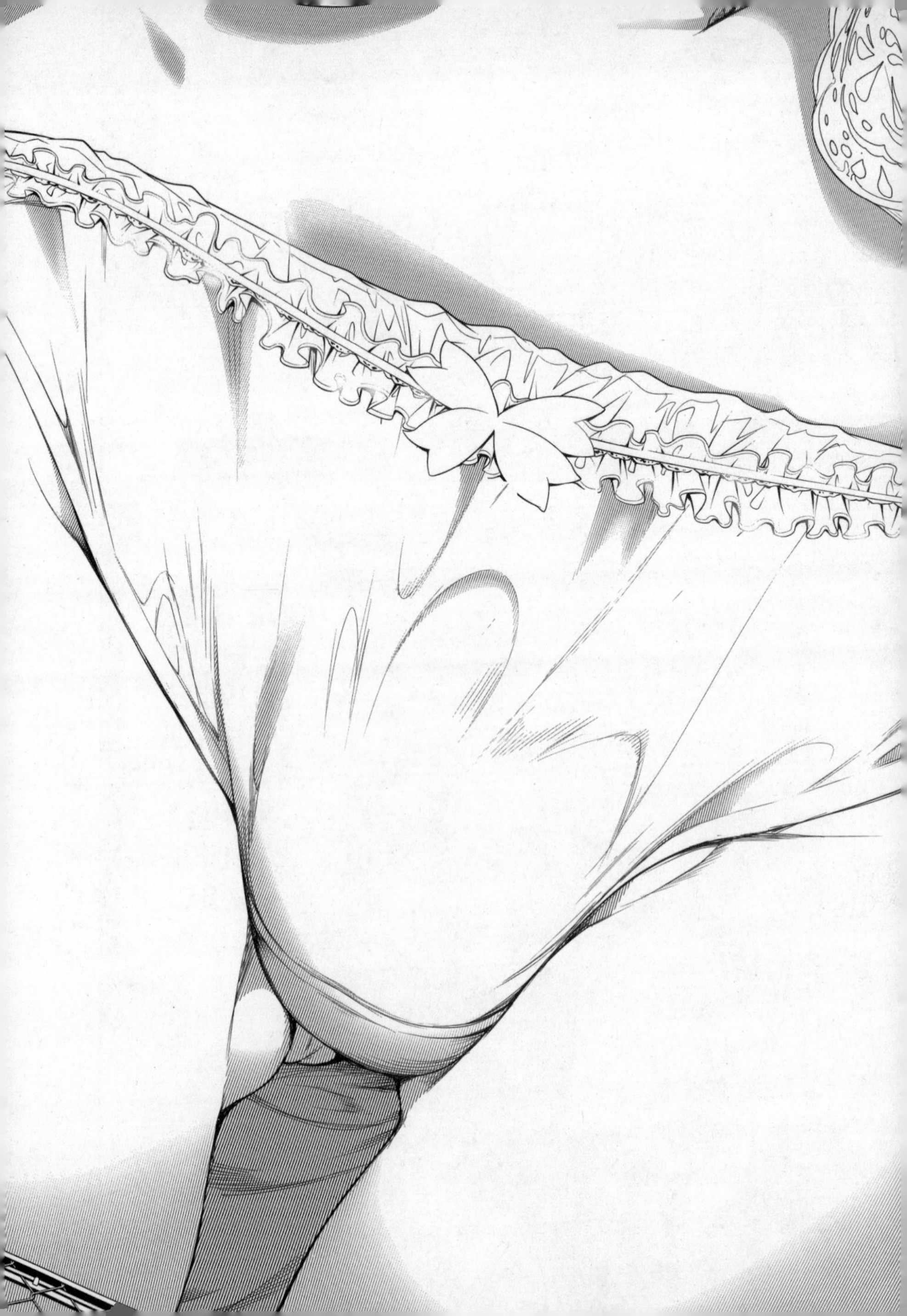

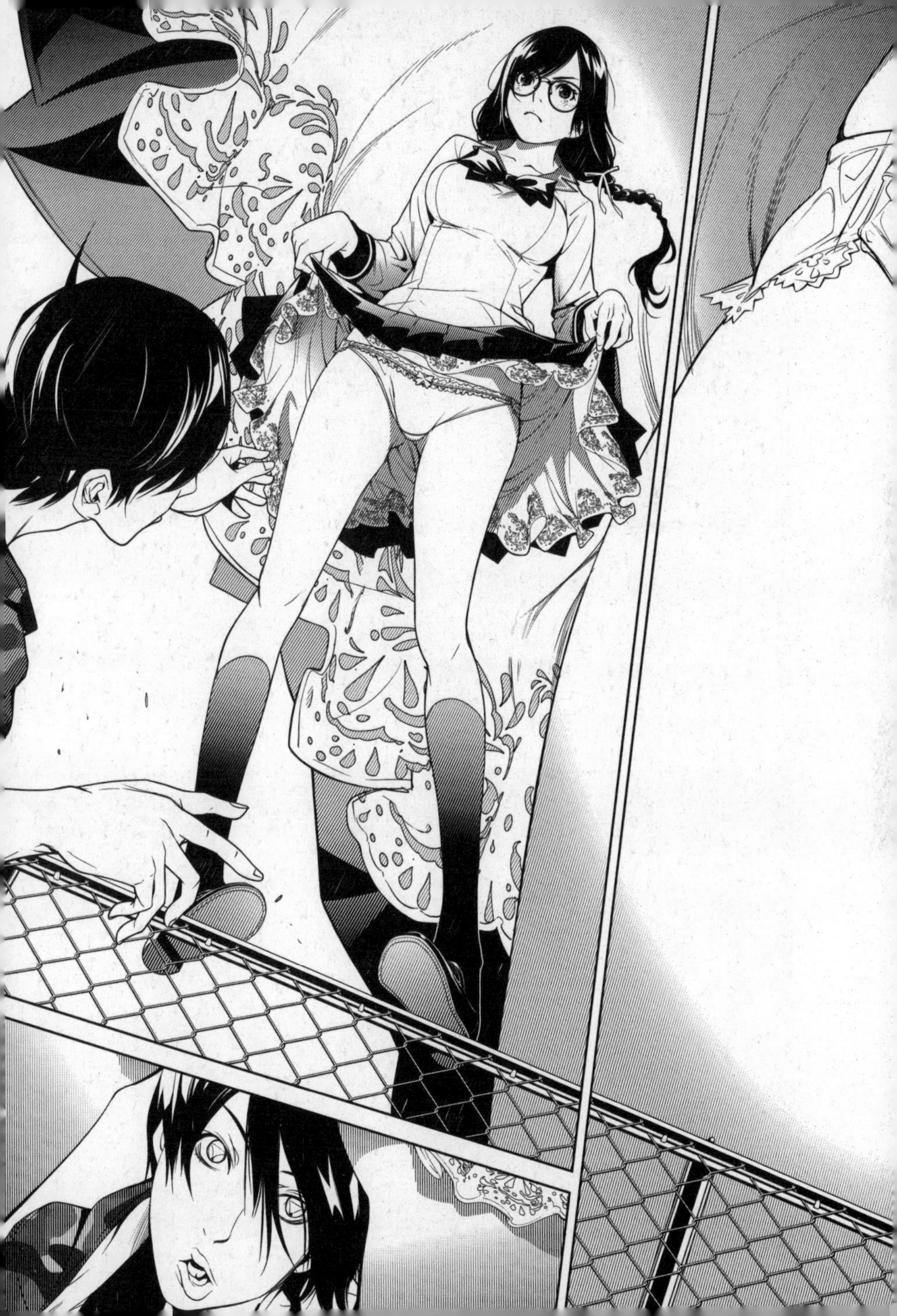

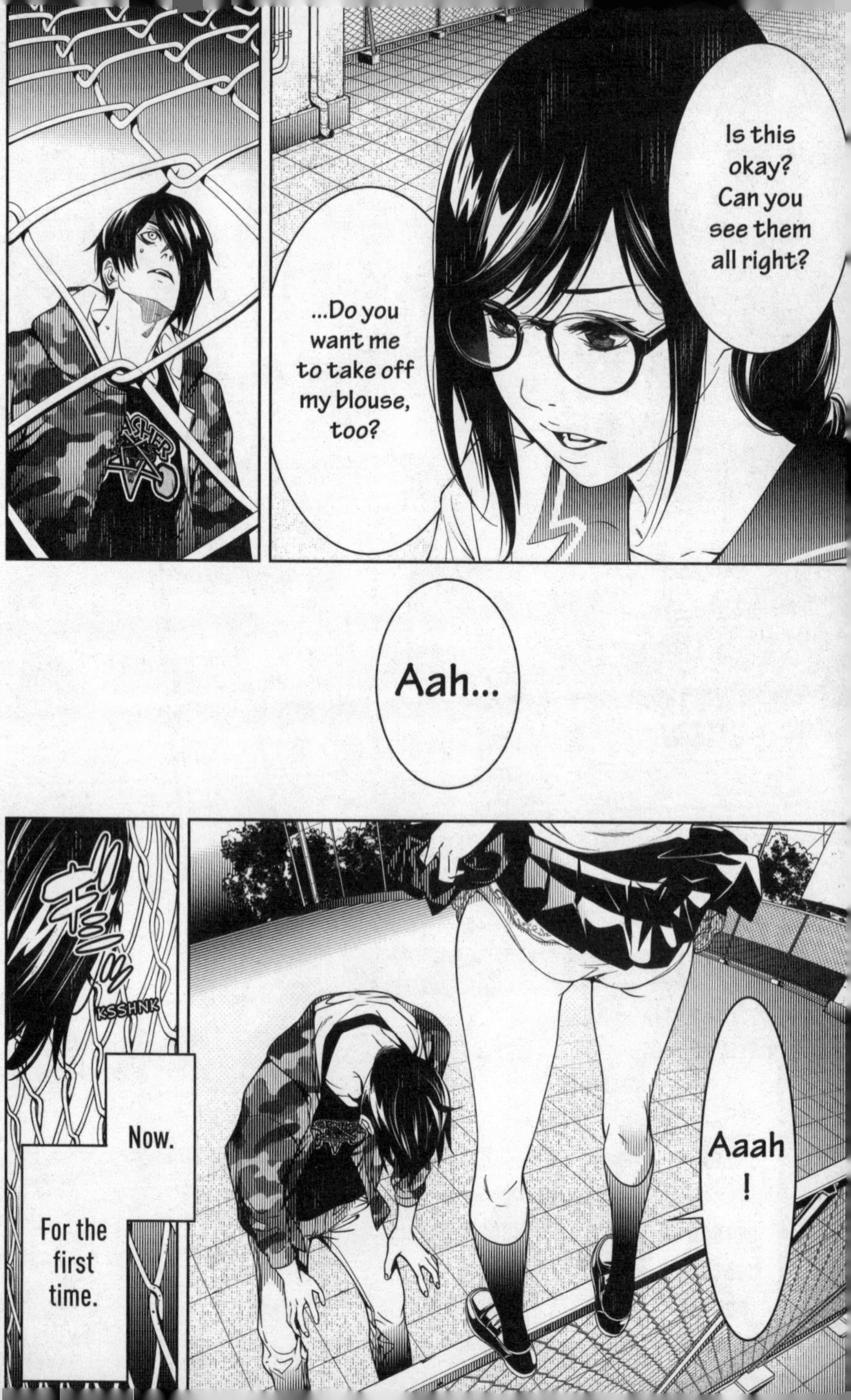
Is this okay? Can you see them all right?
...Do you want me to take off my blouse, too?
Aah...
Aaah !
KSSHNK
Now.
For the first time.

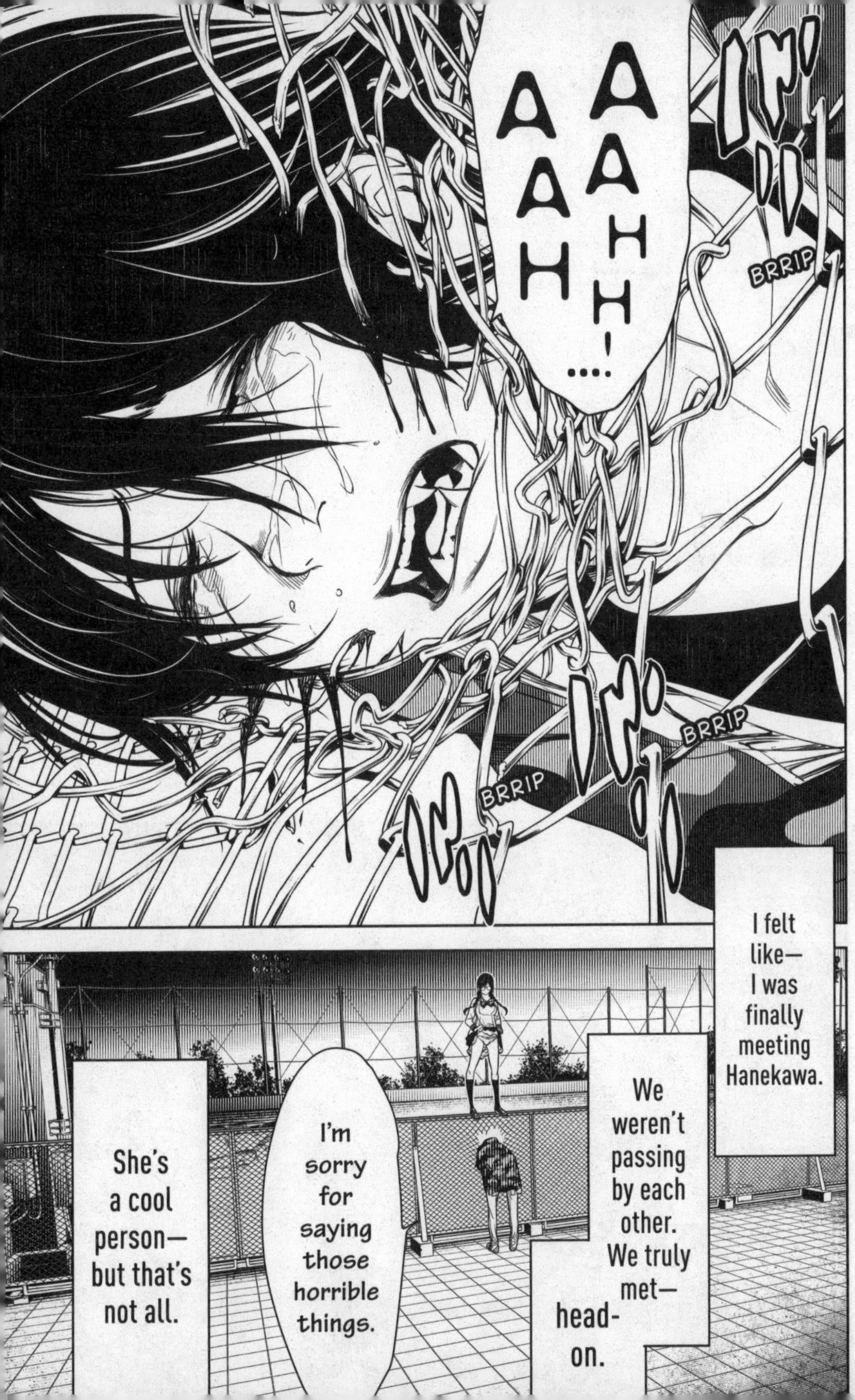
AAH AAH!....
BRRIP
BRRIP
BRRIP
I felt like— I was finally meeting Hanekawa.
We weren't passing by each other. We truly met—
head-on.
I'm sorry for saying those horrible things.
She's a cool person— but that's not all.

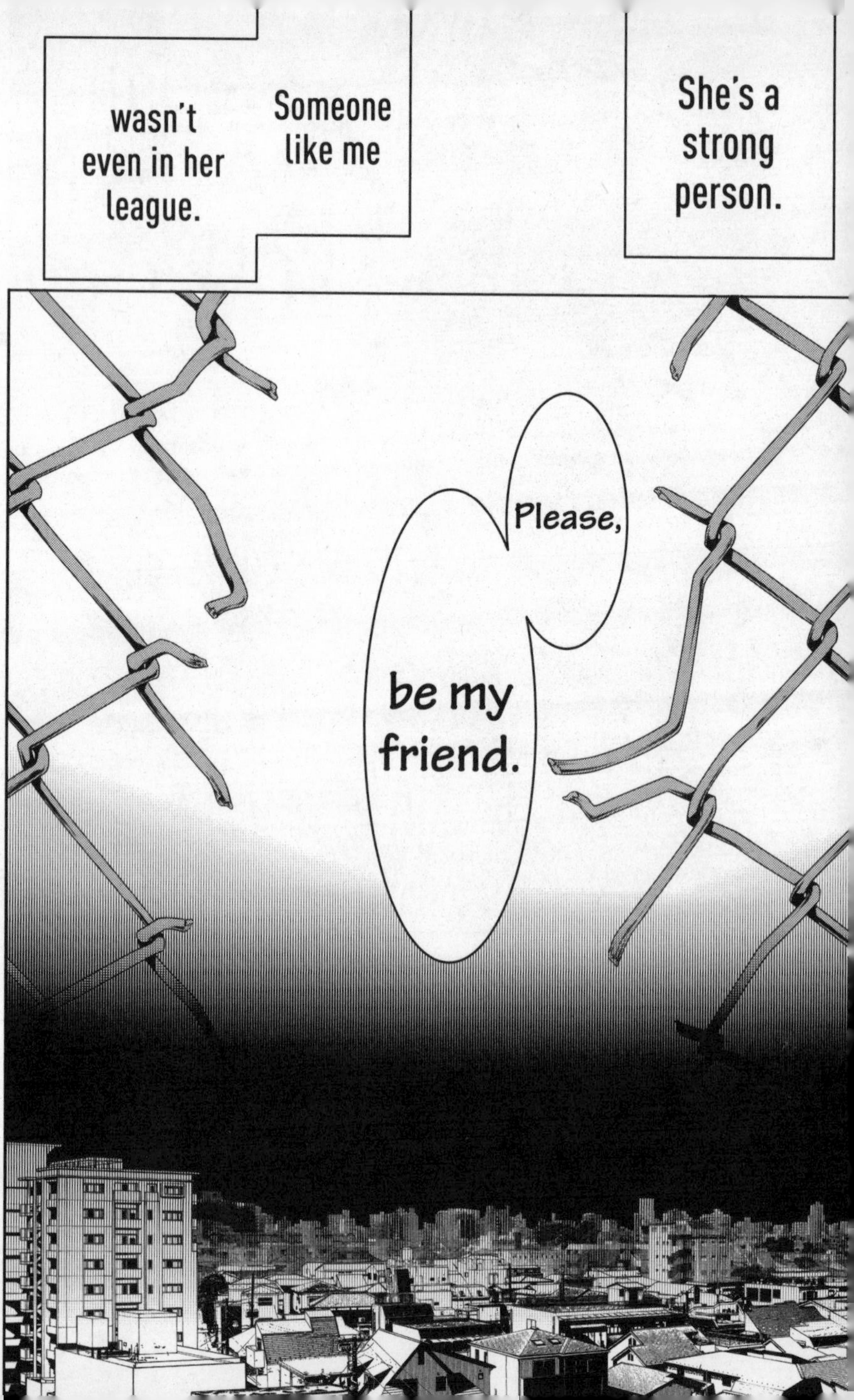
She's a strong person.
Someone like me wasn't even in her league.
Please, be my friend.

BAKEMONOGATARI

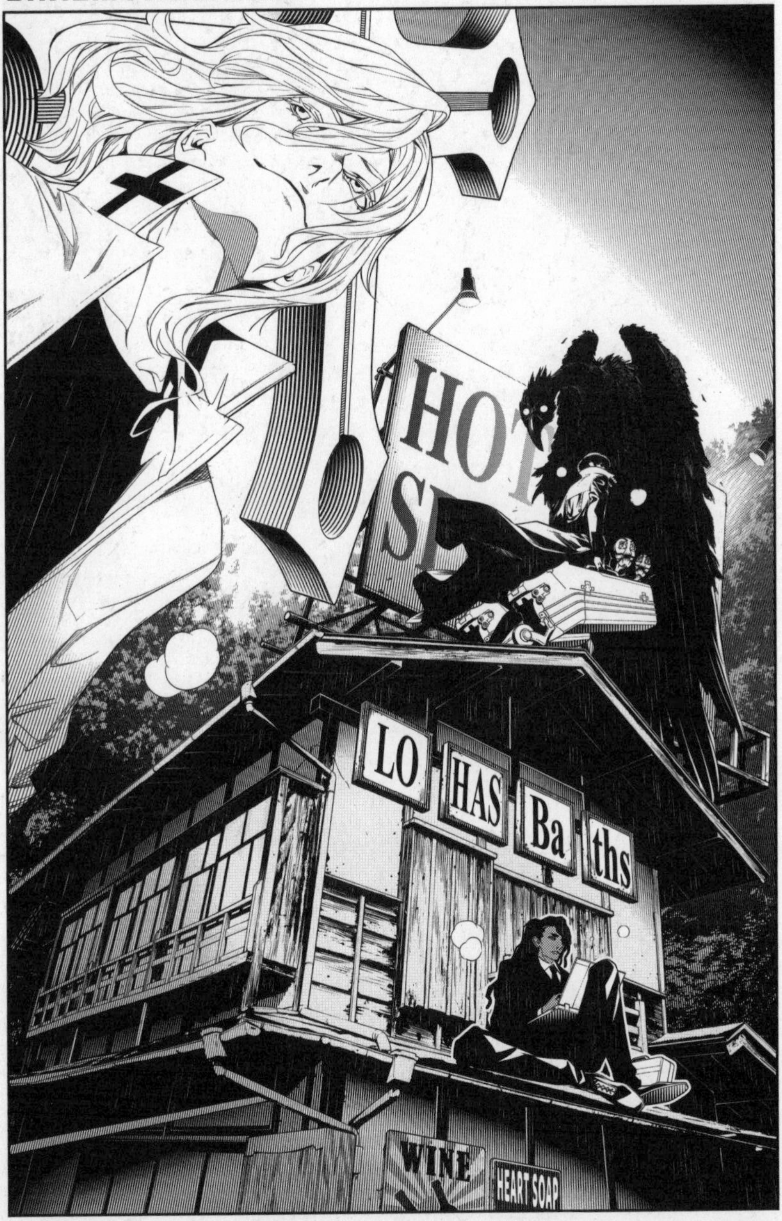
HOT
SP
LO HAS Ba ths
WINE
HEART SOAP

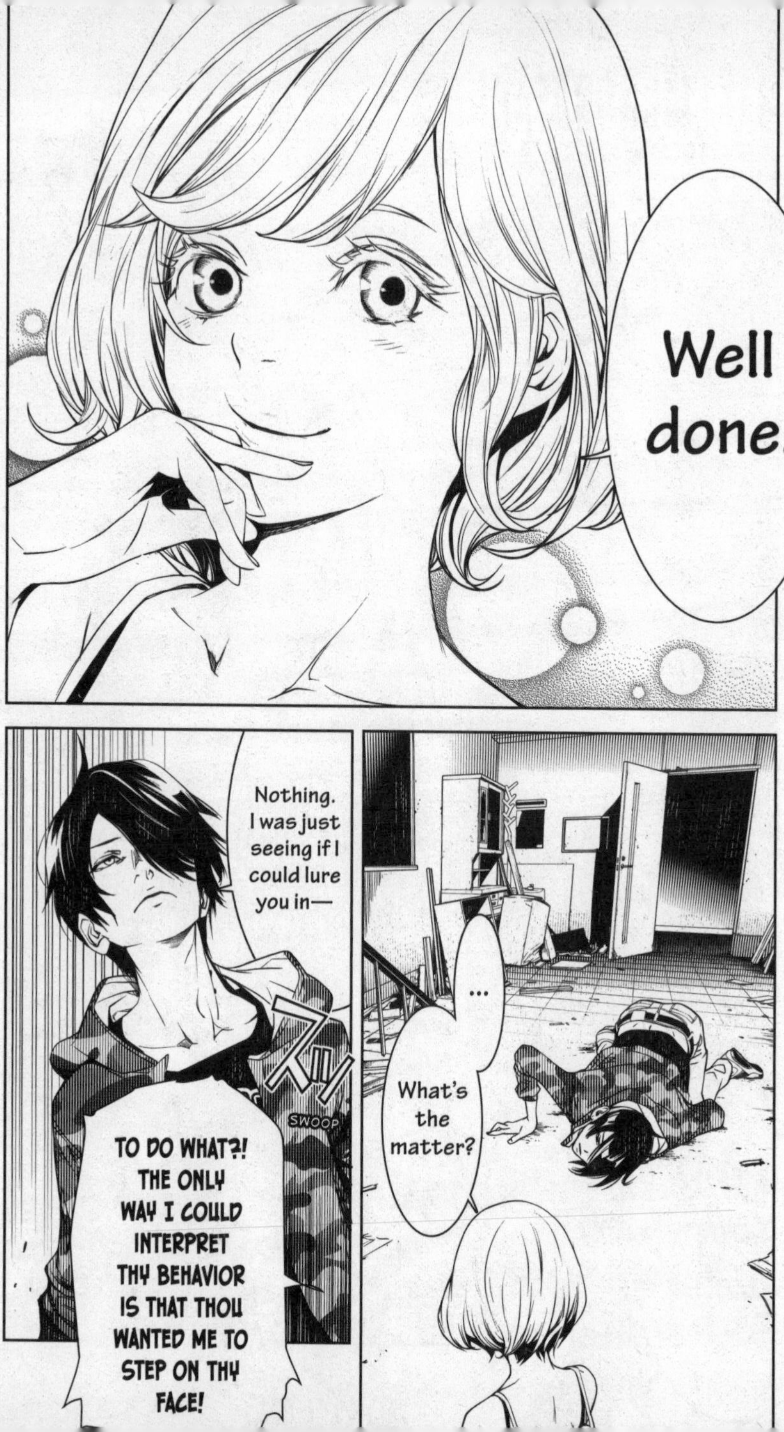
Well done.
...
What's the matter?
Nothing. I was just seeing if I could lure you in—
SWOOP
TO DO WHAT?! THE ONLY WAY I COULD INTERPRET THY BEHAVIOR IS THAT THOU WANTED ME TO STEP ON THY FACE!

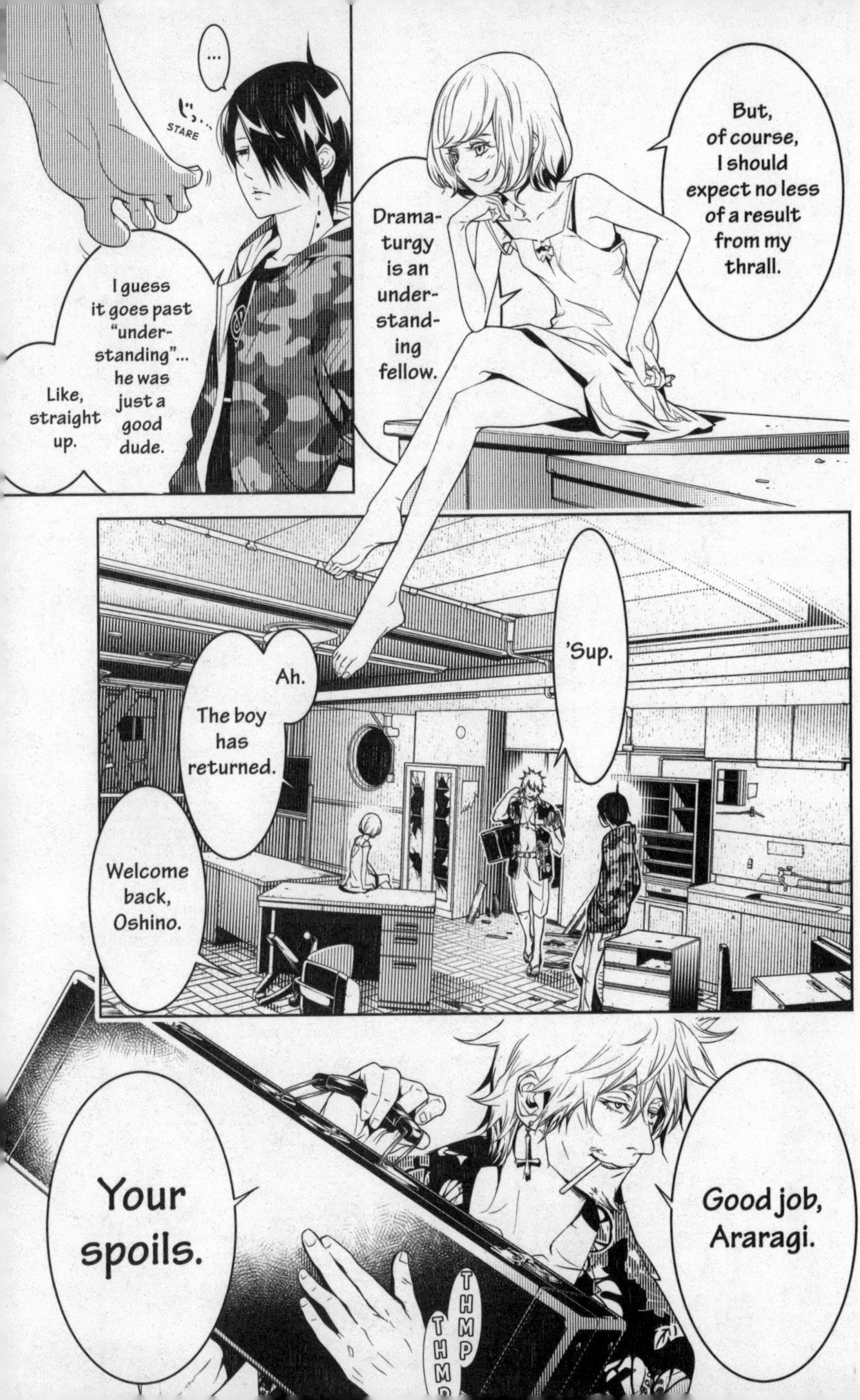
But, of course, I should expect no less of a result from my thrall.
Dramaturgy is an understanding fellow.
...
STARE
I guess it goes past "understanding"... he was just a good dude.
Like, straight up.
'Sup.
Ah.
The boy has returned.
Welcome back, Oshino.
Good job, Araragi.
Your spoils.
THMP
THMP

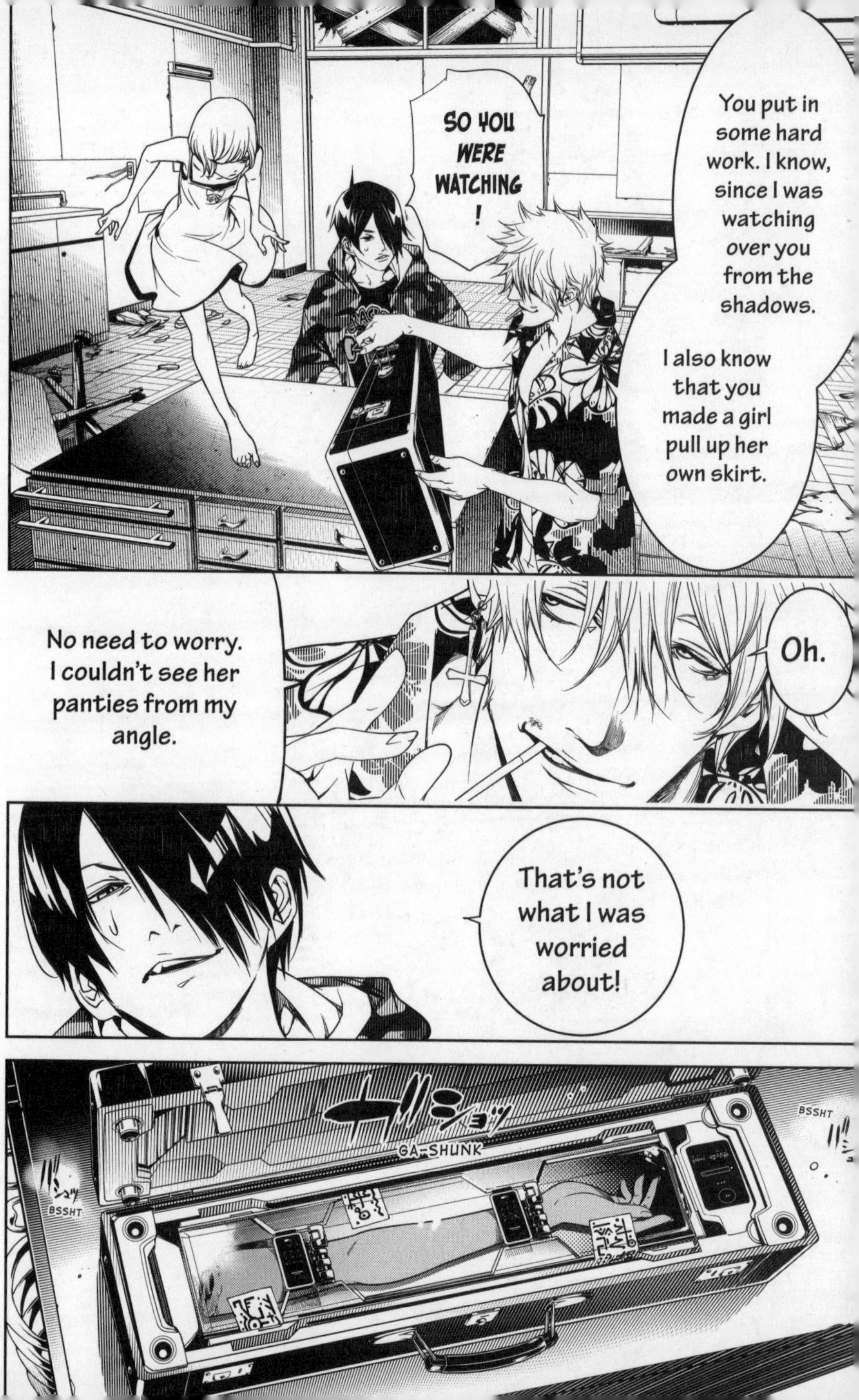
You put in some hard work. I know, since I was watching over you from the shadows.
I also know that you made a girl pull up her own skirt.
SO YOU WERE WATCHING!
Oh.
No need to worry. I couldn't see her panties from my angle.
That's not what I was worried about!
BSSHT
GA-SHUNK
BSSHT

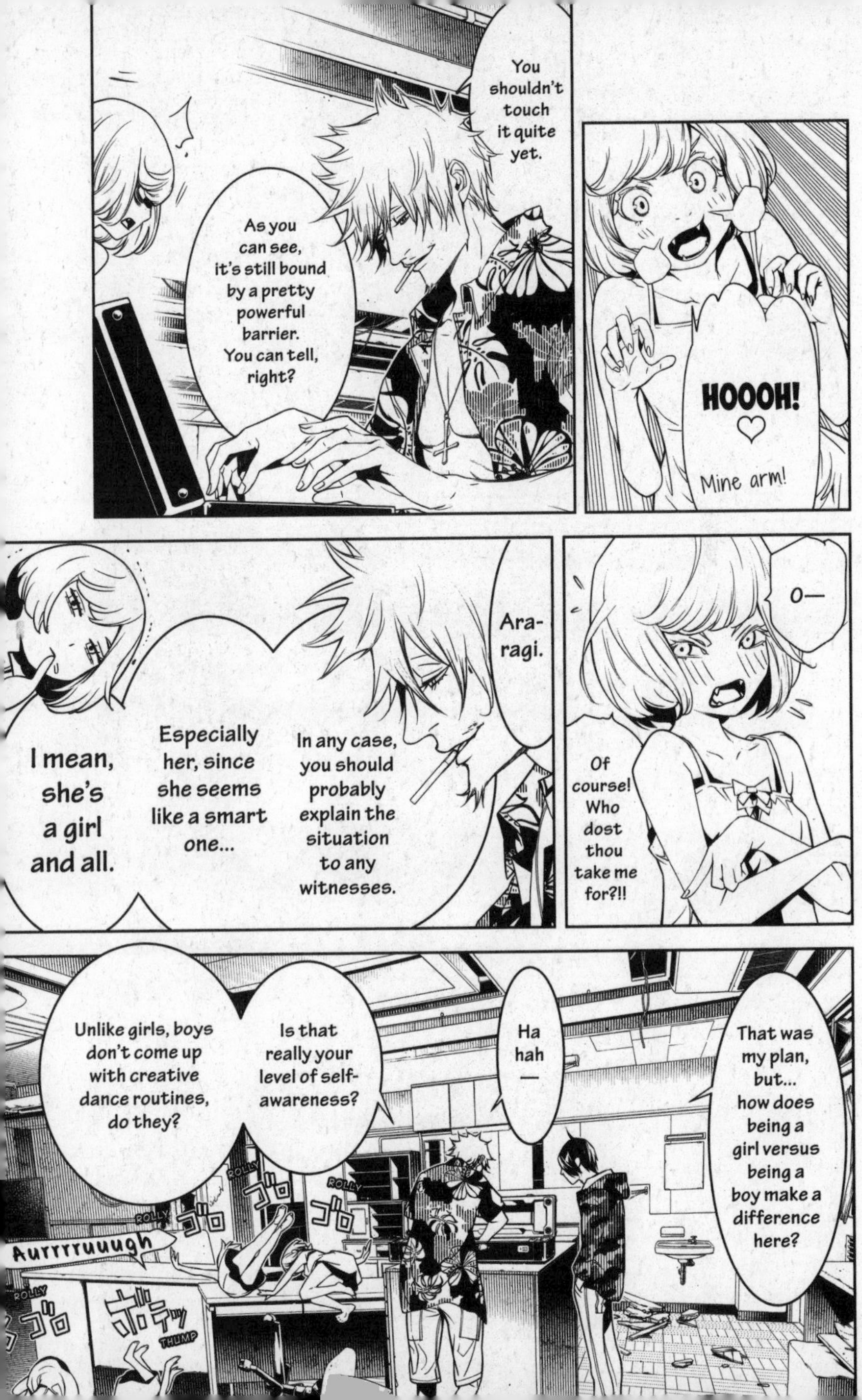
HOOOH! ♥
Mine arm!
You shouldn't touch it quite yet.
As you can see, it's still bound by a pretty powerful barrier. You can tell, right?
O—
Of course! Who dost thou take me for?!!
Ara-ragi.
In any case, you should probably explain the situation to any witnesses.
Especially her, since she seems like a smart one...
I mean, she's a girl and all.
That was my plan, but... how does being a girl versus being a boy make a difference here?
Ha hah—
Is that really your level of self-awareness?
Unlike girls, boys don't come up with creative dance routines, do they?
ROLLY
ROLLY
ROLLY
Aurrrruuugh
ROLLY
THUMP

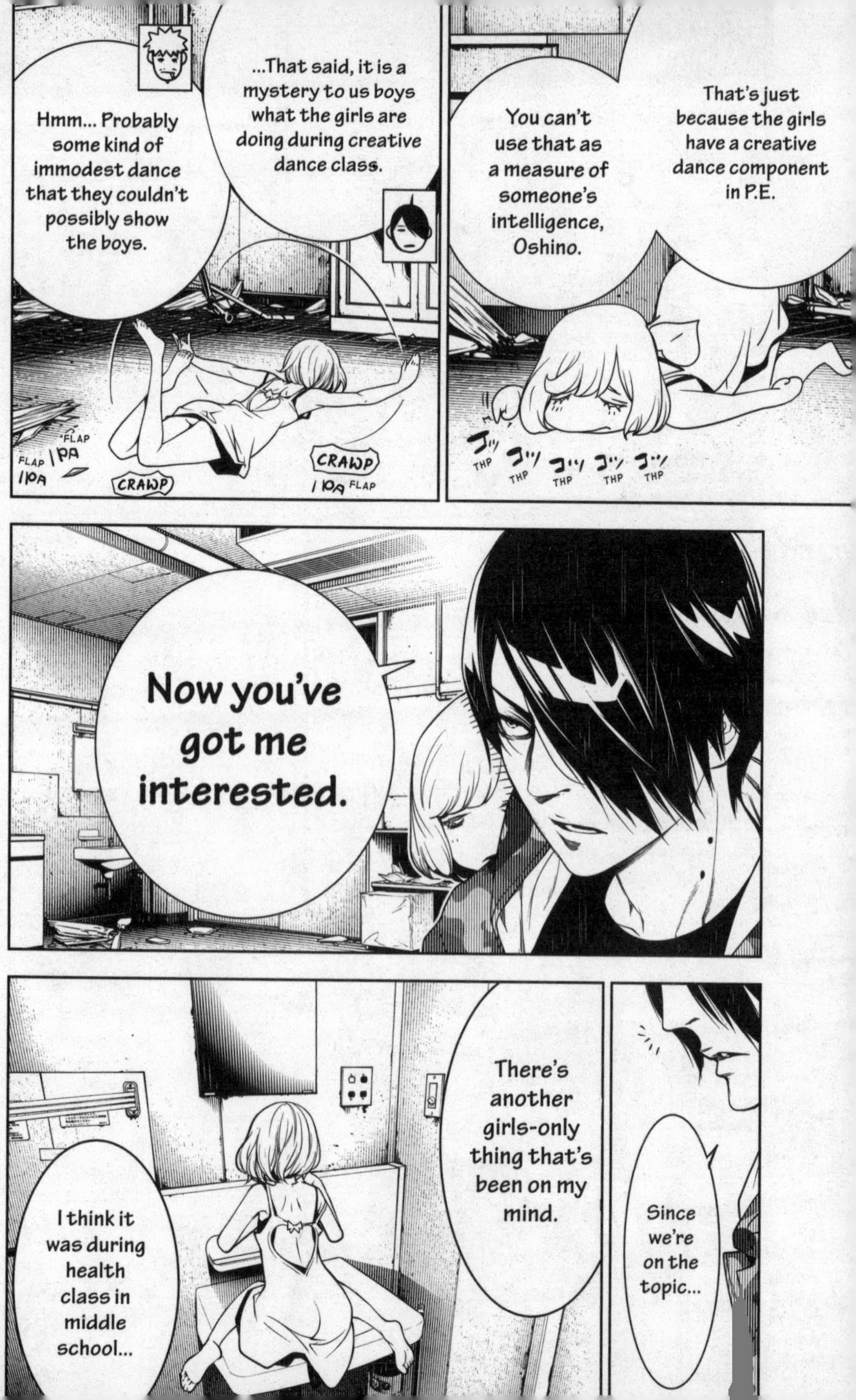
That's just because the girls have a creative dance component in P.E.
You can't use that as a measure of someone's intelligence, Oshino.
ゴッ THP ゴッ THP ゴッ THP ゴッ THP ゴッ THP
...That said, it is a mystery to us boys what the girls are doing during creative dance class.
Hmm... Probably some kind of immodest dance that they couldn't possibly show the boys.
CRAWP
FLAP
FLAP
CRAWP
FLAP
Now you've got me interested.
Since we're on the topic...
There's another girls-only thing that's been on my mind.
I think it was during health class in middle school...

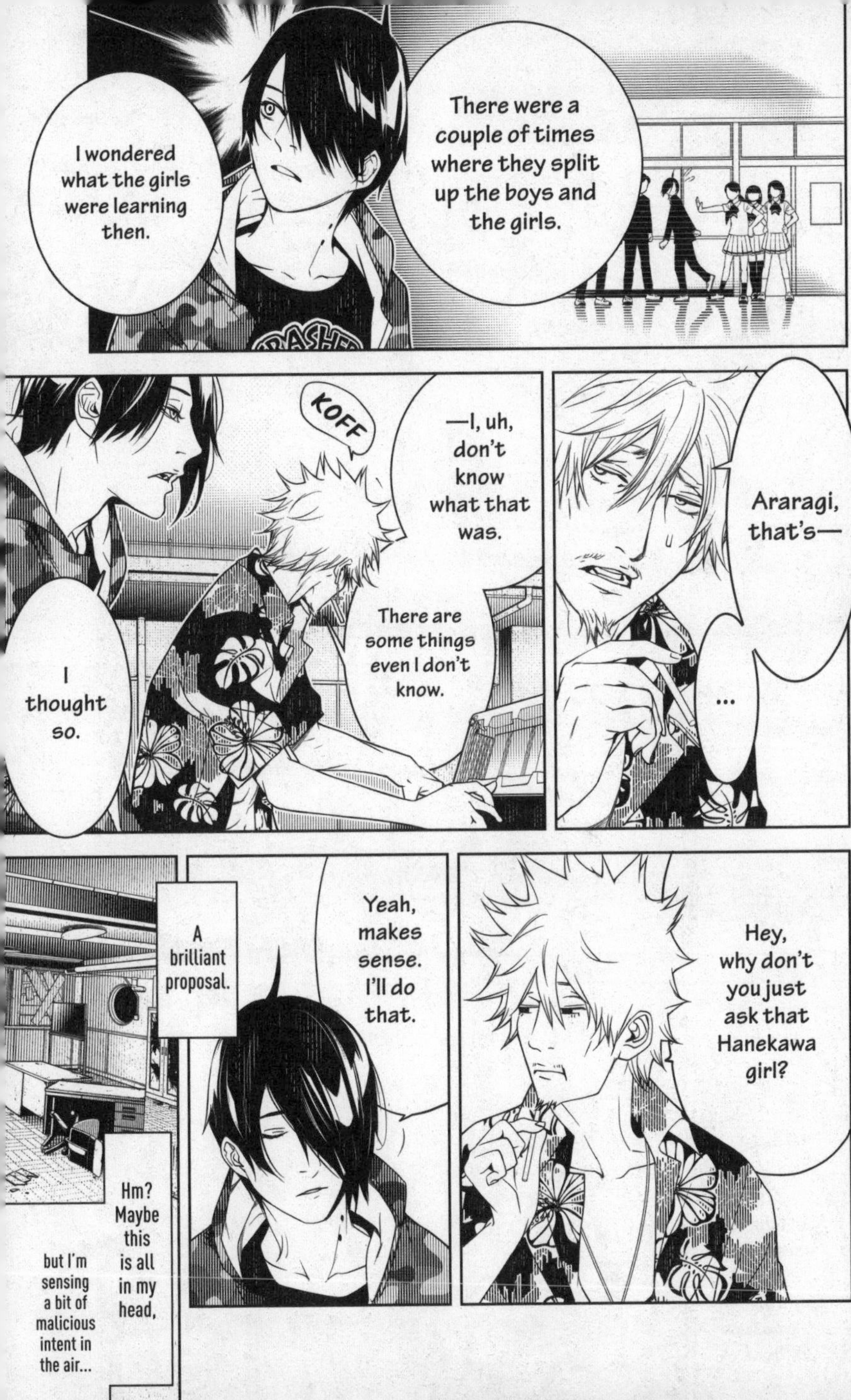
There were a couple of times where they split up the boys and the girls.
I wondered what the girls were learning then.
Araragi, that's—
...
KOFF
—I, uh, don't know what that was.
There are some things even I don't know.
I thought so.
Hey, why don't you just ask that Hanekawa girl?
Yeah, makes sense. I'll *do* that.
A brilliant proposal.
Hm? Maybe this is all in my head,
but I'm sensing a bit of malicious intent in the air...

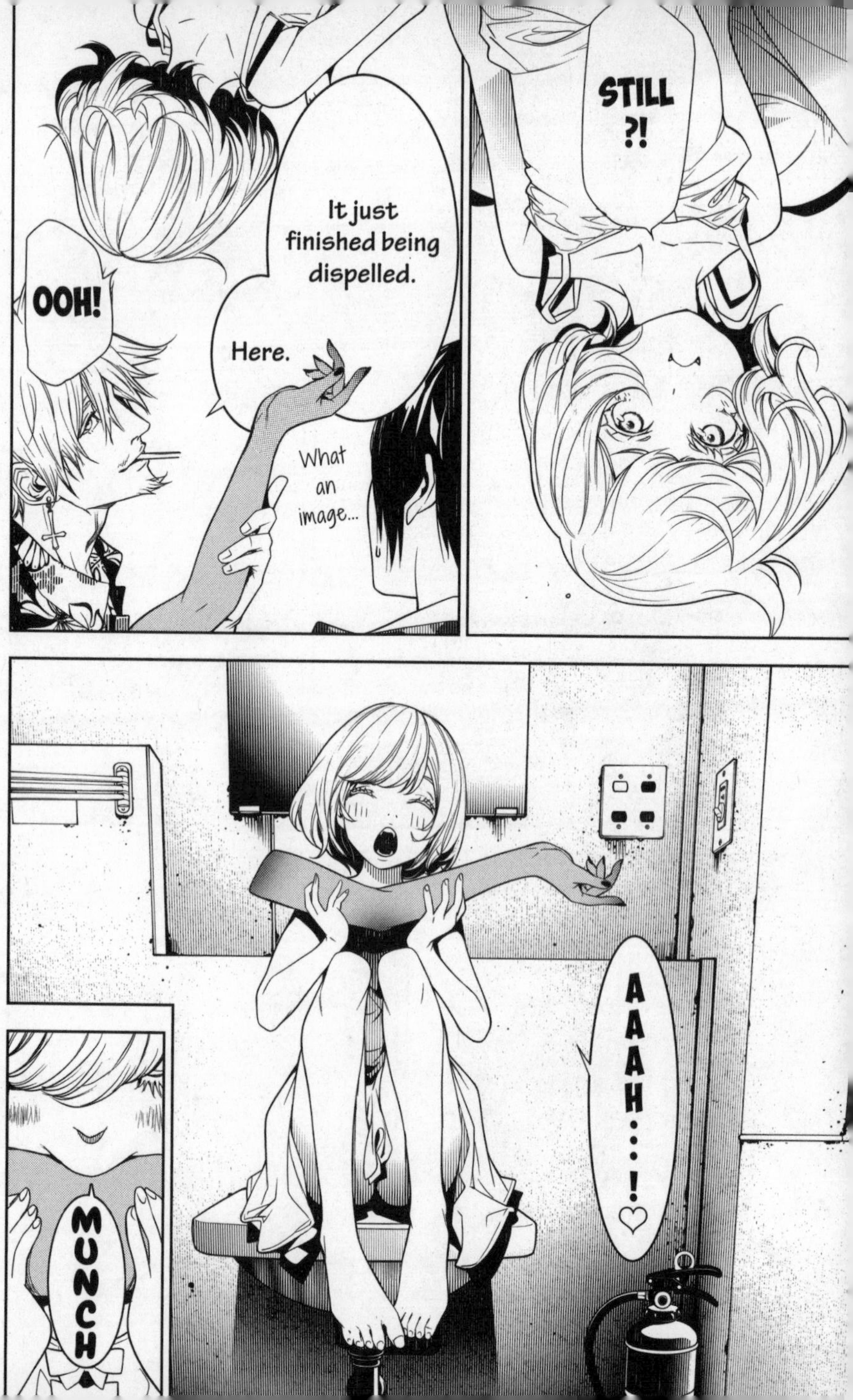
STILL ?!
It just finished being dispelled.
Here.
OOH!
What an image...
AAAH...!♡
MUNCH

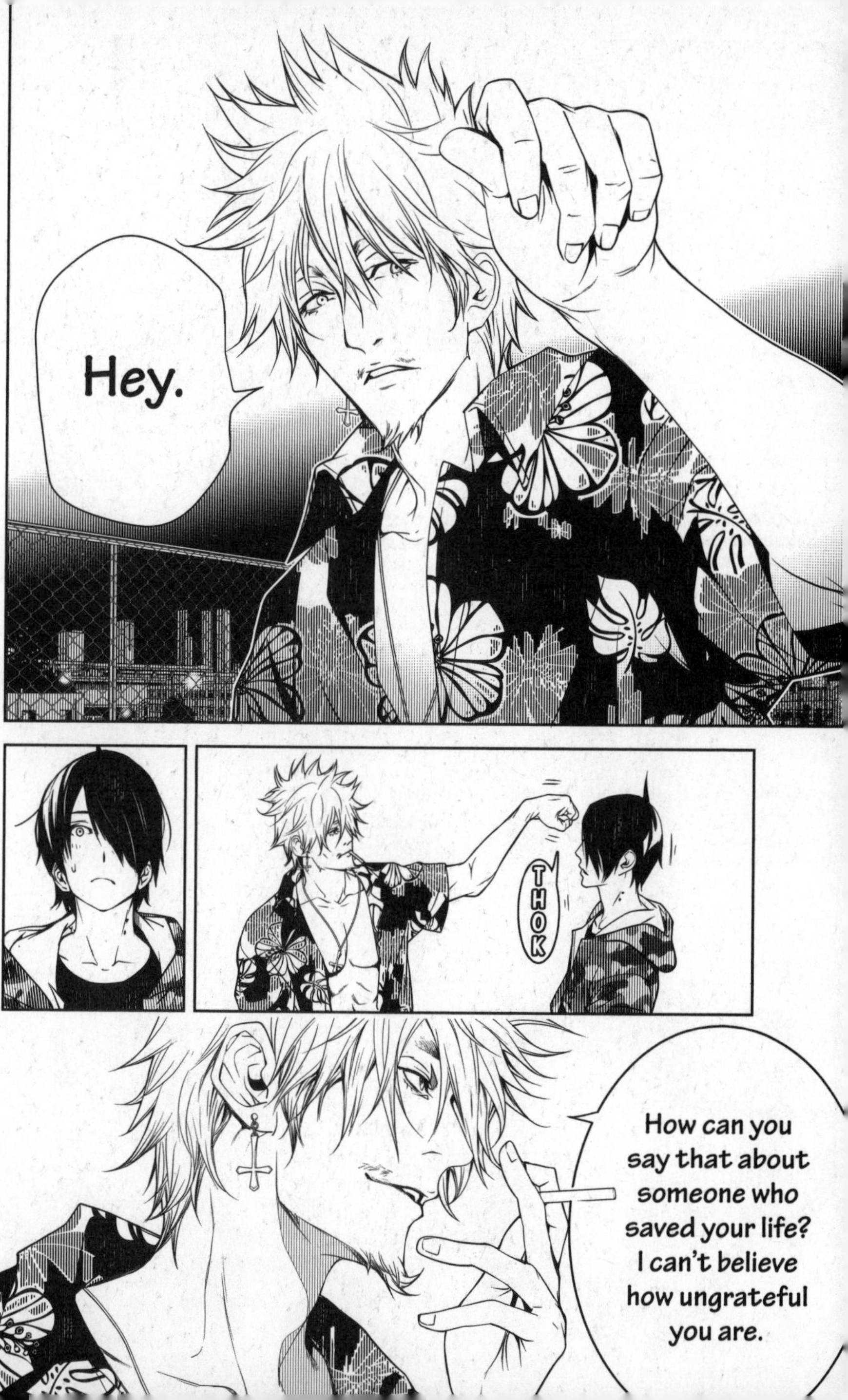
Hey.
THOK
How can you say that about someone who saved your life? I can't believe how ungrateful you are.

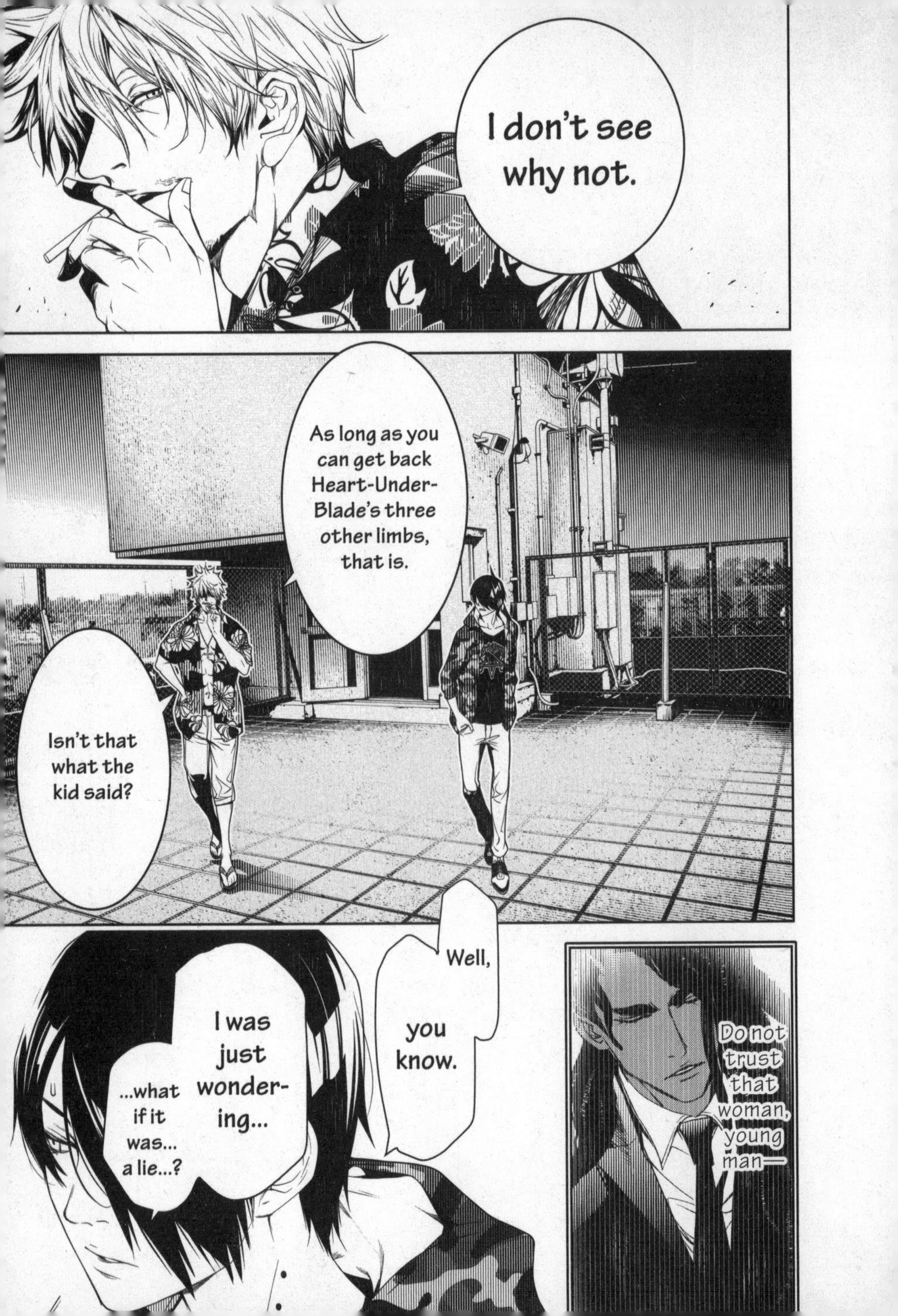
I don't see why not.
As long as you can get back Heart-Under-Blade's three other limbs, that is.
Isn't that what the kid said?
Do not trust that woman, young man—
Well, you know.
I was just wondering...
...what if it was... a lie...?

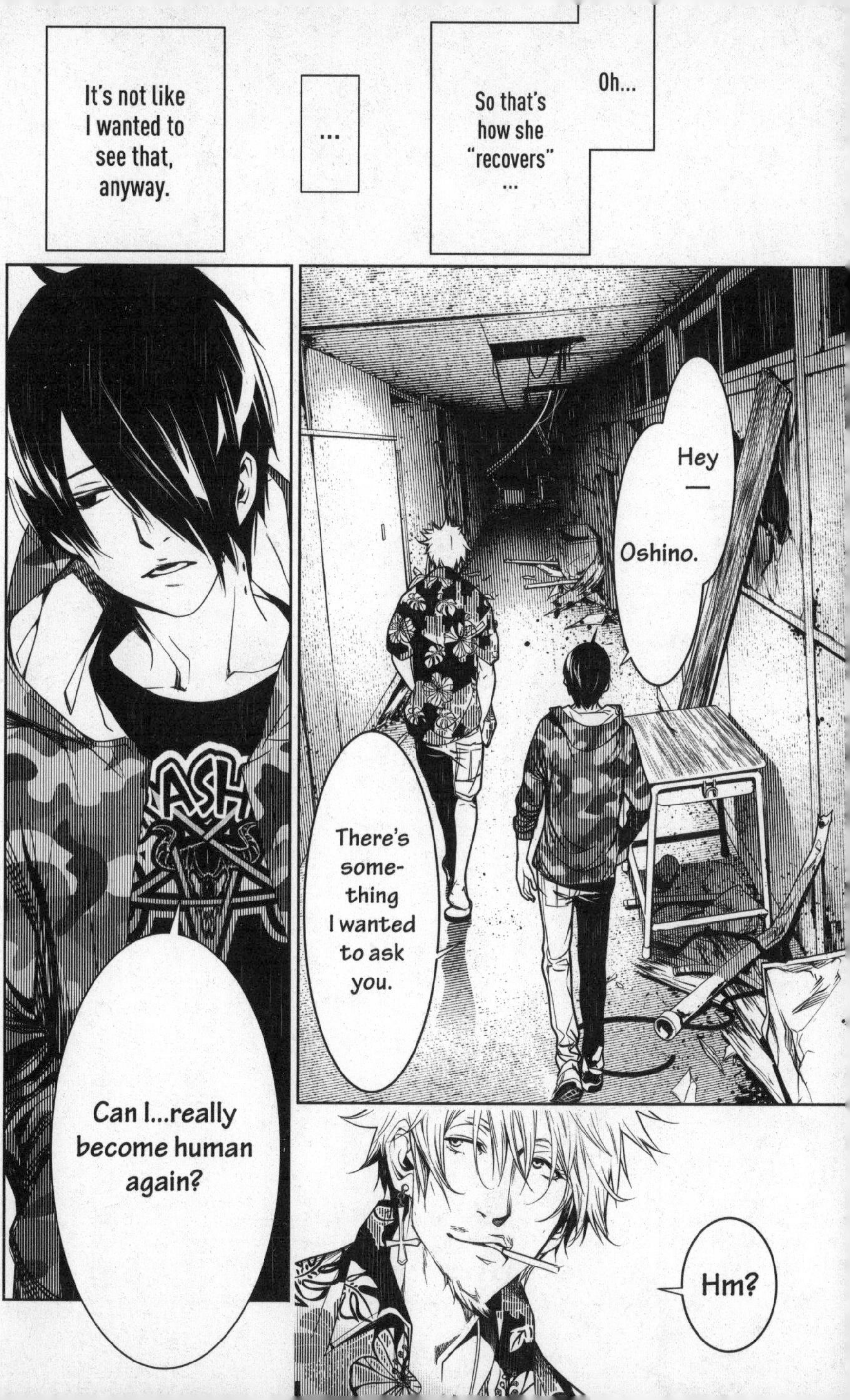
Oh...
So that's how she "recovers" ...
...
It's not like I wanted to see that, anyway.
Hey — Oshino.
There's some-thing I wanted to ask you.
Hm?
Can I...really become human again?

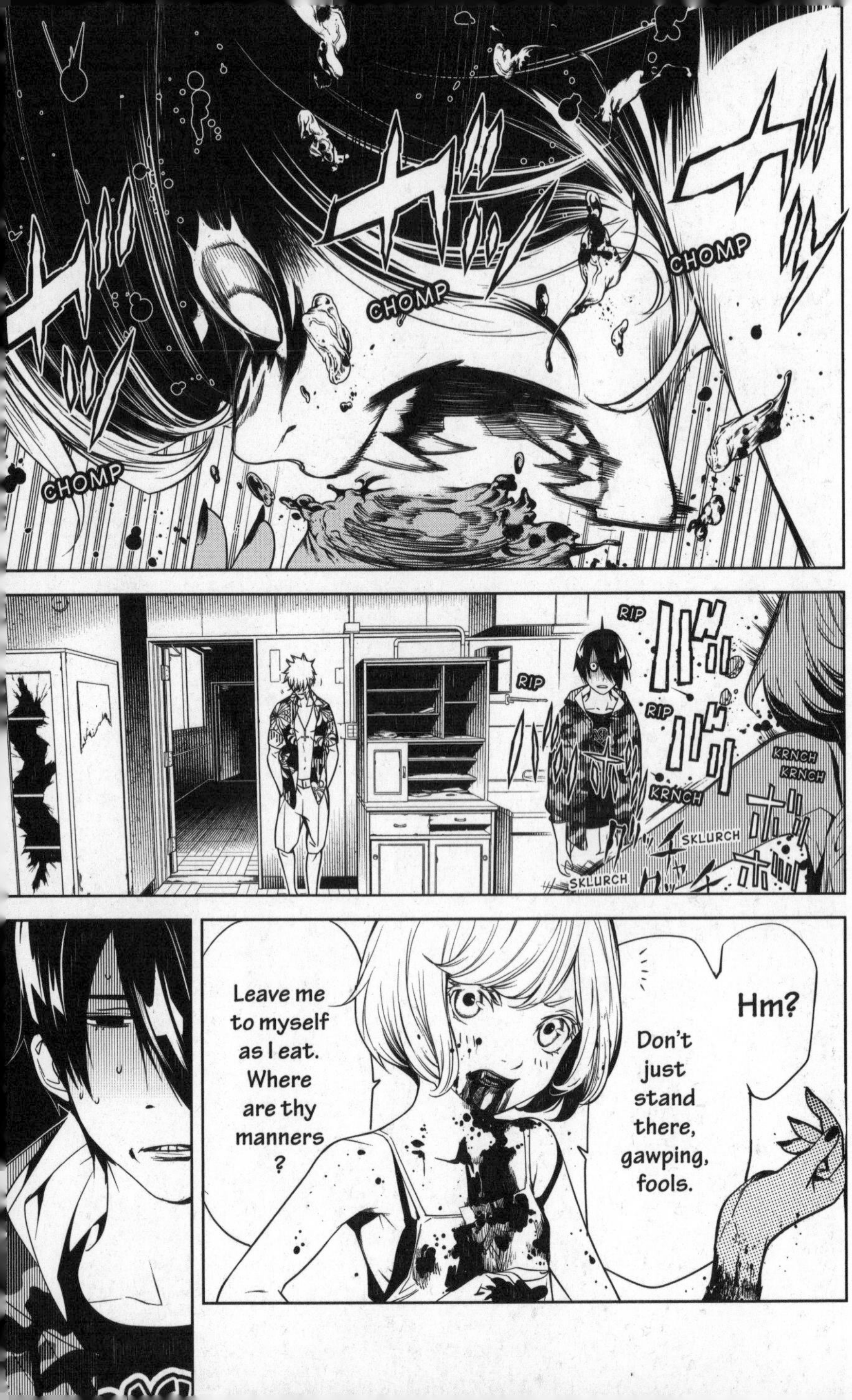
CHOMP
CHOMP
CHOMP
RIP
RIP
RIP
KRNCH
KRNCH
KRNCH
SKLURCH
SKLURCH
Hm?
Don't just stand there, gawping, fools.
Leave me to myself as I eat. Where are thy manners?

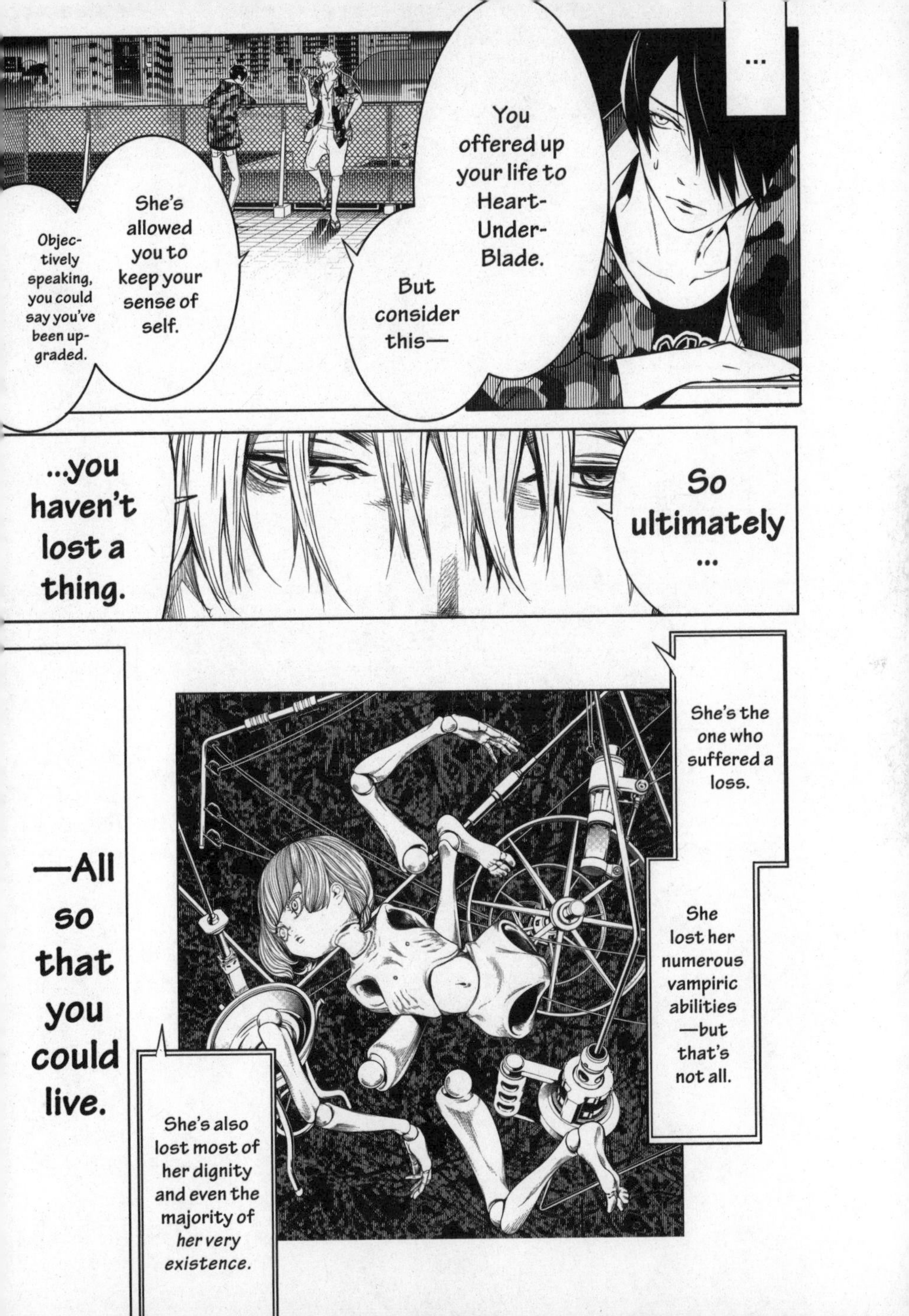
...
You offered up your life to Heart-Under-Blade.
But consider this—
She's allowed you to keep your sense of self.
Objectively speaking, you could say you've been upgraded.
So ultimately...
...you haven't lost a thing.
She's the one who suffered a loss.
She lost her numerous vampiric abilities—but that's not all.
She's also lost most of her dignity and even the majority of her very existence.
—All so that you could live.

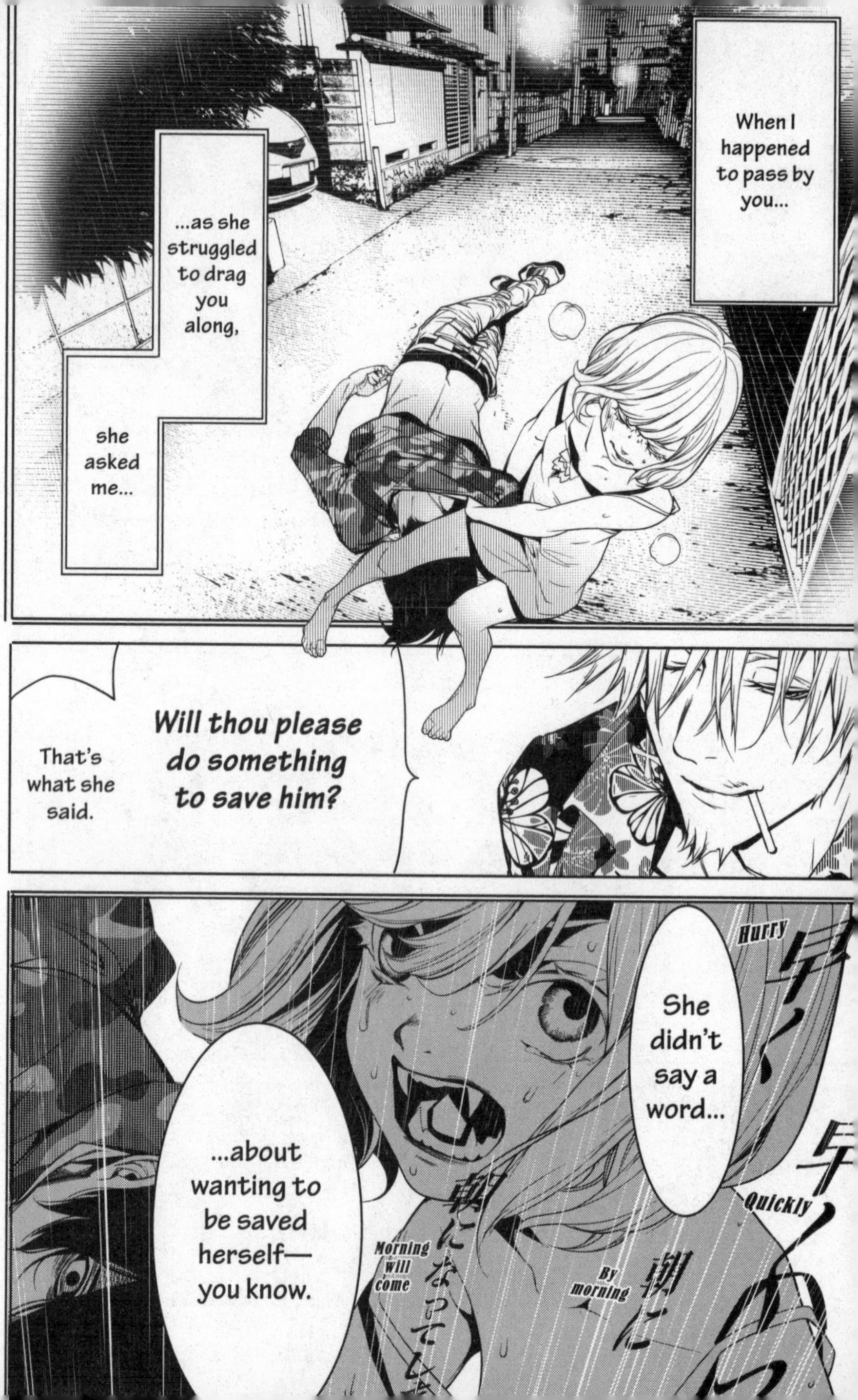
When I happened to pass by you...
...as she struggled to drag you along,
she asked me...
Will thou please do something to save him?
That's what she said.
Hurry
She didn't say a word...
Quickly
By morning
...about wanting to be saved herself— you know.
Morning will come

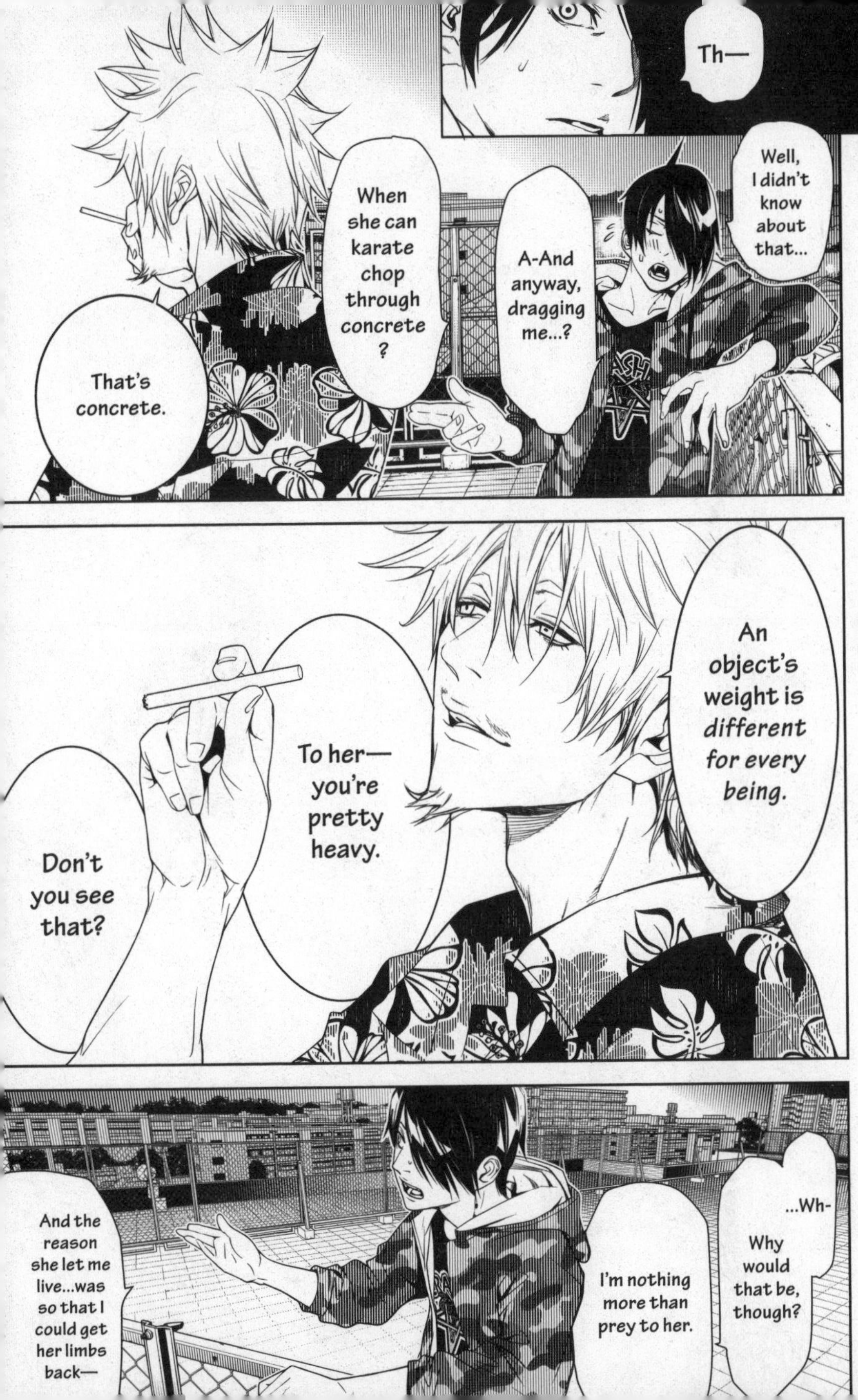
Th—
Well, I didn't know about that...
A-And anyway, dragging me...?
When she can karate chop through concrete ?
That's concrete.
An object's weight is different for every being.
To her— you're pretty heavy.
Don't you see that?
...Wh-
Why would that be, though?
I'm nothing more than prey to her.
And the reason she let me live...was so that I could get her limbs back—

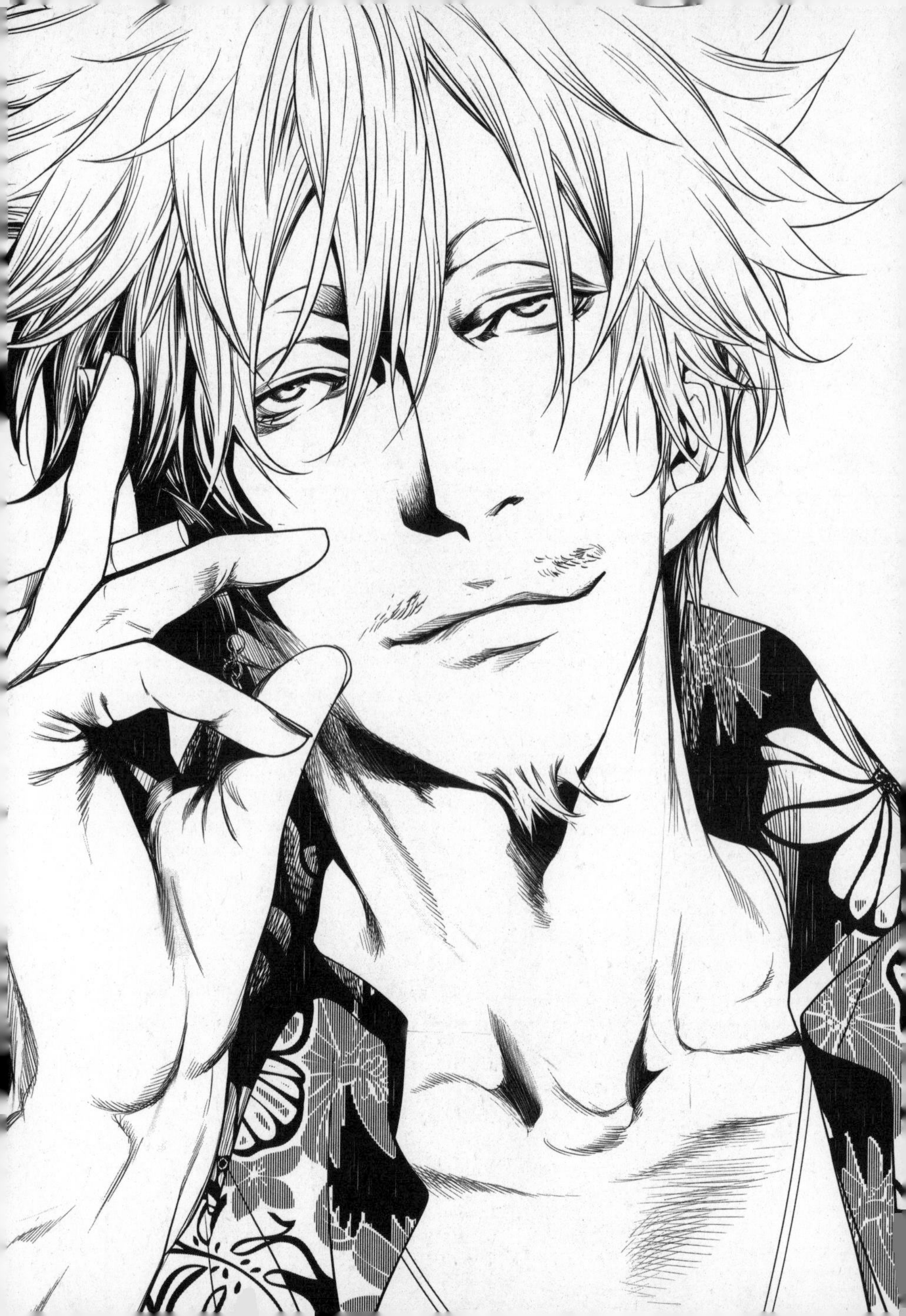

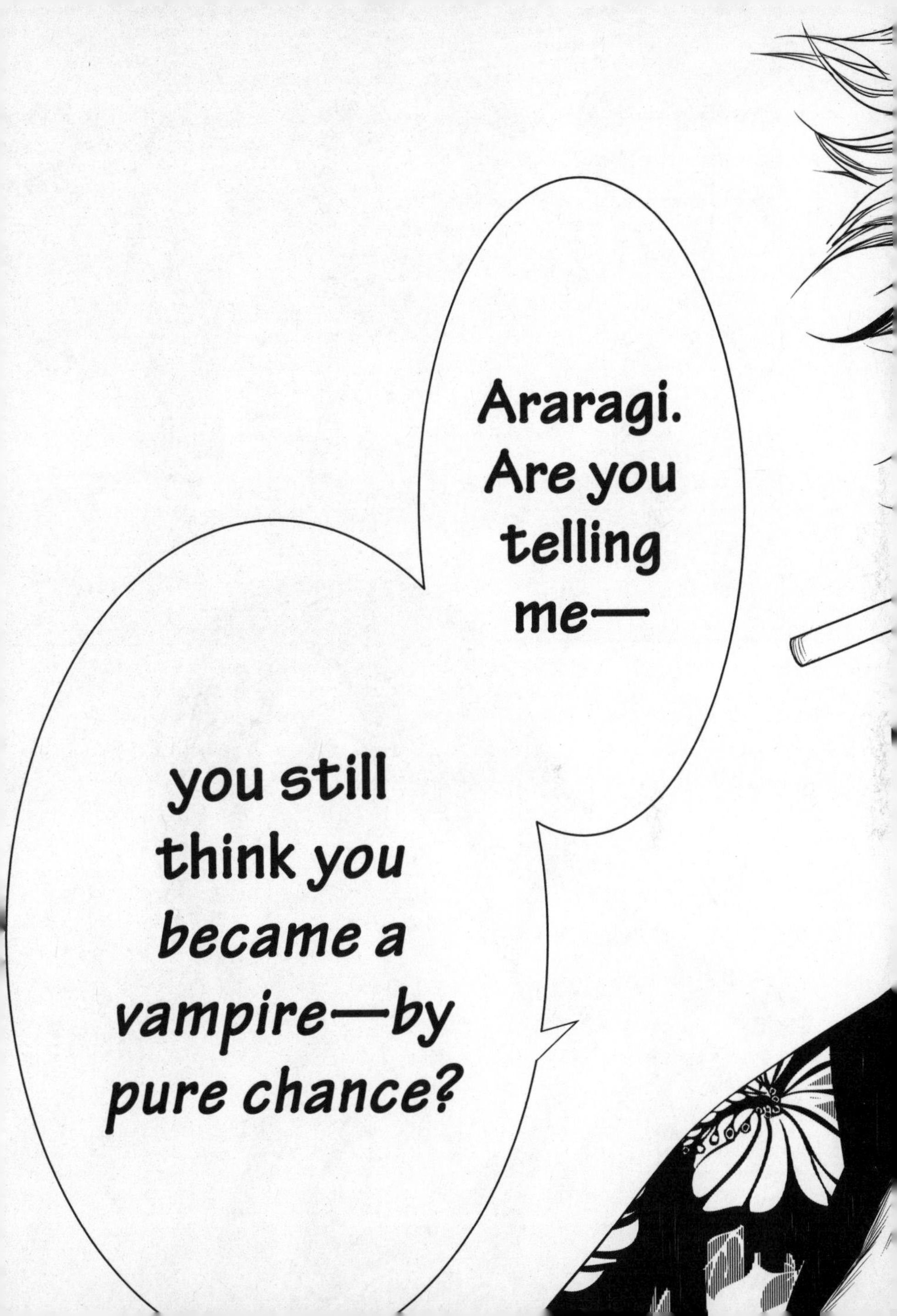
Araragi. Are you telling me—
you still think you became a vampire—by pure chance?

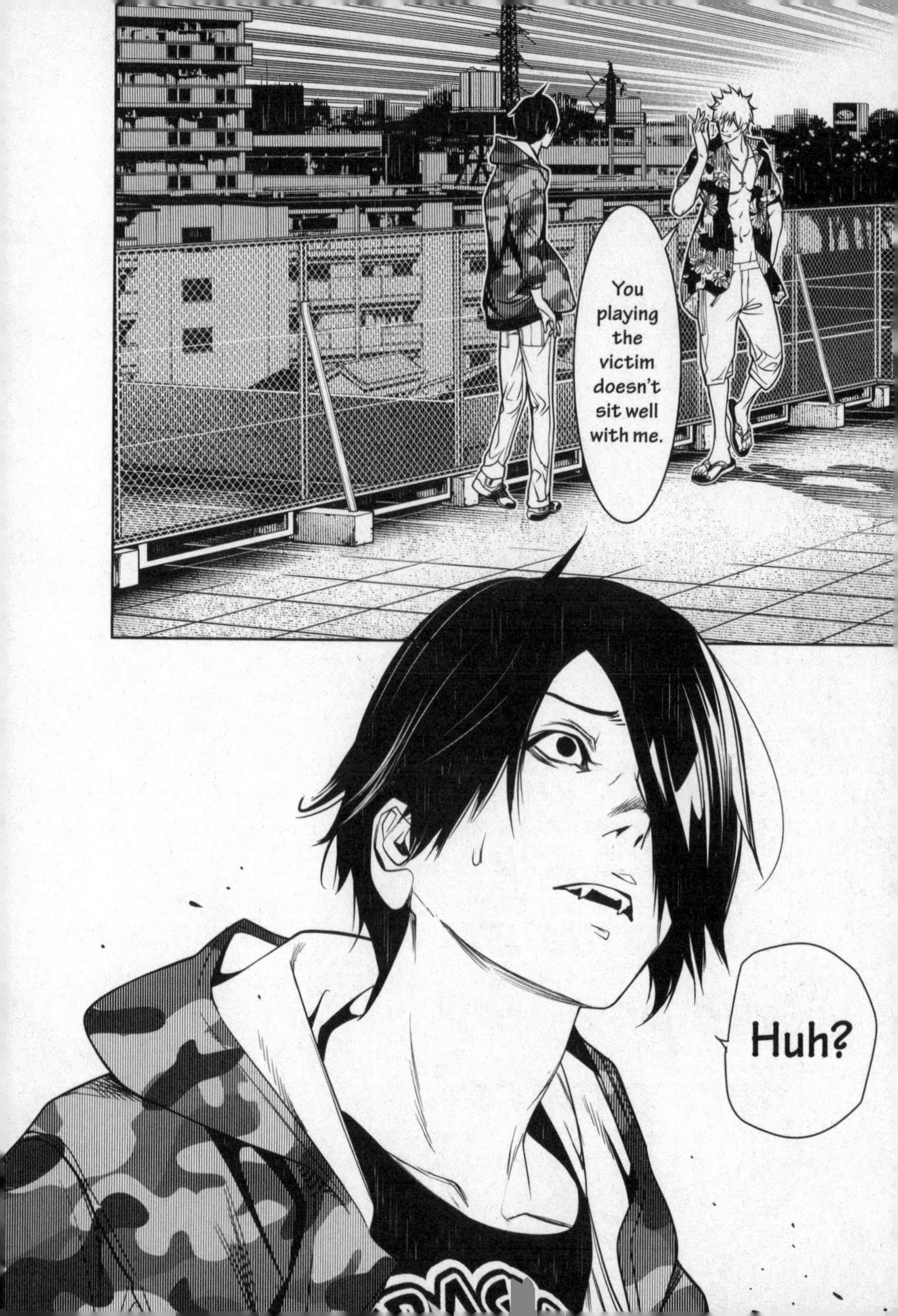
You playing the victim doesn't sit well with me.
Huh?

BAKEMONOGATARI ⑩

After

Right arm

Before

BAKEMONOGATARI ⑩

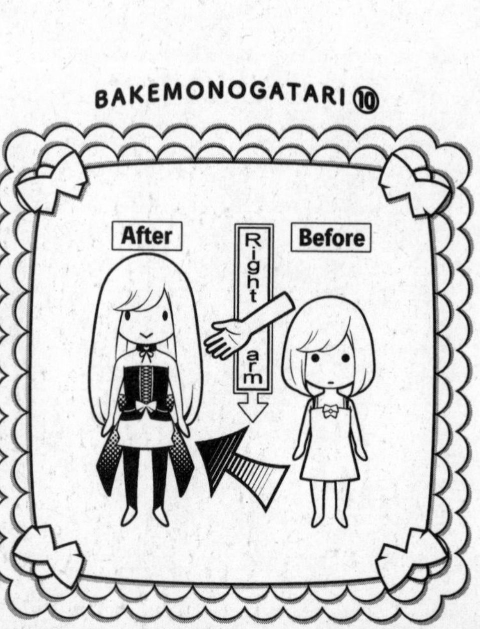
After
Right arm
Before

BAKEMONOGATARI

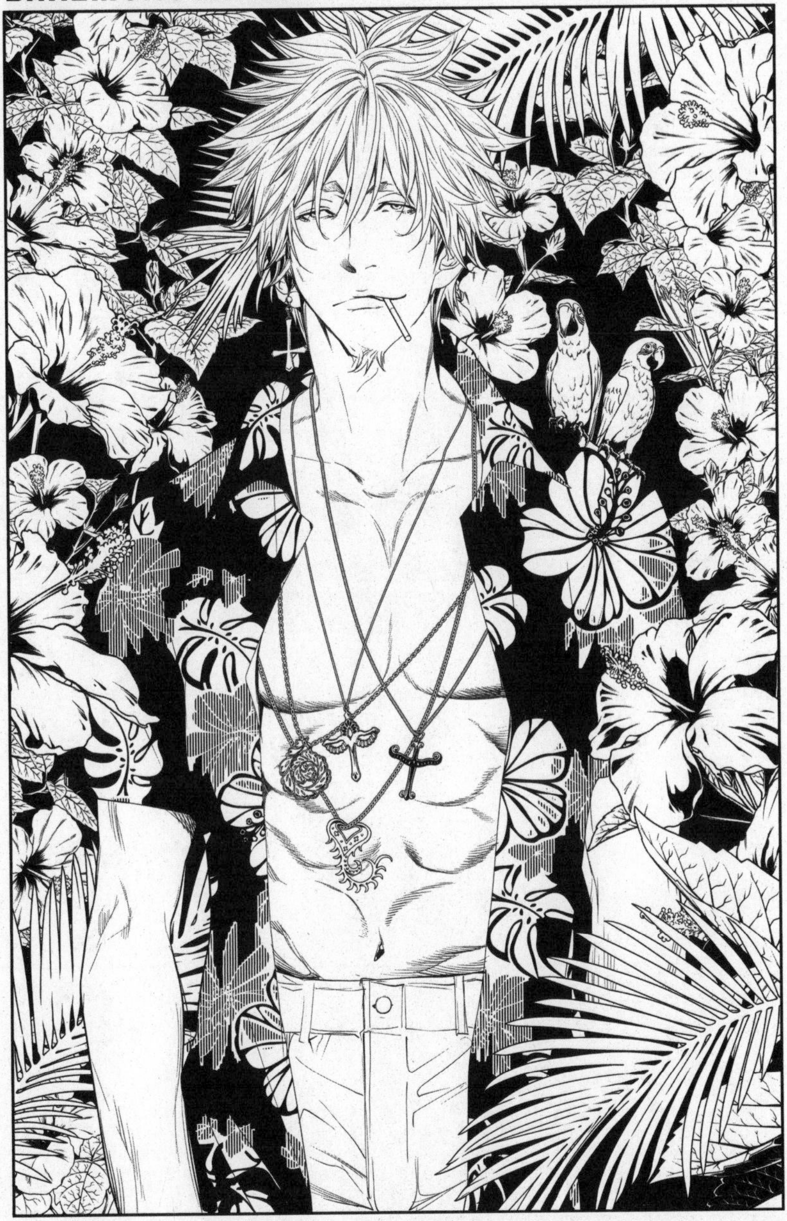

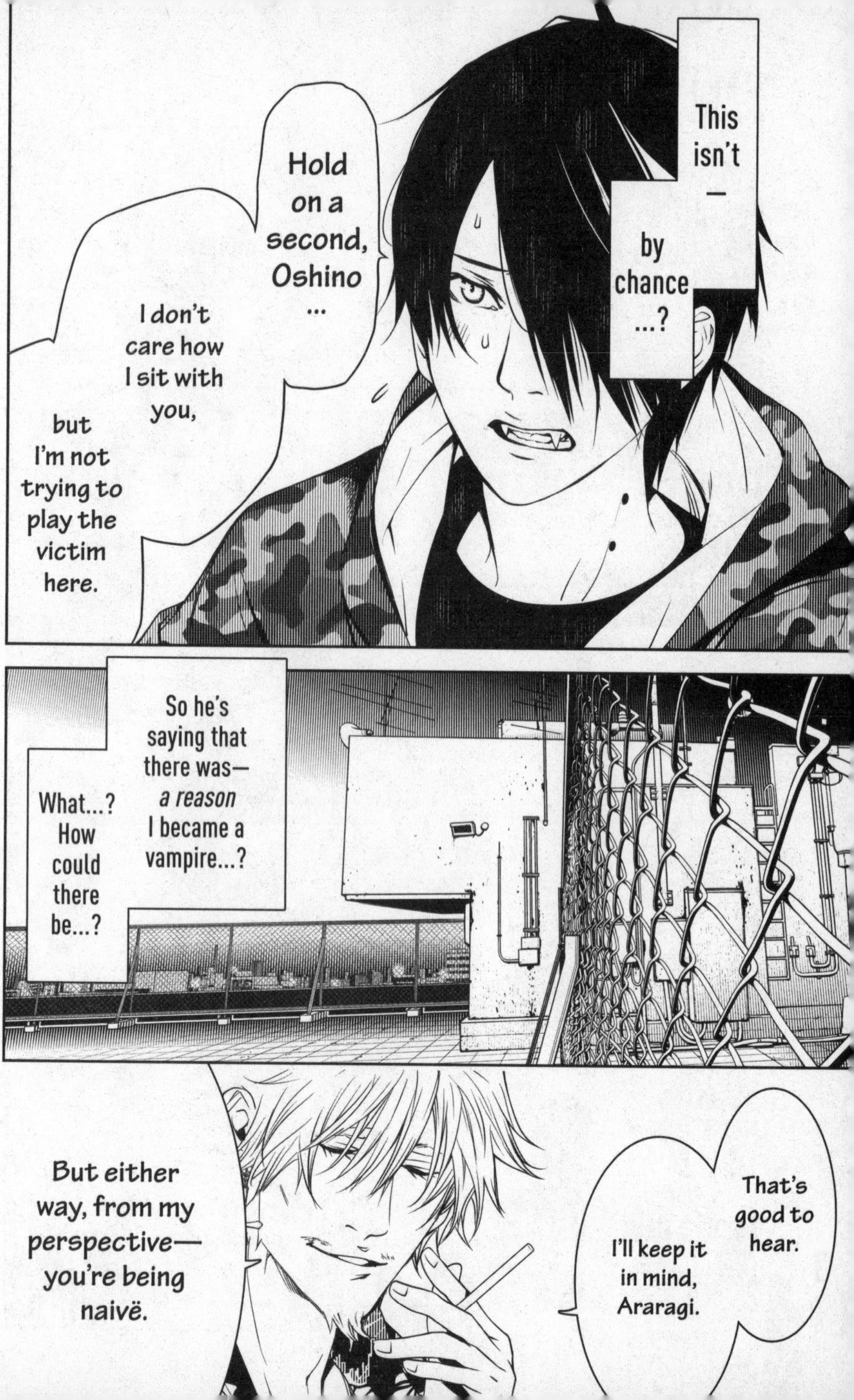
This isn't—
by chance...?
Hold on a second, Oshino...
I don't care how I sit with you,
but I'm not trying to play the victim here.
So he's saying that there was—*a reason* I became a vampire...?
What...? How could there be...?
That's good to hear.
I'll keep it in mind, Araragi.
But either way, from my perspective—you're being naivë.

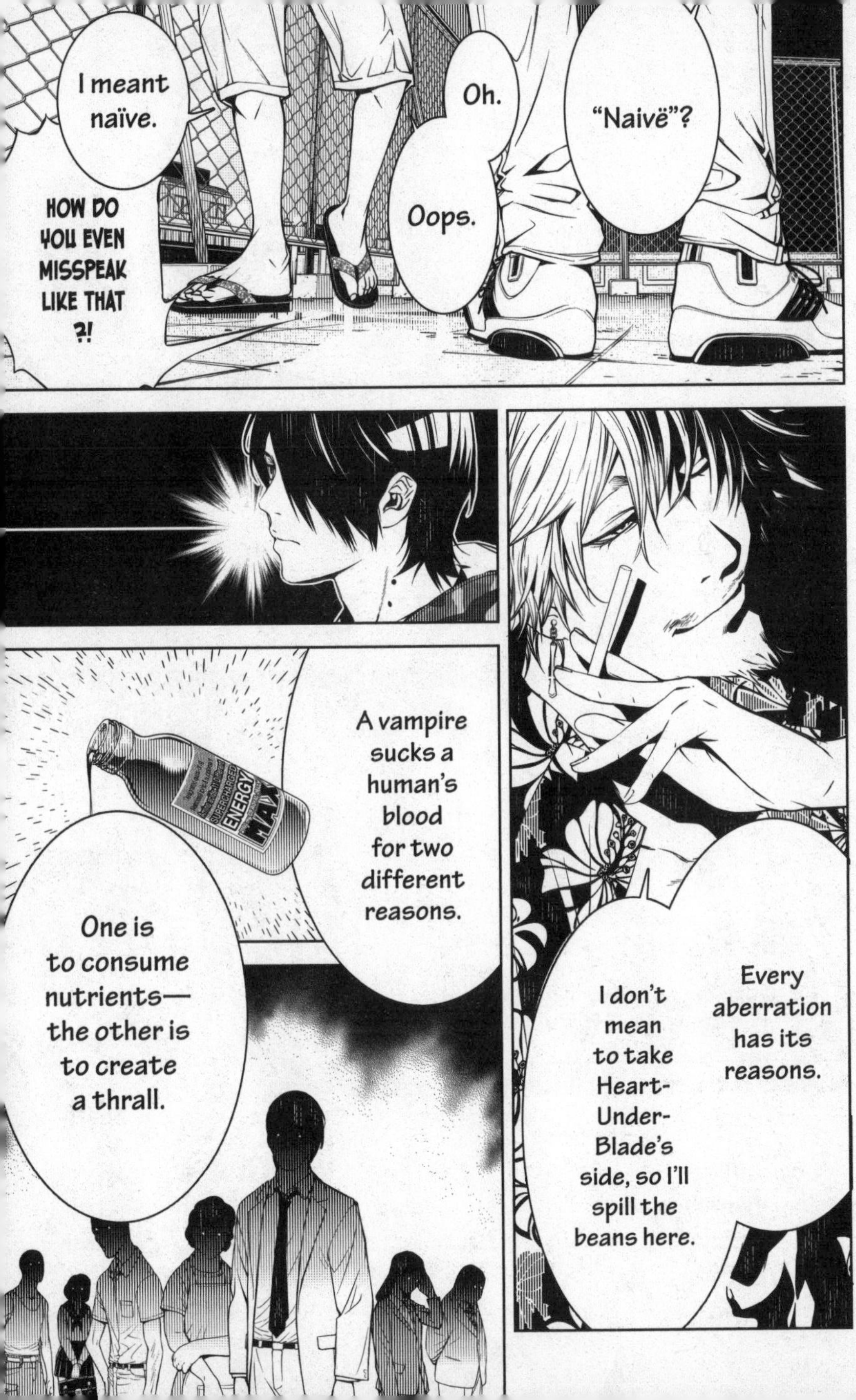
"Naivë"?
Oh.
Oops.
I meant naïve.
HOW DO YOU EVEN MISSPEAK LIKE THAT ?!
Every aberration has its reasons.
I don't mean to take Heart-Under-Blade's side, so I'll spill the beans here.
A vampire sucks a human's blood for two different reasons.
One is to consume nutrients—the other is to create a thrall.
SUPERCHARGED
ENERGY
MAX

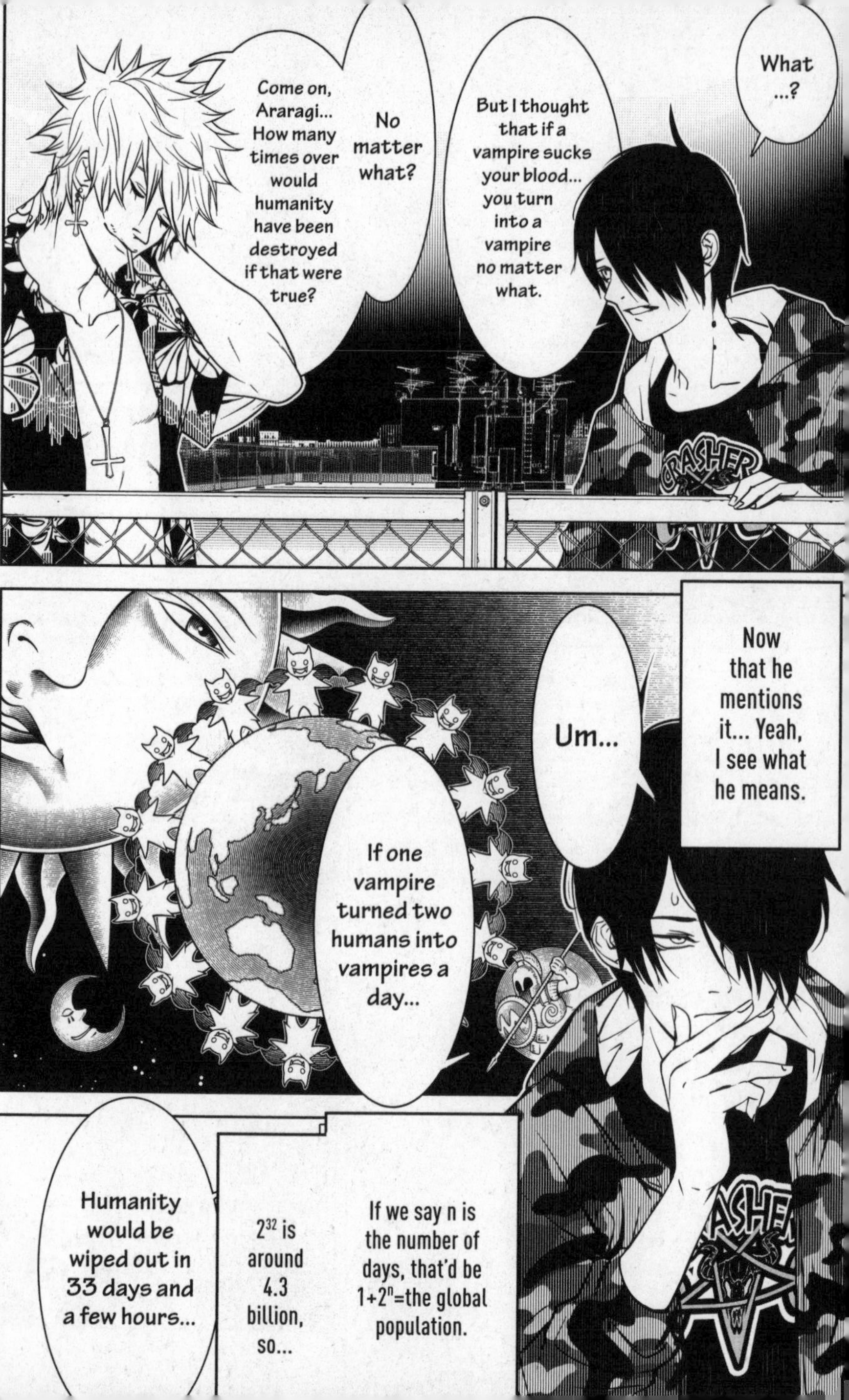
What ...?
But I thought that if a vampire sucks your blood... you turn into a vampire no matter what.
No matter what?
Come on, Araragi... How many times over would humanity have been destroyed if that were true?
Now that he mentions it... Yeah, I see what he means.
Um...
If one vampire turned two humans into vampires a day...
If we say n is the number of days, that'd be $1+2^n$=the global population.
2^{32} is around 4.3 billion, so...
Humanity would be wiped out in 33 days and a few hours...

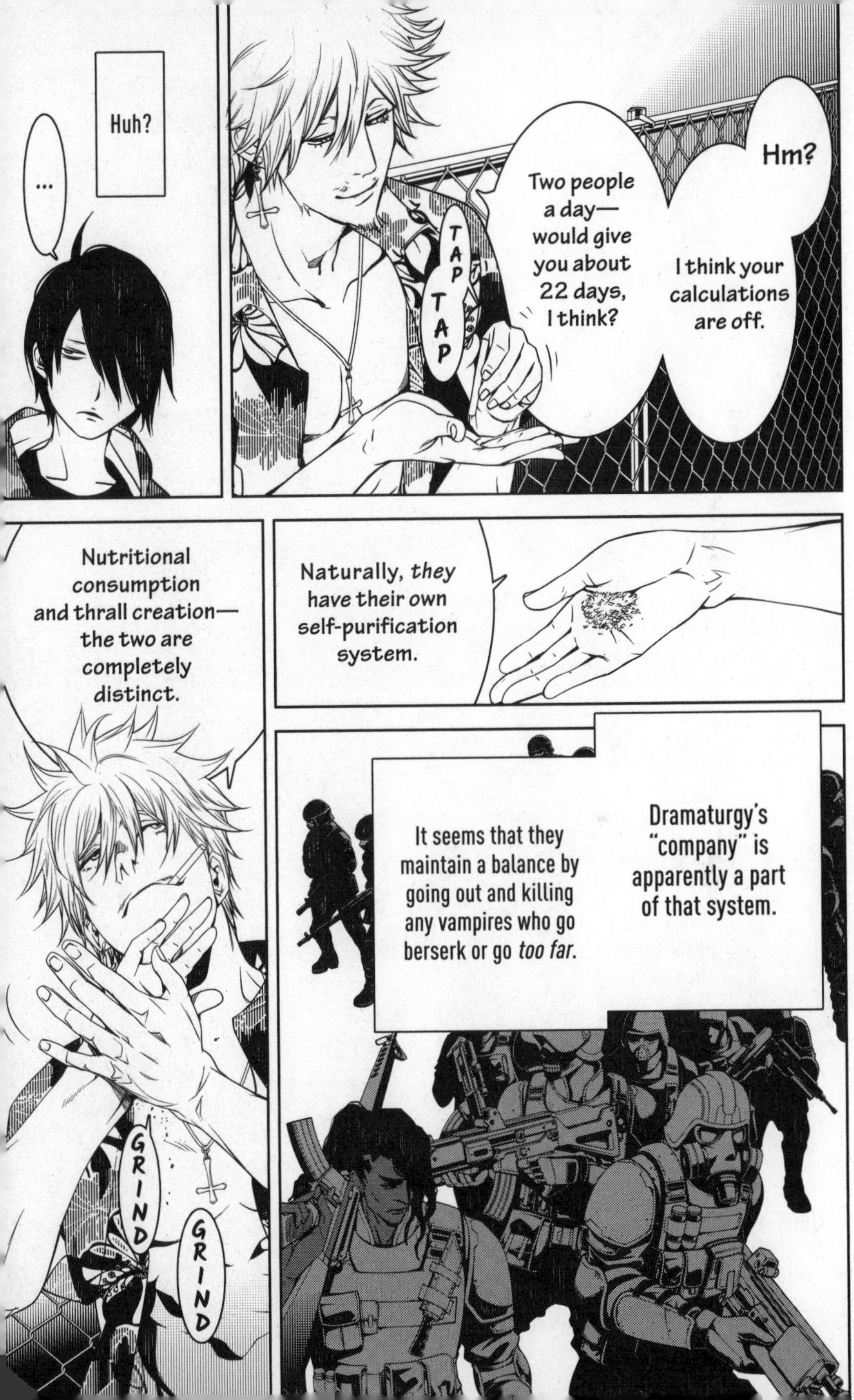
Hm?
I think your calculations are off.
Two people a day— would give you about 22 days, I think?
TAP TAP
Huh?
...
Naturally, *they* have their own self-purification system.
Dramaturgy's "company" is apparently a part of that system.
It seems that they maintain a balance by going out and killing any vampires who go berserk or go *too far*.
Nutritional consumption and thrall creation— the two are completely distinct.
GRIND GRIND

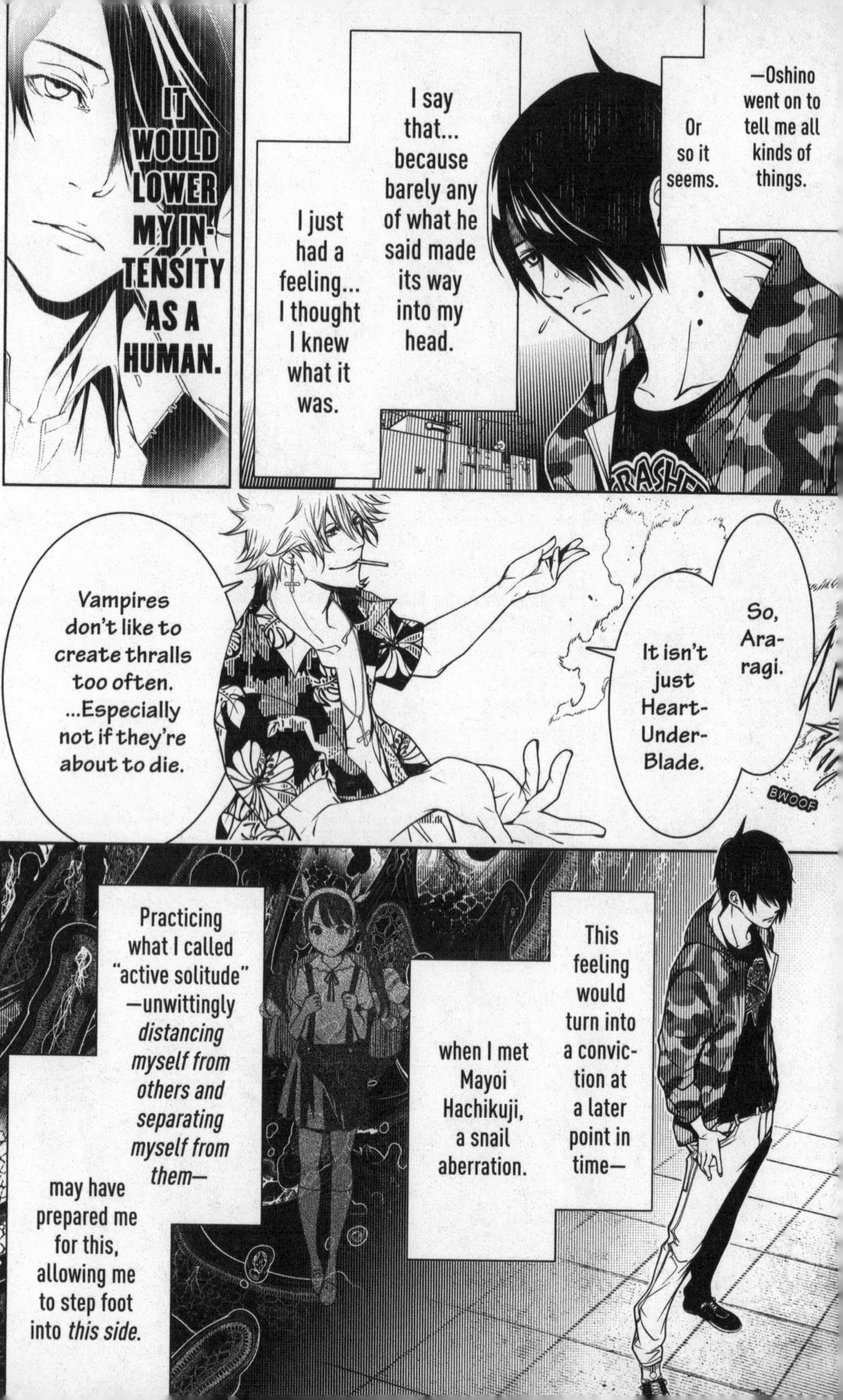
—Oshino went on to tell me all kinds of things.
Or so it seems.
I say that... because barely any of what he said made its way into my head.
I just had a feeling... I thought I knew what it was.
IT WOULD LOWER MY IN-TENSITY AS A HUMAN.
So, Ara-ragi.
It isn't just Heart-Under-Blade.
BWOOF
Vampires don't like to create thralls too often. ...Especially not if they're about to die.
This feeling would turn into a convic-tion at a later point in time—
when I met Mayoi Hachikuji, a snail aberration.
Practicing what I called "active solitude" —unwittingly *distancing myself from others and separating myself from them*—
may have prepared me for this, allowing me to step foot into *this side*.

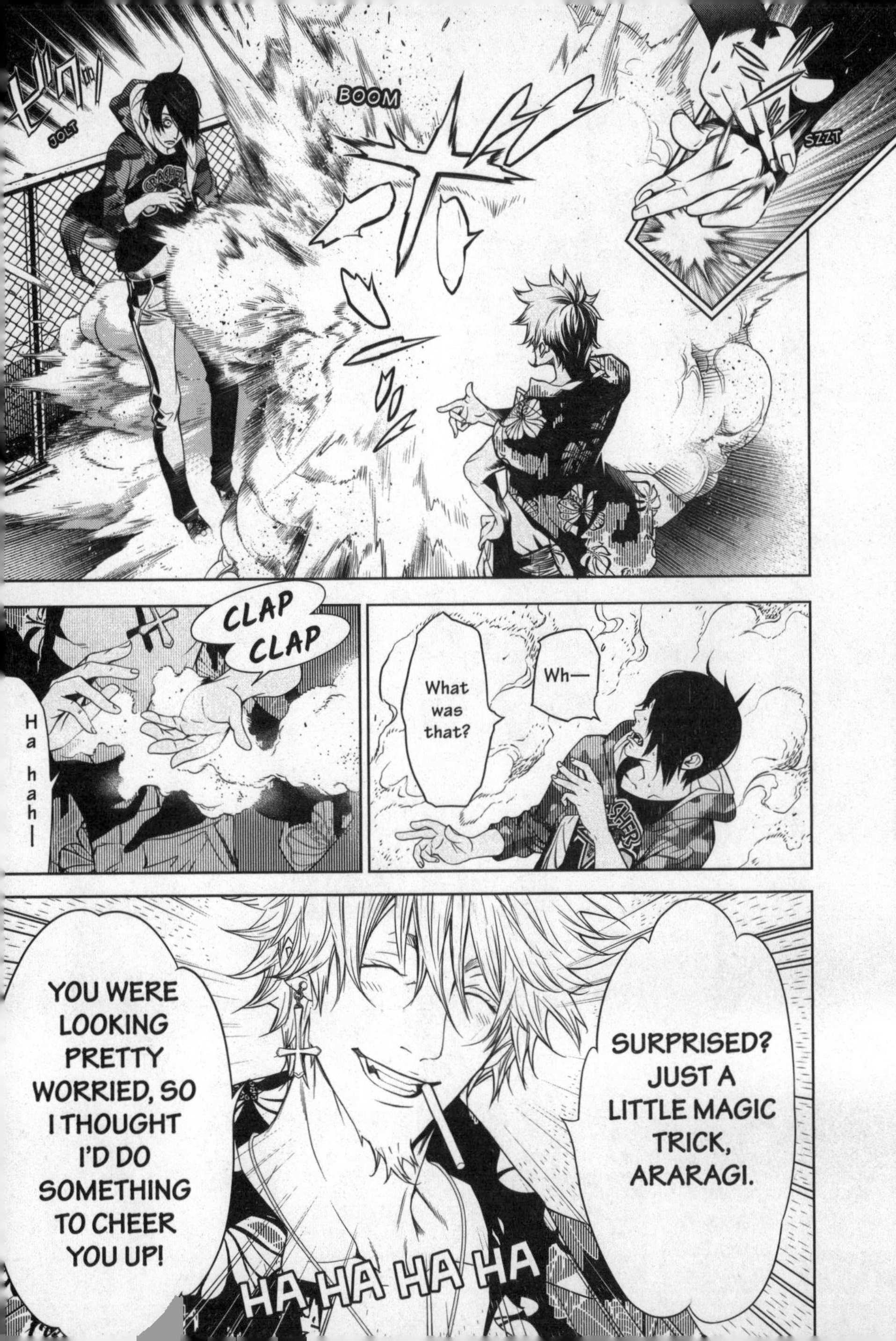
SZZT
BOOM
JOLT
Wh—
What was that?
CLAP CLAP
Ha hah!
SURPRISED? JUST A LITTLE MAGIC TRICK, ARARAGI.
YOU WERE LOOKING PRETTY WORRIED, SO I THOUGHT I'D DO SOMETHING TO CHEER YOU UP!
HA HA HA HA

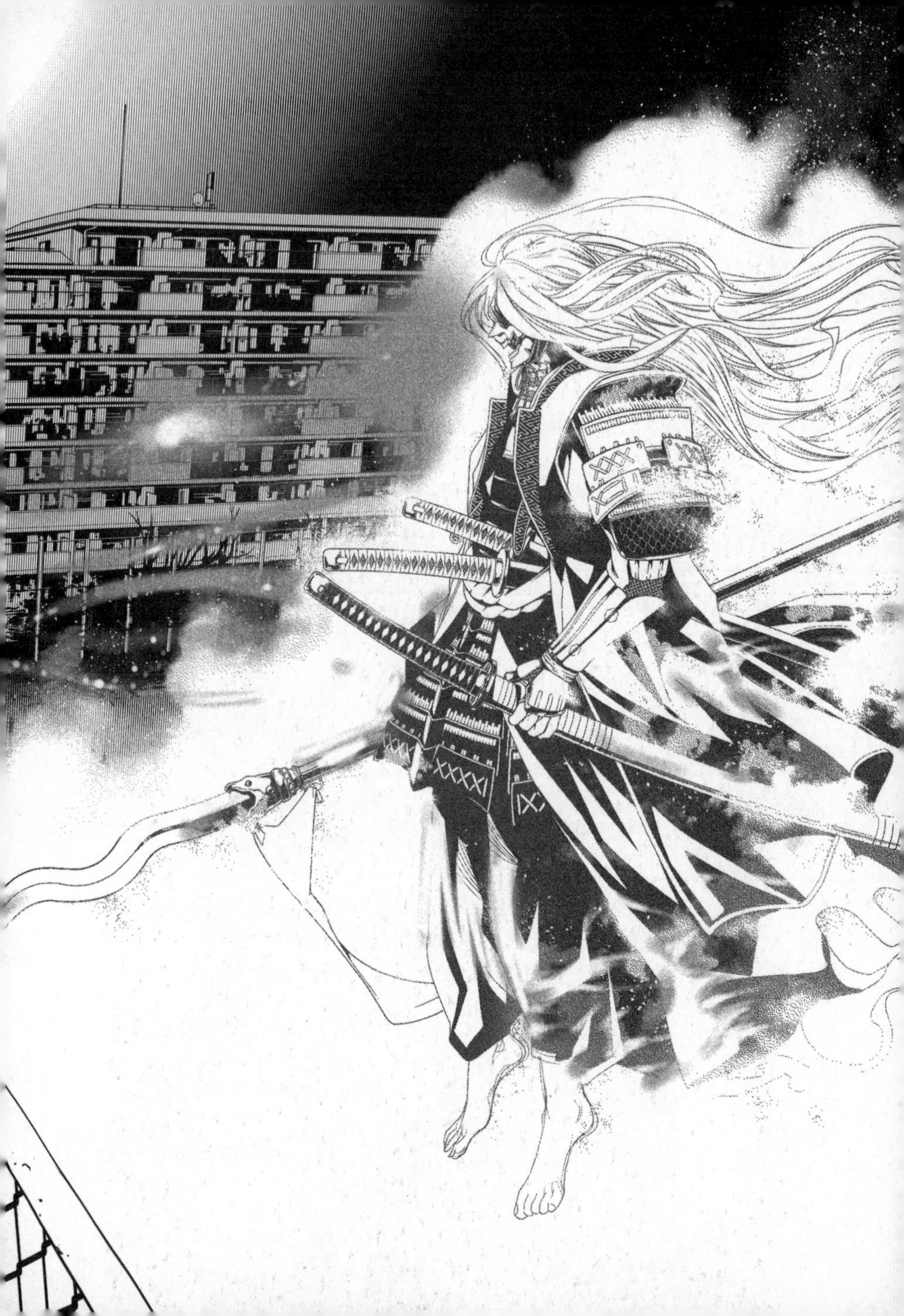

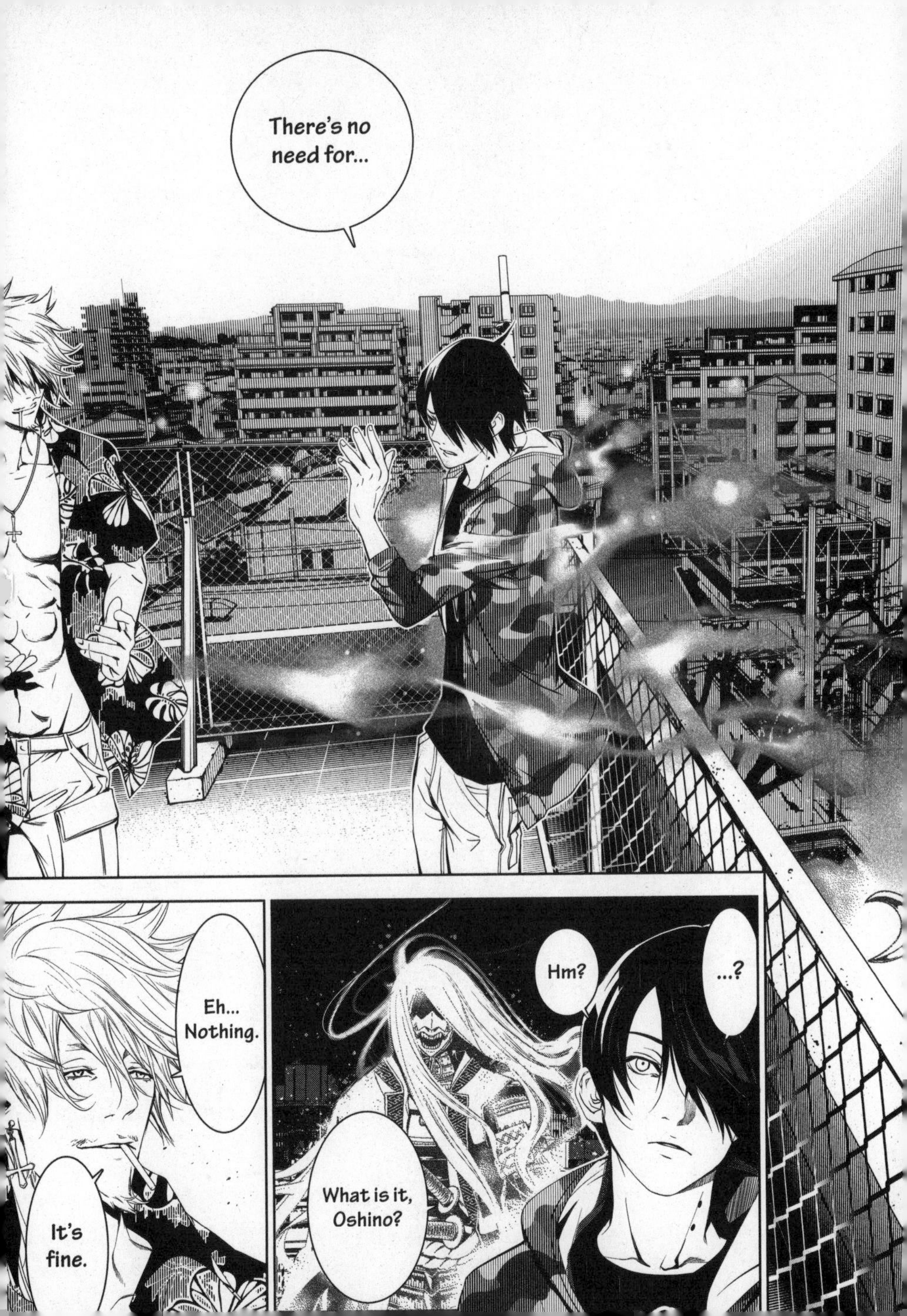
There's no need for...
...?
Hm?
What is it, Oshino?
Eh... Nothing.
It's fine.

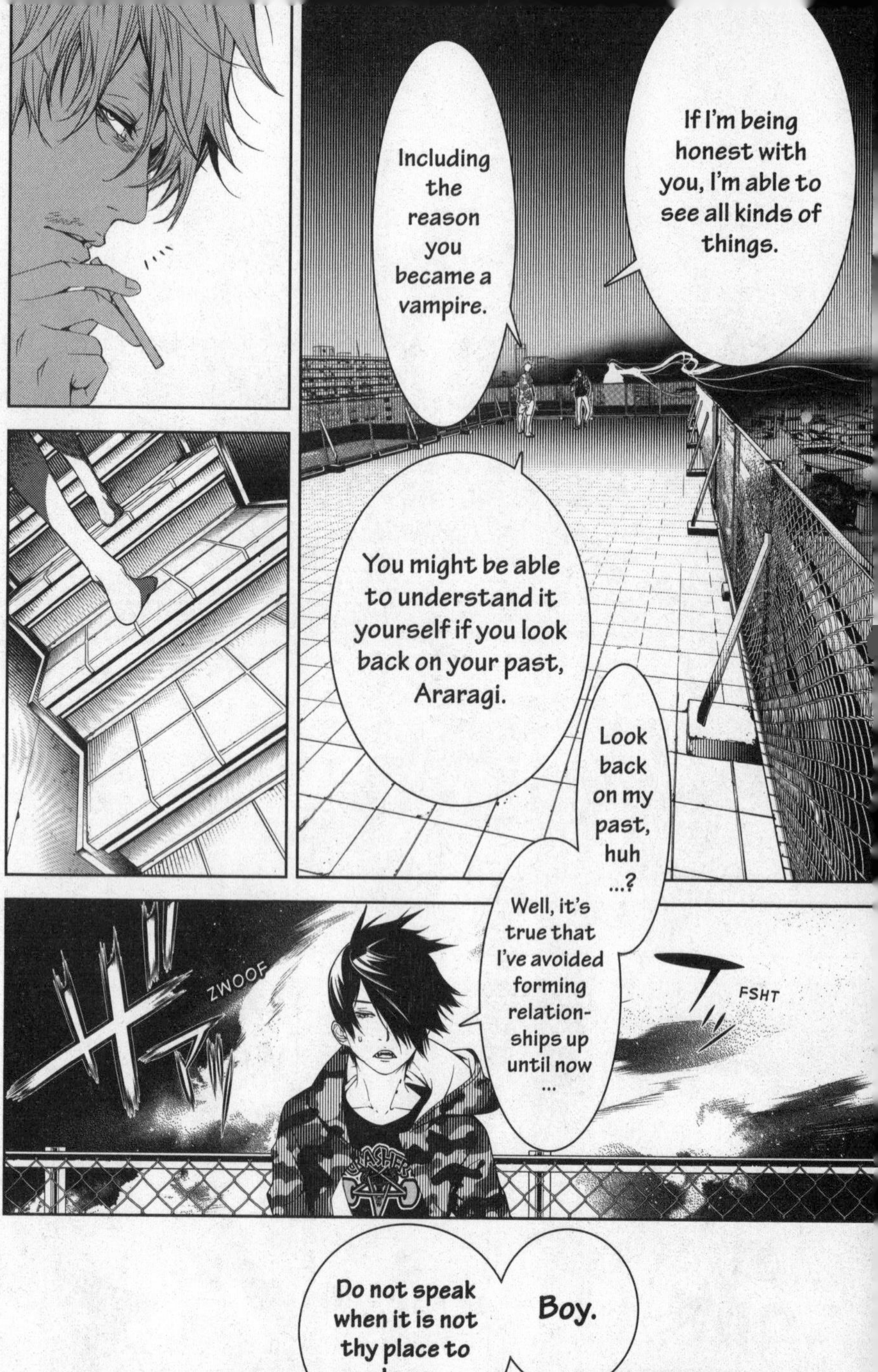
If I'm being honest with you, I'm able to see all kinds of things.
Including the reason you became a vampire.
You might be able to understand it yourself if you look back on your past, Araragi.
Look back on my past, huh ...?
Well, it's true that I've avoided forming relation-ships up until now ...
FSHT
ZWOOF
Boy.
Do not speak when it is not thy place to do so.

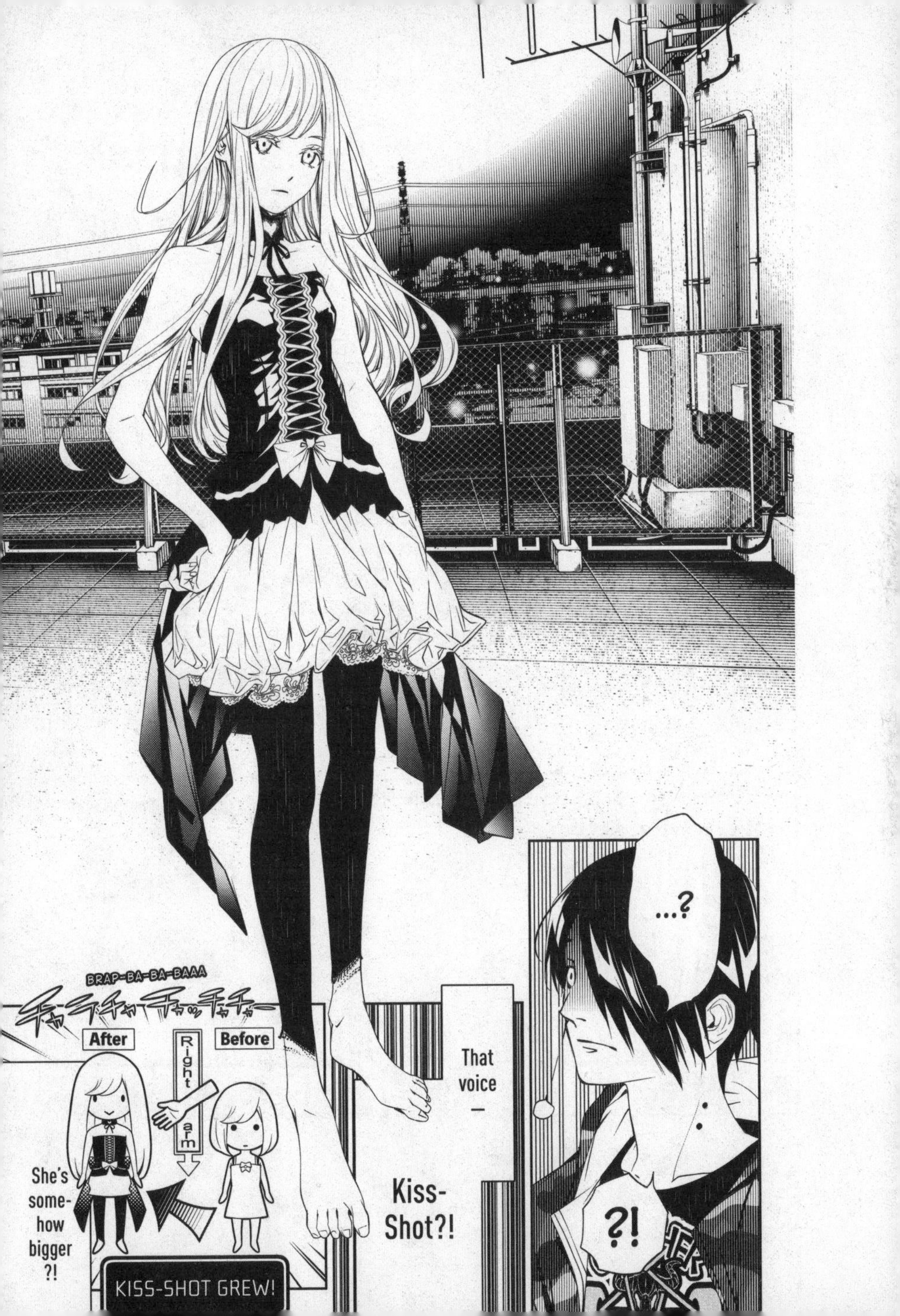
...?
?!
That voice —
Kiss-Shot?!
BRAP-BA-BA-BAAA
After
Right arm
Before
She's somehow bigger?!
KISS-SHOT GREW!

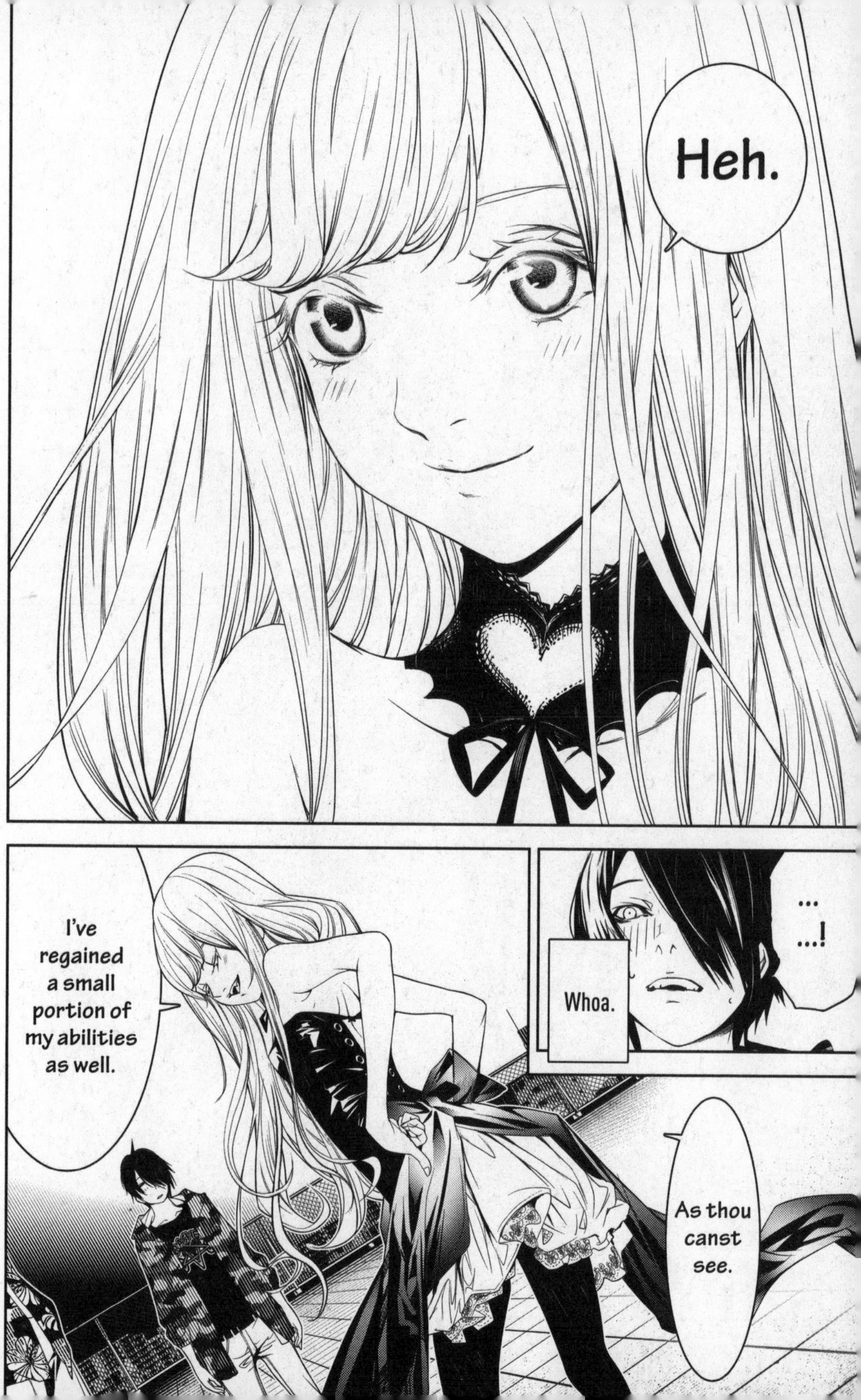
Heh.
... ...!
Whoa.
I've regained a small portion of my abilities as well.
As thou canst see.

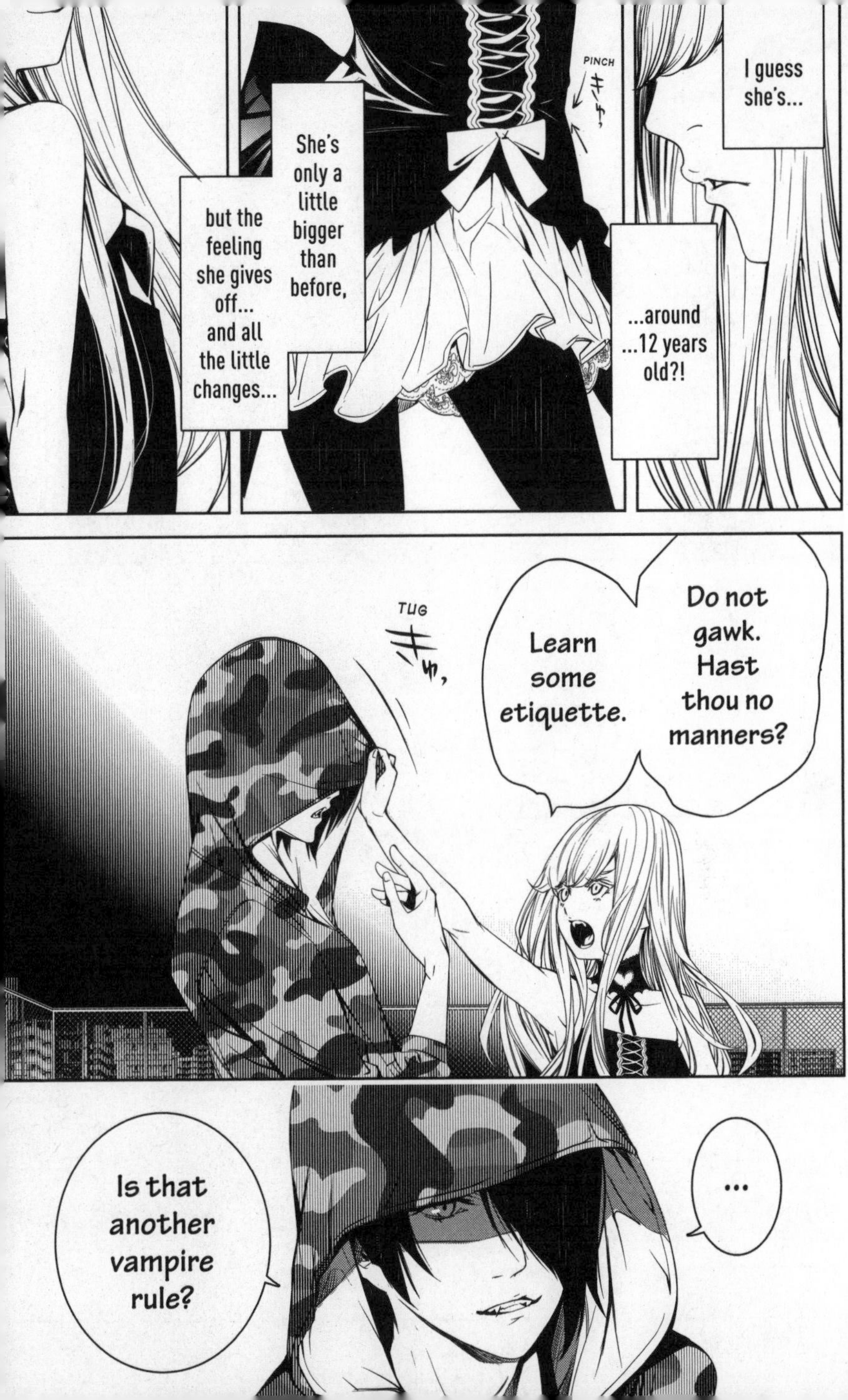
I guess she's...
...around ...12 years old?!
PINCH
She's only a little bigger than before,
but the feeling she gives off... and all the little changes...
Do not gawk. Hast thou no manners?
Learn some etiquette.
TUG
...
Is that another vampire rule?

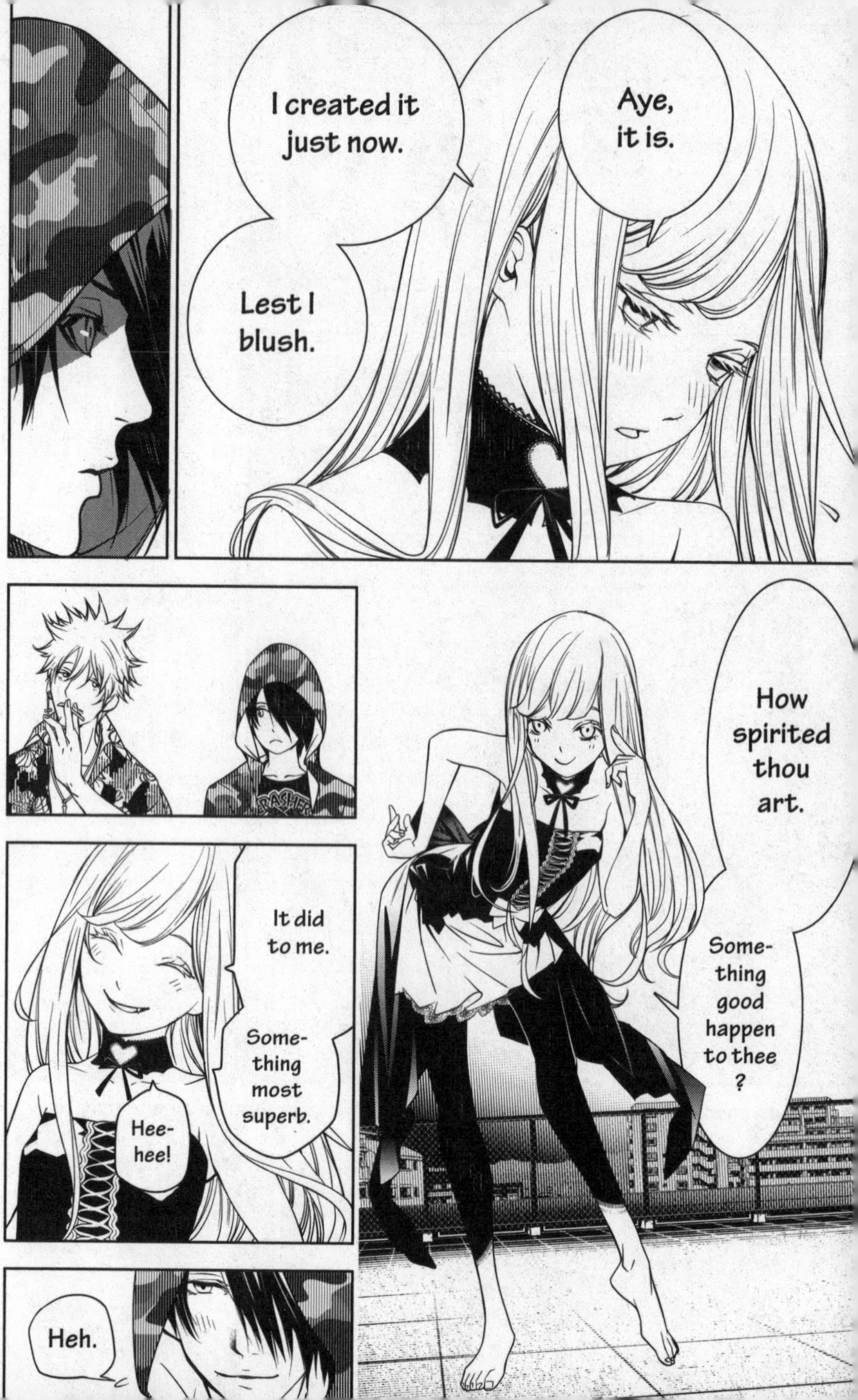
Aye, it is.
I created it just now.
Lest I blush.
How spirited thou art.
Something good happen to thee?
It did to me.
Something most superb.
Hee-hee!
Heh.

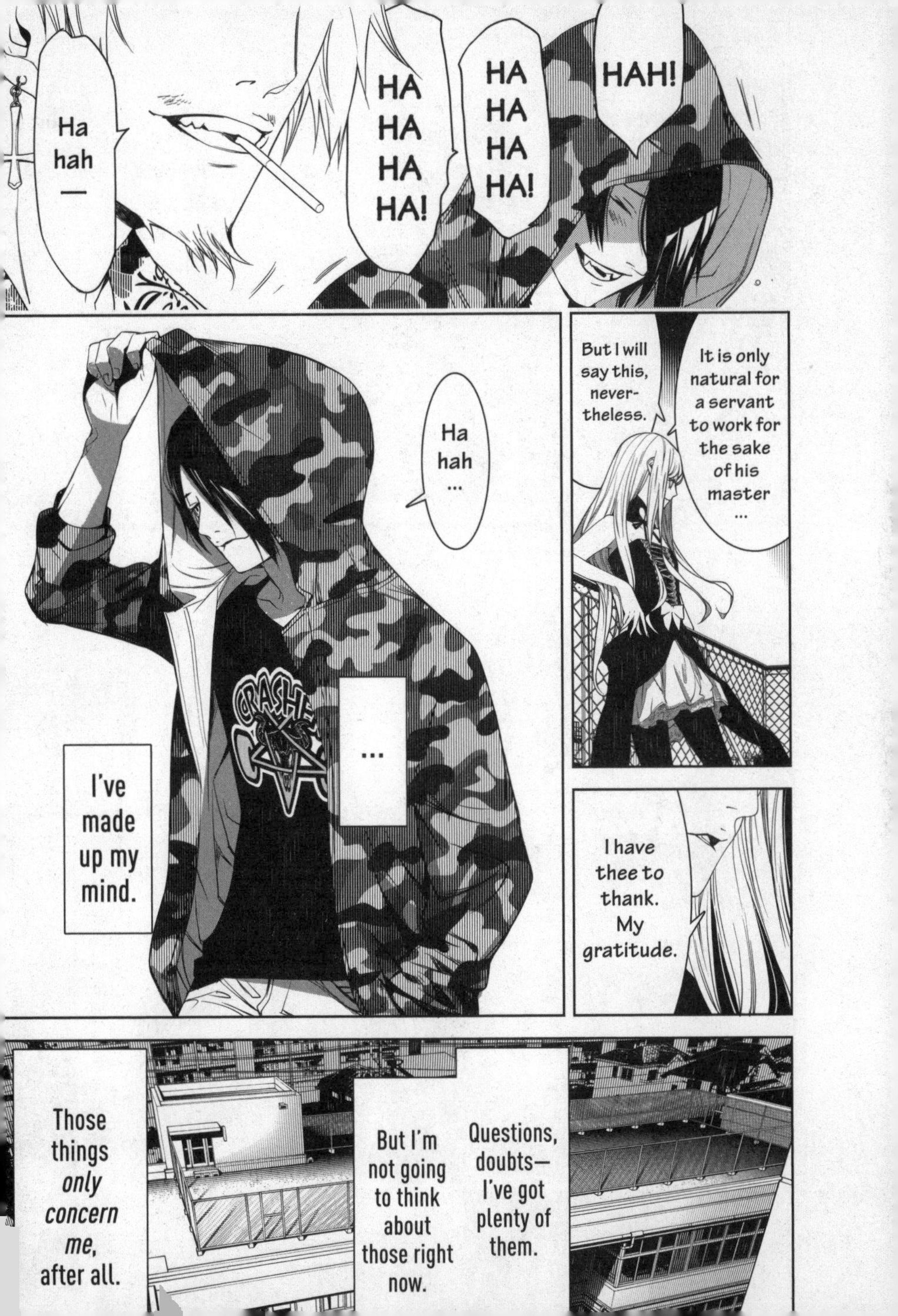

HAH!
HA HA HA HA!
HA HA HA HA!
Ha hah—
It is only natural for a servant to work for the sake of his master ...
But I will say this, nevertheless.
I have thee to thank. My gratitude.
Ha hah ...
...
I've made up my mind.
Questions, doubts— I've got plenty of them.
But I'm not going to think about those right now.
Those things *only concern me*, after all.

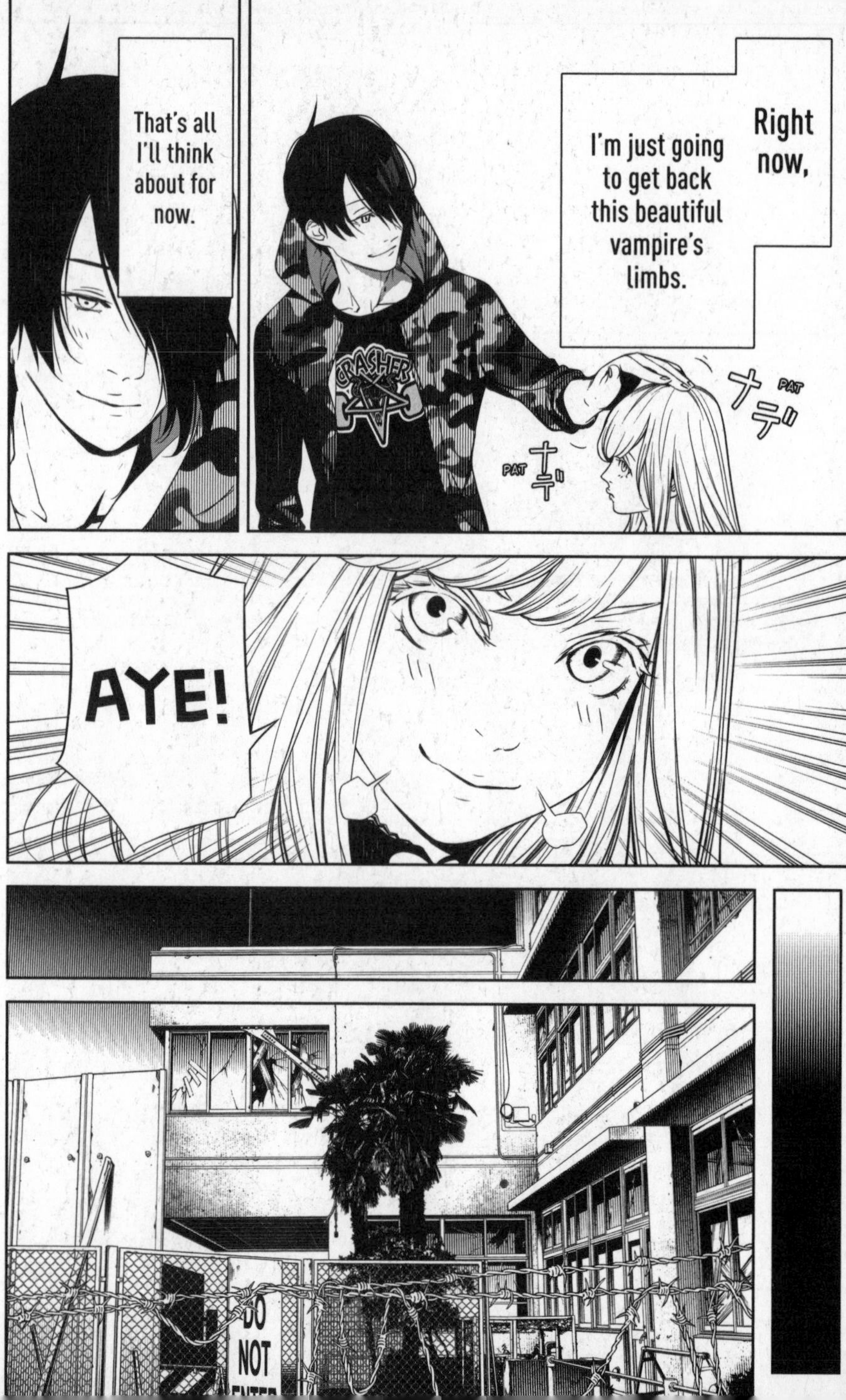
Right now,
I'm just going to get back this beautiful vampire's limbs.
PAT
PAT
That's all I'll think about for now.
AYE!
DO NOT

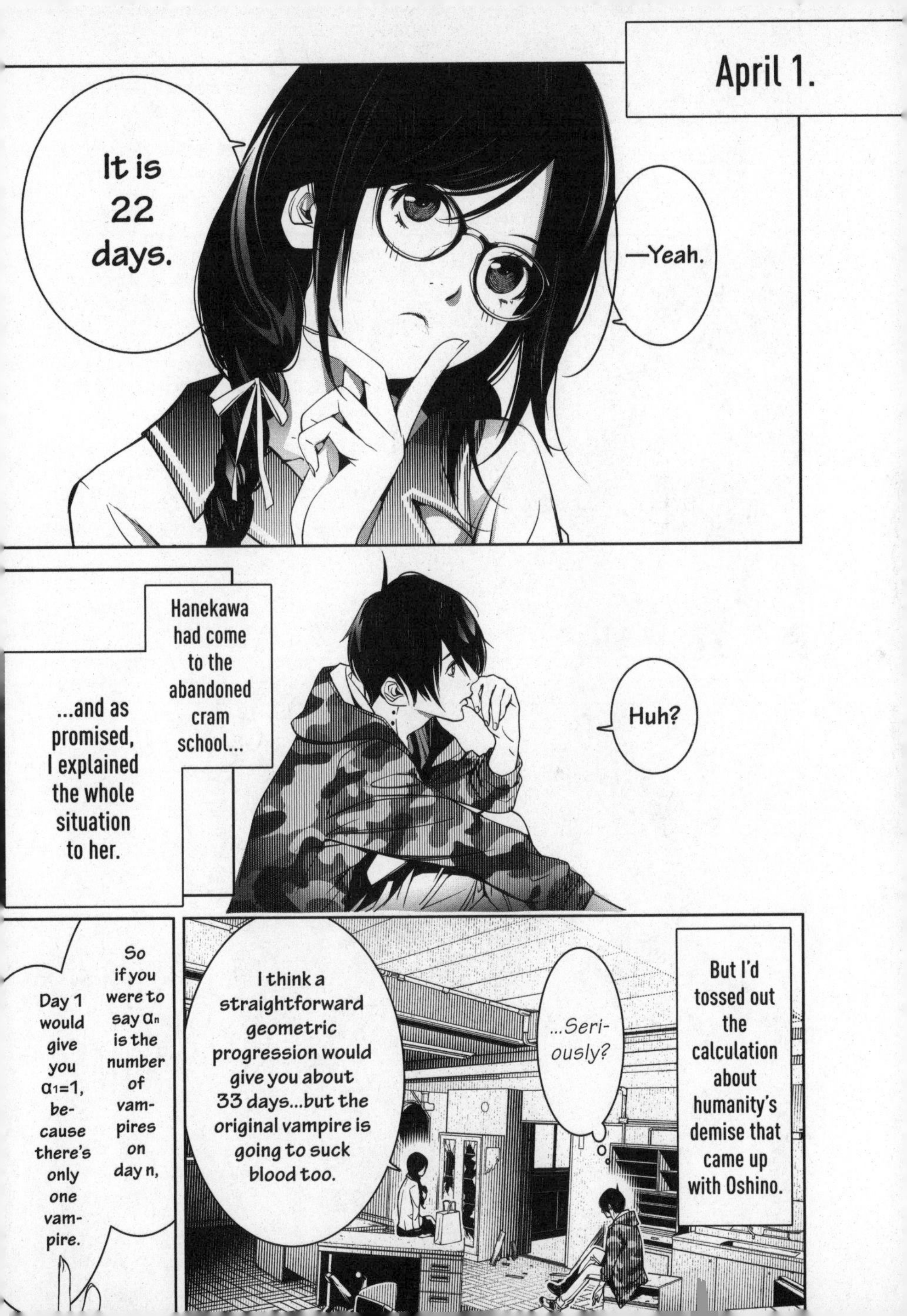
April 1.
—Yeah.
It is 22 days.
Huh?
Hanekawa had come to the abandoned cram school...
...and as promised, I explained the whole situation to her.
But I'd tossed out the calculation about humanity's demise that came up with Oshino.
...Seriously?
I think a straightforward geometric progression would give you about 33 days...but the original vampire is going to suck blood too.
So if you were to say a_n is the number of vampires on day n,
Day 1 would give you $a_1=1$, because there's only one vampire.

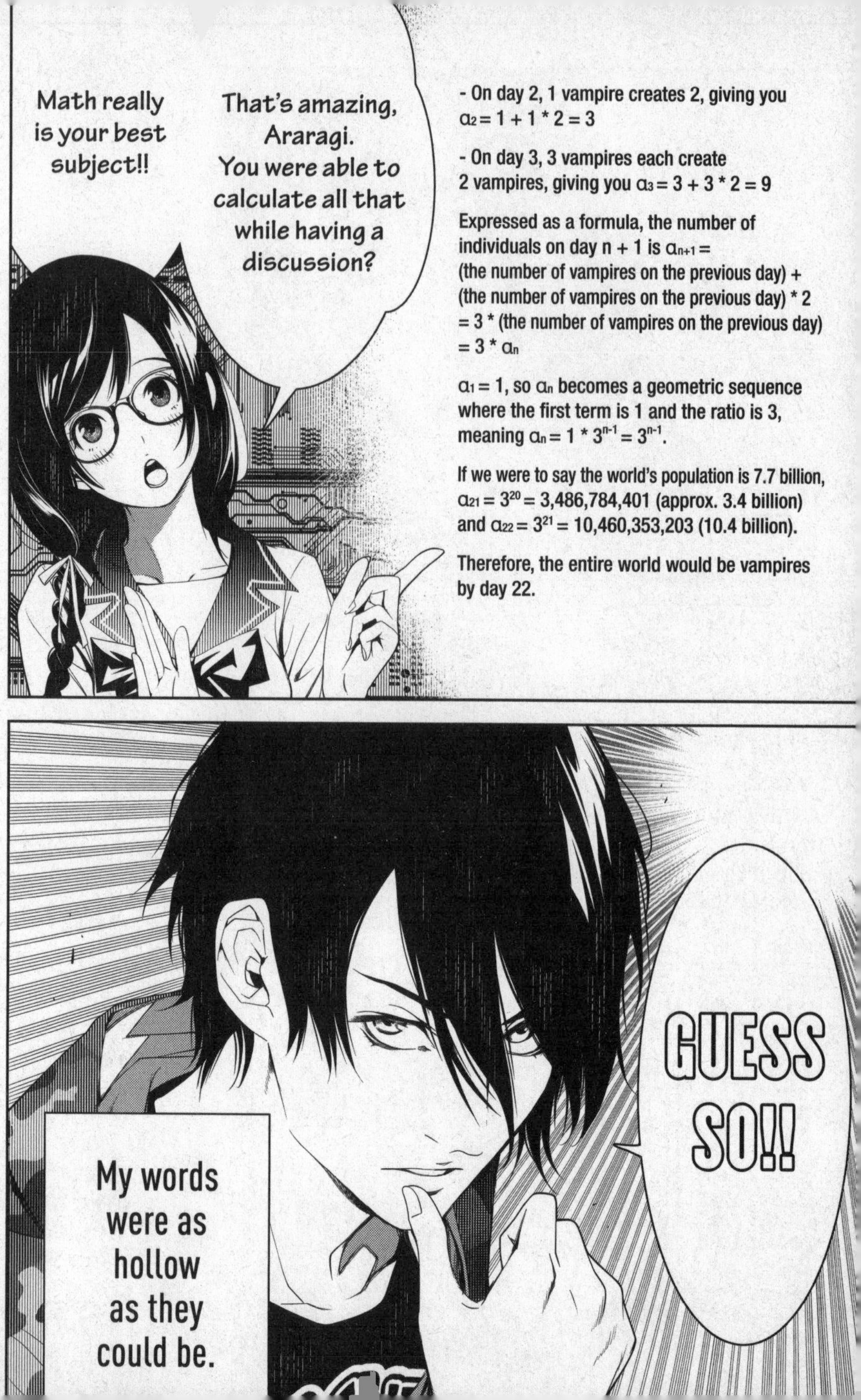
- On day 2, 1 vampire creates 2, giving you $a_2 = 1 + 1 * 2 = 3$
- On day 3, 3 vampires each create 2 vampires, giving you $a_3 = 3 + 3 * 2 = 9$
Expressed as a formula, the number of individuals on day n + 1 is a_{n+1} = (the number of vampires on the previous day) + (the number of vampires on the previous day) * 2 = 3 * (the number of vampires on the previous day) = $3 * a_n$
$a_1 = 1$, so a_n becomes a geometric sequence where the first term is 1 and the ratio is 3, meaning $a_n = 1 * 3^{n-1} = 3^{n-1}$.
If we were to say the world's population is 7.7 billion, $a_{21} = 3^{20} = 3,486,784,401$ (approx. 3.4 billion) and $a_{22} = 3^{21} = 10,460,353,203$ (10.4 billion).
Therefore, the entire world would be vampires by day 22.
That's amazing, Araragi. You were able to calculate all that while having a discussion?
Math really is your best subject!!
GUESS SO!!
My words were as hollow as they could be.

Continued in Volume 11

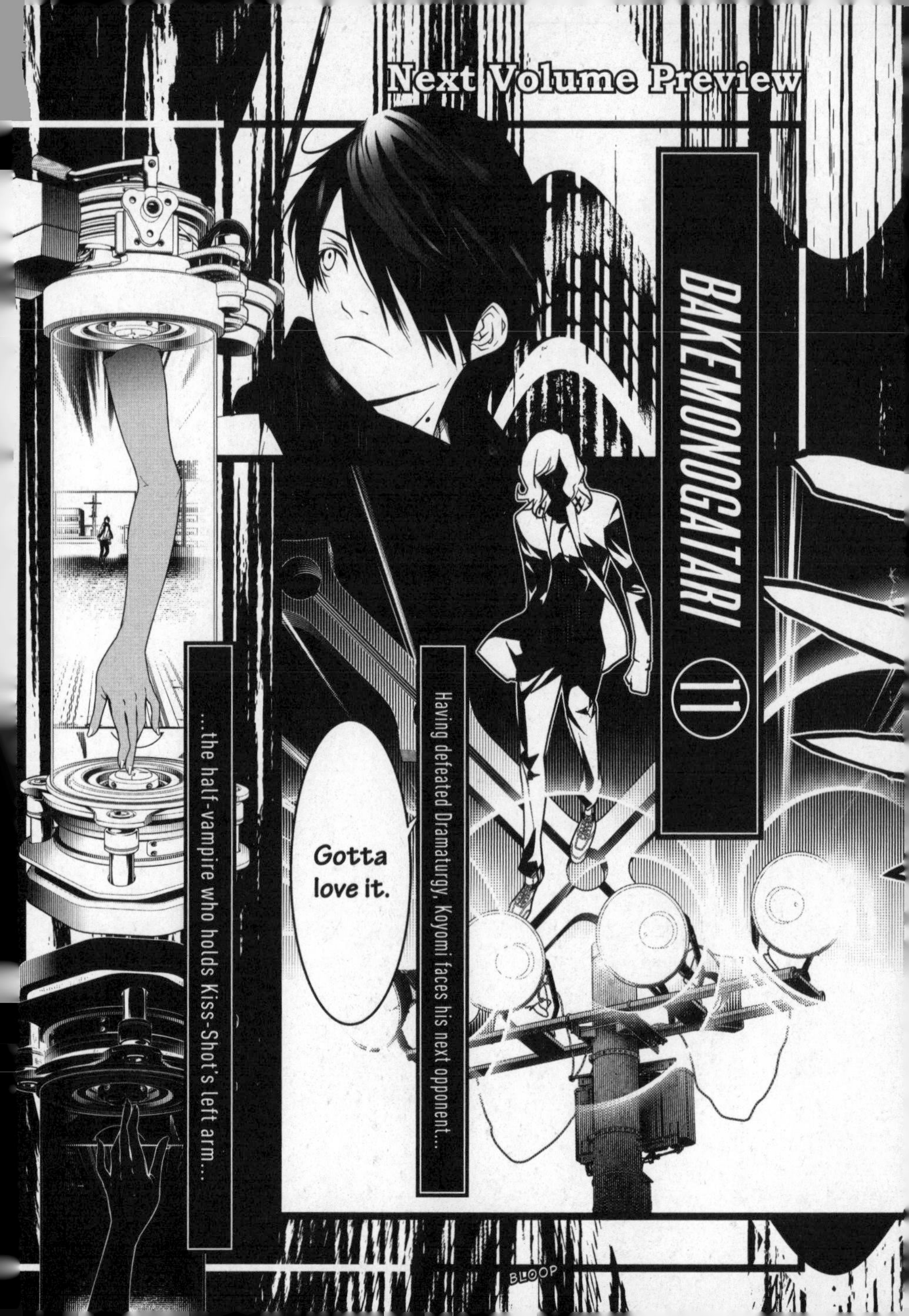
Next Volume Preview
BAKEMONOGATARI 11
Having defeated Dramaturgy, Koyomi faces his next opponent...
Gotta love it.
...the half-vampire who holds Kiss-Shot's left arm...
BLOOP

BAKEMONOGATARI
volume 10
A Vertical Comics Edition

Editing: Ajani Oloye
Translation: Ko Ransom
Production: Grace Lu
           Hiroko Mizuno
           Anthony Quintessenza

First published in Japan in 2020 by Kodansha, Ltd., Tokyo
Publication for this English edition arranged through Kodansha, Ltd., Tokyo
English language version produced by Vertical Comics,
an imprint of Kodansha USA Publishing, LLC

Translation provided by Vertical Comics, 2021
Published by Kodansha USA Publishing, LLC, New York

Originally published in Japanese as *BAKEMONOGATARI 10* by Kodansha, Ltd.
BAKEMONOGATARI first serialized in *Weekly Shonen Magazine*,
Kodansha, Ltd., 2017-

This is a work of fiction.

ISBN: 978-1-64729-007-8

Manufactured in the United States of America

First Edition

Kodansha USA Publishing, LLC
451 Park Avenue South
7th Floor
New York, NY 10016
www.kodansha.us

Vertical books are distributed through Penguin-Random House Publisher Services.

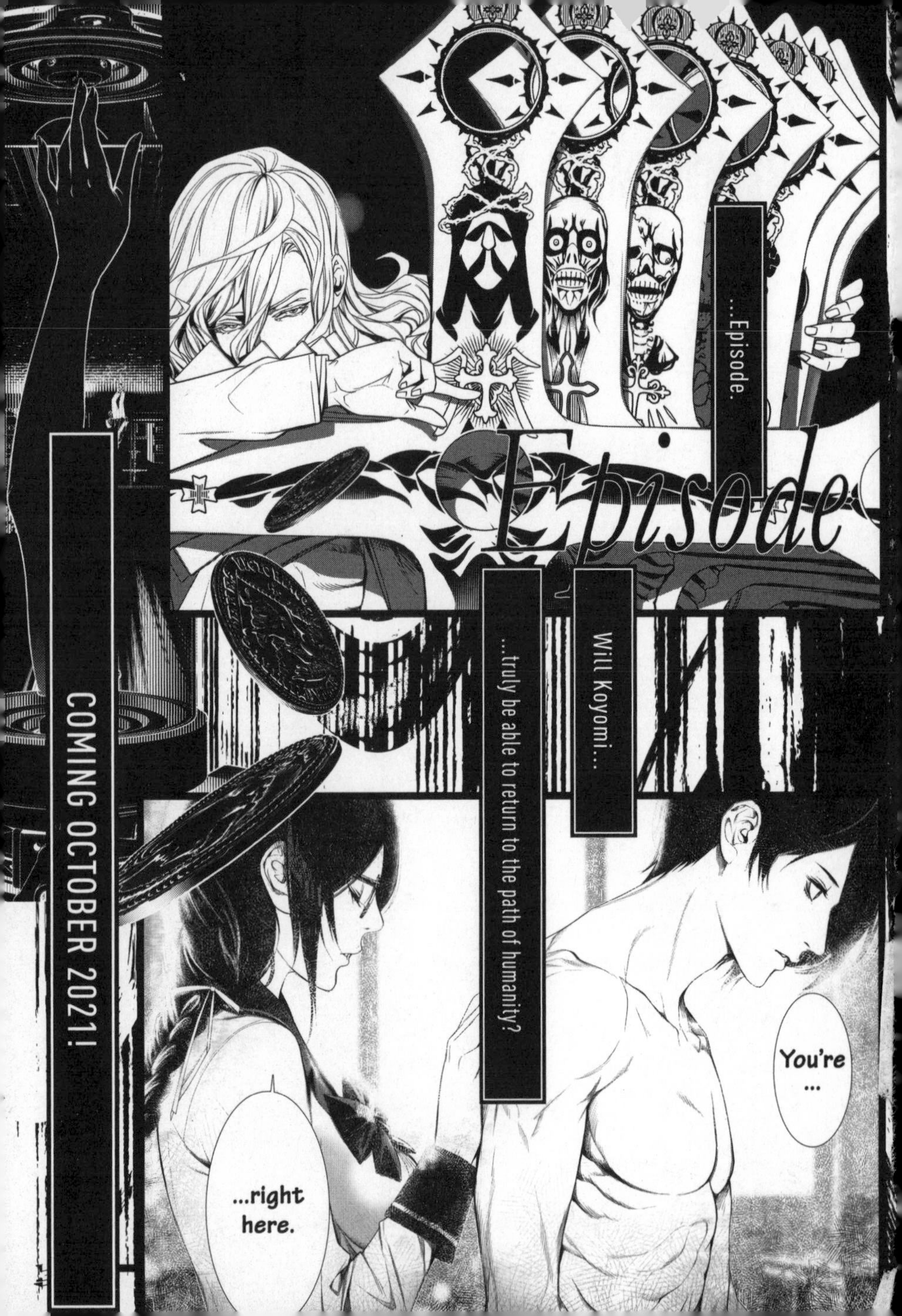
...Episode.
Episode
Will Koyomi...
...truly be able to return to the path of humanity?
You're ...
...right here.
COMING OCTOBER 2021!